following JESUS

THROUGH
THE
GOSPELS
IN A
YEAR

Stephanie
SCHWARTZ

Copyright © 2017 by Stephanie Schwartz

Scripture quotations are from the ESV® Bible (The Holy Bible, English Standard Version®), copyright 2001 by Crossway, a publishing ministry of Good News Publishers. Used by permission. All rights reserved.

No part of this book may be used or reproduced in any manner whatsoever without written permission of the publisher, except for brief quotations in reviews or articles. All rights reserved.

ISBN 978-0-9986274-1-0

Compass Bible Church
150 Columbia, Aliso Viejo, CA 92656
949.540.0699
www.CompassChurch.org

preface

Following Jesus
THROUGH THE GOSPELS IN A YEAR

Get ready to spend a year following Jesus through the Gospels!

Each day of this devotional begins with a small, sequential selection from the Gospel of Matthew, Mark, Luke, or John. After reading the assigned Scripture, return to the devotional for a brief explanation of the text, followed by a call to put a truth from the passage into practice. When the year is up, we will have carefully traveled through every page of all four Gospel accounts.

Please don't neglect reading the Bible text that prompts each daily thought! It would be a mistake to forego the word of God for anything written here. With that said, let's begin our year's journey through the biographies of our Lord, and follow Jesus together.

Oh, and a special thank you to Jennifer Morris, my faithful friend, who helped so much with this work.

Stephanie Schwartz
Director of Women's Ministry
Compass Bible Church

january
ONE

MATTHEW 1:1-11

As we begin our journey through the four biographies of Jesus—Matthew, Mark, Luke and John—it is tempting to "write off" the genealogies as a waste of time. But if we do this, we may end up overlooking many fascinating truths. For example, in Matthew's genealogy of Jesus, we find four questionable women: Tamar in verse 3, Rahab and Ruth in verse 5, and Bathsheba (the wife of Uriah) in verse 6. All four of these women were involved in problematic situations in the Old Testament. Although not from the nation of Israel herself, Ruth was a widow who pursued a Jewish man. Bathsheba, the wife of Uriah, was taken by King David and involved in adultery. Tamar disguised herself as a prostitute and tricked her father-in-law into having sex with her because his sons wouldn't do what was right. And Rahab was both a Gentile and a prostitute. Wow! What a mess! At face value, these women would seem unlikely candidates for salvation. Could God actually use them?

Not only did God use them, but he placed all four of these women in the genealogy of his sinless Son. It's staggering to think that God ordained Tamar, Rahab, Ruth, and Bathsheba to become branches in Jesus' family tree. Those who knew these women, and even the four women themselves, probably never imagined they would be factored into the Messiah's lineage. Let us never forget that although he hates and will judge sin, God is a God of grace. What an amazing reminder for us today as we may feel overly discouraged by our past failures! Do you feel like you've messed up your life so much that God could never use you? A thought like that is simply inconsistent with what the Scripture teaches. God can do anything he wants with repentant sinners. Sure, we all have to deal with the consequences of our sin, but God is able to be glorified even in the midst our regrets. He is a God who specializes in righting wrongs and making the crooked straight. It's day one of another year. What a great time to start your life anew with Jesus. Let's begin this year by asking God to forgive us of our past disasters and purposing to do things his way. Put your spiritual goals at the top of your "to do" list, and make your next year of life about following Jesus.

january
TWO

MATTHEW 1:12-17

In verses 12-17, Matthew completes his account of Jesus' genealogy. Specifically, in verse 16, we arrive at Mary, the fifth and final woman in his record. Before her name, only men are mentioned, along with their fathers, but when we get to Mary a shift occurs. Joseph is not recorded as the father of Jesus, but instead as "the husband of Mary." In the Greek text, the pronoun translated "whom" in verse 16 is feminine. Clearly, Jesus was the son of Mary and set apart from all other men who went before him and came after him. Even the minutest details of God's word are fascinating to explore, study, and think about. It's also worth considering the critical impact of the Jewish people keeping such precise and detailed records. As we begin to focus on the life of Jesus, we should remember that these genealogies prove that the Gospel writers deferred to historical record when compiling the biographies of our Lord. The people, places, and events recorded in Scripture are verifiable, and archeologists continue to discover new artifacts that verify the biblical record as true. Matthew's biography of Jesus is an authentic report, given to us so we can draw closer to our Savior.

As we understand more about our Lord Jesus and follow him by imitating his life and obeying his teaching, we will certainly be viewed as foolish by a world of people who don't want anyone telling them how to live. Many will object to our faith and insist the Bible is make-believe and was created by men to control other men. But honestly examining the historical facts in the Bible only proves its legitimacy. The genealogies provide us with a link between past history and modern study, and we can be confident that the New Testament contains an accurate report of real people, real places, and real historical events. Let's thank God that our faith in Christ is not rooted in myths and fairy tales, but instead grounded in historical truth. Just as ancient details were recorded in Scripture with such care and concern, the things recorded about the present and foretold about the future will come to pass with the same level of precision and accuracy. Choose today to learn and obey God's word like never before, confident that your faith will be validated in the end.

january
THREE

MATTHEW 1:18-25

The birth of Jesus was extraordinary in the extreme. In fact, nothing like it has occurred in all of human history. In considering the supernatural conception of Jesus, we should remember that Joseph and Mary were normal young people, living ordinary but godly lives. In the first century, when a couple became engaged, the woman would continue to live with her parents for a year to prove she had not been sexually active prior the engagement. When Mary was discovered pregnant, naturally, Joseph was ready to divorce her. He planned to get rid of her, yet he wanted to do it in a discreet way that would protect her dignity (v. 19). He clearly knew her character and certainly an unexpected pregnancy made no sense to him. God intervened and sent an angel to tell Joseph that Mary's pregnancy was an act of the Holy Spirit and not the result of extramarital sex, encouraging him not to fear. Joseph believed God's message and took Mary as his wife. Why the virgin birth? It seems a bit odd. Was it really necessary that Jesus be conceived without a natural father? It was. Since Jesus was unlike any other human, in order for him to be fully man and at the same time fully God, his conception had to bypass the sin nature passed on to all born after the fall of humanity in the Garden of Eden.

So Mary knew that she was pregnant, although she was a virgin. And Joseph was made aware of this too. But what about everyone else? As the young couple obeyed God's plan for their lives, imagine the ridicule and mockery they must have endured from friends, neighbors, and even family. From everyone else's perspective, Mary, Jesus' mother, had been sexually active, and Joseph was therefore marrying an unclean woman. Like Mary and Joseph, when we are obedient to God, we can end up misunderstood and mocked by those around us. Let's keep in mind that when we do things God's way, we often forfeit the approval of the world. A lot of what we do and don't do out of allegiance to Jesus can seem strange to those who aren't "on the same page" with us. When trusting in God's plan becomes tough, let's not forget his charge to Joseph: "do not fear." God watches over all those who belong to him.

january
FOUR

MATTHEW 2:1-12

Matthew records what happened some time after Jesus' birth (v. 1). Bethlehem of Judea was a small city located about five miles south of Jerusalem. At this time, Herod "the Great" reigned as the "king" of the Jews. He was put into office by the Romans in 40 BC and remained there until 4 AD. God led a group of men from the east into Israel to meet Jesus. These "wise men" were probably like what we would think of as ancient astronomers, and they saw something in the heavens that let them know the rightful ruler of Israel had arrived. When King Herod discovered these travelers had come into Judea to worship the newborn King, he "freaked out." Herod wasn't even a legitimate Jew. What if the authentic heir to the throne had arrived? Herod quickly went to the religious leaders of the day and asked them where the coming King was to be born. At this time, God's people were waiting for their Messiah, or Anointed One, to come and deliver them from the Romans who dominated Israel. In response to Herod's question, the religious leaders turned to Old Testament prophecy about the coming Messiah and told Herod that according to the book of Micah, written centuries before, the Messiah was to come from Bethlehem.

What's so thought-provoking about all of this is that although King Herod and the religious leaders knew the Messiah had just been born in Bethlehem, they didn't care. They weren't interested in searching to see if Jesus was the One. They just carried on with everyday life, attending to their own needs. And to top it off, instead of seeking God, Herod only worried about losing his own throne! He cared more about protecting what he thought belonged to him, and the last thing he wanted to do was turn his goods over to the rightful owner. In fear of losing his power, Herod lied and told the wise men that he too wanted to worship this new king (v.8). In the end, Herod not only lost his throne, but he missed God as well. How often do we worry about what we will have to give up to worship Jesus rather than rejoice in all we will gain? Keep your hands open and always be willing to give to God what is technically his. Don't be like Herod, willing to lose your soul to save your stuff! Let's make sure we aren't clinging to our agendas or our "thrones" and are instead willing to let Jesus be the rightful King of our lives today.

january
FIVE

MATTHEW 2:13-23

After the wise men from the East left the young Jesus, an angel appeared to Joseph, alerting him that Herod planned to kill the child. The wise men were warned in a dream not to report back to Herod, and when Herod discovered he'd been outwitted, he grew furious. He wiped out all the boys two years and younger in the small village of Bethlehem. According to Herod's logic, it would be safer to get rid of all the town's young boys than to let this new king survive. But Joseph got out before Herod realized what had happened, and Jesus and his parents ended up in Egypt. Later, when the angel let Joseph know that Herod had died, the young family returned to Israel to their hometown of Nazareth in the region of Galilee. Most Jews despised the city of Nazareth because many Roman troops were stationed and living there. Remember, at this time, the Romans were in political control of Israel, and as a result, the Jews despised them. Because of this tension, Jews sought to avoid Nazareth at all costs as part of the great lengths to which they went to keep from defiling themselves with non-Jewish or pagan contacts. Because the residents of Nazareth lived in the same city as the "bad guys," many Jews even judged them to be compromisers who rejected doing the right thing for their own personal gain and convenience.

It's worth pausing here to consider how strange it was that God led Jesus and his family to live in Nazareth. Why would God do this? Why would he want his own Son to live in a "questionable" town? God purposely placed Jesus and his family in Nazareth to foreshadow Jesus' coming rejection by his people. Those soon to encounter Jesus would misunderstand him. God's people sought social and political deliverance, and Jesus just didn't show up in the package the Jewish people were waiting for. Jesus brought spiritual healing, freedom, and release from the penalty of sin. This wasn't the Messiah they had in mind. In the same way, we can reject and even despise God's provision for us because it doesn't come in the packaging we are expecting or hoping for. Let's determine to be open to God's plan for our lives today, even if it looks different from what we anticipated. Remember, he is God and we are not. And he certainly knows what he's doing, even when things seem confusing to us.

january
SIX

MATTHEW 3:1-12

In chapter 3, Matthew transitions to a new character, John the Baptist, the forerunner of Jesus. John was known as "the Baptist" because he preached repentance, and his work included baptizing people in response to his message. In fact, it's hard to read the words of John without feeling convicted and challenged by his bold preaching. Although common belief locates John in the desert, he preached in more of a harsh wilderness than a true desert. In a true desert, it would have been tough to find water for baptism. John was quite straightforward with the religious Jews to whom he preached. They needed to prepare their hearts for the coming Messiah. He let them know that their behavior needed to align with their beliefs and called them to be publicly immersed in water as a symbol of their desire to turn from living sinfully and selfishly to living obediently before God. In verse 9, he sternly warns the religious leaders not to put their hope in their spiritual ancestry, but rather to repent and do things God's way. This was a brand new way of thinking. The religious leaders always assumed that their Jewish heritage automatically qualified them for inclusion in God's kingdom.

Clearly, John taught that God looks at people as individuals. But we can make the same assumption the Jewish leaders did. We can look at the spiritual achievements of our parents, our grandparents, the church we attend, or even our nation, and assume we are good with God as a result. It is critical to remember that in the end each one of us is accountable to God as a unique and responsible soul. Even if we come from a family of dedicated Christians, God does not issue group passes to heaven. Instead, God is going to assess each woman's personal walk with him. Let us each cautiously consider her own relationship with Jesus. Are we putting our hope in our family heritage, or are we making sure that we, as individuals, are right with Christ? Conversely, if we do not come from Christian homes, let's be encouraged that we lose no points with God on that basis. Choose to hear the message of John and live not in the past but in the present, careful to do what God is calling you to do this very day.

january
SEVEN

MATTHEW 3:13-17

Many Jews went to John for baptism, and now it was Jesus' turn. Wait! If baptism symbolizes repentance, then why did Jesus need to be baptized? This seems confusing. It should puzzle us to think about Jesus being baptized. Jesus is the sinless Messiah and actually had no need for baptism. We sense the same bewilderment in John himself, as he protests that he is the one who needs to be baptized by Jesus. In John's mind, things should have been the other way around! We often miss John's humility here. Even though he was the one called by God to prepare the way for the Messiah, he remained aware of his own personal need to be identified as a repentant sinner. Jesus didn't let John keep him from what he came to earth to accomplish, but he clarified things for John by explaining that his actions were "to fulfill all righteousness" (v. 15). In other words, Jesus not only didn't do anything wrong, but he also did everything right, and being baptized was one of the things necessary for him to do in order to live the perfect human life. Every aspect of Jesus' life was exactly on target with God's will for human behavior. After Jesus came up from the water, the Holy Spirit descended upon him, and the Father declared his pleasure with the Son. What a beautiful picture of the Trinity.

Now, what is so amazing about this is that when we repent of our sins and trust Christ as our Lord, we are given his righteousness. This means not only are we released from the penalty of all the wrong we've ever done, but God also chooses to credit us with having done everything right and in accordance with his Law. This is absolutely mind-blowing. We often hear phrases like "Christians aren't perfect, just forgiven." But when we say those words, we are forgetting that because we have been forgiven, we are judged by God as perfect. Wow! If you are a Christian, thank God today for the faultless status you have been graced with as a result of the obedience of Jesus Christ. Because he did everything right, you are blameless. Truly, if this doesn't drive us to love and serve him even more, then we aren't really getting it.

january
EIGHT

MATTHEW 4:1-11

After Jesus was baptized, the Holy Spirit led him into the wilderness to be tempted by the devil himself. Since he had been fasting for forty days, naturally, Jesus was hungry. The devil appeared to him and enticed him to turn the rocks into bread. Matthew records Satan beginning with the phrase "If you are the Son of God." Jesus responded that it would be better for him to obey his Father than to satisfy his own physical hunger. Then Satan tempted him to go to the peak of the temple and jump down, making a grand display of himself. Satan again added, "If you are the Son of God," the angels will rescue you. Jesus told the devil he would not demand a miracle from God by putting his Father to the test. Finally, Satan showed Jesus all the kingdoms of the world, over which Satan presently rules, and offered them to Jesus if Jesus would worship him, tempting Jesus to reign as rightful King without enduring the cross. Jesus told the devil to leave. None but God should be worshipped and served. Jesus flawlessly resisted all three of the devil's temptations.

After reading the account of Jesus' temptation, we may think to ourselves, "Well, of course Jesus resisted Satan. He was God. If I were God, I would resist Satan too!" But we forget that Jesus chose to take on flesh and live life as a genuine human. Although he was the God-man, fully God and fully man, Jesus was tempted just like us. Yet he was without sin. So how did he do it? According to verses 4, 7, and 10, Jesus responded to Satan's temptations with the word of God. He declared, "It is written," and then went on to state to the devil what God revealed through his word. Jesus didn't just say, "Satan, I am God! You can't tempt me!" In his humanity, he relied on the Scripture to battle his enemy. We too must resist Satan's temptations with God's word. But to do this effectively, we, like Jesus, must know the Bible. Let's commit to reading, meditating on, and memorizing Scripture, so that when the enemy comes, even with an offer seemingly too good to refuse, we will be ready with God's authority to say, "It is written," and "Be gone, Satan." Resist the devil today by ignoring his lies and holding fast to the truth recorded in the Bible, God's word.

january
NINE

MATTHEW 4:12-25

After Jesus successfully resisted the devil's temptations, he began his public ministry. When he learned that John the Baptist had been arrested, he left his hometown of Nazareth and went to Capernaum, which basically became the center hub or station of his ministry. Although we might expect Jesus to do the bulk of his three-year ministry in Jerusalem, he actually spent most of his time in the scorned region of Galilee, where both Nazareth and Capernaum were located. This fulfilled the prophecy that the prophet Isaiah foretold about seven hundred years before Jesus' birth that the Messiah would bring light to those in Galilee. Jesus came for the Jew first and then the Gentile, and Galilee contained a mixture of both people groups. John the Baptist prepared the way for Jesus by preaching repentance, and Jesus picked up where John left off, preaching the same message of repentance. Jesus then called those who were to be his disciples and asked them to leave their lifestyles and follow after him. They would no longer throw out nets for fish, but fish for men instead.

Jesus assembled his team, and they accompanied him through the land while he taught, preached, and healed. The signs he performed authenticated his words and his message. It was time for the nation of Israel to receive her Messiah. It can be hard to get through this passage without being struck by the way Andrew, Peter, James, and John responded to Jesus' call. Twice, the text uses the word "immediately" (vv. 20 and 22). *Merriam-Webster's Dictionary* defines "immediately" as "occurring, acting, or accomplished without loss or interval of time." When Jesus called his followers, they responded right away. They left their livelihoods and even their father to obey the Lord's call on their lives. Jesus asks us, as his present-day disciples, to follow him too. How quickly do we respond to the call of the Spirit of Christ in our lives? Do we delay and wonder what will happen with our family or our finances? Or is our obedience to his commands instantaneous, without loss or interval of time? These men didn't delay, and we shouldn't either. What is Jesus asking you to do (or not do) right now? In whatever it is, submit to him without hesitation! May we, like these first disciples, be known for our immediate obedience when it comes to following our Lord.

january
TEN

MATTHEW 5:1-12

Jesus called his disciples and began his ministry, and now, in chapters 5 through 7 of Matthew's Gospel, the author records what is commonly known as the "Sermon on the Mount." Much discussion surrounds the principles Jesus taught throughout this lesson. Some believe that his commands were given to show that no one can be saved by his her own efforts. Others see Jesus' exhortations as motivating behavior that should properly characterize all of his followers. It would seem that both sides are valid. In the first twelve verses of this discourse, Jesus explains to the crowds around him what kind of person is blessed. The word "blessed" in its simplest sense means "happy." Jesus described the kind of people who are happy because they are doing what God wants.

Remember that most of the religious men and women at this time thought God was obligated to accept them into his kingdom because they were good people and of Jewish descent. Jesus painted a beautiful portrait of those who are right with God, describing them in different terms than the religious people of the day valued. Let's look at the eight core qualities of a happy person according to Jesus:

1. Poor in spirit—they realize their spiritual need and depend on God f or salvation; they will inherit the kingdom.
2. Mournful—they are painfully aware of their sin; God will bring them comfort.
3. Meek—they are dependent upon the Spirit; they will have a place with God.
4. Hungry and thirsty for righteousness—they desperately want to live God's way; God will fulfill their longings.
5. Merciful—they extend mercy to others; they will receive God's mercy.
6. Pure in heart—they are clean through faith in Christ; God will reveal himself to them.
7. Peacemakers—they work to bring peace to others by speaking the truth in love; they are like the Father.
8. Persecuted for righteousness—they are willing to do the right thing, even when it means rejection; like the prophets who have gone before them, they will be rewarded.

This is what characterizes people who are more than clean on the outside. They are right with God on the inside. As you meditate on these eight characteristics today, think about where you might want to make changes so that you will be a person Jesus calls "blessed."

january
ELEVEN

MATTHEW 5:13-22

Jesus continued his sermon, leaving much to meditate on and think about. For instance, in verses 21-22, and then five more times throughout this chapter, Jesus states, "You have heard that it was said… But I say to you…" In doing this, Jesus contrasted the difference between what the religious leaders of the day taught and what God really looks for. Clearly, Jesus emphasized that God not only cares about our outward behavior, but about our inner attitudes and motives as well. Backing up, an important section of this passage that is often overlooked reveals the core of Jesus' ministry. In verse 17, Jesus states that he came not "to abolish the Law or the Prophets" but "to fulfill them." The phrase "the Law and the Prophets" was used to refer to the entire Old Testament. In verse 18, Jesus uses the word "truly." This is actually the Greek word we translate as "amen." Jesus commonly prefaced his teaching with "amen" when he was making an intense declaration. Jesus taught that neither an iota nor a dot will pass away from the Law until all is fulfilled. The iota in Hebrew script has been compared to the dot above the English lower case letter "i," and the dot compared to the stroke that makes the difference between the capital letter "P" and the capital letter "R."

So what did Jesus mean when he said, "neither an iota nor a dot" will pass away? Jesus declared that every detail of the Scripture would be obeyed by him and fulfilled in him. He lived in line with what the Law taught, and he brought the Scripture to completion by fulfilling the prophetic words that pointed to him. Because Jesus ushered in the New Covenant, we can forget that he loved, obeyed, and fulfilled the Old Testament. He taught his audience not to "relax" even one of the commandments or instruct others to do so. Though the rabbis of the day made a distinction between light and heavy commandments, Jesus explained that they were all important to God, and they were important to him too. The person who obeys the commands of God and instructs others to obey as well will be called great in the kingdom (v. 19). Let's make sure we embrace the full counsel of Scripture instead of keeping the parts we like and throwing out the parts we don't. Let's choose to love God's law the way Jesus did.

january
TWELVE

MATTHEW 5:23-37

In this text, Jesus continues his Sermon on the Mount, addressing many issues. Concerning anger and broken relationships, Jesus explained how essential it is for those at odds with one another to get things right. If a worshipper about to make an offering to God realized that someone had a complaint against her, she should get her relationship back in order before making the sacrifice (vv. 23-24). The Lord cares about the inward attitude of the worshipper even more than the sacrifice itself. Jesus said the act of adultery is absolutely wrong, but so is an attitude of lust. He taught that God's design for marriage is a lifelong commitment. Jesus also explained that people should be honest. The religious leaders manipulated oaths so they could later get out of statements or commitments they weren't sure about. All of this was ridiculous. A "yes" should mean "yes," and a "no" should mean "no." Jesus says twice, in verses 29 and 30, it is "better that you lose one of your members than that your whole body go into hell."

What did he mean? Was Jesus promoting self-mutilation? No! Jesus stressed that we may have to let God do some extreme surgery, even at the expense of one of our "body parts," to get our hearts right before him. Do you have an angry or a lustful heart? What about a broken relationship? Are you at odds with a brother or sister in Christ? Maybe the tables are turned, and someone in your life has hurt you. If the Holy Spirit is prompting you to reconcile with her, don't hesitate. Contact her and get things right. It can take some radical amputation of our pride to seek reconciliation with someone who has wronged us, or feels we have wronged her, but the more we Christians realize what we have been forgiven of—all our sins and transgressions before a holy God—and what we have been graced with—the righteousness of Christ—the easier it becomes to overlook petty offenses and get our relationships in order. Since Christians are forgiven people, we should be known as forgiving people. When it comes to anger, forgiveness, lust, divorce, or lying, are you holding onto anything contrary to God's will for your life? If so, ask the Spirit to perform his surgery on your heart, and get things right on the inside today.

january
THIRTEEN

MATTHEW 5:38-48

Jesus continued to contrast what the religious leaders of the day thought and practiced with what God actually desires. In verse 38, Jesus quotes the Old Testament, which declares "eye for an eye" and "tooth for a tooth." This principle, if properly enforced, would protect victims and ensure that punishments did not exceed actual offenses. Jesus taught that those who want to do things God's way don't have to take revenge. He didn't mean that sin should run rampant in a community. If someone robs our home, we should call the police. But Jesus pointed out that God doesn't approve of his people seeking private revenge. In addition, the righteous person is not only willing to overlook an offense, but "goes the extra mile" (v. 41) and relinquishes her rights for the sake of others. Again, Jesus wasn't throwing right and wrong out the window, but teaching his followers to put others' interests before their own. Christians should be marked by kindness, generosity, and a trust in God to make things right. In verse 48, Jesus ends his teaching about loving our enemies with an interesting statement: "You therefore must be perfect, as your heavenly Father is perfect." What in the world did Jesus mean? This statement puts us all in a place of tremendous need because we have all failed to meet God's holy standards. And so, we are all doomed without the forgiveness and righteousness of Christ credited to our accounts.

At the same time, Jesus exhorted his followers to keep their standards high. In fact, our standards should be as high as possible. They should be the standards of God. This too serves to level the playing field, since we can all improve our character. No matter how long you've been a Christian, or how much you've matured in your spiritual life, there's always room to grow. Rather than seeing spiritual development or sanctification as a chore, we should see it as a joy and a promise. Those who love God will become more like him. It's a guarantee. Let's be encouraged as Christians today, maintaining an attitude of anticipation, expecting God to get involved in our lives and to help us to become more like him. What area of your life right now isn't meeting God's holy standard? Confess it, ask him for help, and be confident, knowing that he's not done with you yet. He will continue to work in his children. How exciting is that?

january
FOURTEEN

MATTHEW 6:1-15

The Sermon on the Mount continues through Matthew's sixth chapter. And Jesus again explains how important our motives are to God. When we do good deeds or give, we should never do so to impress others. Instead, we should perform acts of kindness from a grateful heart, even doing things in secret, knowing that God sees all of our actions and won't overlook any of our service to him. Then Jesus contrasts the wrong way to pray (before others) with the right way to pray (before God). After instructing his disciples to begin prayer with worship, Jesus taught his followers four things to ask for: God's kingdom and will, daily bread, forgiveness, and deliverance. It's fascinating to think about the phrase "daily bread." First, the request for daily bread comes immediately after the request for God's will to be done in our lives and the lives of those for whom we pray. It seems like a jump from one realm to the next as Jesus moves us from God's kingdom directly to our physical needs. Yet, how encouraging to know that God takes our needs seriously. When Jesus taught his audience to ask for bread, he included the word "daily." We are to pray continually or daily that God would grace us with the resources we need for life. He wants us, in humility, to depend on him for literally everything.

Do you ever feel like your physical needs aren't important to God? We often look at the template for prayer Jesus gave his disciples and get so caught up in the wonder and majesty of it that we forget how valuable we are to him. The model Jesus gave us shows that God desires our continual dependence upon him. What a contrast to "checking the box" when we pray, simply going through the motions. God wants our total trust. Are you relying on God for your daily bread? Do you come to him often, asking him to meet your needs? Or do you wait until circumstances become really difficult before you pour your heart and requests out to him? Make sure dependence on God through prayer is the habit of your life. The more you ask him for help, the more humble you will become and the more you will see his hand of provision. Let the phrase "Give us this day our daily bread" remind you to pray without ceasing.

january
FIFTEEN

MATTHEW 6:16-24

As we move through the Sermon on the Mount, we see Jesus continue to point out the difference between the practices of the outwardly religious and the way God desires people to live. At the time, those who sought God fasted as an act of self-denial to focus on spiritual things. Many of the religious leaders made it obvious to others that they were fasting in an attempt to be recognized as "spiritual." Jesus clarified that if they fasted to gain the approval of man, then man's approval was their reward. God isn't interested in commending those who do the right thing for the wrong reason. Then Jesus hit hard on the topic of money. In verses 19 through 20, Jesus warns against the opinion of the day that said money was a measure of righteousness. The Pharisees believed that God financially blesses those he loves. So, to be seen as righteous, they put much effort into amassing for themselves material possessions on earth. Jesus revealed the foolishness of investing merely in the things of this life and instructed his audience to invest in the life to come.

What's exciting about Jesus' teaching is that we actually can "lay up for ourselves treasures in heaven." When we choose to do things God's way, even if it means loss for us now, we can be certain of gaining eternal reward. Many say, "All I want is to go to heaven. I don't need an eternal reward." Though this can sound humble and right, it may betray a form of spiritual laziness. Jesus clearly stressed the need to live in a way that will bring eternal gain. Jesus explains in verse 21, "For where your treasure is, there your heart will be also." It takes more faith to live for treasure in the life to come than to live for treasure in this life. The one who lives to amass the biggest eternal reward possible is ultimately employing the greatest amount of faith. Is your heart in heaven or on earth? Do you seek an eternal reward? If not, you aren't exercising the faith that Jesus calls his followers to live by. If you are seeking an eternal reward, be encouraged! You are living consistently with your desire to please God. Let's rejoice today that as Christians we can look forward to treasure that will never be taken from us.

january
SIXTEEN

MATTHEW 6:25-34

Jesus continues his Sermon on the Mount, moving from the subjects of money and eternal rewards to anxiety. Three times in this passage, Jesus exhorts his listeners with the command, "Do not be anxious" (verses 25, 31 and 34). We might think, "Are you kidding me, Jesus? Don't be anxious?! You have no idea what kind of stress I am under." It can seem counterintuitive to "not be anxious." There are so many things to worry about: finances, relationships, and health, to name just a few. Are we really not to worry about any of this? We can easily forget that Jesus actually lived in a time and culture in which lack of food was a common problem. The majority of people woke up wondering if they would get to eat that day or that week. We may battle many issues that make us feel insecure, but we usually aren't struggling to get something to eat. The problem with most of us is that although we have food, it might not be the kind of food we like. How many of us don't have any clothes? Again, we are usually troubled not because we don't have clothes, but because the ones we have are out of fashion. For most in the Western world, food, drink, and clothing aren't legitimate problems.

Then Jesus adds that all the worrying we do won't make anything better anyway. In verse 27, he asks, "And which of you by being anxious can add a single hour to his span of life?" Jesus said worrying is a waste of your time. Stop and think about how much more we could focus on God and his kingdom if we weren't worried about eating in nice restaurants and wearing the latest shoes and purse. Remember, Jesus addressed an audience that actually had to wonder where these things would come from, yet he still challenged them not to worry. How spiritually effective could our lives be if we were satisfied with what we have?! No angel in heaven is feeling sorry for us because we don't have a nicer dress or a loaded Starbucks card. Think about what makes you anxious. Is it going on social media, reading magazines, or watching TV? If something you're doing is triggering anxiety, work to eliminate it. Let's get the point Jesus makes here and stop stressing out about the things of this life!

january
SEVENTEEN

MATTHEW 7:1-11

In this section, Jesus teaches about making judgments and begins with a statement that has been misused by many. He says, "Judge not, that you be not judged." If no extra explanation were given, we might believe the error that many opponents of Christianity have concluded: Christians should not judge. But as we read the passage in context, we see that Jesus does provide clarification. It's not that we shouldn't judge. It's that we shouldn't judge wrongly. So, how do we judge wrongly? Three key truths about wrong judging emerge from verses 1-3. First, we should not be people who are habitually critical or harsh. Second, we need to realize that those we judge are probably judging us in return. And finally, we must guard against practicing the very things we are condemning in others. Jesus taught that the point of judgment is to "get the speck out of our brother's eye" or to help a brother deal with sin in his life. But to get that "speck" or splinter out, we need to be aware of the potential "log" or wooden beam in our own eye. At the same time, we can't try to beat wisdom into someone who really has no interest in the things of God. When the gospel is blatantly rejected, we need to move on.

What Jesus said about the speck and the log is actually pretty funny. Can you imagine someone struggling to get a small splinter out of another person's eye with a giant beam stuck in her own? How strange we must look to God when we jump all over one another without dealing with the sin in our own lives. Christian judgment should be loving, kind, honest, and purposeful. Remember, Jesus was not saying that we should never judge, but when we do, as we should, we need to be incredibly careful to judge rightly. What about you? Are you a critical person? Do others know you as a fault-finder? When you judge people, are you aware of the fact that they may be judging you for the very same thing you are pointing out in them? And when you judge, are repentance and reconciliation your goals? Jesus doesn't tell us to just leave the speck there. Let's help our sister get that splinter out of her eye! But let's make certain that when we judge, we do it in a way that is pleasing to God.

january
EIGHTEEN

MATTHEW 7:12-23

After reading this passage, it's hard not to be struck by the intensity of verses 21-23. Honestly, these words of Jesus sound pretty scary. And they are. To begin with, Jesus was clear that only two eternal destinations exist. In the next life, people will either be inside the kingdom of heaven or outside the kingdom of heaven. In love, Jesus explained to his audience that their destiny would not be based on what they said or even what they did in his name. Instead, it would be determined by whether or not they had a legitimate relationship with him. The people Jesus described had accomplished many things for him, even acknowledging him as God ("Lord, Lord!"), but they refused to do the will of the Father. The result was total and complete rejection. So what does it mean to do the will of the Father in heaven? We must begin by acknowledging that we cannot earn a right relationship with God through our own goodness. Instead, we must enter by the narrow gate of repentance and faith. This means that we don't come to God offering him a package of obedience that we have created, but we come completely broken, confessing our sins, placing all our trust in Jesus and ready to do his will. When this happens, God's Holy Spirit transforms us from the inside out and we begin a relationship with Christ that lasts for eternity.

If you have never turned from your sin and put all your confidence in Jesus, please don't hesitate any longer. Admit your sin to God, thank him for the righteousness of Christ credited to your account, and decide with the help of the Holy Spirit to live for him and his kingdom. If you are confused, ask Jesus to show you whether you have honestly come to the place of willingness to exchange your life for his. Clearly, we can't enter a relationship with Jesus if we aren't really willing to do so. If you are honestly in Christ, then thank God that you will be with him forever. May this truth encourage you more today than ever before, even in the midst of difficulty. And pray for those around you who haven't fully trusted in Jesus yet. Just as God opened your eyes to see your need for him, he can do the same for the people in your prayers.

january
NINETEEN

MATTHEW 7:24-8:4

When Jesus concluded his Sermon on the Mount, the crowds were astonished by his teaching. They were literally overwhelmed as Jesus taught them new things from God rather than deferring to what well-known rabbis had said in the past. The cleansing of the leper in verse 3 is the first of ten miracles Matthew records in chapters 8 and 9, which provide a series of snapshots from the healing ministry of Jesus. The leper was a most unlikely candidate for Jesus' ministry as lepers were excluded from Israel's healthy population. Leprosy, a horrible skin disease, was contagious, and once caught, some forms were incurable. Thus, anyone found with leprosy had to live outside the city and away from its residents. If a leper did happen to cross paths with a non-leper, he was required by law to call out, "Unclean, unclean!" signaling the potential danger of his presence. Can you imagine what life must have been like for those with incurable leprosy? They were not only subject to this terrible disease, but cut off from all social life, including their families. We often feel discouraged by our circumstances. But how many of us suffer the hopelessness that ancient lepers felt?

We see this despair in the leper's approach to Jesus. He knew full well that Jesus could heal him. So his question wasn't "Can you heal me?" but "*Will* you heal me?" It was as if he asked, "Jesus, will you heal someone as insignificant and castaway as I am?" Let's not miss what happened here! Not only did Jesus heal, but he also displayed incredible compassion as he purposely stretched out his hand and touched the man. This was totally counter-cultural. How long must it have been since this man received a physical touch? Wow! What about you? Do you feel "unclean" because of past sin? Have you confessed it and asked Jesus to forgive you or heal you? If so, know that not only has he completely cleansed you from your unrighteousness, but he also embraces you and causes his Spirit to live in you. Just as the leper was made whole again, so is the Christian. Let's remember as we go through our day that Jesus himself has shown great compassion on us and cleansed us from all of our sin. Let's show compassion to others as we demonstrate the wonderful things our Savior has done.

january
TWENTY

MATTHEW 8:5-13

Jesus went back to Capernaum, the central hub of his ministry, and performed the second of ten miracles recorded by Matthew in chapters 8 and 9. Again, we find another unlikely candidate for the ministry of Jesus: the Gentile servant boy of a Gentile centurion. The centurion, an officer in the army and probably Roman, recognized who Jesus was and believed Jesus had the power to heal his servant. The boy suffered great pain, and the centurion was quite concerned. In verse 7, Jesus responds to the centurion's faith by saying, "I will come and heal him." Think about Jesus' compassion for this man and his servant. Jesus was actually willing to enter a Gentile home to heal this suffering boy. The centurion knew the Jews considered it "unclean" to enter the residence of a Gentile, and so, to keep Jesus from an awkward position, he demonstrated tremendous faith. The centurion told Jesus he was aware of his ability to heal without even being present. The centurion gave orders, and men under him followed. In the same way, Jesus could give orders, and all creation would follow. Jesus was more than impressed with the great faith of this man. According to verse 13, "The servant was healed at that very moment."

No record of Jesus healing from a distance exists before this incident, yet the centurion didn't limit the scope of Jesus' rule. Instead, he trusted in Jesus' ability to do whatever he wanted. How often do we limit God's power to work in our lives? We can wrongly think that "A" or "B" must be in place for God to act. This centurion realized the authority of Jesus. When he addressed Jesus as "Lord," he showed that he knew Jesus is the ultimate boss with influence over not only the seen realm, but the unseen realm as well. Determine to be like the centurion today. Acknowledge that Jesus can do whatever he wants, however he wants, and whenever he wants. Jesus is the Lord of all, and nothing is too difficult for him. Bring him your toughest requests, confident that no matter what answer you get, he is completely able to do whatever is best for your life. If it appears he is saying "no" to your request, trust that he's got a reason. The "no" is never because your desire is too difficult for him to accomplish.

january
TWENTY-ONE

MATTHEW 8:14-27

Jesus' healing of Peter's wife's mother is the third of ten miracles Matthew records in chapters 8 and 9. When the fever left her, she was immediately restored and even able to get up and serve Jesus. News traveled fast, and soon many people were brought to Jesus. He healed and delivered them too, just as Isaiah foretold seven hundred years earlier. Because of all the miracles that took place, a crowd began to form around Jesus. He knew many came to him for the wrong reasons. They wanted what Jesus had to offer, but they didn't want Jesus himself. And so that none were confused, Jesus explained to the crowd what it really meant to be his disciple. In verses 19 and 20, a scribe, or a teacher of God's law, says he wants to follow Jesus. But Jesus, knowing the scribe's heart, revealed to him that if he were to come with the group, it would mean less than a "middle-class" existence for him. Jesus didn't own a home, and those who came after him left the comforts of this life as well. In verses 21 and 22, a second man asks to bury his father before coming after Jesus. This shouldn't have been unreasonable, right? He wanted to take care of his father, and then after his father died, he would follow.

Jesus responds with a seemingly strange statement: "Follow me, and leave the dead to bury their own dead" (v. 22). What does that mean? Jesus used this conversation to teach that discipleship isn't something we can turn on and off. This man probably wanted to make sure he received his proper inheritance when his father passed away. After that, he said he would be ready to go. When Jesus said, "Leave the dead to bury their own dead," he meant that anyone could manage funeral arrangements. Following Jesus means we will probably risk at least some of our comforts on earth as God must always be the top priority in our lives, even when there's a cost involved. What are some of the securities and conveniences of life you are afraid to give up to fully follow Jesus? Ask God to show you whether you are wholeheartedly living for him. If the answer is "no," be willing to do whatever it takes to sincerely embrace what it means to be a disciple of Christ. In the end, nothing this world has to offer is better than loving, living for, and serving Jesus.

january
TWENTY-TWO

MATTHEW 8:28-34

Jesus had just calmed the storm on the Sea of Galilee, the fourth of the ten miracles recorded in chapters 8 and 9, and now he and the disciples arrived ashore in the country called the Gadarenes, which was the land of the Gentiles. This was unclean territory; the Jews would never be found herding pigs like their non-Jewish neighbors. When Jesus walked past the local cemetery, two violent, demon-possessed men approached him. The demons in these men knew who Jesus was, and they addressed him as the Son of God. They literally screamed at Jesus, telling him that it wasn't the time for their torment in hell yet. Then, when they realized that Jesus was going to command them to leave the men's bodies, they pleaded to be sent into the herd of unclean animals nearby. After Jesus performed the fifth of the ten miracles, casting the evil spirits out of the men, the pigs ran down the hill and drowned themselves. Wow! What a sight that must have been! But the herdsmen were in big trouble. The entire group of possibly two thousand pigs was dead. What would they tell their bosses, and how would they explain this great loss? They rushed back to town to let everyone know that it was all Jesus' fault.

Instead of welcoming Jesus, the one who had all authority over the unseen realm and who had just freed two of their fellow humans from demonic bondage, the townspeople rejected him and begged him to leave. If Jesus' presence meant financial loss for them, then get him out! It's sad that the local people were more upset by the deaths of their pigs than they were gladdened by the deliverance of the two men. We live in a world that places supreme importance on finances and material goods. What if Jesus came to your town and everyone lost their homes as a result? Would you welcome him, or would you tell him to go away? What if your community suffered monetary loss, but two men were saved? Would it be worth it to you? Accounts like this remind us that eternal souls are more important than stuff. Let's make sure we value Jesus more than our bank accounts. Pray for a proper attitude toward your money and things today. And be willing to part with some of your resources so that others might be spared.

january
TWENTY-THREE

MATTHEW 9:1-13

Jesus returned to Capernaum, where he lived at this time. Nazareth was his hometown, where he grew up, but Capernaum, near the Sea of Galilee, was the center of his ministry. A paralyzed man was presented to him, and Jesus addressed the paralytic by saying, "Take heart" or "Take courage." Then Jesus made a radical declaration to the man in the hearing of all those present: "Your sins are forgiven." Why did Jesus charge him to "Take courage"? Was he about to experience something painful? No! Instead, according to Jesus, even though this man was quite sick, he had absolutely nothing to fear because all his sins were taken away. When Jesus told the man his sins were erased, the crowd began to reason, "This is crazy! Jesus is claiming to be God! Only God can forgive sins!" Jesus knew exactly what they were thinking, and to prove he had the authority to release this man from his sins, he completely healed his broken body. When Jesus asks, "which is easier to say, 'Your sins are forgiven,' or 'Rise and walk'?" we would think the answer would be "Your sins are forgiven." That would be much easier "to say" because no one could verify the truth of that statement. To say, "Rise and walk" would be harder because everyone could clearly see whether or not a man was healed, right?

The real answer to Jesus' question was that it is easier to say "Rise and walk." Any healer can say that. But only God can pardon sin. Jesus forgave the man of his sins, and he healed his broken body. This was the sixth of ten miracles Matthew records in chapters 8 and 9. We can forget what an incredible miracle our salvation is. If we are Christians, God has chosen to release us from the punishment we deserve for our sins. Yet, we can know we are forgiven and still mope around, thinking other issues in our lives are too difficult for God to deal with. How foolish we can be! If God has freely given us the blood of his own Son, he's not going to keep us from anything else we need in this life. God won't withhold any truly good thing from his kids. Let's rejoice that our sins are forgiven, and as a result, remember nothing else necessary for us is too hard for God to accomplish.

january
TWENTY-FOUR

MATTHEW 9:14-26

In verse 14, the disciples of John are puzzled by what Jesus has done, and they ask, "Why are we fasting, but the disciples of Jesus aren't?" Jesus let them know the time would come when his followers would fast too, but at the time of this text, since he was still physically with them, it wasn't yet appropriate. Then he explained that he brought something new. Jesus said it would be absurd to patch an old, ragged piece of clothing with a fresh piece of material. When the mended garment endured strain, the strong new patch would pull away from the thin, tattered material. The resulting tear would be worse than if the patch were never even used. The same principle held true for wine and wineskins. Old wineskins lost their elasticity. If new wine, which was still fermenting, was placed in old wineskins, the chemicals produced during the fermentation process would cause the old skins to burst. The point Jesus made would have been clear to his audience. Jesus was not trying to patch up the old system of Judaism. Now, Jesus was in no way dismissing the Old Testament. Instead, he rejected many of the religious practices that had grown out of Jewish tradition.

Then Matthew records the seventh and eighth of ten miracles in chapters 8 and 9. Jesus healed two daughters: the child of a synagogue ruler and a woman he addressed as "daughter." Jesus continued to powerfully demonstrate the principles he taught. Thinking back on the patch and the wineskins, how attached are we to traditions? Are we unwilling to budge when it comes to our favorite practices? We need to make sure we hold fast to biblical law and principle, yet remain flexible in areas that aren't moral issues and may need to adapt over time. Should women wear pants to church? Should drums and an electric guitar be included in worship? Should the weekly bulletin be published in paper or digital format? If we get too hung up on the way things used to be, we can lose our ability to be effective for the gospel in a rapidly changing world. Remember, we are saved to let go of ourselves and lead others to Jesus. So, hold fast to God's absolutes, yet bend wherever Jesus would bend to reach as many people as possible with the good news.

january
TWENTY-FIVE

MATTHEW 9:27-34

Matthew records Jesus' healing of two blind men and the deliverance of a mute man, the ninth and tenth of ten miracles found in these two chapters. Clearly, Jesus has power and authority over all of creation, so it is important that people listen to and obey what he taught. Jesus wants people to follow him for the right reasons. The two blind men followed Jesus because they desperately wanted sight. They addressed Jesus as the "Son of David," a title used for the Messiah as the Messiah was to be a descendant of King David. Interestingly, the text says Jesus didn't acknowledge the blind men until they entered a house. Then he healed them. After Jesus restored the eyes of the blind men, he ordered them not say anything about what had just occurred. Didn't Jesus want people to know he was the Messiah? Why was he hiding who he was from the people?

It seems Jesus didn't want people seeing him as a political Messiah who was there to overthrow the government, so he waited until he and the blind men had entered a house before engaging with them. He also didn't want people coming simply to get a physical healing. He came to set people free from sin. The supernatural healing and deliverance that took place were to confirm the truth of the claims he made. What is your motive for coming to Jesus? Do you want your marriage fixed, your finances ordered, or a bad habit overcome? Though all these things may be byproducts of obedience to Christ, they shouldn't be the reason for our faith. Instead, we must see our desperate need for spiritual forgiveness. We can improve our marriages, get our finances in order, and overcome all our bad habits, but still remain in our sins. And the opposite may be true too. We could come to Jesus and still have problems in our marriages, finances, or even new hardships to deal with in life. But if we are delivered from the penalty of our sins, our daily difficulties pale in comparison to the pardon we have freely received. Make sure your motive for following Jesus is right. If it's not, recognize your deep need for his forgiveness and turn to him in full surrender today.

january
TWENTY-SIX

MATTHEW 9:35-10:4

While Jesus traveled throughout Galilee, visiting various cities and working from the local synagogues, he met many people. Jesus took on flesh and became a man so that souls would be saved from the eternal consequences of their sins. His ministry involved continual teaching, preaching, and healing (to authenticate his message). As Jesus saw the crowds around him, he had compassion on them. The Greek word for compassion implies that intense emotion was involved; he felt deep sympathy for them. Why did he feel sorry for them? Because they were like sheep without a shepherd. If a herd of sheep had no shepherd, there would be no one to care for them and protect them. Jesus also said they were "harassed and helpless." These words describe sheep that have been injured by bushes with thorns or dangerous animals. Without the shepherd's protection, sheep often ended up on the ground, or cast down, with no one to assist and no way to get out of their predicament. Jesus saw the crowds were in spiritual danger and unable to rescue themselves.

Sheep are incredibly needy animals because they are basically defenseless. Shepherdless sheep would have been easy prey for any attack. When Jesus looked at all those around him, he saw them as sheep in the midst of wolves. Those wolves were the religious teachers of the day who led the sheep away from Jesus, the shepherd they so desperately needed. Even when no aggressive animals lurk nearby, sheep must be directed to green pastures and quiet waters for food and drink. The bottom line is that sheep really can't do much on their own. They need someone to deliver them from the perils of life. We are all, in a spiritual sense, like sheep. We can't provide salvation for ourselves, and we are continually open to the attack of false doctrine. If we are under the care of the Good Shepherd, we need to utilize the resources he's provided for us by staying in his word, depending upon his Spirit, and participating in his church. If you are neglecting any of those, then change that. On the other hand, if you are making use of what Jesus has given you, then, out of gratitude for his care, tell someone else about your compassionate Shepherd today. All people need the protection Jesus offers, whether they realize it or not.

january
TWENTY-SEVEN

MATTHEW 10:5-15

Jesus commissioned his twelve apostles to announce the same message that he and John the Baptist preached: "The kingdom of heaven is here!" As they went from place to place and town to village, the apostles were to embrace those who accepted the news they brought and reject those who didn't accept what they proclaimed. Jesus declared the severe consequences for those who would not receive the twelve. In verse 15, he begins with the phrase "Truly, I say to you." This signaled to the listeners that the next statement was critically important. Jesus then says, "It will be more bearable on the day of judgment for the land of Sodom and Gomorrah than for that town." Most remember Sodom and Gomorrah as the twin cities known for their incredible wickedness. Because of their evil practices, darkness, and the hardened hearts of those who dwelt there, God completely overthrew and destroyed Sodom and Gomorrah.

Jesus' teaching here is a truth we should all stop and think about for a few minutes. What did he mean by "it will be more bearable" for Sodom and Gomorrah than for the towns that deliberately rejected the apostles? Those who spurned the message of Jesus' sent ones would be punished more severely than the outlandish sinners of ancient history chronicled in Genesis. In a time and a place where most have come face to face with the gospel, if we continue to reject his message, how do we think we will escape the judgment of God? If you have family or friends who are refusing the good news, understand that Jesus takes this dismissal very seriously. If you are faithfully communicating the message Jesus preached, know that God continues to stand behind those who proclaim his word. Even though we may face rejection from the world now, it will be nothing compared to the eternal wrath that those who snub him will face in the life to come. Pray for those close to you who have not surrendered to Christ in repentance and faith. Be confident as you continue to petition God on their behalf and speak the truth in love to them. God has put specific souls in your life for a reason. Share the good news! Though the majority may not listen, you never know who will, and who may even be saved today.

january
TWENTY-EIGHT

MATTHEW 10:16-25

Jesus teaches another tough message in this text. As the disciples did what he charged, they would be like sheep in the midst of wolves, implying exposure to constant danger. In response to the trouble they would face, Jesus cautioned them to be "Wise as serpents and innocent as doves." What did Jesus mean when he asked them to be like serpents and doves? Although Jesus previously called them sheep, which are defenseless, he wasn't asking them to be stupid. Being as wise as serpents, which are considered cunning, means followers of Jesus need to be careful and thoughtful when they face tough situations. At the same time, they are to be like doves, which are considered gentle and kind. What a tough balance the Christian is called to! We need the empowerment of God's Spirit to aid us in our weaknesses as we employ wisdom and kindness in all that we do. In verse 23, Jesus makes a statement that has been the source of much controversy. When he said his disciples would not have gone through all of Israel before he returns, he probably meant that after his ascension to the Father, he will return again before all the Jews have been evangelized. In other words, followers of Jesus have much work to do because many souls are in need of salvation.

Despite the strong warning in this passage, Jesus gave the disciples encouragement. Even if they ended up facing rejection from their own family members (v. 21) or extreme hostility (v. 22), they were to remain confident, as their salvation and eternal protection were secure. Another layer of hope exists here as well. Although the followers of Jesus will suffer much difficulty for the gospel, God was and is already aware of every detail and factors each trial into his predetermined plan. Nothing escapes his knowledge! The call to stand up for Christ in an unreceptive world is truly a high charge. The believer is to be thoughtful and smart, yet gracious and merciful, even in the face of rejection and hostility. How are you doing at handling the persecution God has allowed in your life? Are you overwhelmed by the pain and choosing not to see his grand design in all things? Or are you using every opportunity to speak the truth in love? Let's determine to press on today in the work God has prepared for us to do, remembering that even if we are despised, we are to follow in the footsteps of Jesus.

january
TWENTY-NINE

MATTHEW 10:26-33

After warning the disciples about the persecution they would face in his name, Jesus exhorted them nevertheless to be found faithful in proclaiming the truths he proclaimed (v. 27). They were to speak his message boldly and without fear because God was with them and involved in every circumstance of their lives. Two sparrows could be purchased for a penny, yet God is attentive to each and every bird. God also knows exactly how many hairs are on every person's head at all times. The point Jesus made was clear: God is in control. Although men could physically hurt the disciples, no human has the ability to harm any soul who belongs to Jesus. It is remarkable that Jesus used sparrows and hair to illustrate God's concern for all of his creation. He taught that God is involved in the trivial details we might consider beneath his notice. Even though a pair of sparrows weren't worth more than a cheeseburger in the economy of Jesus' time, God took note of every single one. If God is interested in so-called worthless birds and takes notice of hairs on heads, then he is obviously not too busy or too lofty to be intimately involved with every detail in the lives of those who place their trust in him.

While reassuring the disciples of God's care and concern, Jesus made a strong declaration throughout his teaching. He reasoned that because the God of the universe is so intimately involved in every area of the believer's life, his followers have no need to be afraid. Three times in this discourse, Jesus says, "Do not fear." Jesus never promised that harm or trouble would bypass those who belong to him. In fact, he said the opposite. Yet he encouraged his followers to stop being afraid. On the other hand, in verse 28, Jesus says all should fear the Lord, who can destroy the whole person in hell. What a graphic reminder of what Jesus has saved his people from. Why should we turn from fear? What's wrong with it? Fear paralyzes us and keeps us from doing what God has called us to do. It also reveals a lack of trust in God. What are you afraid of? Choose to let God's truth override your insecurities. Say goodbye to your fears and embrace full obedience to Jesus today.

january
THIRTY

MATTHEW 10:34-42

Jesus delivered another strong teaching to his disciples. Because he purposefully came to bring peace between God and man, which included overcoming sin, tension was bound to arise between those who responded positively to him and those who did not. Jesus warned about this natural hostility by saying he came to bring a sword. At times, the ones who reject Jesus are just as intense about their hatred of him as believers are passionate about the Lord. The gospel "polarizes" or puts people on opposite sides of one another. Does a soul love Jesus, or not? The answer to that question will have eternal consequences and generates a strong emotional response. Doing things the way Jesus asked will lead to rejection, even from beloved family members. Nevertheless, all Christians must be ready to pay this price. In fact, the follower of Jesus must take up her cross and follow Jesus or endure extreme hostility, even to the point of death, out of allegiance to him (v. 38). In this time period, when a criminal carried his cross, it symbolized his full agreement with the Roman government's determination that his offense merited death. When the followers of Jesus carried their crosses, they acknowledged that Jesus had rightful authority over their lives. Yet, ironically, in giving up themselves for him, they would find true life.

In verse 39, Jesus gives his followers tremendous hope as he explains that to focus on self is destructive, but to exist for the glory of God is really to experience life. Even more, Jesus let his disciples know that a mere drink of water, given on his behalf to the least of his followers, would not go unnoticed by God. Do you feel discouraged when you face rejection for standing up for Jesus? It's easy to feel overwhelmed as the world around us thinks very differently than we do as Christians rewired from the inside out to serve God. Remember, Jesus warned his followers on multiple occasions that following him would cost them. Yet the benefit so outweighs the price. Those who abandon themselves to follow Jesus live for the glory of God, and not one detail of what is done for him goes unnoticed. Be encouraged today as you speak and live consistently with biblical Christianity. Everything you do for Jesus will be worth it in the end.

january
THIRTY-ONE

MATTHEW 11:1-19

Jesus continued to travel around Galilee, teaching and preaching. John the Baptist was in prison and heard about all that Jesus was doing. Naturally, John was a bit confused, so he sent his disciples to Jesus on his behalf to get clarification. The disciples of John asked Jesus if he truly was the one they were waiting for, since their leader was in prison. Wasn't the promised deliverer supposed to overcome evil, judge sin, and establish his kingdom? Jesus responded by quoting Isaiah's prophecy about the coming Messiah who would heal, raise the dead, and preach the gospel, which is exactly what Jesus did (v. 5). Jesus affirmed that he was the Messiah they waited for. He then explained that John was not weak to question this. It would have been hard for the Jews to think of anyone attaining a higher place than a prophet, but in Jesus' mind John the Baptist did. As both prophet and the fulfillment of prophecy, John was the highest of prophets. He was the forerunner of the Messiah of whom Malachi spoke. In fact, John was the greatest among all men and women (v. 11)! And yet, even the least in Jesus' new kingdom was greater than John. Wow. What a privilege to be a follower of Jesus today.

Jesus went on to describe how the people were never satisfied. John came preaching repentance, and they rejected his message. Jesus embraced the outcasts, yet his teaching was ignored too. He then illustrated this truth by using children he had seen at play. During a wedding game, some children played the flute, but none of the other children would dance. At a funeral game, the children wailed, but none of the other children would mourn. In the same way, the people refused to join in with John and Jesus. Nothing was good enough for them. What about you? Are you critical of the messengers God brings, saying, "He is too harsh," or "He is too welcoming?" Let's not be like John's and Jesus' audience, never satisfied and missing God as a result. Jesus declares, "Wisdom is justified by her deeds." The wise one will accept the teachings of Jesus, remaining flexible about the manner or style in which they are carried out. Let's never be found dictating to God how he should manage things, but instead allow him, rather than our preferences, to lead the way.

february
ONE

MATTHEW 11:20-24

Jesus pronounced judgment on Chorazin and Bethsaida, the cities that witnessed some of his most significant healing miracles. He verified the message he preached with great signs and wonders, performing them right in the midst of the people in these towns, yet they did not put their trust in him. He added Capernaum, his hub of ministry, to the list too. The residents there would go down to the depths in judgment because they refused to respond to his message. Interestingly, Jesus also announced that some of the most notoriously wicked Gentile cities, Tyre and Sidon, along with Sodom, would have repented if he had done his works among them instead. This truth made the condemnation pronounced upon those who rejected his testimony even more severe. When Jesus performed a miracle, he wasn't looking for awe and astonishment like a magician; instead, he longed for people to repent (v. 21). The residents of Chorazin, Bethsaida, and Capernaum never took to heart the intended effect of Jesus' miracles. God was present with them, but they didn't turn from their sinful ways.

Jesus called for people to stop living for themselves and instead live for the glory of God. He didn't come so that people would simply feel sad and sorry about their sins. He came so that people might be reconciled to God through a genuine relationship with him. We may think, "If God would answer my one prayer, then I would really start living for Jesus," or "If God would only do this or that, then I would give my life over to him." But that thinking is foolish. Let's not remain numb to what we know God wants us to do by turning a deaf ear to the voice of the Lord. Respond to the Holy Spirit's conviction today. Just as Jesus worked in the midst of these ancient cities, he is still working and deeply desires men and women everywhere to repent. With all that we have been privy to on this side of the cross, there's no excuse for us if we do not get our lives right with Jesus. Stop seeking more signs from God and choose instead to turn your life over to him fully today. And if you already belong to him, then no matter how crazy your day gets, rejoice in knowing that you will never ever experience the wrath of God.

february
TWO

MATTHEW 11:25-30

Jesus addressed God in prayer as "Father" on many occasions, and he taught his followers that the Father is not far off but accessible to all who belong to him. Jesus also addressed the Father as "Lord of heaven and earth." This was a reminder to his disciples that every created being will bow before God, willingly or unwillingly. He thanked God for choosing to show himself not necessarily to the wisest and most educated, but instead to those willing to simply trust him. God intended the good news of his plan for redemption to be made known to all. Jesus was the revelation of the Father, and as the God-man, he knew the Father in a way no one else could (v. 27). As a result of Jesus' relationship to the Father, he asked the disciples to "come to" him (v. 28). Jesus called all who labor or are "tired from hard toil" and heavy laden or "loaded down" to come. The greatest burden a human can carry is the burden of sin and its consequences.

The word "yoke" (v. 29) describes a wooden frame placed over the heads of animals to make them work in tandem while ploughing. A yoke was also an emblem of submission to a conqueror or authority. Without Jesus, all humanity is in slavery and bondage to disobedience. Weariness is inevitable when people try to carry their own burdens, particularly the burden of sin and its effects. Those who place themselves under Jesus' yoke find rest for their souls. Anyone run down from labor can approach Jesus for spiritual relief and enjoy life with renewed strength. To serve Jesus is no burden. Are you tired from hard toil and loaded down with sin and its consequences in your life? If so, then come to Jesus. If you turn to him in simple faith, he promises to take the weight of your iniquities upon himself and give you the greatest rest possible, rest for your soul. Then you will be able to serve him instead of sin as you get back to the work he has called you to with confidence and energy. Jesus is our ultimate rest. Stop and thank him for taking all your burdens upon himself, confess any sin, and serve alongside and underneath him like never before.

february
THREE

MATTHEW 12:1-8

On the Sabbath, the one day of the week that the Jewish people set aside as a day of rest, Jesus and his disciples walked through grain fields and ate from the unplucked wheat. The Pharisees were furious when they saw Jesus and his followers doing this, and they accused the group of working on the Sabbath. Jesus explained three errors in their thinking to them. First, in the time of the Old Testament, King David ate bread from the tabernacle that was reserved only for the priests. Second, the temple priests worked on the Sabbath when they offered the required sacrifices. And finally, Jesus announced himself as the Lord of the Sabbath! The third point was the real key. Although the Lord was present to a degree in the tabernacle and temple, the greatest revelation of God walked right in their midst. Jesus was God in the flesh, and they didn't recognize him. Then Jesus got to the root of their problem. The Pharisees took much pride in their knowledge of Scripture, so Jesus reminded them of what they should have known. God desires "mercy, and not sacrifice" (v. 7). The religious leaders were obsessed with the formalities of their religion, but they neglected to care for basic needs, like hunger. Sacrifice was important, but it was never to take precedence over compassion.

As the Lord of the Sabbath, Jesus had the authority to declare what could and couldn't be done on that day. The religious leaders accused Jesus of violating the very law that he originated. Jesus demonstrated the rightness of showing mercy and kindness every day. Worship is never intended to become so mechanical that the worshipper forgets the heart of God while serving him. In the Old Testament, the word often translated as "mercy" is hesed. This is a rich word, expressing God's steadfast love for and commitment to his children. Since God has graciously extended his mercy to his people, they should always be found showing the same compassion to others. Do you ever get so caught up in the formality of your practices that you forget to be kind to those around you? If you are a follower of Jesus, then in light of all God has done in Christ for you, pray that the Lord would enable you to be known by all as a woman full of compassion.

february
FOUR

MATTHEW 12:9-21

After the grain field incident, Jesus and his followers entered a local synagogue. Jesus encountered a man whose hand was crippled. This handicap would have made it hard for the man to earn a living. Jesus asked him to stretch out his hand, and then he completely healed the man. Now the Pharisees must have expected Jesus to show up there; they probably even planted the man with the withered hand in their synagogue to stir up trouble. When they asked Jesus if it was lawful to heal on the Sabbath, he responded by asking them if it was lawful to lift a sheep from a pit on the Sabbath. Jesus brilliantly shut their argument down by showing them the foolishness of their reasoning. If mercy could and should be extended toward an animal, then of course mercy should be extended toward another human being, even on the Sabbath. A prophecy from Isaiah spoke to what happened next. Jesus withdrew from the mainstream crowds, as was foretold (v. 19). And continuing the theme of mercy, Isaiah spoke rightly of Jesus when he said, "A bruised reed he will not break, and a smoldering wick he will not quench, until he brings justice to victory."

What an incredible description of the compassion of our Lord! Reeds could be used to create products as various as a flute, a measuring rod, or a pen. They were super easy to obtain, and a broken or damaged one would be immediately tossed away. A smoldering wick on a candle was also considered useless. Not only would it fail to put forth the light it was designed to give, but it would have created a lot of annoying smoke. To work with a bruised reed or a broken wick would take much time and patience. Think of verse 20 as "Jesus will not break the bruised reed, and he will not quench the smoldering wick." Jesus invested an unconventional degree of care into people as he fulfilled God's agenda of saving souls. The picture Isaiah painted of Jesus should convict us all. Though he was the blameless God-man, he was longsuffering, kind, and merciful. He continued to work with any in whom he saw potential. We should pursue this same kind of patient hope. As we follow Jesus, may we ask God to help us never to cast out the "bruised reeds" and "smoldering wicks" in our lives. We simply don't know who may turn out to be the next useful tool or bright light for the Lord and his kingdom.

february
FIVE

MATTHEW 12:22-32

A man unable to see, unable to speak, and oppressed by a demon was brought to Jesus. Wow! What a nightmare! Imagine the horror this man must have experienced. Although there was basically no way to communicate with him, Jesus cast the evil spirit out and completely healed the man. In an instant, he was set free. The crowd around Jesus stood amazed. They asked one another, "Can this be the Son of David?" But the Pharisees refused to believe. Instead, they insisted that Jesus did this great work by the power of Satan. How frustrated Jesus must have been! He explained to them that their logic was ridiculous. Why would Satan use his power to cast himself out of a man? That would make no sense. Then Jesus asked why they believed that their Jewish exorcists could cast demons out, yet failed to believe that he could do the same. Jesus also pointed out that he had just overthrown the enemies of God. The Pharisees should have realized that he was operating under the power of the Holy Spirit. God's kingdom had clearly arrived.

Jesus called those present to make a choice. Would they be with him or against him (v. 30)? The need to respond rightly to Jesus is so critical that eternal condemnation would result for the people present who attributed the Holy Spirit's work to Satan. Though Jesus continued to prove that his preaching was true via miracles, many people remained unwilling to believe. Many times, resistance to Jesus isn't an intellectual problem. In fact, most often, it's an issue of the will. If he is who he said he is, then we must do things his way, and we can no longer live as we please. The need to live under Christ's authority can be more of a stumbling block than the reality of Jesus' origin, life, and death. If you are currently rejecting Jesus because you don't want to do things his way, ask him to make you willing to do his will. Let today be the day of full surrender to him. And if you are a follower, pray that those in your life who are resisting the Holy Spirit's witness would make the choice to be found with him. Pray that they would feel no peace until they also decide to do things God's way.

february
SIX

MATTHEW 12:33-45

Jesus compared people to two types of trees: good trees that bear good fruit and bad trees that bear bad fruit. The fruit produced reveals the type of tree. Then Jesus drew a parallel between the heart and what people speak or say. He rebuked the Pharisees for failing to recognize the Holy Spirit's work and exposed the reason for their harsh words against him: their hearts were evil. Jesus repeated the words "good" and "evil" multiple times as he explained that what comes out of the mouth is consistent with a person's character. What a person does reflects who she really is. Jesus went even further by warning that people's spoken words will play a critically important role in God's final judgment. Of course, Jesus wasn't saying that our words are the only thing that will matter in the end, or that all mutes will be justified apart from Christ. But he did say God takes our words very seriously since they are intimately interwoven with who we really are.

The heart was considered the center of the person or the inner man; it encompassed the emotions, the intellect, and the will. Just as the Pharisees' words were driven by what was in their hearts or their characters, so our inner person drives what crosses our lips. Even the thoughtless or the careless words we speak are a reflection of our hearts. We often hear people excuse their sin by saying, "Well, God knows my heart." Although this is true, God does know our hearts, even better than we do, Jesus would add, "And people can get a good estimate of your heart based upon the words you speak too." In our natural state, we all have issues with our hearts. So, for anyone who is not a Christian, "God knows my heart" should be a terrifying thought. Not one heart will prove wholly good before the Lord. This is why we all desperately need Jesus. But everyone in Christ has been given a new heart, called a "heart of flesh" and not stone. Because we have been graced with new hearts, we need to make sure our words reflect the work that God has done in us. May we care as much about what we say as God does, and ask the Holy Spirit to keep our speech right and pure.

february
SEVEN

MATTHEW 12:46 - 13:9

As Jesus concluded his teaching, he learned that his mother and brothers wanted to talk to him. His brothers, who were technically his half-brothers, wouldn't believe in him until later, after his resurrection. His family may have hoped to prevent him from saying or doing anything foolish, so they probably showed up to "rescue" Jesus from himself. Jesus replies to the man who told him his mother and brothers were looking for him with a surprisingly counter-cultural statement: "Who is my mother, and who are my brothers?" Then he goes on, "For whoever does the will of my Father in heaven is my brother and sister and mother" (vv.48-50). In that society, a good son and brother would never reject his family for the unrelated crowds. Whatever the reason his family members came to him, Jesus affirmed that blood ties do not equate to spiritual bonds. Because the Lord's agenda must come first, even above mother or brother, Jesus could not neglect what God called him to do in order to please his relatives. He physically pointed to the disciples around him and said those who serve the Lord with him have become his family. The true "mother and brother" of Jesus are the ones obedient to God. Jesus in no way dismisses love and loyalty to one's relatives. Instead, he elevates love and loyalty to the family of God.

The family is an important unit in the world and in the church. We should love our husbands and our children, honor our parents, and look out for the interests of our brothers and sisters. At the same time, we must honor and look out for the interests of our spiritual family. How do you feel about your church family? Would you be comfortable calling them your mother and your brothers? Jesus was. Just as Jesus' own family members didn't understand him, some of our natural family members won't understand us either. Let's ask God to help us love our church family with a new passion, knowing that according to Jesus, they are related to us too. Again, we aren't called to neglect our natural family and should always seek to love them. But at the same time, we must remember we are called to love our brothers and sisters in Christ. How are you showing love to your church family today?

february
EIGHT

MATTHEW 13:10-17

After Jesus' parable of the sower, the disciples wondered why he taught using such stories because up to this point Jesus hadn't used them as a method of instruction. The Greek word translated in English as "parable" comes from two words which mean "to throw" and "alongside." A parable throws two truths alongside each other, or makes a comparison between something familiar or understood and something not easily understood. So why did Jesus suddenly start teaching in parables? Parables helped the disciples "to know the secrets of the kingdom of heaven" (v. 11). By comparing something known to something unknown, the disciples would be able to understand a truth or idea unfamiliar to them. At the same time, Jesus used parables to hide kingdom truths from unbelievers. Since the Jews had rejected him, the parables became a judgment against them. They didn't want truth, and now they weren't going to get it. In addition, the prophet Isaiah was told by God that both his own message and the Messiah's message would be as parables to the people. Many would hear, but few would perceive. Jesus let the disciples know God had blessed them as they were seeing and hearing what the prophets of the Old Testament pointed to.

The disciples were expected to appreciate the great honor God had bestowed on them in allowing them to experience what truly righteous people had longed for (v. 17). Stop and consider how much more blessed we are, since we live two thousand years after the cross! We can see and hear through gifted biblical scholars, the record of history, those who have hammered out doctrine, the ability to read, commentaries, sermons, solid churches, the Old and the New Testaments, the Holy Spirit, and the blood of Christ. We are truly blessed! If we are honest about all that we have, we must admit that even the "poorer" among us have a lot. Let's stop fussing about and focusing on the things we don't have, and instead be grateful, realizing that many who lived before us would have loved to access the countless resources with which God has blessed us. Take fuller advantage of the resources God has blessed you with.

february
NINE

MATTHEW 13:18-23

Jesus explained what his parable of the sower meant to the disciples. The farmer's seed fell on four different soil types, representing four different responses to the message of the gospel. The first, the path, signifies the heart that rejects his message. The second, the rocky ground, is full of stones, and although the plant begins to grow in it, the rocks keep the seed from proper root progress, and the plant dies. The third, the thorny ground, is full of weeds that choke out and overtake the growing plant, and again, it dies. The hearts symbolized by the rocky and thorny ground appear to truly understand the gospel, but they only seem to make progress for a time, revealing that they never responded rightly to the good news. Only the fourth, the good soil, produces a harvest. Some harvests are larger than others, but the harvest comes because the conversion is genuine. Note that in all four cases, the seed is exactly the same. The same gospel was preached. The different results were due to the nature of the soils or the hearts on which the seed fell.

It is fairly easy to discern whom the first and fourth soils represent, as many clearly reject the gospel and never produce a harvest for the kingdom. It is harder to discern whom the second and third soils represent. In the second case, testing or persecution arise, which cause the heart to walk away from Jesus. In the third case, the heart loves this life more than the life to come, and again walks away. We may have friends or family members of the second or third type. We might have witnessed a response to the gospel in their lives, but only temporarily. Jesus' parable helps us to understand what "happened" to them. At the same time, it's great to remember that there's no reason a person can't go from being type two, type three, or even type one to type four. Let's pray for our family and friends that God would prepare their hearts to receive his word in soil that he has made "good" and ready to bear a harvest. If you aren't sure which soil type you are, confess that to God, and ask him to make you a fruitful ground for his work today.

february
TEN

MATTHEW 13:24-35

Jesus taught about a sower again, yet from a different angle. In this parable, the farmer sows his seed, but his enemy sows weeds right alongside the good seed. When the farmer's wheat grows up, weeds crop up too. The farmer's servants ask as if they should pull up those weeds. The farmer tells them to wait until the end, so that none of the wheat will be harmed. At the right time, God's agents will remove the wicked from the righteous. Then, in verse 31, Jesus compares the kingdom of heaven to a mustard seed. Although the mustard seed is very small, it grows into a large tree. Jesus drew attention to the contrast between the little seed itself and the result of the seed's growth, which was a magnificent tree. In verse 33, Jesus describes the kingdom of heaven as leavened bread. A little amount of leaven, or last week's dough, mixed into flour, would soon spread throughout the entire loaf. Again, the contrast is between the small portion of leaven and the result of its dispersion throughout the entire bread.

Many of Jesus' opponents considered his work insignificant. Jesus certainly didn't arrive with a lot of pomp and spectacle, so he was often rejected. But he encouraged those who were with him to be forward-thinkers. Just like the tiny seed became a huge tree and the small amount of leaven affected the entire bread loaf, so too would the efforts of Jesus and the disciples have large and widespread results. Even in the face of continual opposition, the disciples were to keep things going. It only takes a spark to create a forest fire. Do you ever feel like your effort for the kingdom of God isn't really making a difference? Do you feel your contribution to the work Jesus has called you to is trivial or insignificant? If so, put yourself in the mindset of the disciples. As they followed Jesus, they didn't own much, they were few in number, and they were continually criticized and rejected. Yet we can clearly see how God used their work of faith to turn the world upside down. If you are serving Jesus today, keep going! Your labor in his name will have lasting results. And if you aren't serving Jesus, get on board. Let's not miss out on what God can do through our obedient choices. Your sacrifice for Jesus makes an eternal difference.

february
ELEVEN

MATTHEW 13:36-46

Jesus left the crowds, but continued to teach his disciples in parables. After explaining the meaning of the parable of the weeds, he compared the kingdom of heaven to a treasure hidden in a field and a pearl of great value. Both of these illustrations emphasize the worth of the kingdom. In verse 44, a man finds treasure hidden in a field. Today, we use banks and safes to keep our valuables, but in Jesus' time, people buried important possessions for safe-keeping. If the owner of the treasure went on a trip and didn't return or died, his valuables remained underground until someone else found them. Legally, when the abandoned wealth was discovered, it belonged to the finder. So to guarantee his right to title, the man in Jesus' parable sells everything to purchase the field with the treasure to avoid any possible dispute regarding lawful ownership.

Jesus explained that the man in the parable was incredibly happy when he found the fortune. And because of his joy, he gladly sold all that he owned to buy the field containing the treasure. Jesus used this parable to teach his disciples that losing everything for the gospel is worth it. Even if the treasure is buried, or veiled to the world, it's worth all the time and energy invested into it. Was Jesus saying we can buy our way into the kingdom? Of course not! We become citizens of heaven when we place our faith in Jesus and repent of our sins. Jesus made the point that even if all were lost on earth for the good news, it would be worth it. Have you sacrificed for the kingdom of heaven? Have you lost relationships, titles, or given time and money to advance God's agenda? If so, you are like the man who sold everything to buy the field. Just as the man experienced joy, you should rejoice too, knowing that nobody and nothing can take what belongs to you in Christ. If you are holding back from doing what God has called you to because you fear missing out in this life, know that no cost is to too high when it comes to living for the Lord. If we experience any remorse in heaven, it will be over not doing more for Jesus. No one will regret her decision to do things God's way.

february
TWELVE

MATTHEW 13:47-58

After Jesus finished teaching his disciples through parables, he returned to his hometown of Nazareth, where he spoke in the local synagogue. The synagogue was the place where Jewish instruction took place, and when a visiting teacher came to town, especially one from that very region, he was customarily invited to speak. When Jesus taught, the people of Nazareth were astonished. They were amazed by his wisdom and the miracles they had heard he performed. The people were confused as to how the son of a carpenter had more insight than the wisest men they ever heard. They couldn't figure out the source of this supernatural power. As they discussed where Jesus' ability came from, they began to ask questions: What was the source of his skill? Wasn't this just the local carpenter's son? Weren't his parents and brothers and sisters living in their community? What was going on here? They didn't take offense at his wise teaching or his wondrous works. Their problem with Jesus was that they thought he was an ordinary villager, a man just like them.

The people of Nazareth wondered what Jesus was thinking. What right did he have to teach and perform miracles (vv. 54-57)? Jesus responded by saying, "A prophet is not without honor except in his hometown and in his own household." In other words, when people are familiar with a person, they often can't see past the fact that he is one of them. What about us? Do we reject God's gifts because they come through avenues that are too familiar to us? When we are looking for the spectacular, we can fail to see God moving right in our midst. What if a young man or woman you knew as a child became your spiritual leader in the church? Would that bother you? Could you receive instruction from someone you watched grow up? That's what stumbled the people of Jesus' hometown. If you are failing to accept someone because he or she just doesn't seem "special" enough to you, acknowledge the foolishness in that thinking. Let's not be like the people of Nazareth who missed out on Jesus because they couldn't see past their image of the carpenter's boy. Instead, choose to listen to the Lord through whatever vessels he desires to employ in your life today. God uses ordinary people with ordinary lives to accomplish extraordinary things.

february
THIRTEEN

MATTHEW 14:1-12

Matthew prepared the minds of his hearers and readers for the rejection of Jesus by recounting John the Baptist's execution. Herod the tetrarch was the son of Herod the Great, who murdered the young boys in Bethlehem back in chapter 2. A tetrarch was a title for a ruler just below an ethnarch, who in turn was just below a king. So Herod the tetrarch, also known as Herod Antipas, had a lot of power. When Herod heard about Jesus, he responded, "This is John the Baptist." What a strange reaction! Herod's conscience was troubled because of what he had done to John, and he couldn't stop thinking about him. So what had Herod done to John? Well to back up a bit, Herodias was the granddaughter of Herod the Great. She married her uncle Herod Philip, and they had a daughter together named Salome. Herod Antipas was married too, but he fell in love with Herodias, although she was married to his half-brother Philip and was his niece. Because of this love affair, Herod's first wife ran back to her father, reported what happened, and an actual war broke out. What an absolute mess! It was as bad as any reality TV show!

John the Baptist openly spoke out against this unlawful marriage between Herod Antipas and Herodias, ended up in prison, and was beheaded as a result. Although Herod didn't take the advice of John, he knew John was a man of God and did not want him executed (v. 9). Nevertheless, Herod had John killed because of his desire to please Herodias, her daughter, and his party guests. What a sad story. Although Herod's conscience bore witness to the message of John the Baptist, he rejected the truth because of his desire to do things his own way. The Herods may have thought they were above the law, but as John clearly pointed out, no one is above the Law of God. If the Holy Spirit is convicting you of sin today, be quick to respond and repent. Don't be like Herod, who foolishly ignored God. Even after John's death, he was still tormented by John's voice. Whether we want to please people or just do things our own way, let's stop and put an end to our disobedience today. God completely forgives those who turn to him in readiness to do things his way.

february
FOURTEEN

MATTHEW 14:13-21

After Jesus learned about the death of John the Baptist, he wanted to be alone. As Matthew's Gospel records, from this point on Jesus focused on instructing his disciples, since the nation had rejected him. Nevertheless, the people tracked Jesus down and caught up to him. As much as Jesus and the disciples wanted to be alone, the people wanted to find him. Jesus had compassion on the crowd and healed the sick. When the afternoon came to a close, the disciples asked Jesus to send the people away so they could find something to eat since they were in a remote place. Strangely, Jesus says in verse 16, "You give them something to eat." Now, how could the disciples possibly feed this crowd? They brought all the food they had to Jesus: five loaves of bread and two fish. Jesus took the food, prayed to God, and a miracle took place. From that small amount, five thousand men, plus women and children, about fifteen to twenty thousand people, ate until they were full (v. 21). This miracle is known as "the Feeding of the Five Thousand" and is the only miracle recorded in all four of the Gospels. Jesus used this event to show his disciples that just as he fed people, they would feed people too.

We have to remember how difficult it was for these people to get food. They couldn't just drive through McDonald's on the way home. They needed to eat! Just as this crowd needed physical food, the disciples would soon provide people with necessary spiritual food after Jesus' departure. The true source of the bread and fish for the thousands and thousands present was Jesus, and the source of spiritual food in the future would continue to be Jesus. Although the disciples didn't see how God would provide, they were still called to move out in faith and do what Jesus asked of them. Jesus taught the disciples to take their eyes off the apparent hopelessness of the situation and instead step up to see what they could do. Is God asking you to meet a spiritual need that you can't see a way to meet? Jesus can do great things through even the smallest of resources. When God calls you to bring physical supplies, or more importantly, the gospel to those around you, ask him to take whatever you have to offer, and expect him to multiply it to carry out his purpose today.

february
FIFTEEN

MATTHEW 14:22-23

After teaching and then miraculously feeding the thousands upon thousands with the 5 loaves of bread and two fish the disciples collected, Jesus finally got a chance to pray to the Father by himself. He stayed back alone in the mountains and sent the disciples ahead of him across the lake in a boat. Early in the morning before dawn (between 3 a.m. and 6 a.m.), when the disciples were about three miles away from the shore, Jesus came to them—walking on the water! They panicked, thinking he was a ghost. We must admit, a ghost makes more sense than a man walking on the water. Jesus told them to take courage, and he identified himself. But Peter wanted further evidence. Peter said to Jesus, "If it is really you, then I want to walk on water too." Jesus replied something like "Okay then, Peter, do it!" Only two men in human history have ever walked on water: Jesus and Peter. In faith, Peter stepped out of the boat and literally walked to Jesus. But when Peter saw the rough waves the wind created, he became frightened.

As Peter lost focus, he began to sink. Jesus caught him and questioned why he began to doubt. After he and Peter got in the boat, the storm stopped, and the awestruck disciples worshipped Jesus. Clearly, they knew they were in the presence of the one who had control over all creation. They were face to face with God incarnate. Too bad that Peter stressed out and sank. Who knows what would have happened if he continued to exercise faith without fear when he walked on the water. But before we look down on him, we should remember that he was the only disciple who had the courage to go to Jesus. It was when his focus drifted off of Jesus and onto the storm that he began to sink. In a sense, we have the same choice in our lives. We can either look right at Jesus, trusting in him and doing his will, or we can look at the circumstances around us. Like Peter, even in the midst of storms, we can do above and beyond all that we can imagine if our lives and actions are fully dependent upon the Lord. Ask yourself this question today: "Who is bigger, Jesus or my circumstances?"

february
SIXTEEN

MATTHEW 14:34 - 15:9

Jesus and his disciples crossed over the Sea of Galilee and reached a highly populated area. The men there recognized Jesus and immediately announced his presence to the people in that region. Verse 35 says all the sick from that region were brought to him. When they came to Jesus, they simply made contact with him, and because of their trust in who he was, they were healed. It was clear to all that Jesus not only had authority over the water and the wind, but over sickness as well. Right after Jesus administered healing to the hurting souls brought to him, his opponents criticized him. It's worth noting that although Jesus was continually harassed for healing and teaching the people, he kept doing the good works the Father called him to. Whenever we find Jesus reaching out to help those around him, we see his opponents scheming to discover new ways to accuse him, find fault with him, and shut his ministry down. Right after the healings in the region of Gennesaret, the Pharisees jumped on Jesus and the disciples. The Pharisees wanted to break them and wear them down so that they would stop their mission.

Jesus let them know Isaiah was right when he said, "This people honors me with their lips, but their heart is far from me." Despite all the seemingly righteous words and deeds of Jesus's opponents, they weren't really interested in God's glory, only their own. In the same way, when our enemies attack us, it is tempting to stop doing good. We can feel discouraged and want to "throw in the towel," especially when the opposition is continual. But Jesus and his followers didn't grow weary in doing good, and neither should we. If you have been rejected, condemned, mocked, harassed, or just bombarded by faultfinders in your life, realize that Jesus faced the same hostility. God will make all things right in the end when he one day silences those who tried to thwart his work. Remember, the disciple is not greater than the master, and if they harassed Jesus for doing good, and they did, they will harass us too. Those who determine to please God won't always please people. Even in the face of criticism from people in religious "packaging," continue to follow Jesus and keep doing the right thing!

february
SEVENTEEN

MATTHEW 15:10-20

After the Pharisees questioned Jesus about his hand-washing practices, he called all the people around him to listen. It was critical that they understand what makes a person unclean before God. In Jesus' time, the Jews demanded careful ritual washing before food was consumed. But Jesus says, "It's not what goes into the mouth that defiles a person." This was completely different from what the Pharisees practiced. Jesus goes on to say in contrast to their teaching, "What comes out of the mouth; this defiles the person." Contamination, according to Jesus, happens not on the kitchen counter, but in the heart. The Pharisees were not happy with Jesus dismissing this practice they had worked hard to adhere to all of their lives. In verse 15, Peter asks Jesus for further explanation. Ceremonial washing didn't matter anymore? This made no sense to the disciples. Jesus was a bit surprised that they still didn't get it (v. 16). With respect to food, we eat, we digest, and we eliminate waste. But words are totally different because they come from the heart, or the mind, or the soul. Jesus goes on to explain that all sins come from the inner person. It was therefore a waste of time to follow the Pharisees' hand-cleaning processes when God is actually interested in character.

In this teaching, Jesus emphasized the necessity of an upright heart. He let the disciples know that evil and ungodly behavior begins in a person's mind. We all need to keep our inner woman pure. When we indulge in wicked behavior, it's a sign that we have a heart problem before God. Even if we are Christians who have been given a new heart, our old nature wants to creep back in and attempt to suffocate the new life within us. In our busyness, let's be careful to take time to check our hearts. Are you holding a grudge against someone or unwilling to forgive? Are you dissatisfied with what you have and even jealous of those who are blessed with more than you? Are you bitter about something that didn't go your way? If we find any darkness within us, let's confess, repent, and determine to avoid whatever triggers that thinking in our minds. Ask the Holy Spirit to purify your heart. How wonderful to consider that he cleanses us and graces us with new beginnings each and every day.

february
EIGHTEEN

MATTHEW 15:21-28

Jesus traveled to Tyre and Sidon, located in the coastal region of Phoenicia. This was Gentile territory, as Sidon was 60 miles away from Galilee. Jesus and the disciples were far from home, and some say the round-trip journey could have taken months. The woman who approached Jesus was a Canaanite. The Canaanite culture went back thousands of years and had a long history of problems with the people of God. The text says this woman was literally shouting again and again, pleading with Jesus to have mercy on her or take pity on her. She never says she deserves help from Jesus, but instead, she appeals to his compassion. What's fascinating is that this Canaanite woman calls Jesus the "Son of David" and the "Lord." Why would she acknowledge Jesus as King of the Hebrew people with whom she had nothing to do? She heard about Jesus, his teaching, and his work, and she realized that he was the promised Messiah. Jesus firmly told her he came for the nation of Israel. Then he said Israel was like a family gathered for dinner, eating food provided by the father. The Canaanite woman acknowledged that while she didn't belong at that table, she could still, like a dog, partake some of the crumbs discarded by the family.

Jesus was impressed with the woman's faith. She believed in him, and she trusted in his compassionate nature. He said "no" to her in order to make a point to his disciples and to us. Jesus was looking for the kind of faith this Gentile woman had. And he expected the same from the leaders in Israel, but he didn't find it. She was determined to get Jesus' help. Do you believe that if Jesus is saying "no," it is so that he might be glorified? She could have just said, "Forget it!" and walked away. When our circumstances don't make sense, or when things work out differently than we anticipate, we can become discouraged and even tempted to give up. Pray that God would increase your faith today, and continue to cry out to him with full trust in the character of Jesus. God can do whatever he wants, when he wants, and he is good. He promises not to withhold one good thing from those who walk uprightly before him. Believe that he knows what's best.

february
NINETEEN

MATTHEW 15:29-39

Matthew records that crowds of people came to Jesus for healing, followed by another occurrence of Jesus multiplying food for them to eat. This incident was not the same as the Feeding of the Five Thousand detailed in Matthew 14:13-21. This time, four thousand men were in attendance, the number of loaves and fish was different, and a different amount was left over. In addition, these people had been with Jesus for three days, and even the word for "basket" was different from the word Matthew just used in the last account. To top it off, because he came to the Sea of Galilee from Phoenicia, Jesus was still in Gentile territory. The crowds here were not Jews, but Gentiles. We see this detail revealed as the foreign people "glorified the God of Israel" (v. 31). Jesus calls his disciples to himself and says, "I have compassion on the crowd." The Greek verb used for "compassion," *splanchnizomai,* means that Jesus felt deep pity or sympathy for the people. Why did he feel this compassion? The people stayed with him for three full days, and they ran out of whatever food they had brought. Jesus didn't want them to return home hungry. They came to him for help, and he wouldn't have them fainting on the way back.

Out of sympathy for the people, he supernaturally provided an abundance of fish and bread, and all who were there ate and were satisfied or full. Again, the meal Jesus provided was more than enough, and 7 baskets full were left over. This miracle revealed to the disciples that Jesus blessed both the Jews and the Gentiles. Though this this was not a crowd of Hebrew people, Jesus had genuine compassion upon them. We can forget that Jesus has compassion for all people. He is interested in people from all ethnicities, religious backgrounds, social and educational levels, and genders. Do you feel that certain people groups are "too far gone" or too distant to receive God's blessing and saving grace? If so, stop thinking like that and trust in Jesus' ability to turn even the heart of the greatest sinner toward him. Remember, if you are a Gentile yourself, you were brought near to God by nothing less than the grace and mercy of Christ. Let's make sure we are ready to bring the good news of Jesus to anyone who will listen today.

february
TWENTY

MATTHEW 16:1-12

After Jesus returned to the land of his own people, the religious leaders came at him again. The Pharisees and Sadducees didn't get along with each other, but they willingly joined together in their common goal to get rid of Jesus. This time they wanted to see a "sign from heaven." In other words, all the miraculous healings, demonic deliverances, and signs up to this point weren't good enough for them. They wanted to see something really spectacular, and then they claimed they would believe. Jesus was not happy with them and called them an "evil and adulterous generation." They could and would predict the weather based on physical signs of coming rain or sunshine, but they refused to see the spiritual signs right in front of them. Jesus let them know they would be given no further signs. Jesus didn't come to work signs for the sake of a show. He told them they had the sign of Jonah, and just as Jonah was in the fish for three days and nights, Jesus would be dead for three days and nights. It's worth noting that if they waited for this sign, the sign of Jonah, to come to pass, then they wouldn't realize the prophecy's meaning until after Jesus' crucifixion, burial, and resurrection. So in declaring this, Jesus actually foretold his rejection as the promised Messiah.

These people had every sign necessary to believe, but it just wasn't enough because they weren't willing to submit to Jesus' authority. Do we want more signs from God before we will truly believe in him? We can think it would make more sense for God to just appear in the sky or write in the clouds for all to see, but even if God did that, those unwilling to believe would just explain it away or call it a cosmic fluke. We can see the creation of God all around us, and we have been given a conscience that testifies within us to our guilt and need for forgiveness. We know that Jesus died to ransom us from the judgment we deserve and rose from the grave, proving that he accomplished what he set out to do. What other signs do we need? Let's choose to turn from depending on signs and wonders, be satisfied with all that God has provided for us, and move ahead with our lives, fully trusting in him for all that he is calling us to do today.

february
TWENTY-ONE

MATTHEW 16:13-20

Jesus and his disciples entered Caesarea Philippi. They were back in Gentile territory and apparently experiencing a break from the crowds. Jesus used this time to help his disciples think through all that they learned, saw, and experienced while traveling with him. Jesus initiated this process by asking them what others thought of him. The disciples listed some of the great speculations they heard others make about Jesus (v. 14), but none was correct. Then, getting to the heart of the matter, Jesus asks the disciples directly, "Who do you say that I am?" Peter replies to Jesus, "You are the Christ" or the Messiah, the Anointed One, of Israel. And Peter adds, "You are the Son of the living God." Jesus let him know he was absolutely right. Then Jesus added that Peter didn't come up with this on his own. Instead, God himself revealed it to Peter. It's interesting that Peter's name, *Petros*, means "rock, and Jesus used the word *petra*, which means "massive rock" or "bedrock," to describe the truth that Peter or Petros declared. By using a play on words to highlight this concept, Jesus let Peter know that the affirmation he just made was the bedrock on which he would build his church. The disciples learned that Jesus himself is the ultimate foundation or cornerstone of the church.

Then Jesus let the disciples know that nothing, not even the gates of hell, considered strong enough to keep the dead locked in, would be able to stop God's program for his church. If you are a Christian today, you, like Peter, have realized that Jesus is the promised Messiah. You have put your faith in the truth that Jesus has taken your sin upon himself and given you his righteousness. If you understand this, then it was God, by the Holy Spirit, who revealed it to you. As Christians, we need to stop and ponder the marvelous reality that God has chosen to reveal himself specifically to us. That ought to humble us and fill us with a sense of gratitude that nothing else can compare to. Again, God made Jesus known to you. Let that knowledge guard your heart and mind as you face the challenges of your busy day with more thankfulness than ever before. As Jesus says to Peter in verse 17, "You are blessed," he says the same to us. We *are* blessed!

february
TWENTY-TWO

MATTHEW 16:21-28

Jesus let his disciples know what the near future held for him. Soon he was going to be killed and then rise again on the third day. Peter, who was just commended by Jesus for rightly stating that Jesus was the Messiah and the Son of the Living God, went in the opposite direction and chose now to rebuke Jesus. Peter thought Jesus' statement made no sense. How could the Messiah be killed? That wasn't a part of Peter's plan for the future, especially after he had just received Jesus' praise and promise of blessing. It is startling to read that Jesus then addressed Peter as Satan (v. 23). Jesus had just told Peter that God himself revealed Jesus' identity to Peter. Matthew records these incidents back-to-back to show us that right after Peter was praised for listening to the Holy Spirit, his focus slipped back to his own agenda. Satan wanted to keep Jesus from the cross, and the enemy used whomever he could to try to thwart our Savior from carrying out the plan the Father sent him to accomplish. Jesus used this opportunity to teach Peter and the disciples that following him would always involve a cost.

As Jesus went on to say, gaining everything in this world is not worth it if the cost is our soul. Yet, Jesus clearly told his disciples that in losing their lives, they would find even better ones (v. 25). Jesus was prepared to endure the coming darkness, knowing that the great joy on the other side could only be accomplished if he walked head-on into the storm. Like Peter, we can be foolish too. We can make great decisions and act rightly on them one minute, and then immediately afterward make silly and selfish moves. We can track with God, hold fast to wise choices, and then suddenly get tripped up when something doesn't fit into our agenda, and shift our focus back to the cares of this life. Let's be watchful as we walk along the path that God has in mind for us today. When something doesn't go our way, let's remember our potential to react selfishly, keep our guard up, and make sure we are responding in a way consistent with what we truly believe. Let's learn from Peter to trust God, even when things aren't going as we planned.

february
TWENTY-THREE

MATTHEW 17:1-13

Immediately before the chapter break, Jesus tells his disciples that some standing with him would not die before seeing the Son of Man coming in his kingdom. Six days after that statement, Jesus took Peter, James, and John up to a high mountain and was changed before them. His "face shone like the sun, and his clothes became white as light." During those moments, the disciples present saw Jesus in his transfigured, heavenly state. Moses and Elijah appeared and talked with Jesus. In the minds of the Jewish people, Moses was the lawgiver, and Elijah represented the prophets. Having the two of them present signified that the whole of the Old Testament pointed to Jesus. Peter, possibly thinking it was time to fulfill the Feast of Tabernacles, suggested to Jesus that tents be made for the three men. While Peter was proposing this, the voice of God said from a cloud, "This is my beloved Son" and "Listen to him" (v. 5). Between these statements, the Father also said he was pleased with his Son. Jesus did everything according to the eternal purpose and plan of God.

When the disciples heard the Father's voice, they were afraid and they fell down prostrate on the ground. They must have been absolutely overwhelmed at this point. But Jesus graciously placed his hand upon them and said, "Have no fear," or "Do not be afraid." He was with them, and it was time to get back to work. According to the voice of the Father, Peter, James and John, the other disciples, the people of Israel, and the entire world should listen to and follow the teaching of the Son of God. Do you ever wonder what God would tell you if he spoke directly to you? What kind of specific insight or guidance would he give you for life? God exhorted Peter, James, and John that the right thing to do was to listen to his Son. God has also spoken directly to us in and through Jesus. By this point, Peter, James, and John had given up everything to follow Jesus. Did they make the right choice? Yes! Let's be encouraged, knowing that following Jesus is exactly what God desires all people, especially his children, to do. Even though you may run into many obstacles and difficulties in this life, God wants you to listen to and obey Jesus today.

february
TWENTY-FOUR

MATTHEW 17:14-23

Jesus returned from the high mountain where Peter, James, and John witnessed his transfiguration, and they were immediately faced with the failure of the other disciples. As soon as they approached the crowd, a man with a demon-possessed son came to Jesus and respectfully begged him to heal his boy. The man's son suffered from epilepsy as a result of the possession, and he would fall into fire and water in his "fits." This must have created tremendous stress on the family as they continually rescued the boy from great danger. Jesus not only rebuked his disciples for their lack of faith, but the crowd as well. Jesus cast the demon from the boy, and he was instantly restored to health. The nine disciples wondered why they were not able to cast the demon out like Jesus did. They clearly realized they needed something. Jesus let them know that their problem was a lack of faith. Their relationship with Jesus and faith in God and his word was enough to do whatever they were called to do, but they needed faith to boldly step out with confidence and trust that God could and would carry out his will through them.

The disciples had "little faith," meaning a weak faith in Jesus' ability to work through them. Even a small amount of genuine faith, like a grain of a mustard seed, in the power of God can move mountains. So did the disciples not even have a little bit of faith? What happened to them? It could be that they thought the power to heal the sick and cast out demons came from themselves rather than from Jesus. He wasn't there with them, so maybe they began to rely on themselves to do God's work. It's easy to forget that God always wants us to look to him and call upon him in humility. What about you? Is God prompting you to do something for him that seems impossible? Do you feel you have had little success as you struggle to obey to his word? Ask him for faith and courage, and be willing to step out boldly and act on whatever he is calling you to do. Don't shrink back from his promptings because of your weaknesses. Remember who he is, and trust that he is with you. Small faith in a great God can move mountains.

february
TWENTY-FIVE

MATTHEW 17:24-18:9

Jesus and his disciples arrived at Capernaum, and the Jewish temple tax collectors approached Peter, asking why Jesus hadn't paid the temple tax yet. Apparently, the collectors thought Peter handled the everyday affairs of Jesus, the rabbi. According to custom, all Jewish men twenty years and older (except the priests) were required to pay a *didrachma*, or half a shekel, annually for the upkeep of the temple. Peter let them know that Jesus would pay the tax and did not intend to break the customary law. Even before Peter talked to Jesus or mentioned a word about this, Jesus asked Peter a question: "From whom do kings of the earth take toll or tax? From their sons or from others?" Peter responded with "others." Jesus added that the sons of the kings would not be required to pay kingdom taxes (v. 26). Jesus let Peter know that since he was the King, he should not be required to pay temple taxes. In addition, the disciples shouldn't have to pay taxes either. They were like the sons of the kingdom, who held positions of honor. If Jesus paid the tax, he would look like an outsider rather than the rightful ruler. But if he didn't pay it, people might think he didn't support the temple.

Jesus solved the dilemma perfectly. He told Peter, the fisherman, to catch a fish and open its mouth. There, he would find a coin to pay both his and Jesus' tax. Jesus wouldn't have to pay from his own money as an outsider, and he wouldn't have to stumble or offend anyone (v. 27). So although Jesus technically wasn't required to pay the tax, he did so to avoid perplexing the tax collectors and others around him. It's easy to overlook how careful Jesus was to stand up for the truth of the gospel, yet at the same time refrain from unnecessarily confusing anyone. Jesus never compromised God's law or principles, and at the same time, he spoke and acted with wisdom, sensitive to how others would receive his message. Let's seek to be just like him. Let's rejoice in the great liberty we have as a result of being in Christ, and at the same time let's be careful not to stumble those around us. Let's always be willing to limit our liberty because of our love for people.

february
TWENTY-SIX

MATTHEW 18:10-20

Jesus taught that every human life is important to God. All little ones are under his care, and he doesn't want any of them to end up lost. In verse 15, Jesus discusses what Christians, who are also incredibly valuable to the Father, should do when one sins against another. According to Jesus, the first step is for the two to try to reconcile on their own without involving anyone else. Jesus said that the one sinned against needs to state the problem to the sinner. The text literally says, "Go," meaning the one sinned against needs to start this process. If the two resolve the issue, the sin can be repented of and forgiven, and the matter should never be brought up again. It is critically important to Jesus that believers work out their differences. so much so that he adds if the sinning sister won't repent, then two or three witnesses should be brought into the discussion (v. 16). This process is all done with the goal of making things right. Finally, if the sinner still refuses to listen, then church leadership should come alongside the parties to mediate restoration. If that fails, and the sinner still refuses to turn from her ways, then the church leaders are called to remove her from the congregation until she is ready to repent (v. 17).

How wonderful if Christians would follow the pattern Jesus gives here! Far too often, we go to others before we go to the one who has sinned against us. And when we finally approach the sinning sister, we go with a harsh and critical attitude, not with a heart motivated to achieve reconciliation. Most of our problems with one another could be handled in a way that honors God if we worked them out on our own. But sadly, for some, the thrill of the fight brings excitement to their lives, and they don't seek reconciliation because they don't want to drop the matter. Let us be careful, extremely watchful, and always sure to initiate reconciliation with our sisters one-on-one when we have been sinned against. Let's do whatever we can to promote holiness and harmony between all believers. God is our Father. We are his kids. He wants us to get this right. What a testimony we could be to the love and life of Jesus if we put this admonition into practice.

february
TWENTY-SEVEN

MATTHEW 18:21-35

In response to Jesus' teaching on reconciliation, Peter asks, "How often will my brother sin against me, and I forgive him?" And he questions further, "Seven times?" There must be some limit to the number of times we have to forgive, right? The rabbis of the day said three times was enough. So Peter doubles that and adds one, "just to be safe." To forgive seven times had to be enough. Jesus answers Peter's question with "seventy-seven times." This was Jesus' way of saying there is to be no limit to forgiveness because the believer must always keep in mind the forgiveness she has received from God. We live in a world where all people, even Christians, still sin, and we must learn how to deal with relational conflict. Jesus then told the story of a king who ran across one of his servants who owed him literally millions of dollars. The man had no way to repay and was put in prison along with his family as punishment. He could never repay the debt he owed, so he fell on the ground and begged the king for more time. The king pitied the man, and so freely and completely forgave him all that he rightfully owed. But, as we read, the man was owed a few dollars himself, and he sought out his debtor and demanded payment. The debtor begged for more time, but the man said, "No," and threw him into jail.

The parallel is crystal clear here. Like the man, we have been forgiven an unpardonable debt before God. How absurd we must look before him and the angels if we refuse to fully forgive others. Christians should be the most forgiving people on the planet as we continually reflect on the radical forgiveness that God has lavished upon us. We have received grace and mercy at the expense of Jesus. If we don't extend grace and mercy to those who have sinned against us, we can't expect to bathe in the forgiveness of Christ. Jesus adds that God won't be fooled by false forgiveness when we fail to "forgive your brother from your heart" (v. 35). May we never be found holding grudges against one another. If you have not genuinely and completely forgiven someone today, then stop and do so now. This is very serious to God, the Father of all believers.

february
TWENTY-EIGHT

MATTHEW 19:1-12

Jesus was met again by both the large crowds and the skeptical Pharisees. The Pharisees were troubled by one of the debated questions of the day: "Is it lawful to divorce one's wife for any cause?" The accepted practice within Judaism was that a husband could divorce his wife, but a wife was not allowed to divorce her husband. So the Pharisees were actually asking under what circumstances a husband could divorce his wife. They wanted to see how Jesus would respond and hoped to put him right in the middle of a heated argument. Jesus affirms what the Scripture says. In marriage, a man and a woman are joined in an inseparable union that is to take priority over all relationships, even over parent and child (v. 5). Because of God's original design, Jesus says, "What therefore God has joined together, let not man separate." In other words, there should be no divorce. This wasn't what the Pharisees wanted to hear, and they reacted to Jesus' statement by recalling Moses's provision for divorce in the Old Testament. Jesus responded that Moses allowed this because the people's hearts were hard. In the days of Moses, a man could throw his wife out of the home, but because she was still married to him, she couldn't seek a new relationship. Moses allowed for the certificate of divorce to protect a wife from being both rejected and claimed by her husband. The certificate declared her freedom to remarry.

Jesus teaches strongly in verse 9 that a husband divorcing his wife and seeking another commits the equivalent of adultery. Those who heard Jesus realized that he is totally opposed to divorce, so much so that the disciples thought, "Wow. We may be better off not to marry at all!" (v. 10). In the case of adultery, divorce was allowed, but even then the marriage could still be saved. According to Jesus, divorce should only be permitted when there is literally no other option and all means of saving the marriage have been exhausted. If you are married today, thank God for your one-flesh union and do whatever you can to make it or keep it your priority relationship. If you are not yet married, be careful to choose a husband who will be faithful to you, who loves Jesus with all his heart, mind, and soul, and who will love you as Christ loves his church.

march
ONE

MATTHEW 19:13-22

In verses 13-15, Matthew records Jesus engaging with children again. Many religious teachers of the day, and really all throughout history, have considered themselves and their disciples to be above children. Yet here we have Jesus, the God-man, taking time out for young kids. Although parents chose to bring their children to Jesus, hoping he would pray for them, the disciples assumed it was a waste of Jesus' time. They didn't think he should exert his effort and energy on behalf of kids. So the disciples literally "rebuked," meaning "spoke sternly to" or "scolded" the parents for bringing their children to Jesus. Verse 14 begins with "but." In contrast to the way the disciples handled the situation, Jesus said, "Let the little children come to me," and continued, "For to such belongs the kingdom of heaven." Earlier in Matthew's Gospel, Jesus comments on children playing games. He also talks about how we need to humbly become like children, praising their dependent attitude. He says that whoever receives a child receives him, but whoever stumbles a child would be better off drowning himself. Clearly, children are incredibly important to Jesus. The disciples' attitudes and actions were wrong here, and Jesus did end up praying for the children brought to him (v. 15).

With our extremely busy and stressful schedules and agendas, it can be easy to overlook children and scoot them off. But that's not the way of Jesus. Children are important to him, and they should be important to us as well. If you have children, be sure to make time to listen to them, dialogue with them, encourage them, instruct them, discipline them, and pray for them. If you don't have children, you still have the potential to make a significant impact on their lives. Remember, Jesus didn't have any kids of his own, but that didn't discourage him from reaching out to them. Keep an eye and an ear open for all children, whether they are yours or not. The time you invest in their hearts and minds has the potential to impact the way they see God and themselves for years to come. Take a moment to pray for the children you know, asking God to bring them to repentance and faith soon that they may shine for Jesus like bright lights in our dark world.

march
TWO

MATTHEW 19:23-30

The rich young man walked away from Jesus sorrowful because Jesus asked him to sell his stuff and give it to the poor. This wealthy man owned great possessions that he couldn't imagine parting with, even to follow the Lord. Jesus then told the disciples that it is difficult for the rich to enter the kingdom of heaven. Jesus didn't say the rich can't be saved, but he spoke frankly about their temptations. The wealthy are more tempted to trust in their riches than the poor. Jesus also said, "It is easier for a camel to go through the eye of a needle than for a rich person to enter the kingdom of God." Jesus reinforced the point that wealth can slow down or even stop spiritual progress. This surprised the disciples, who viewed wealth as a sign of God's blessing. The disciples then thought, "If a rich man with God's blessing upon his life can't be saved, then who can?" Verse 25 states that the disciples were not merely surprised but astonished. This just didn't add up to them. The Pharisees had long taught that God gives wealth to those he loves. Their culture believed the rich were wealthy because God favored them. How could those favored by God not be saved?

The disciples asked Jesus, "Well, who then can be saved?" Jesus replied to this that all things are possible with God. Only God has the power to save souls. What do we wrongly view as indicators of God's favor on a person's life? Intellect? Beauty? Marriage? Children? Money? Power? Popularity? All these things can be gifts from God, but we must be careful never to let his gifts end up being the very things that keep us from him. If God has graced you with much, be thankful. Use the gifts he has given you for his glory. But always keep your hands open before him. As he has freely given to you, he has the right to freely take away. If God has seemingly withheld from you in your current season of life, thank him for that as well. Realize your "poverty" could be just what you need for spiritual growth. Either way, let's keep our focus off of the "stuff" and on him as we rejoice that he can save anyone, rich or poor.

march
THREE

MATTHEW 20:1-16

The conversation between Jesus and the disciples about the rich young man ended with Jesus adding, "But many who are first will be last, and the last first" (19:30). The disciples were convinced that the rich man would be first because he was wealthy, but Jesus taught that things won't always turn out the way people imagine. To illustrate this, Jesus told the story of a landowner who hired day laborers for his vineyard. His grapes were ready, and he needed them harvested. The workers he hired early in the morning agreed to a denarius for their day's labor. As the day progressed, fruit still remained to be harvested, so the landowner hired more men, even up to the last hour. At the end of the day, more workers lined up. The ones who began last were paid a denarius, just like the ones hired first. The ones who started first assumed they would be paid more than a denarius because they had worked longer and under the heat of the midday sun. But they were paid the same, so they grumbled. Why should they be paid the same amount as those who only worked a fraction of the time? They felt this was totally unfair. The landowner explained he had done no wrong. The early group got exactly what they agreed to work for. The owner had the right to be generous with whomever he pleased, and nothing unfair took place.

Jesus clearly showed the disciples that salvation is all of grace. Many who are not yet born again believe that if they live a good life God will have to accept them into his kingdom. But this is just not true. On judgment day, God is not going to weigh good deeds against bad deeds to decide one's destiny. Salvation is a gracious act of God, and he owes no man eternal life. In fact, if God gave us what we deserved, no one would be saved! If we have been Christians for any length of time, it is easy to begin thinking we have somehow contributed to our own salvation, especially if we have been faithful to his word. Let's drop that thinking from our minds immediately. Instead, let's thank God for his grace and ask him that many others, even those we deem unworthy, be blessed with the same favor he has freely bestowed on us.

march
FOUR

MATTHEW 20:17-24

Verses 17-19 show that Jesus knew what lay ahead for him in Jerusalem. In verse 20, Matthew notes that sometime after Jesus' announcement of his impending suffering, the mother of James and John brought her sons before Jesus and requested that her boys be granted seats of honor in his coming kingdom. The mother of these two men took the posture of a lesser in the presence of a greater when she knelt, a stance used when one desired to make an appeal to an authority. Jesus asked her personally what she wanted. Next to a king, the right and left hand were seats of honor, and she let him know she wanted these seats next to Jesus for her boys. Jesus responded to the request with "You do not know what you are asking." The "you" used is plural, so Jesus spoke to James and John along with their mother. Jesus added, "Are you able to drink the cup that I am to drink?" This "cup" referenced the great suffering and death on the horizon for Jesus. The two men answered, "Yes." They believed they could endure the hardship he foresaw. These three recognized that Jesus was about to set up his kingdom, and they wanted positions of prominence.

In verse 22, Jesus reveals that the three didn't understand what the coming kingdom was about. The disciples were expecting Jesus to throw off Roman rule. They still didn't realize that Jesus' kingdom involved rejection by the world. James and John did end up drinking the cup of suffering when James was executed and John was exiled as a prisoner. How many times do we ask God for things without realizing the suffering that may result if we get our requests? Are we begging God for a spouse, a better job, homeownership, children, or a prominent role in our church? Although these may all be wonderful things, they come with a price tag of responsibility or sacrifice that we may not understand at the time of our asking. There's nothing wrong with seeking great things, as long as we remember that greatness is often accompanied by a high cost. Let's be careful to make all of our requests to God in humility, adding, "If it is best," or "If it is your will, Lord." Let's make sure we keep ourselves in our rightful place before God, even in our prayers.

march
FIVE

MATTHEW 20:25-34

The other disciples were furious because James and John had asked their mother to request that they be seated in the positions of honor, the right and the left hand, in Jesus' coming kingdom. But why were the disciples so mad? They were angry because they wanted those spots too! It wasn't fair! Why did James and John have to ask first? So Jesus gathered them together and taught what real greatness in his kingdom looks like. It isn't about self-promotion. Jesus reminded them of a truth they all knew: rulers of nations exercise authority over their subjects. Most people want to climb to the highest possible place of leadership to get others underneath them. Those who gain positions of authority can end up harshly treating the common people or the ones over whom they have power (v. 25). But the followers of Jesus are to behave totally differently. In fact, the one who wants to be first must be the slave of others. In the Roman world, there was no status lower than that of a slave. The slave's role was to make sure someone else's needs and desires were met. The slave was to put the interests of another before his or her own interests. This is exactly what Jesus did. He humbled himself and took on human flesh. He allowed himself to go all the way down the social ladder to a slave's death of execution on a cross, all for our benefit. He calls those who trust in him to imitate his example.

Do you want to be great in the kingdom of God? There's nothing wrong with that! But we must remember that to be considered great in heaven, we are called to serve. The goal of the Christian should be building into others instead of ruling over them. In whatever areas of our lives God has graced us with authority, let's use our "power" to better the lives of those around us. Where can you serve others today in your church, in your community, and in your home? Remember, those who serve give themselves up when they focus on and are attentive to the well-being of others. Let's follow the example of Jesus and let go of our own interests for the glory of God and the good of others. By doing so, we can choose to be truly "great" in the eyes of the Lord today!

march
SIX

MATTHEW 21:1-11

Jesus told two of his disciples to go into the nearby village, find a donkey with her colt, and bring them both back to him. He instructed them to tell anyone who questioned them, "The Lord needs them." Two men marching into a city and walking out with a donkey and colt would look very strange and suspicious. Many believe that "the Lord needs them" was a prearranged code between Jesus and the animals' owner should anyone notice what the disciples were doing. Jesus then rode into Jerusalem on a donkey as the prophet Zechariah had predicted hundreds of years before. This act demonstrated that Jesus truly was the King of the Jews. At the same time, according to Zechariah, not only was he the King, but he also was the humble King. Normally, when a king entered his capital city, he would come in pomp and glory, riding on a war-horse. The lowly donkey was known only as a "beast of burden." A king riding into his capital city on a donkey made no sense. When Jesus did this, he displayed his mission to those watching. Jesus didn't come as Messiah to overtake the Romans with armies and weapons. Instead, he came to bring peace between God and man through his impending and ultimate sacrifice on the cross.

The crowds that followed after Jesus shouted repeatedly, "Hosanna in the highest! Blessed is he who comes in the name of the Lord!" The anxious and eager masses just couldn't wait for Jesus to set up his kingdom. They were tired of Roman rule, and they wanted Jesus to bring the political deliverance they longed for. God wants us to give him our attention here. Jesus came to earth in full humility to deal with our sin problem. For this, we praise him. Let's be sure that our worship of him isn't rooted in our wish to get stuff in the here and now. We never want to follow Jesus solely because of what he can do for us in this life. He can and does choose to bless us with much during our time on this planet. Nevertheless, our adoration of him is grounded in the greatest gift of all: freedom from sin and death. If you are a Christian, give praise to Jesus today for living and dying so that you could belong to his eternal kingdom.

march
SEVEN

MATTHEW 21:12-22

Jesus entered the temple, which was supposed to be a place of prayer, and discovered people using both God's house and God's people for personal financial gain. In response, Jesus boldly drove out those who sought to make a profit there and overturned the tables of the money-changers. The money-changers were like people who exchange currency today. Because travelers came from all over to worship and make sacrifices to God, a variety of currencies were brought into the temple. The money-changers traded the coins the worshippers brought with them for coins that could be used to buy animals or pay the temple tax. But this all came with a substantial fee. No one was changing money for free. Verse 12 also states that Jesus overturned the seats of those who sold pigeons. There was nothing wrong with selling animals for sacrifice, as people who traveled far couldn't bring their own birds with them. But Jesus' anger emanated from the fact that the temple was not the place for the buying and selling of animals. These transactions should have taken place outside of God's house. How could people seek the Lord in prayer amidst the clamor of buying and selling? In addition, Jesus said the "house of prayer had become a den of robbers." Many who sold animals for sacrifice were overcharging the worshippers. This was never God's design for his house or his people. Jesus let them know what he thought about their practices.

There have always been and will always continue to be people who seek to use God's house and God's people for personal financial gain. Although we don't go to the temple to make sacrifices, we do go to church to worship, learn about, and serve the Lord. The church is not a place where people should peddle their wares, goods, and services. Of course, there's absolutely nothing wrong with supporting one another's businesses, but we must resist any desire to look at God's people as sources of potential monetary profit. Our financial ventures cannot motivate our relationships in the church, and we must be careful not to encourage or support those who even unknowingly use God's people for profit. If you attend a church that keeps Christ and his word as its focus, thank God for that today. If you don't, then find one as soon as you can!

march
EIGHT

MATTHEW 21:23-32

In verses 28-32, Jesus teaches a parable about two sons. He asked his audience to think about this one. A man asked his sons to work in his vineyard. The first son responded, "No," but later changed his mind and complied. The second son responded, "Sure," but he didn't follow through. Jesus asked the audience, "Which of the two did the will of his father?" The crowd answered that the first son did the will of the father. Then Jesus made the parable more practical for his hearers. The religiously self-righteous listening to Jesus heard the preaching of John the Baptist. They went out to John and even agreed with what he said. But they didn't do anything about it. The sinners, tax-collectors, and prostitutes, who were considered the "rejects" of society, heard the preaching of John and responded with repentance and faith. Jesus said that these so-called "wicked" were the ones who did God's will. The audience must have been shocked to hear Jesus say that "sinners" were more obedient to God than the "righteous." Jesus used this parable to teach his listeners that it is not enough for a person to say what she will do; her good intentions must lead to action.

We can say all day long, "I am going to get a college degree," or "I am going to get a driver's license." But unless we put the effort in and move on it, we don't have a college degree or a driver's license. In the same way, it's easy for us to say what we are going to do spiritually: "I am going to read the Scripture every day," "I am going to pray continually," or "I am going to have a better attitude when I serve at church," and so on. But until we actually do these things, saying what we are going to do benefits no one. What have you been saying you are going to do? How long have you been saying it? We can actually deceive ourselves into feeling like we have done something simply because we said we were going to do it. Choose to put an end to simply declaring what you are going to do, and instead put what you are going to do into action today. Until you have actually done it, despite what you say you are going to do, you haven't actually done anything at all.

march
NINE

MATTHEW 21:33-46

Jesus told another parable describing his rejection by his own people. A landowner leased his prized vineyard to tenants to take care of it in his absence. His servants returned at harvest time to get the owner's share of the fruit, but time after time, the tenants beat and even killed the servants that the landowner sent. Finally, the landowner sent his own son to get his percentage of the fruit, thinking the tenants would respect his son, but they killed him as well. They killed him outside the vineyard so they wouldn't defile their fruit, since the tenants were hoping to rid themselves of the landowner and keep the vineyard for themselves. In the parable, the landowner represented God, the vineyard stood for Israel, the fruit stood for righteousness, the tenants represented the Jewish religious leaders, the servants represented the prophets, and the son represented Jesus. So Jesus asked the listeners what the landowner would do to the tenants. They answered that he would put those tenants to death and lease the vineyard to other tenants. Jesus responded in kind that the kingdom would be given to Gentiles who would produce fruit in like manner.

Jesus also quoted Psalm 118 to his audience, showing that the rejected Son was the "capstone" of the faith. In the first century, buildings were made of stone. The capstone was the stone set in the foundation of a building's corner wall, around and against which all the other stones were measured. Jesus challenged his audience, "And the one who falls on this stone will be broken to pieces; and when it falls on anyone, it will crush him." We can either fall on Jesus and his message, be broken and found in him bearing fruit, or he will, in judgment, fall on us and we will be ruined. God sent men with his messages to his people, and those men, the prophets, were harshly treated and their words ignored. God's people even rejected the ultimate prophet, Jesus. What about you? Do you listen to those who speak God's word, or are you critical of those who preach the gospel? Do you nitpick God's messengers and fail to hear Jesus through them because you find fault with them? Let's not be like ancient Israel and refuse the message of the Lord, but rather let us be careful to pay attention to those God has placed in our lives to teach us his word today.

march
TEN

MATTHEW 22:1-14

Jesus told another parable, this time using a royal wedding banquet to explain his rejection by his own people. A king gave a grand wedding feast for his son. When all the magnificent preparations were ready, his servants told those invited to come. To the king's shock, the guests ignored their invitations. So the king sent the servants out and tried again. This time, the guests harmed and even killed the king's servants. When the king found out, he was enraged. He destroyed those would-be guests and demolished their cities. Rejecting a royal invitation was unthinkable. And to top it off, the guests had no good reason for their refusal. They were just too consumed with their own agendas. One went back to his farm and one to his business. They couldn't be bothered with the banquet. The king reminded his servants that the banquet was ready. He asked them to go to the main roads where the poorest people would be found and invite them. The unlikely and unacceptable, the "bad and the good" (v.10), responded and came to the feast. But when the king came in, he saw that one of the guests had not put on the proper clothes that the king had made available to those in attendance. He kindly asked this guest how he got in without the right clothes, but the man didn't respond, so the king ordered him to be thrown out of the kingdom. Jesus adds, in verse 14, "Many are called, but few are chosen."

What a challenging parable this is! Jesus clearly taught that the king, who represents God, is willing to accept anyone, including the poor, the good, and the bad, to his son's (Jesus') feast. But there are conditions. The "right clothes" must be put on. We must do what God asks us to do. Jesus showed us that even if someone has heard the call of God, agrees to the facts about the gospel, and understands his grace, that doesn't necessarily mean she is right with God. She must respond to God's call, turning from sin and trusting the good news. Let's never be found like the man without the right clothes. If you have not repented and placed your faith in Christ, today is the day to do it. And if you have, rejoice, knowing that one day you will dine with the King and his Son! Thank God that you have been both called and chosen!

march
ELEVEN

MATTHEW 22:15-22

The Pharisees joined with the Herodians, who supported the Herods, and schemed to entrap Jesus in his own words. These bitter enemies, the former protecting God's Law and the latter loyal to Rome, suddenly became friends when it came to getting rid of Jesus. They attempted to flatter Jesus, saying they knew he was a man of integrity who taught the truth about God regardless of what others thought (v. 17). They fully expected Jesus to answer honestly, and so attempted to trap him by asking, "Is it lawful to pay taxes to Caesar, or not?" Did it align with the Law of God to give money to Gentiles? If he said "no," the Herodians would see him as disobedient to the government. If he said "yes," many Jews would see him as compromising. The questioners hoped Jesus' answer would place him in a no-win situation and stomp out much of his recent popularity. Jesus asked them for a coin, and they brought him a day's wage, the denarius. Many Jews wouldn't even carry this coin because it had an image of Caesar engraved on it. Jesus said they should pay Caesar, or the government, what it is owed. The Jews were clearly under Roman authority, and whether they liked it or not, they had to subject themselves to the laws of the land. At the same time, they should pay God what he is owed as well.

Just because they were under Roman rule didn't mean that the Jews shouldn't have lived their lives for the glory of God, making his concerns their priority. We too should live within our government in a way that brings glory to God. We must do whatever we can to abide by the laws of the land and be known as people who would never break the rules unless they ask us to violate biblical law or principle. We should pay taxes and vote and take part in government if possible. We should also remember that as Christians, we are called to give and serve within a church. We must never get so involved in the affairs of the land that we neglect our place within the people of God. May we, by the help of the Holy Spirit, master the balance that Jesus spoke of and fully invest in our church while living as peaceful members of the civil administrations God has ordained for us to live under.

march
TWELVE

MATTHEW 22:23-33

The Pharisees failed to break Jesus with their question about paying taxes to Caesar, so a different group came to test him. The Sadducees were more liberal than the Pharisees. They didn't believe in angels, resurrection from the dead, or any form of an afterlife. The Sadducees attempted to baffle Jesus with a question they were certain he would not be able to answer. They appealed to a teaching of Moses in which if a man died and had no children, his brother had to marry the widowed wife to carry on the name of the dead brother. The Sadducees asked in essence, "Suppose there were seven brothers who died one by one, and each one successively married the widow before he died. Then the widow died. Which one of the seven brothers would have her as his wife in the next life?" The Sadducees were confident they had Jesus stumped now! Jesus told these men, who considered themselves the elite thinkers of the day, that they didn't know either the Scriptures or God's power to bring people back to life (v. 29). In heaven, no one will be married. Once we have our glorified bodies, there will be no more death. No more death means no more need to reproduce and no more need for marriage. Jesus also used Moses as an example. Jesus quoted from when God spoke to Moses out of the burning bush and said, "I am the God of Abraham, Isaac, and Jacob." Abraham, Isaac, and Jacob had been dead for some time, but God spoke as if they were still alive, saying, "I am," not "I was." Jesus cleverly showed the Sadducees how God's declaration proved the truth of an afterlife.

It may seem like people have begun to deny any existence after death only within the last hundred years or so. Yet we read about the Sadducees, two thousand years ago, arguing that death is the end of man's existence. Jesus himself confirmed that God is able to and will bring the dead to life again. The question isn't "will we live forever?" but "where will we live forever?" Some will be resurrected to eternal life and some to eternal death. Let's pray for our friends and family who, like the Sadducees, are still blind to the coming resurrection. This life is a vapor compared to eternity. Let's choose today to make decisions consistent with a belief in the life to come.

march
THIRTEEN

MATTHEW 22:34-40

First, the Pharisees tried to trip up Jesus; then it was the Sadducees' turn, but neither group had any success. And so the Pharisees went at it again for "round three." In this attempt, an expert in the Law sought to trap Jesus by asking him what the greatest commandment was. The Pharisees believed some commandments were more important than others. They counted 613 commandments in all, so they really believed this question would confuse Jesus; they hoped to make him look foolish and discredit him. At this point, they figured that no matter what Jesus said, someone would disagree with him, and his popularity would decline as a result. Jesus responded to the lawyer's question by stating that the greatest commandment was to love God with all your heart, soul and mind, quoting Deuteronomy. It is interesting to note that even though the lawyer only asked Jesus to give the one great commandment, Jesus decided to throw in another. The "second is like it," he said: "You shall love your neighbor as yourself." Jesus taught that the one who loves God will also love other people. The two go hand-in-hand. All people are important to God and have great value in his sight. You can't love God without offering compassion and kindness to those who have been created in his image. And so again, for the third time, Jesus answered in a way that silenced his enemies.

Some may protest, "Of course I love God. I just don't really like people." But it isn't possible to truly love God without loving those he loves. Jesus added the second commandment for a reason. It feels easy to love God because God is perfect. He makes no mistakes, and we can fully trust in his character. But people are not perfect. Even those who have been redeemed still battle sin, and as a result, they may let us down at some point. Yet Jesus says we must love them. He calls us to extend to other people the same kindness, understanding, forgiveness, and grace that we allow ourselves. If you haven't loved someone in your life as much as you love yourself, choose to change that today. Don't make excuses for yourself anymore, but just step out and do the right thing. Make sure you are seeking to obey both of the great commands of Jesus.

march
FOURTEEN

MATTHEW 22:41-46

After the religious leaders failed in their numerous attempts to trip up Jesus, he turned the tables around and tested the Pharisees with a question of his own. He asked them what they thought about the Messiah, adding the question "Whose son is he?" Who did they believe would be included in the ancestry of the Messiah? The natural answer was what the Scripture taught. The Messiah would come from the line of King David. Jesus then quoted Psalm 110 where David, under the inspiration of the Holy Spirit, says, "The Lord said to my Lord." When he made this declaration, David admitted the Messiah was his Lord and would be greater than he. The Pharisees were puzzled. How could the Messiah be both from David and greater than David? When the Jews remembered King David, they thought of a fearless warrior who delivered the nation of Israel from her enemies. Even from David's humble beginning as a boy, he stood up against the giant Goliath to win victory for the people of God. Those eagerly awaiting the Messiah expected this kind of deliverance. When Jesus asked the Pharisees, "If then David calls him Lord, how is he his son?" he was challenging them to consider that there were still things they just didn't understand about the one who would be the Messiah of Israel. The Pharisees, in the end, were the ones stumped by Jesus.

Neither the chief priests and elders, the Herodians, the Saduccees, nor the Pharisees could not trip up Jesus in his words. No matter what they asked him, he gave a brilliant response. Yet with one question from Jesus, they were silenced. Do we want to question God? Do we think we know more than he does, or are wiser than he? Often, when we see the sin and suffering in this world, we are tempted to think we could have done things better. Like the religious leaders, if we were to question God, he would not only be able to respond to our accusations, but would stop us in our tracks. If you are questioning the wisdom of Jesus, learn from these conversations and realize that you will never win. Jesus is the Lord to whom King David referred. Jesus is both the son of David and the Lord of all. Decide to humble yourself before him in full and complete trust today.

march
FIFTEEN

MATTHEW 23:1-12

Jesus turned to those who overheard his "Q and A" sessions with the religious leaders and told them that the religious leaders taught true things that all should follow, but no one should follow the leaders themselves, as they failed to practice the things they preached. In fact, much of what they did was motivated only by the desire to be noticed by others. They made their "phylacteries" wide and their "fringes" long. Phylacteries were small boxes which contained copies of select passages of Scripture and were tied to the arms or even the forehead. The fringes on their robes represented the Laws of God. By lengthening the fringes, the Pharisees and scribes wanted others to know how serious they were about obedience to the Law. The places of honor, the best seats, and the greetings of others that Jesus spoke of all referred to the Pharisees and scribes feeling superior to those around them. They honestly thought they were better, and they expected others to treat them as such. Jesus said those listening should not be called "rabbi." Since rabbi means teacher, was Jesus saying no one should be called teacher? No. Rabbi, used here, meant one exalted above the crowd. Teaching wasn't the problem. The same was true of calling another "father." Jesus was calling out those who put on an attitude of supremacy over others in the name of religion.

Using these examples, Jesus addressed the religious leaders' misuse of their power. In their actions and attitudes, the Pharisees and scribes loved to be recognized by others. We can slip into the same trap. Do we obey Jesus because we love him and are grateful for all that he has done on our behalf? Or do we obey to garner the attention of others? Many use the name of Jesus and the Law of God to get those around them to think more highly of them. Yet these same people neglect to show love, mercy, and kindness to their family, friends, and neighbors. We should want to follow God's Law, but we should follow because we want to please God, not because we want to impress others. Ask God to show you if you are obeying for the wrong reason. If you feel he is saying "yes," then make the necessary changes and instead serve and obey from a heart of love.

march
SIXTEEN

MATTHEW 23:13-22

Jesus continued to speak against the scribes and Pharisees, pronouncing seven "woes" upon them. The first three of the seven are found in verses 13-22. A "woe" is a "verdict of punishment" or an "expression of sorrow." The first woe resulted from the scribes and Pharisees keeping others from entering the kingdom of heaven. Many in the crowd heard the teaching of Jesus and may have wanted to follow him, but because of the scribes' and Pharisees' disdain for Jesus, and the people's fear of displeasing the religious leaders, many in the crowd turned away from the gospel. The second woe resulted from the scribes and Pharisees pursuing converts, because those who followed their ways ended up just as messed us as they were, if not worse. The third woe concerned the religious leaders' use of oaths. Jesus taught that we should always be truthful and shouldn't need to add anything for emphasis. The Pharisees and scribes employed an intricate system of oaths. For example, if one swore by the temple, it wasn't binding, but if he swore by the gold in the temple, that really meant something. Jesus spoke against this craziness. How ridiculous to think that God would consider some oaths as obligatory yet not enforce others because of the clever way they were worded.

The distinctions created between the temple and the gold, or the altar and the gift, were ways the religious leaders used to manipulate the rules to justify breaking their own promises. Jesus let his audience know that the final judgment for the scribes and Pharisees would be terrible and filled with sorrow. He warned the religious leaders of doom if they continued to reject him. At the same time, we shouldn't miss the compassion and concern Jesus showed the scribes and Pharisees as he exhorted them to respond to his teaching and get this right before it was too late. When people in your life are rejecting the message of Jesus, sometimes you just need to do what Jesus did and "tell it like it is." For those who continue to turn their backs on the gospel, judgment is promised. Let's not shy away from this fact. Pray that God would give you the courage to speak the truth in love today, just like Jesus did.

march
SEVENTEEN

MATTHEW 23:23-28

Jesus pronounced three more woes upon the scribes and Pharisees. All three times, he denounced them as hypocrites. First, Jesus addressed the issue of tithes, which were paid to the Levites. The Jews were required to pay a tenth of all God had blessed them with. The religious leaders went above and beyond this requirement, tithing even from every herb in their gardens. They wanted to make sure they weren't missing anything. Next, Jesus drew attention to their extreme concern with their appearance before others--they were like cups cleaned only on the outside. And they obeyed every rule to impress others like whitewashed tombs, which were externally beautified for others to see. So what made them hypocrites? What did they do wrong? Jesus didn't condemn them for trying to give much to God, keeping their outsides clean, or living consistently with God's law. All these things were good. The problem was that they focused on the details, but neglected the important things and failed to deal with their hearts. Jesus said God is more concerned with the "weightier" matters, such as fairness, showing others the mercy received from him, and faithfulness. Jesus revealed that the fruit of genuine love for God manifests itself in the way we treat others.

When a person is clean on the inside, it affects her outside too. Because the religious leaders were focused on external righteousness, not caring to make that righteousness an inward reality, they were lawless (v. 28). What about you? Are you more concerned with the way you appear before others than with your inner man? Do you work and strive to impress people by trying to show them you are following every rule, yet live with a heart that lacks love? When we become angry because others think poorly of us but don't mind when others think poorly of someone else, it reveals that our hearts are out of step with God's design for humanity. If you are lacking in Christian love, ask God to cleanse you from the inside out. Only Jesus can make your heart right. Pray that he would replace your heart of stone with a heart of flesh. And if he already has, then pray that he would help your inner woman be satisfied in him as you put the needs of others before your own today.

march
EIGHTEEN

MATTHEW 23:29-24:2

Jesus pronounced the last woe, the seventh of seven, upon the scribes and Pharisees. He called them hypocrites again because they spent time building the tombs of the prophets and decorating the monuments of the righteous. In other words, they looked at those whom the nation's leaders persecuted in the past and honored them, insisting they would never do or have done such a thing. Yet ironically, Jesus, the very God-man and the ultimate prophet, sat right there in their midst and they were plotting to kill him. Their attitudes and actions toward Jesus showed that they were just like their fathers and would indeed have done the same thing. Jesus then spoke firmly with the religious leaders. He told them clearly that they were like snakes, and their destiny was the same hell that those who persecuted the prophets earned. Jesus recalled Abel, the first righteous man killed in the Scripture (Genesis), and then Zechariah, whose murder is recorded in 2 Chronicles, the last book in the Hebrew Bible. The Hebrew Bible contained the same books found in our Old Testaments, but they were arranged differently. So Jesus was saying that from Genesis to 2 Chronicles, or from cover to cover, the religious leaders had always killed those God sent to them.

It is easy to look at tragedies of the past with the advantage of hindsight and insist that we would never have done such things. The scribes and Pharisees really believed they would never have persecuted God's messengers like their ancestors did, yet they were plotting and planning to get rid of the Messiah. Too often, we think more highly of ourselves than we should and believe we would have done things differently if given the chance. On the other hand, we can also feel doomed to repeat the mistakes of our ancestors and follow their bad habits, even practicing sinful behaviors we once insisted we would never be found doing. But with God's help, we can put an end to ungodly patterns today by saying "no" and refusing to do what's always been done. You don't have to repeat the past. It may not be popular, it may not be easy, and we may be rejected because of it, but let's do things God's way. We don't want people looking back at our lives and insisting they would never be found doing what we did.

march
NINETEEN

MATTHEW 23:37-24:2

These passionate words are the last ones Jesus spoke directly to the crowds of Jerusalem as recorded in Matthew. Jerusalem was the place God chose to set up his kingship and the city that flourished under King Solomon when the nation reached her height of economic and political influence. It was the city founded as the center of Israel's religious activity. It was known as the city of God, the city of David, and a place set high upon the hill. How bizarre to think that this was the city where the Son of God was sentenced to rejection and death. Verse 1 of chapter 24 almost symbolically states that Jesus left the temple. As the disciples admired the beauty of the temple, Jesus prophetically warned them not to be too enamored, because soon it would be destroyed. And yet, there was future hope. Jesus will set up his final and glorious kingdom, and all will acknowledge that he has come in the name of the Lord.

Jesus didn't take the things he spoke of lightly. He was deeply grieved, and moved with compassion. He felt like a mother hen, longing to bring her chicks under her wings to protect them and shelter them from harm, whose little ones were unwilling. In times of danger, chicks naturally run to their mother for protection. But instead of turning to Jesus for refuge, the people of Jerusalem sought to put him on a cross. Their opportunity was over. They chose condemnation over salvation. When we see sin and evil and death in the world, we can grow overly discouraged. We must remember that this was not the way God designed things to be. He is patient with all so that as many as possible might come to repentance, but never confuse his patience with tolerance of sin. He hates sin more than we can imagine. It is sin that turned the Garden of Eden into a land of thorns and thistles, subjected the entire creation to decay, and caused men to toil by the sweat of their brows. May we learn to hate sin as much as we should! We shouldn't be found taking sin lightly, laughing at it, or holding it close to us. Pray that Jesus would help you to see the destruction that sin has created, and ask God to help you turn from it quickly and completely.

march
TWENTY

MATTHEW 24:3-14

The disciples came to Jesus privately and asked him two questions. First, "When will these things be?" referred to Jesus' previous prediction of the destruction of the temple. Second, "What will be the sign of your coming and of the end of the age?" The disciples believed these two events would happen at or around the same time. Their questions led to the next two chapters of text in Matthew, known as the Olivet Discourse, named after the place where Jesus' teaching occurred, on the Mount of Olives. The disciples knew the words of Zechariah the prophet, who foretold that Jerusalem would be destroyed and the Lord would return on the Mount of Olives--just where Jesus happened to be at the time. Nevertheless, Jesus' response to the question on the end of the age was "not yet." Many things needed to occur first, including the gospel being proclaimed throughout the world (v. 14). It is interesting to note that up to this point in Matthew's biography, Jesus is the one who preaches the gospel. Now, Jesus hints to his disciples that his followers would be the ones to finish the work he began in bringing the good news to all the earth's inhabitants.

What must it have been like for the disciples gathered with Jesus as he proclaimed these words? Can you imagine their shock when Jesus said things won't wrap up until the gospel is proclaimed throughout the world? They were just a small band of followers, waiting for the Messiah to establish his kingdom. They may have thought, "Are you kidding, Jesus? How are we going to get the gospel to the entire world? No one can handle this task!" And yet two thousand years later, we live in a world throughout which the gospel has spread and changed countless people, families, governments, and groups. Still, there's more to be done! God wants his people to preach the good news of salvation through his Son Jesus Christ to those who would turn to him in repentance and faith. If it doesn't seem like you've been very successful in evangelism, pray that God would bring you someone to share with today! And if you are thinking, "How will I do this?" Remember it's his work, not yours! If we are willing, God can do wonderful things through us, his followers.

march
TWENTY-ONE

MATTHEW 24:15-22

The disciples asked Jesus when the temple would be destroyed and what would be the sign of his coming and the end of the age. Jesus explained to them what must happen before the end. He focused on what many have called the most marked sign of the tribulation: the "abomination of desolation." The disciples were familiar with this term because the prophet Daniel spoke of it over five hundred years before Jesus did. Jesus taught about the time when an ultimate leader or world dictator will gain power and set himself up to be worshipped as God in the future temple, thus defiling it. When the abomination of desolation comes to power, the end is near. Jesus warned the reader that when this event begins, people should run! The danger will be so great that to stay alive, men and women will need to flee, even leaving their belongings and possessions behind. Jesus said the distress coming upon earth will be unlike anything that has ever gone before or will ever occur again in the future (v. 21). It will be like pressure to the point of bursting.

It is interesting that Jesus added, "If those days had not been cut short." Even in the great tribulation, we still see God's incredible mercy. If this time of great suffering were to go on indefinitely, no one would survive. But because God has elected some to salvation during this horrible period, the tribulation will come to an end. Reading about the great tribulation should make us shudder. Jesus alerted the disciples of the massive tribulation that will come upon the earth so that men and women might listen and repent now. The New Testament teaches that God has not destined believers for wrath. That means if you are a follower of Jesus today, you will not be present on earth during this future time. What a relief! If you are a Christian, pray that the spiritual eyes of those you love will be opened so that they may flee from the wrath to come by turning to Christ now before this terrible time comes upon our world. In addition, if you are a Christian, thank God for delivering you from his coming wrath against sin by pouring it out on Jesus. The great tribulation will be horrible, but hell will be even worse. And hell won't be cut short, because none of the elect will be there.

march
TWENTY-TWO

MATTHEW 24:23-28

Jesus told his disciples that people will come in the future, declaring that they are the Messiah. He counseled his followers not to believe those who make such claims. Jesus also warned his followers not to pay attention to anyone who suggests that he knows where the Messiah is located. For example, if someone claims the Messiah is in a desert or in a closet, the followers of Jesus should not believe the report. Why should they reject any such claim? The second coming of Christ will not be a secret thing. After the great tribulation is over, his return will be like lightning flashing in the sky. All will see it. Jesus followed this caution and exhortation with a strange statement in verse 28. He says, "Wherever the corpse is, there the vultures will gather." A corpse is dead. Those who are spiritually dead, who have not been born again through repentance and faith in Jesus, will attract vultures. The vultures represent the judgment of God upon sin. Just as a corpse draws vultures to itself, so the unbeliever will draw God's judgment down upon herself. No one can say when the last judgment will occur, but it is inevitable. It will take place. God will deal with sin.

Often, people ask, "If Christianity is the truth, then why are there so many religions?" Jesus told his followers in advance that false religious leaders would arise. He didn't say they might come, but he said they would come, even doing great things to substantiate their claims. If someone declares he has a new way to reconcile others to God, or has received new revelation from the Lord, even by an angel, his message should be immediately rejected. We live on a planet where the god of this world is at war with our Lord Jesus. But this war will not continue forever. God will put an end to it soon. Until then, the Christian must remain on guard and live defensively. Our enemy, the devil, would love to get us sidetracked onto some supposedly new or different path to Jesus, or even get us listening to "new words" from the Lord. Avoid these things. Keep your focus on the gospel and stick to the message that was given once for all believers. Don't allow yourself to get distracted today by any "new revelation" from any so-called Jesus.

march
TWENTY-THREE

MATTHEW 24:29-31

Jesus explained to his followers what would occur right after the great tribulation. He said the sun and the moon and the stars will no longer give their light, and as a result the world will be engulfed by total darkness. Some have suggested that Jesus meant the sun will literally stop shining, while others believe this is symbolic of the world's rulers losing all power. Either way, the bottom line is the same: "the powers of the heavens will be shaken." Whatever or whomever these powers of the heavens are at the time, God will bring them down at the second coming of Christ. Jesus will then appear before the entire world. And will they rejoice? No. Instead, they will mourn as they realize their security in this life has come to an end. When Jesus first came to this planet, he arrived in absolute humility. He was born an infant and placed in a manger. And he continued to live his life in utter humility, even going all the way to a slave's death—death on a cross. But, the day will come when Jesus will return again. And this time, he will fully exercise his power and authority. Those who have chosen to surrender to his lordship in this life will be the subjects of his amazing kingdom. But those who refuse to obey him will be shut out from his presence forever.

The day will come when everything in our world system will come undone and Jesus will reign as the rightful king forever. We live in a culture that seems to elevate celebrities such as politicians, intellectuals, athletes, pop stars, and models to a height where people can value them as somehow worth more than the average soul. But clearly, they're not! In fact, the day is coming when anyone and everyone not right with Christ will be brought down, no matter how powerful or popular they are now. If you are a Christian, make sure your thinking is consistent with truth. If you tend to elevate those whom the world venerates and esteem them above other "common" people, you need to stop. Ask God to help you to see others as he sees them. It's not wrong to look up to people, but Christians should admire those who will be great in the kingdom of our Lord.

march
TWENTY-FOUR

MATTHEW 24:32-35

Jesus instructed his disciples to learn the lesson he taught, using the fig tree as an illustration. Many trees in Israel kept their leaves year round, but the fig tree lost its leaves in the winter and grew new ones in the spring. Jesus reminded his followers that they could tell summer was coming when the fig tree's branches began to put forth new leaves. In the same way, when the signs that Jesus spoke of appear, his followers will know the end is near. This promise was so certain that Jesus stated it would be easier for the physical universe to end than it would be for his words to fail (v. 35). Jesus said, "This generation will not pass away until all these things take place." Many believe that Jesus was referring to the fact that the temple would be destroyed a few decades after this conversation, especially since the words of Jesus that triggered the entire Olivet Discourse were "There will not be left here one stone upon another that will not be thrown down" (24:2). Many alive at the time would live to see the temple and Jerusalem fall to the Roman army. In addition, he spoke of the coming tribulation. Some future generation of Israel will see the great tribulation, the abomination of desolation, and the second coming of Christ.

What Jesus declared and taught is absolute truth. We can know with confidence that what he said will come to pass. We live with an assurance that the sun will appear with the morning, the earth will continue to spin day in and day out, and the moon will remain in the heavens. We should be even more certain that the words of Jesus are true. We don't know when we will leave this planet, but we do know that none of us will live here forever. We have a choice to make. Are we going to listen to the words of Jesus, which are firm, factual and will never fail? Or are we going to listen to the voices of the world, the sinful desires of our flesh, and the promptings of our spiritual enemy? Let's choose to follow Jesus. Even if we are already Christians, let's determine anew today to listen to and obey the words of our Lord.

march
TWENTY-FIVE

MATTHEW 24:36-51

Jesus addressed the timing of his return with his disciples. He began by teaching that no one knows when he will return. On earth before the flood of Noah, people carried on with regular life until, unexpectedly, the worldwide flood wiped all humanity off the face of the earth except for Noah and his family. It will be the same with the return of Christ. People will be carrying on with regular life until, unexpectedly, Jesus will come again. In the days of Noah, people were not ready for the judgment of God. When Jesus returns, people again will not be ready for the coming judgment. With that warning, Jesus explained to his followers that they must "Be ready, for the Son of Man is coming at an hour you do not expect." The main point Jesus stressed was that his followers are always to be ready for his return, as no one knows when judgment will arrive. Jesus then used the illustration of a criminal breaking into a home at night. If the residents knew the thief was coming, they would have stayed awake and been ready for him. There's no way they could sleep if they knew a criminal was on his way to their home. In the same way, people should always be ready and prepared for Jesus and his return.

Many Christians throughout the years have tried to speculate about when Jesus will return, when the earth will be destroyed, or who the antichrist is or will be. Although these events are sure to happen, Jesus taught his followers that no one knows. If we did know, we might relax about his return and fail to live like people ready for judgment. And even if the Lord's return is still hundreds of years away, it doesn't change the fact that we will all leave this planet. We don't know when. We could live for fifty more years, fifty more days, or fifty more hours. Only God knows when your existence on earth will come to an end. Listen to the warning of Jesus today. Prepare for your future, but live each day as if it were your last day on earth. Be ready to leave this planet without regret for what you did or didn't do when you stand before your King.

march
TWENTY-SIX

MATTHEW 25:1-13

With another parable, Jesus emphasized how critically important it is for people to be ready for his return. This time, he related the kingdom of heaven to ten virgins or girls going out to meet a bridegroom. Weddings in the time of Christ were different from weddings today. First, engagements were much more binding than our engagements, and a broken engagement necessitated a formal divorce. The engagement usually lasted a year, and then the wedding took place. On the wedding night, the bridegroom and his party would go to the home of the bride to meet her and her party. When the two groups came together, the wedding took place. This would often happen at night, so the attendants carried lamps or torches. In Jesus' parable, the ten girls waiting to meet the bridegroom are part of the bride's party. But half of them fail to prepare for the groom's coming. They don't have enough oil for their lamps. The parable calls these girls "foolish," or more literally "stupid." The smart girls realize they don't know when the bridegroom will show up, so they make sure to have enough oil and to stay ready to go at any time. The bridegroom ends up coming late (v. 5), and the foolish girls have to live with the consequences of their lack of preparedness. By the time they are able to wake up a merchant from whom they can buy oil in the middle of the night, the bridegroom is gone, the wedding feast has begun, and the foolish girls are locked out.

Jesus used this story to teach his followers what his return will be like. When the foolish girls arrive at the wedding feast, they assume there is still a place for them. But they are too late. The bridegroom answers them harshly in verse 12, "Truly, I say to you, I do not know you." Wow. That must have been a shock. Why didn't the five who had oil just share it with the foolish five? We must remember that readiness for Jesus' return is not something that can be shared. Each person is accountable for herself. In the same way, we must be prepared for Christ's return. If you know God is expecting something from you and you are putting it off, stop procrastinating today. Don't neglect what you should do. You never know when it will be too late.

march
TWENTY-SEVEN

MATTHEW 25:14-30

Jesus taught a parable illustrating our need to be faithful with what we have. In this parable, a man, a wealthy landowner, is called to leave the country, but before he leaves, he gives each of his servants a considerable amount of money. He wants to make sure his money is making more money, even during his absence. The amounts he gives to each servant are different, but all receive a sizeable sum. He trusts them to work hard on his behalf. Two of those three servants choose to do what they were charged and use the money to make even more. When the man returns and finds they have done the right thing, he thanks them and richly rewards them. The third servant is different. He doesn't work to make more money for the master. He reasons that if he buries the money and the master returns, he can just give the money back. Why should he go to all that hassle for someone else? Plus, if the master doesn't return at all, the servant could just keep the money. No one would even know he had it. When the boss returns and finds the servant has done nothing with what was entrusted to him, he is angry and takes away what that servant has. The servant's excuse is "I knew you to be a hard man, reaping where you did not sow, and gathering where you scattered no seed." Basically, he complains that his boss expected too much from him. The third man is considered wicked, lazy, and worthless, and so is sentenced to judgment (v. 26, 30).

One day Jesus will "settle accounts" with us too (v. 19). What "talents" has God given you? Have you faithfully used them to build his kingdom? Are you sharing your talents with the church, or burying them for yourself? Do you feel like you don't want to work for God's kingdom while he is gone, or think he won't really care when he comes back anyway? If so, stop thinking like that! If you are a Christian, you have been given resources you are expected to use for God's glory. Don't let laziness or selfishness drag you down to the place of the third servant. Use whatever God has given you to be faithful to him today, trusting that he will reward you greatly when he comes back.

march
TWENTY-EIGHT

MATTHEW 25:31-40

Jesus taught his followers that the day is coming when he will judge every person from every ethnicity on the earth. In his earlier parables, he taught about the need to be ready for the coming judgment. In this parable, he gave his disciples instruction regarding what to expect at the judgment. He described himself as a king sitting on a royal throne. By using this illustration, he let his followers know that he will be the one judging. He then compared this judgment to a shepherd separating a group of sheep from a group of goats. Shepherds would often let sheep and goats graze together for a while and then separate the two. Goats are less insulated and get colder at night than sheep normally would. The two groups were separated so the goats could sleep someplace warmer than the sheep. After Jesus divides the two groups, he will command those on the right, the sheep, to enter the place they inherited before the foundations of the world. Something inherited is not earned, but given as a gift because of a relationship. Jesus cites the good things the sheep did. He is not saying they earned their entrance into the kingdom, but they lived consistently with their election. This separation was planned before the world even began and is not an afterthought of God. If we belong to Jesus, then we will live like it. It's our destiny.

What are the good things listed here? Jesus declared that when his followers provided food, drink, and hospitality to strangers, took care of someone's financial needs, or even visited them when they were sick or imprisoned, he viewed it as if they had done it for him. The sheep wondered when they had done these things for Jesus. Again, they did these things not to earn their salvation, but as a natural result of their salvation. Because they loved Jesus, they loved others. If you are a Christian, do you long to love and serve Jesus? Of course you do. God has rewired you from the inside out and made his desires your desires. How can we love and serve him? By loving and serving others who have been made in his image! Let's choose to see Jesus when we look at other people today. Think of something tangible you can do to minister to someone else, and then do it as if you were doing it for the Lord.

march
TWENTY-NINE

MATTHEW 25:41-46

Jesus let his followers know what will happen to those on his left, the goats, who are not in a relationship with him. Instead of hearing "enter in" from Jesus, they will be told to "depart." They are sentenced to the eternal fire, which was prepared for Satan and his evil angels. It's worth noticing that those who are believers will go to the kingdom prepared for them from the beginning of the world (25:34), but those who have rejected Jesus will be sent to the place made ready not for them, but for Satan (v. 41). Jesus then goes through the same list he outlined with the earlier group. Even though these people did not know Jesus, he still holds this group responsible for not providing food, drink, and hospitality to strangers, or taking care of someone's financial needs, or visiting them when they were sick or imprisoned. In fact, he explains to them that when they didn't do these things for others, they didn't do these things for him. These people were shocked. They questioned, "When did we not do these things for you, Jesus?" They didn't realize loving other people was so important to God.

Many think that God is only concerned about their bad behavior. They may protest, "But I am not doing anything wrong!" When they say this, they don't realize that God requires people to refrain from wrong and to do what is right. Both are essential. Loving and serving others is a necessary byproduct of a right relationship with Jesus. If you are a follower of Jesus today, you will look for and meet needs in other people. Now there have always been people who don't know Jesus, yet live sacrificially. Even though they live uprightly, if they are lacking the right motive, gratitude for the work Jesus has done in saving them, their good deeds will come up short. We all need the forgiveness of God and truly can't afford to leave earth without it. This was Jesus' final teaching to his followers in Matthew's Gospel. His last sentence was, "And these will go away into eternal punishment, but the righteous into eternal life." Take some time to meditate on the word "eternal." As you will discover, eternity is a really, really long time. Ask God to help you make decisions today that are appropriate for one who possesses eternal life.

march
THIRTY

MATTHEW 26:1-5

Jesus finished the Olivet Discourse and let his disciples in on what was going to happen next. He reminded them that the Passover was coming in two days. Passover always began on a Friday after sunset, so Jesus probably spoke these words on a Wednesday. The Passover was celebrated annually in remembrance of God's people being delivered from bondage in Egypt. At the temple, a male lamb was sacrificed, and its blood was thrown on the altar. This act commemorated the blood that God's people painted on the doorposts of their homes the night of the first Passover, while they were still enslaved. When the angel of death came that evening to kill the firstborn of the Egyptians, the blood on a home's doorposts signaled to the angel to "pass over" that house. After the lamb was sacrificed, it was taken home and eaten together by a family or a group. Although the religious leaders planned to kill Jesus, with all the activity going on in Jerusalem, they definitely didn't want his arrest and execution to happen during the Passover. Worshippers were literally everywhere preparing for and participating in this great feast. It was certainly not the right time for a crucifixion. The chief priests and elders were willing to wait until the celebration was finished. But God had other plans. Jesus was killed during the feast, because God predetermined all the details surrounding his death.

The Passover was a memorial feast, which celebrated both the freedom of God's people and their deliverance from the angel of death. At the same time, the Passover pointed to the crucifixion, where Jesus would become the last sacrifice for sin. The payment he made on the cross would provide for the believer's pardon. Men may plot and scheme, but in the end God is in the details of life. The religious leaders said they wouldn't kill Jesus during the Passover, but Jesus knew his death would occur in two days. Man cannot thwart God's plans and purposes. When we want to get our agenda done by a certain time or in a certain way, we should always keep in mind that God may have something totally different prepared. Let's remember this short passage as we deal with the schedules we create. Keep your hands open before God today, trusting that in the end his plans are far better than ours.

march
THIRTY-ONE

MATTHEW 26:6-16

Jesus spent time during the last few days of his life in a town called Bethany. One night, while he was enjoying a meal with friends, Mary, his follower, poured very expensive oil on his head. The other disciples strongly objected to her action. They accused Mary of doing something foolish, since the perfume was worth an entire year's wage. They scolded her that she could have sold it and given the money to help the poor. But Jesus opposed their objections and let them know that they would always have opportunities to help the poor. But he would not be with them much longer, so what she did was right. In the culture at that time, it was normal for a Jewish host to provide oil for his guests' heads. The oil used for anointing would have been fairly cheap, but the more honored the guest, the more expensive the oil. If a dignitary or even a king were coming for dinner, the best oil possible would be used. Mary realized things about Jesus that the others may have missed. She knew Jesus was the Messiah—the Anointed One—and the King, and she knew that his time with them was coming to a close. So Mary held back nothing and gave her very best to Jesus. The disciples just didn't get it. They were poor and lived humbly, and so had the Lord. Why waste so much money on a one-time anointing? The apparent excess shocked and outraged them.

Jesus never instructed his followers to neglect the poor. But in this instance, he did begin to reveal to them that in a few days he would die a death designed for a criminal, and his body would not be properly anointed. It seems that Mary understood and may have had more insight into what Jesus had taught his followers up to this point, and she responded by giving generously before his departure. What about you? What is Jesus calling you to give him? Is he asking you to be generous in response to his love for you? Do you find yourself hesitating to do what his Spirit is prompting you to do because you fear what others may say or think? Even if it seems extravagant, do exactly what the Scripture and the Spirit are calling you to do for the Lord today. Mary's act became her memorial and should remind us that we will never regret what we give to Jesus.

april
ONE

MATTHEW 26:17-29

In this passage, Matthew describes the very first Lord's Supper. The disciples wanted to prepare the Passover meal to share with Jesus, so they asked him where they could do this. Jesus prearranged this celebration with his friends. He knew his time was short and kept the place a secret to thwart his enemies' attempts to find him until after this important meal. The disciples got everything in order, and Jesus ate together with the twelve. It was during the meal that Jesus made the shocking announcement, "One of you will betray me." Interestingly, none of the disciples said, "Of course, he must mean Judas." They had no idea whom Jesus was talking about, and each one assumed he could be the "betrayer." When Judas finally asked, "Is it I?" Jesus answered him with "You have said so." Judas must have been surprised, but he went ahead with the evil act anyway. How sad for Jesus that the one to hand him over to torture, crucifixion, and death was his so-called friend. Yet Jesus declared these things were all part of a predetermined plan. Nevertheless, Judas was fully responsible for his sin and would have been better off had he never been born.

The Scripture foretold all these events, yet Judas was still accountable to God for what he did. We may wonder whether those who commit sinful acts that are clearly a part of God's predetermined plan will be excused, since God knew or even ordained what would happen. The answer is "absolutely not." Even though God is able to take sinful and evil acts and work them together for his glory, the sinner is in no way "off the hook." God is able to bring good from bad situations without neglecting justice. Judas was not an honest follower, and he would suffer the consequences of rejecting Jesus. The other disciples addressed Jesus as "Lord." But in verse 25, Judas addresses him as "rabbi." Judas could no longer call Jesus his Lord. If you are a Christian today, thank God that Jesus is more than just your teacher; he is your Lord. Pray for your friends and family members who still see him as merely a great teacher. God can enable them to see Jesus for who he really is, just as he allowed you to see. Keep praying! You never know what God has planned.

april
TWO

MATTHEW 26:30-35

Jesus and his disciples finished their Passover meal together. Traditionally, the Jewish people would sing from Psalm 115 to Psalm 118 while celebrating the Passover. These four psalms are known as the Hallel Psalms. The Hebrew word *hallel* means "a song of praise." Jesus and his disciples probably sang directly from these four psalms, praising God, before they moved on to the Mount of Olives. Our Lord Jesus worshipped God right before he prayerfully prepared to experience the greatest trial presented to any human in history. After they departed, Jesus warned and prophesied to his disciples that they would fall away from him on that very night. At this point, the disciples still didn't think anything unusual was happening, but Jesus clearly knew otherwise. "Fall away" didn't mean they would or could lose their salvation or become apostates, but it did mean they would have a severe lapse of faith, acting out of character due to fear. In verse 31, Jesus quotes Zechariah, letting the disciples know that all of this was right in line with God's predetermined plan. Peter affirmed to Jesus that he would never fall away. He was totally loyal to Christ! After Peter's declaration, all the disciples chimed in and said the same thing (v. 35).

As the text reveals, Jesus knew exactly what was going to happen. But the disciples were clueless. Jesus let Peter know that he would fall away, and even went on to tell Peter how he would fall away! In the same way that Jesus knew what Peter was going to do, God knows exactly what all of us would do in any and every situation, real or hypothetical. God knows how you would respond if you got that new car or home you have wanted, how you would behave if you were the one promoted at work, what you would do if that relationship panned out the way you want, or how things will unfold if he gives a "yes" to that prayer request you have been making. God already knows what you would do and how things would turn out in these situations and any others. Like Peter, you may think you know what you would do in a given circumstance, but God knows the truth. Pray today that he would only give you what you can handle. God often says "no" because he clearly knows far more about us than we know about ourselves.

april
THREE

MATTHEW 26:36-46

Jesus and his disciples went to the Garden of Gethsemane on the Mount of Olives. Jesus often met with his disciples in this place, so nothing yet was out of the ordinary for them. Jesus knew what he was facing, and he had to get time alone with God in prayer. He took Peter, James, and John with him and asked them to wait with him. Verse 37 says he began to feel sorrowful and troubled. The Greek words used here for "sorrowful" and "troubled" mean "grieved and deeply distressed." It is impossible to imagine what Jesus was feeling at this point. Jesus adds, "My soul is very sorrowful, even to death." This clearly was not normal human anxiety or stress. It wasn't death that disturbed Jesus. It was the kind of death he faced that was so dreadful. Then Jesus dropped down and put his face to the ground. This posture signified the lowliest kind of prayer possible. Jesus addressed God as his Father and asked, "If it is possible." Jesus was hoping for some other way to go about all of this, but clearly deferred to the Father's plan over his own desires as he stated, "Not as I will, but as you will." When he asked, "Let this cup pass," he acknowledged the severity of what he would undergo. In the Old Testament, the cup often symbolized God's wrath against sin. Nevertheless, three times he prayed for God's will to be done.

In verse 40, Jesus speaks directly to Peter. Just before this, Peter insisted he was strong and would never fall away. Now he didn't have the stamina to stay awake for even an hour. Jesus then said, "The spirit indeed is willing, but the flesh is weak," and he asked his disciples to pray. When we pray, we acknowledge before God that we need his help. We declare that we don't have the ability to do what he has called us to do, or live the life he has called us to live when left to ourselves. Imagine yourself in the garden with Jesus. What if he told you to watch and pray? Would you do it? If so, then respond by spending some good time in prayer today, no matter how tired you may be. Our willingness must be met with God's power, and the two come together when we pray.

april
FOUR

MATTHEW 26:47-56

Jesus was still speaking to his disciples in the garden when Judas showed up with both Roman soldiers and Jews from the Temple Guard. They came armed with swords and clubs. How strange this must have been for Jesus and his followers. Jesus pointed out, "Day after day I sat in the temple teaching," yet now they came to him as if they were in pursuit of a dangerous criminal. Maybe they were afraid the crowds gathered for the festival would come to Jesus' aid if others saw what was happening. Little did the soldiers and guards know, but even Jesus' own disciples were about to abandon him. Nevertheless, Peter quickly attempted to rescue Jesus. Peter had been sleeping. When he heard the commotion and awoke, he realized this was no longer an ordinary Passover night. He immediately responded by cutting off the ear of the high priest's servant. Jesus told Peter to stop, as he didn't need Peter's help. If Jesus wanted to, he could have called for seventy-two thousand angels to defend him (a Roman legion consisted of six thousand soldiers). After this, the disciples realized they would probably go down with Jesus, so they panicked and scattered. They fled just as Jesus told them they would, and he went toward the cross alone.

Having poured himself out in prayer to God, Jesus was now calm and totally in control. His followers, however, panicked and ran away. But Jesus knew with certainty that this path for his life and death was foreordained, and there was no getting out of it. This route was best. What about you? Do you follow Jesus' example of total trust? After you pour yourself out in prayer to God, how do you face the trials and challenges he keeps before you? When we have prayed and done all we can, we are left with the will of God. We cannot change what God has determined to do with us. But we can change our attitudes. We can go through our trials screaming, yelling, crying, pouting, and feeling sorry for ourselves, or like Jesus we can maintain our calm, composure, and confidence. Maybe we aren't in control the way he was, but we are in him. And nothing can mess up his perfect plan for our lives. If you are a Christian, decide to put on the attitude of Christ in whatever difficulty he allows you to meet today.

april
FIVE

MATTHEW 26:57-68

After Jesus was arrested, Peter secretly followed him into the courtyard of Caiaphas to see what would happen. Caiaphas was the Jewish high priest, so this "trial" was not a civil affair but a religious trial. But Caiaphas was interested in Roman support. The Romans appointed him to the office of high priest, which was a lifetime role. So Caiaphas didn't want Jesus or anyone else messing up his position. The scribes and elders showed up too. Together, and under the leadership of the High Priest, this group was known as the Sanhedrin, the most powerful Jewish council. Verse 59 reveals that the purpose of this gathering wasn't to collect information and conduct a fair trial. Instead, these leaders were looking for a way to kill Jesus. False witnesses spoke, but didn't offer the information the leaders were looking for. Finally, two witnesses said Jesus had claimed he could destroy the temple and rebuild it in three days. Jesus didn't reply to their accusation. The high priest was enraged and commanded Jesus to tell them whether he was the Son of God. Jesus responded with "You have said so." Then he added, "But I tell you, from now on you will see the Son of Man seated at the right hand of Power and coming on the clouds of heaven." That was it! They all agreed that death was the only acceptable punishment for a claim like this.

Normally, when a person is falsely accused, he will do whatever he can to argue his case. But Jesus didn't. Instead, he remained basically quiet. His silence infuriated the religious leaders. They couldn't understand why he didn't plead for his life. We know that Jesus had already done so in the Garden of Gethsemane before his Father. The cross was inevitable. In verse 63, Caiaphas adds, "I adjure you by the living God." In doing this, he put Jesus "under oath," and Jesus had to respond. Jesus gave Caiaphas more than he hoped to hear, declaring that he held an office equal to God's. What Jesus said was incredible. If anyone tells you, "Jesus never claimed to be God," just have her read Matthew 26:64. Under oath, Jesus boldly declared his identity. All humans have two options: reject Jesus or surrender to him as Lord. Which one will you do today?

april
SIX

MATTHEW 26:69-27:2

Matthew shifts the reader from Jesus back to Peter, who waited in the courtyard of the high priest to see what would happen next. While there, a servant girl remarked in passing to Peter that he was a follower of Jesus, but Peter denied it. The servant, both a female and a slave, was practically the most unintimidating person imaginable in comparison to Peter. But since Peter was in the home of enemies, he was scared, and he refused to be identified as "belonging" to Jesus. Feeling awkward, Peter relocated to the gate of the courtyard. Another servant girl did the same thing: she acknowledged that Peter was with Jesus. Peter grew more aggressive and denied it with an oath. Finally, bystanders commented on the same thing again, declaring that Peter had to be a follower of Jesus. This time, Peter panicked. He cursed and swore, insisting that he did not know Jesus. Immediately after this, Jesus' prophecy came true, and a rooster crowed. Peter must have felt horrible. He had insisted he would never deny Jesus. He even shadowed him into the home of the high priest. Now, fearing his own safety, he denied ever even knowing Jesus. He failed the very one he loved. And he did it three times in a row! Peter wept bitterly (v. 75). He was embarrassed before Jesus, sorry to God for his sin, and wept tears of genuine repentance.

Even as dedicated followers of Jesus, we all fail God on occasion. Like Peter, we sin against God when we think of ourselves. We want protection from suffering and harm, we want to escape others looking down on us, or we want to indulge ourselves in something inconsistent with the character of our Lord. If we are saved, like Peter, we feel awful afterward. But feeling awful isn't enough if it doesn't lead to real repentance. If you know you shouldn't have done something, or you should have done something and didn't, and you feel embarrassed or badly about it before God, turn your grief into repentance today. Let him know you are genuinely sorry, and ask him for help to keep from repeating the same behavior again. God wants us right with him more than we want it for ourselves. May we learn to love repentance as much as we love faith. The two really go hand in hand.

april
SEVEN

MATTHEW 27:3-10

Judas realized that Jesus wasn't going to use his divine power to deliver himself from imprisonment. Instead of escaping, Jesus stood condemned as a result of the betrayal. Judas began to feel awful, and he changed his mind about the "hand Jesus over for thirty pieces of silver agreement." He went back to the chief priests and elders, who should have given Judas good spiritual advice. But the religious leaders didn't care about Judas. They let him know that his conscience was his own problem and not theirs. They wanted nothing more to do with him. They were concerned with making sure that Jesus was executed. Like Peter, Judas felt dreadful about what he had done. He confessed that he had sinned and betrayed innocent blood. He threw the thirty pieces of silver back into the temple. It is absolutely ironic that the religious leaders wouldn't take the money because it was used to buy the death of another since they were the ones who paid Judas in the first place. So it was fine for them to pay Judas to betray an innocent man, handing him over to the Romans, but they wouldn't accept that same money back into the treasury. What a mess their hypocrisy had gotten them all into! They couldn't see their right hands from their left anymore and had lost the notion of what it meant to live for God.

So why was Peter right with God after his betrayal, but not Judas? Both felt awful about what they had done. Both responded emotionally to their sin. Although both seemed repentant, their actions revealed the nature of their sorrow. Peter's was godly sorrow. He repented and met up with the rest of the disciples. Judas' was worldly sorrow. He was frustrated with what he had done, but instead of rejoining the disciples, he hung himself. Had the repentance of Judas been genuine, he would have run to God instead of away from him. Although it is possible to take one's own life and still be saved, in this case, Judas was never an honest follower of Jesus. He was with Jesus physically but not spiritually. Most believe Judas was "in it for the money," acting as group treasurer and betraying Jesus for silver. Actions reveal the nature of faith. Pray that those in your life who are sorry about their sin will be moved all the way to genuine repentance, and that the source of their genuine repentance would never need to be "repented of" again.

april
EIGHT

MATTHEW 27:11-23

After the chief priests and elders bound Jesus, they sent him to trial before Pilate, the Roman governor of Judea, who asked Jesus whether he was the King of the Jews. This question is recorded in all four Gospels, and the "you" is emphatic, meaning, "Are YOU the King of the Jews?" It is as if Pilate were looking at Jesus and thinking, "Wow! This guy is not what I expected. No way is he going to try to take over Rome." Jesus answered, "You have said so." The religious leaders accused Jesus of many other things, but Jesus refused to answer them. This amazed Pilate. This was no ordinary trial, and Pilate recognized that Jesus should not have been there. He knew Jesus was on trial because the religious leaders were jealous of him (v. 18). To top it off, Pilate's wife was tormented in a dream about Jesus. She realized he was innocent too. At the time, as an act of mercy, one prisoner was customarily released during the Passover. Pilate offered to release one of the two prisoners there, certain they would choose Jesus. The other prisoner was a man named Barabbas, a murderer. Pilate figured even though the religious leaders didn't support Jesus, the crowd certainly would. And he couldn't imagine them choosing the murderer over the Messiah. But Pilate was wrong. The crowd wanted Barabbas released and Jesus killed.

Just days before, this same crowd "rolled out the red carpet" for Jesus and shouted, "Hosanna to the Son of David! Blessed is he who comes in the name of the Lord!" They were thrilled by the thought of their Messiah finally delivering them from Roman rule. Now the very same crowd chanted, "Crucify!" over and over again like frenzied fans at a football game. They didn't get what they wanted from Jesus, and they were done with him. Many people today treat Jesus the same way. They get involved with Christianity, they find their lives don't "improve," and they toss him off, saying, "I tried Jesus. He didn't work for me." If you feel frustrated because your life, even as a Christian, is still hard, remember that while things may seem unfinished here, they will all come together in God's kingdom. Don't forget that Jesus came to do God's will, not ours. As a result, even though we still struggle physically, our spiritual need has been forever satisfied.

april
NINE

MATTHEW 27:24-31

Pilate couldn't believe that the crowd begged for Barabbas instead of Jesus. His plan to have Jesus released backfired, and a notorious criminal was freed as a result. Now that the crowd was riled up, there was no going back. Pilate was frustrated, and in protest, he washed his hands, declaring to the crowd, "I am innocent of this man's blood." Washing the hands was actually a Jewish custom used to demonstrate innocence. Pilate realized that Jesus was about to be unjustly murdered, and he did not want to be liable for Jesus' execution. The crowd, however, had a completely different response. In fact, they willingly accepted full responsibility for Jesus' death upon themselves and their children (v. 25). They clearly did not see Jesus as innocent. The religious leaders successfully infuriated the crowd and convinced them that the claims Jesus made about himself were worthy of his murder. The crowd must have been ecstatic at this point. They forced Pilate to release a murderer and they dictated that Jesus be crucified. They felt totally in control and powerful, and they gladly took responsibility for their choices.

Even though Pilate "washed his hands," in the end, he was the one who had the legal authority to either release or execute Jesus. Pilate knew Jesus was innocent, but he stood by and allowed him to be murdered anyway. Washing his hands was a cop-out. He should have stood up to the mob and said, "No." But Pilate feared the crowd's reaction and the potential loss of his honored position if he let things get out of control. So to keep the peace and his job, Pilate allowed Jesus to die. We can do the same thing when we get caught up in wrong thinking like Pilate did. We can feel that if we say we don't want any part of something, then we are off the hook. But if we have the power to stop injustice and do nothing, we are guilty. Search your heart today. Are you allowing something to happen because you don't want to "rock the boat" and upset people? Are you afraid you will suffer loss if you speak up for someone being mistreated? Take a stand today and say, "No more!" to the wrongdoing around you. You may not be popular as a result, but remember, pleasing God always takes priority over pleasing man.

april
TEN

MATTHEW 27:32-44

At some point along the route to the crucifixion, the procession ran into a man from Cyrene named Simon. Cyrene was a city in North Africa where many Jews lived. Simon was probably in Jerusalem to celebrate the Passover. Whatever the case, Simon was forced to carry Jesus' cross (actually it was the crossbeam that would be nailed to a supporting beam to form the cross we think of). By this point, Jesus had no more strength. He had been up through the night undergoing various trials, beaten, and then brutally scourged with whips. He was absolutely exhausted physically. One of the Roman soldiers could have carried Jesus' cross, but since the custom was that the guilty would carry his own cross, there was no way any Roman was going to do that. They finally arrived at Golgotha, the place of the skull. As Jesus hung on the cross, they offered him wine and gall to numb his senses, but he wouldn't take it. Those who were crucified hung totally naked from their execution racks and had no need for their garments, so the soldiers divided up Jesus' clothing. This was the most humiliating form of death possible. Over the heads of those crucified was written their crimes. The sign over Jesus read, "This is Jesus, the King of the Jews" (v. 37).

Matthew doesn't go into great detail about Jesus' physical suffering. We often think about all that Jesus endured physically, and it makes us cringe. But we can forget that what he endured physically was nothing compared to what he endured spiritually. No human can imagine what it would be like to have God's justified wrath toward the sin of humanity poured out upon a soul. God is holy, and his hatred for evil is something we don't have the ability to comprehend. Somehow, as Jesus willingly became sin for us, his perfect and eternal relationship with the Father was interrupted. Again, no one can fathom what this was like. The physical beatings he endured were just a sign pointing to the real pain Jesus embraced for those who would follow him. If you are a Christian today, stop and thank Jesus for allowing himself to be punished instead of you. In the crucifixion, we see more love than our minds can ever comprehend. If you ever doubt God's love for you, remember the cross.

april
ELEVEN

MATTHEW 27:45-56

Matthew records that from the sixth hour until the ninth hour, or from noon until 3 p.m., darkness covered all the land. This supernatural darkness resulted from Jesus acting as a sin offering before the Father and climaxed with Jesus calling out, "My God, my God, why have you forsaken me?" Jesus said this loudly enough for others to hear. As he called out to God, "Eli" in Aramaic, bystanders thought he was calling out to Elijah. They waited to see if Elijah would come and rescue him. After this cry, Jesus chose to give up his spirit (v. 50). This was all in God's predetermined plan and happened exactly as he intended. Many readers of Matthew overlook the three incredible events that transpired next. First, the curtain separating the Holy Place from the Most Holy Place in the temple was torn in two. Next, an earthquake split even rocks in half, and finally, to top it off, many believers who had died were resurrected and went into Jerusalem. Wow! Jesus was in control of both the living and the dead! It is no wonder that the centurion and his companions were terrified and recognized that Jesus truly is the Son of God (v. 54).

It is incredibly significant that the curtain in the temple was torn in two with the death of Christ. This heavy curtain separated the Holy Place into a Most Holy Place that very few could ever enter. In fact, only the high priest could go into this space, and only one time per year. The "regular" priests were not permitted in the Most Holy Place. Verse 51 tells us the curtain was torn from top to bottom. This top to bottom tear revealed that it was God himself who ripped the curtain in half. The curtain was no longer necessary, as access to God's throne was not limited as it had been before. With the death of Jesus, all believers may enter into the presence of God. The Messiah dealt with sin on the cross once and for any who might place her trust in him and turn in repentance from self to God. After reading today, take a couple of minutes to pray. When you pray, realize that the open and direct access you have to God was made possible only by Jesus' work on the cross.

april
TWELVE

MATTHEW 27:57-66

Jesus died on the cross. Proper burial and treatment of the dead were very important to the Jews, but when a criminal was executed, the body was often tossed away. But that's not what happened with Jesus' body. A rich man from Arimathea named Joseph, a Jewish religious leader who believed in Jesus, asked Pilate for Jesus' body. This Joseph must have been an important man, given his ability to access Pilate directly. Pilate agreed to his request, and Joseph took Jesus' body off the cross to properly prepare the corpse for burial, according to the custom of the day. It is interesting that Jesus' family and close friends didn't do this. Joseph then put the body in a rock tomb he owned and rolled a stone in front of it, which was how these tombs were typically closed. Jesus' enemies continued to work as well. The chief priests and the Pharisees also went to Pilate. They remembered that Jesus said he would rise from the dead. They assumed he intended deception, and that his followers would figure out a way to trick people. They wanted to post security by the tomb's entrance. That way, after three days, they could prove the corpse was still there. Pilate agreed again to their request, and the religious leaders did whatever they could to make the tomb secure by sealing the stone and setting a guard there. They could rest now, knowing that no one could reach the body of Jesus.

Little did the enemies of Jesus realize they were helping his cause! When Jesus did actually rise from the dead, because of the intense security, no one would be able to say his disciples did it. Pilate provided guards to stand by the tomb, and to top it off they sealed it with a Roman seal, using wax so that no one could tamper with anything. God used the plans of his enemies to carry out his purposes. Do you ever feel discouraged by those who plot or scheme against you? Do you feel like God's agenda will not be accomplished because of the efforts of his enemies? Even though things may seem crazy at times, we can rest assured, knowing that God's hands are not tied. God is able to take every single thing and work it together for good for the followers of Christ. Take comfort in this truth today as you struggle against the sin around you.

april
THIRTEEN

MATTHEW 28:1-10

Early in the morning, the two women who had watched all that happened to Jesus went back to his tomb. After another giant earthquake, an angel appeared. This angel rolled back the stone protecting the entrance to the tomb, and he sat right on the giant rock. The angel was striking in presence, and the mighty Roman guards were terrified. Paralyzed with fear, they fell to the ground like dead men. The angel spoke to both Marys, telling them Jesus' body was no longer present. Just as Jesus had promised, he had risen from the dead! The angel rolled away the stone so the women could gaze inside. He asked them to look in the tomb and see with their own eyes. These were the same women who watched Joseph of Arimathea put Jesus' dead body in that tomb and then close it with the stone. (There was no point in wasting time at an empty tomb.) The angel encouraged them to rush back and let the other disciples know that Jesus was no longer there. He was going to meet them "back home" in Galilee. As the women ran, Jesus showed up! They fell down at his feet and worshipped him as God.

The angel from heaven encouraged the women not to be afraid (v. 5), and Jesus encouraged them not to be afraid as well (v. 10)! Both the angel and Jesus personally comforted these women. In the first century, women were not considered to have the same worth as men, yet this angel and Jesus appeared to them before appearing to the other disciples! These women stayed by Jesus at the cross, followed when he was placed in the tomb, and got up early to return to his place of burial. They were on the front lines for Jesus, and he chose to show himself in his resurrected state to them first! What about you? Do you ever feel like you aren't in on all the action when it comes to God's work? Do you feel like you miss out on his presence or power? Maybe you haven't been out on the front lines of ministry. If these women had been home watching TV, they would not have been the very first to see Jesus. Let's choose to get off the couch today and get involved in what God is doing here on earth. You never know what he will do next.

april
FOURTEEN

MATTHEW 28:11-20

While the two Marys were running to deliver the good news to the other disciples, the Roman guard rushed to tell the Jewish religious leaders what happened as well. The Jews would believe the story before the Romans ever would, so the guards figured it was smart to report to them first. The Jewish religious leaders decided to pay the soldiers to say that the followers of Jesus stole his body while they slept. One thing was certain: no corpse lay in the tomb anymore. Some explanation had to be given. But how could the soldiers know what happened while they were asleep? If they knew the disciples were stealing the body, why didn't they stop them? There were some problems with the lie, but it was the best they could come up with. Then the eleven disciples (Judas was dead, so eleven remained) met with Jesus in Galilee. There, Jesus charged them with what is known as "The Great Commission." He instructed them to make new disciples by doing three things: going, baptizing, and teaching obedience to his directives. He encouraged his followers with his promise to be with them to the end. Looking carefully at verse 19, note that it literally says "the name of," not "the names of." This is one place where Jesus undoubtedly taught that the Father, the Son, and the Holy Spirit, three persons, are in essence one God with one "name."

Matthew records Jesus' final charge to his followers. Most people are aware that Jesus instructed his followers, including us as Christians, to make disciples. We know that. But one thing we often overlook is that Jesus unmistakably said, "Teaching them to observe all that I have commanded you" (v. 20). In other words, "Teach them to do what I say." This should be common sense to us, but we live in a day where many, even Christians, would say that obedience to Jesus doesn't really matter. All we need is faith or to "believe in" him. But when we truly believe in him, we do what he said. If we don't seek to do what Jesus said, then it's safe to say we don't "really" believe. If you are a Christian today, when you communicate the gospel or pray for those around you, make sure that your words are consistent with the truth. Followers of Jesus will follow Jesus. It's not that complicated.

april
FIFTEEN

MARK 1:1-8

Mark's account of Jesus begins with a title which could be read "The Good News about Jesus, the Messiah and Son of God." Mark starts with the ministry of John the Baptist, the forerunner, or the one who went before Jesus. He prefaces the information about John with Isaiah's Old Testament prophecy, pointing to the forerunner. Aside from Jesus' quotations, this is the only time Mark uses the Old Testament in his biography of Christ. As Mark introduces John, he reveals that Isaiah specifically prophesied that the forerunner would be heard in the wilderness or desert (v. 3). He then transitions to John, who was baptizing and proclaiming repentance in the wilderness. Clearly, John the Baptist was the promised forerunner of the Messiah, about whom Isaiah spoke. But John's baptism was a little different from what the Jews were familiar with. Prior to this time, Gentile converts to Judaism were required to be baptized. Now, under John's transitional ministry, those who prepared themselves for the Messiah were baptized as a result of their repentance and their desire to get right with God. The verb "baptize" literally means "to immerse." According to verse 5, people were "going" and "confessing" as they were immersed by John in water, symbolizing what took place in their hearts through the cleansing forgiveness of God. The people continued to stream from all over the country to John. As one group left, another replaced it.

The Jews who came to John were willing to be publicly identified with their repentance by the act of baptism. They acknowledged their sins and their need to turn from living for themselves to living for God. Although it took humiliation for a covenant Jew to acknowledge his need for the forgiveness of God, any discomfort was well worth the benefit of the Almighty's forgiveness. What about you? Is anything too embarrassing for you to do before others when it comes to standing up and out for the truth? These Jews could have faced hardship and rejection as a result of embracing John's baptism, but they wanted to be right with God. Search your heart today. If fear of others is keeping you from doing what God has called you to do, then repent! Choose to turn around and do things God's way instead of living in fear of what people may think.

april
SIXTEEN

MARK 1:9-20

In this section, Mark turns from John the Baptist to Jesus. We read of Jesus' baptism by John, Jesus' temptation in the wilderness, and the beginning of Jesus' preaching and calling of his first disciples: Simon, Andrew, James, and John. Mark's account so far is brief and to the point, yet many thought-provoking facts are worth noting. For one, right after Jesus' baptism, Mark records that the Holy Spirit immediately drove him into the wilderness. The Greek word we read in English as "drove" means just that. It is a term of force and can be translated as "drove out, expelled, or sent away." The Spirit empowered Jesus at his baptism, and then drove him out to test his obedience. Would he use his power to serve himself, or to serve God? It is also interesting to see what Mark records as the content of Jesus' preaching in Galilee. In verse 15, we read, "The time is fulfilled, and the kingdom of God is at hand; repent and believe in the gospel." Jesus preached two responses to the gospel: repent and believe. It has been said that belief and repentance are like two sides of a coin. We cannot separate the "heads" from the "tails," and if we did, we would no longer have a full coin. In the same way, we cannot separate belief from repentance. Both are necessary components of the proper response to the good news Jesus brought. This was the message of John the Baptist, and it was the message of Jesus.

Because the kingdom of God is at hand, those who want to follow Jesus must repent and believe. Another way of saying this is "turn and trust." To follow Jesus, we must choose to trust in what he has accomplished to make us right with God. We cannot for one minute think we are qualified to access the Father without the Son. We must also choose to turn from living for ourselves and instead live for him. This means we stop doing the things that displease God and in their place do the things that are consistent with his will for us. Can you say you have truly "turned and trusted"? Would those closest to you say you have? If not, what's keeping you from a proper response to the gospel? The verbs used for "repent" and "believe" are present imperatives, meaning "keep on repenting" and "keep on believing"!

april
SEVENTEEN

MARK 1:21-28

While in Capernaum, Jesus went into the local synagogue. The synagogue was not the same as the temple. Animal sacrifice took place only in the one Jewish temple where priests presented offerings to God for the people. The temple was in Jerusalem, and to make sacrifice, the Jews who lived outside of Jerusalem had to travel there. The synagogue was like an assembly hall. Synagogues, or gathering places, were located throughout Israel, and Jewish men would gather there on the Sabbath for Old Testament "Bible studies." All that was necessary to form a synagogue was ten or more Jewish men over the age of thirteen. The ruler of the synagogue probably invited Jesus to teach that day. When the Jews heard Jesus teach, they said his teaching was not like what they normally heard from the scribes. At this time, the scribes were considered experts in the Law of God. They were so admired that when they made decisions about how the Law should be practiced people responded as if those decisions were from God. In fact, the Jews had so much respect for the scribes that they rose up when the scribes entered a room! When Mark says Jesus "taught them as one who had authority," this would have meant a lot to the first century reader. The scribes did have authority! But Jesus' teaching had supernatural authority.

When you read or listen to the words of Jesus, how do you respond? Anyone familiar with the New Testament can think, "Yeah, yeah… I have heard all that before. 'Blessed are the so-and-so.'" We can yawn our way through the words of Christ as if he were a familiar voice we've grown accustomed to. The Greek word used for "astonished" in verse 22 can literally be translated "struck out of their senses." When was the last time you were struck out of your senses by the teaching of Jesus? As we read the book of Mark, or the other Gospels, or any of the Scripture for that matter, let's respond to it for what it is, God's direct communication to us! Jesus spoke to you, and his message is recorded in the Bible. May we love the teaching of Jesus today like never before, and may we be changed as a result.

april
EIGHTEEN

MARK 1:29-39

Right after Jesus left the synagogue in Capernaum, he went to Peter (Simon) and Andrew's house. Peter's mother-in-law was sick. It is interesting to note that Peter had a mother-in-law, which means he was married. Clearly, God does not oppose marriage or desire spiritual leaders in the church to remain unmarried, contrary to what some may teach. Jesus simply walked up to Peter's mother-in-law, took her by the hand, lifted her up, and she was healed. No magic formula or drawn-out process was needed. In fact, Peter's mother-in-law was so restored to health that she was able to serve immediately without weakness. Jesus went on to heal many who were sick or demon-possessed. Then the crowds came to Jesus at sundown because the Sabbath had ended. The people heard about his teaching and healing power and wanted help from him. Verse 33 says, "The whole city was gathered at the door." Jesus extended his compassion toward this crowd in Capernaum and healed many people that evening. He also delivered the people from evil spirits, and yet he commanded the demons to remain silent, as he didn't want any advertisement from them at this time. Jesus was in absolute authority over sickness and the demonic realm.

The whole city of Capernaum came to Jesus for help. But to be healed or delivered, they had to admit they needed help. These people realized Jesus possessed a supernatural authority and was able to restore their broken bodies. We too must see our need for help. We are all spiritually sick and in desperate need of Jesus' touch. We have all sinned or done things our own way instead of God's way. Because God is absolutely holy, or morally pure, and we are not, our sin creates a separation between God and us. And when we come to Jesus' door, confessing and asking for help, he will heal us. If you are a Christian, thank the Lord that he has allowed you to see your spiritual need and respond accordingly. Yet many think they are whole or complete without the help of Christ. When they stand before God in judgment, they will see that they didn't meet God's perfect standard for human life. Stop and pray for those who think they are well without Christ. Ask the Lord to allow them to see their tremendous need for a Savior today.

april
NINETEEN

MARK 1:40-45

Leprosy was a devastating skin disorder in the ancient world. If someone contracted the disease, her life was basically over. She had to isolate herself from the community and, to keep others from contacting the horrible condition as well, the Law required her to shout, "Unclean! Unclean!" when people approached her. Many with leprosy spent their lives away from their family and friends. And to top it off, the general population believed leprosy was a sign of God's judgment, so the misery associated with the sickness was dreadful. What a nightmare! It was almost like a living death sentence. Now when Jesus met the leper, verse 40 tells us he didn't remove himself from the leper's presence, which was very unusual. The leper begged Jesus to make him clean. He didn't ask Jesus to heal him, as one might typically request, because the unique nature of leprosy meant that it required "cleansing." The infected were not only seen as sick but as contaminated too. What's so incredible is that Jesus not only engaged this leper, but actually stretched out his hand and touched the man. Mark records that Jesus did this because he was "moved with pity." Though others would have been made unclean by contact with a leper, Jesus remained unscathed.

Leprosy was also a symbol of sin. It reminded those who saw it of the separation sin works between God and man. Jesus completely cleansed and healed this man, so that he went from uncleanness to immediate purity. In the same way, Jesus completely cleans the broken sinner too. Looking again at his request, the leper didn't ask Jesus, "Can you heal me?" Instead, in faith, he declared, "If you will, you can make me clean." Do we come to Jesus like this? Are we confident he can do whatever he wants to do when he wants to do it? The issue wasn't Jesus' ability but his will. Even if you are already a follower of Jesus, if any sin remains unconfessed in your life, stop and ask Jesus to cleanse you. We know that if we come to Jesus, begging to be washed from our sin, he is both willing and able to heal us. Let's be restored to spiritual health today by confession and repentance, thanking Jesus for his pity upon and power over our weak and sinful flesh.

april
TWENTY

MARK 2:1-17

Jesus returned to Capernaum, which he considered home. Commentators believe Jesus lived with Peter and Andrew in Capernaum. Many gathered around the home to hear from Jesus, even completely blocking the doorway. While Jesus was preaching to the crowd, four men tried to get a paralyzed man close to him. But they just couldn't push their way through this group of people. No one gave up his spot for the paralytic. The four men grew desperate. They went up the staircase alongside of the house, dug an opening in the roof, and lowered the paralyzed man on a mat right in front of Jesus. Talk about persistence! As Jesus was teaching, he looked at the paralyzed man and said, "Son, your sins are forgiven." Jesus didn't scold the men for literally dropping in during his teaching, but simply stated that the paralytic was forgiven. Can you imagine what the crowd was thinking? The four didn't bring the paralytic there to have his sins forgiven. They wanted him healed! In addition, the scribes thought, "Wait a minute! Jesus is claiming he can forgive sins! No one can do that but God!" Jesus knew what the scribes were thinking and went on to heal the paralyzed man with the words "Rise, pick up your bed, and go home." Immediately, the man was restored to health, proving Jesus could heal and forgive sins. The amazed crowd gave glory to God.

The faith of the paralytic's four friends is fascinating. Even Jesus was impressed (v. 5). But it is interesting to consider that Jesus clearly responded to the faith of the group of men, and it's evident that the paralytic's faith is included in this "group faith" the text speaks of. Jesus forgave the paralyzed man's sins and healed him in response to the faith and actions of his friends. It is easy to forget that Jesus responds to our faith, even when we come to him on behalf of someone else. Who in your life needs the help of Jesus? Are you continually bringing them before him in prayer? Are you passionate? Would you push through a crowd, climb stairs, or dig a hole in a roof so that Jesus might consider them? Don't grow weary in asking the Lord to save those you love. Bring them before the throne of God in prayer today. You never know when Jesus might do a work in their lives.

april
TWENTY-ONE

MARK 2:18-28

Mark records an occasion when Jesus and his disciples were going through grain fields on the Sabbath. One of the Ten Commandments instructs God's people to refrain from work on the Sabbath, an important time for the Jews that marked them off from the nations around them. The Sabbath ran from Friday at sundown to Saturday at sundown. The 24 hours in between these sunsets marked the official Sabbath. God's people were to stop working because God himself "rested" from his work on the seventh day of creation and set the pattern for humanity of six days of work and one day of rest. The Jewish people were to do no work on the Sabbath, unless work was necessary to save life. Now, Jesus and his disciples plucked grain and ate as they passed through the grain fields, on the Sabbath. There was nothing wrong with plucking and eating leftover grain, but the Pharisees complained that Jesus and his disciples were "working" on the Sabbath. Jesus responded with Scripture and reminded them that in the Old Testament David entered the tabernacle court and asked for the consecrated bread, which was only for the priests. David gave this bread to his men as they were hungry and in desperate need. The ceremonial laws about tabernacle practice were important, but human life took precedence over ceremony.

Jesus finished by saying, "The Sabbath was made for man, not man for the Sabbath" (v. 28). In other words, people weren't made for the purpose of holding fast Sabbath regulations, but rather the Sabbath was instituted to bless people. Then Jesus added, "The Son of Man is lord even of the Sabbath." Wow! Now Jesus declared that he had authority over the Sabbath. God set the Sabbath in motion for the benefit of man, and Jesus had supremacy over it. Jesus put himself in the place of God. Jesus never discarded the Law of God; rather, he came to fulfill the Law. God has provided the Christian with ultimate rest through his Son. Jesus is our Sabbath! If you are a Christian, choose to live like one free from the *bondage* of work so that you may embrace the *blessing* of work. For those in Christ, work provides a wonderful opportunity to express our gratitude to God for all he has done.

april
TWENTY-TWO

MARK 3:1-12

Jesus entered the synagogue, probably in Capernaum, on the Sabbath, and a man with a deformed hand happened to be there. The Pharisees present kept their eyes on Jesus to see if he would heal the man. They desperately wanted to accuse Jesus again of working on the Sabbath. How strange. The Pharisees were waiting to see if Jesus would do good so they could accuse him of doing evil. Since a deformed hand wasn't life-threatening, Jesus wasn't supposed to heal on the Sabbath based on the manmade rules of Judaism. Sure enough, with everyone watching, Jesus called the man to stand up. Can you imagine what the man with the deformed hand was thinking? What was Jesus about to do? Jesus then asked the religious leaders, "Is it lawful on the Sabbath to do good or to do harm, to save life or to kill?" In other words, is it illegal to do good on the Sabbath? They couldn't answer. Jesus asked the man to stretch out his hand. Would the man do it? If he did, he would face the rage of the Pharisees. The man stretched out his hand to Jesus and was immediately healed. The Pharisees now had their reason to eliminate Jesus.

It greatly distressed Jesus that the Pharisees didn't answer his question about whether it was right to do good on the Sabbath. He was very angry at their unwillingness to show kindness to their fellow man, especially one with a need (v. 5). The answer should have been, "Of course it is right to do good on the Sabbath. In fact, to have the ability to do good and withhold it would be the true evil." But the Pharisees could not care less about the man's hand. They weren't rejoicing when Jesus healed him. All they were interested in was seeing Jesus break their rule. If we ever find ourselves hoping someone will sin, or rejoicing when someone falls, our hearts are not right. In fact, wanting to see someone do evil is an evil wish in itself. Check your heart. Can you think of anyone whom you hope to see fail? If so, confess and repent. Let's make sure we aren't as hard-hearted as these Pharisees. Let's instead choose to love mercy and offer kindness to all people today.

april
TWENTY-THREE

MARK 3:13-21

Jesus specifically called twelve men from those who were following him to be apostles. Typically, students would take time to ponder which rabbi they wanted to study under, and the student would then approach the rabbi for consideration. But when Jesus called the men he desired, the exact opposite happened. Jesus knew exactly whom he wished to be his twelve apostles, and he appointed them according to his command. He both chose them to be with him and to be sent. The twelve would be charged to do two specific things: preach the gospel and have authority over demons (v. 15). The apostles were commissioned to declare to others what they had seen and heard in and from Jesus. In this sense, these men were the initial representatives of all disciples who would follow the Lord, as the Christian is someone who is both with Jesus and sent by Jesus to do his will. After Jesus called the twelve, he went back to eat, but so many people pursued him that he wasn't even able to eat a meal. At this point, his family thought it was "intervention time" for the religious fanatic. They believed Jesus had gone crazy, and they desperately tried to bring him back to his senses.

It is worth considering the fact that no one "does Jesus a favor" by choosing to follow him. Instead, if you are his disciple, you are indebted to his call on your life. Think about the moment when you came to the place of genuine repentance and faith. How did God orchestrate the details of your life so that you could respond to his summons? The honest heart will see that salvation is truly all of God from start to finish. If you are in Christ, spend a few minutes thanking God for his choice of you. The Christian is a living testimony to the sovereignty of God. And the Christian is a continual reminder to those watching, seen and unseen, of not only God's sovereignty, but his goodness too. As God continues to unfold his timeless plan before even the angels in heaven, those who have been called out as believers play an important role in his grand demonstration. Allow your knowledge of his authority to encourage and strengthen you to further obedience and joy, knowing that he can and will complete what he sets out to do.

april
TWENTY-FOUR

MARK 3:22-30

The scribes became even more aggressive with their accusations against Jesus. They declared Jesus cast out demons by using the power of demons. The scribes couldn't deny what Jesus was doing, so they chose to attack the source of his power. Instead of admitting God cast out demons through Jesus, they claimed the evil spirits were leaving men because Jesus relied upon Satan for power. They charged Jesus with being possessed by Beelzebul, which was another name for the devil. Jesus called them together and told them their logic was ridiculous. If Jesus' work was against Satan and his kingdom, then how could Satan be empowering it? That made no sense. Jesus also declared that no one could enter into a strong man's house and take what he had, unless the strong man were first bound. Jesus would not be able to rescue men from Satan's clutches unless he were more powerful than Satan. The mightier one, Jesus, is able to rescue souls from the realm of the devil, the lesser power. And that's just what Jesus did. Jesus certainly didn't need Satan's power to help him out. In fact, Jesus took what "belonged" to the devil.

What if you were there as an eyewitness of Jesus casting out evil spirits from men and delivering them from demon possession? What would you do? Would you believe? Would you turn from living for yourself and instead live for him? The scribes saw Jesus' mighty works, but it sure didn't help them. They were still not willing to do things God's way. Many today will argue that if God simply appeared to them, gave them a sign, or answered a specific prayer, then they would believe. But what kind of appearance or sign or answered prayer would satisfy our doubt? People often reject Jesus not because they don't believe the facts about who he was and what he did, but they reject him because they aren't willing to give him their lives. Those who agree to the facts about Christ but don't repent are no different from the unbelieving scribes. Those who believe will obey. Jesus says in verse 28, "All sins will be forgiven against the children of man." There is no sin you've committed that Jesus isn't willing to forgive. If you know in your heart that Jesus is Lord, be willing to do whatever he asks you to do today.

april
TWENTY-FIVE

MARK 3:31-35

Mark takes the reader back to the story of Jesus' family and the crowded house (found in Mark 3:20-21). Jesus' relatives arrived to help him restrain his "fanatical" activity. When they got to the house, it was so packed with people that they had to send someone to get him. The crowd inside and around him let him know his family was outside looking for him. The original word used for "seeking you" implied some authority over him. Jesus responded, "Who are my mother and my brothers?" (v. 33). Jesus used this opportunity to teach the crowds around him about the connectedness of his followers. Jesus looked at those sitting around him and said, "Here are my mother and my brothers!" Jesus demonstrated that those who sat and listened to his teaching, ready to do his will, made up his spiritual family. He didn't dismiss the idea of responsibility to physical family, but he did elevate the spiritual bond to include those who follow him into a new kind of intimacy that actually surpasses blood relatives.

What an honor to be a part of Jesus' family! Although we know Jesus was never married and never had children, hypothetically, what if someone let you know that records were uncovered revealing your descent from the family line of Jesus? How would you feel? What's so fascinating is that Jesus offers much more than blood intimacy to those who turn to him. Your ethnicity, gender, and economic status do not matter! If you are in Christ, he considers you family. So, how do you know if you are a member of Jesus' spiritual family? Jesus declares in verse 35, "For whoever does the will of God, he is my brother and sister and mother." Are you doing the will of God? Remember that those physically related to very spiritual people, even physically related to Jesus, are still on the outside if they aren't doing the will of God. His brothers, though related to him by blood, weren't necessarily part of his spiritual family. In the same way, those who refuse to do things God's way, no matter how they view themselves, are not spiritually "related" to Jesus. During Jesus' ministry on earth, there were essentially two groups of people: those who sat inside with Jesus, attentive and obedient to him, and those who stood outside. Where would you have been found? Does Jesus see you sitting inside or standing outside?

april
TWENTY-SIX

MARK 4:1-9

Mark transitions from the house where Jesus taught to the Sea of Galilee. Again, a very large crowd followed him. In fact, the crowd was so large that Jesus had to get into a boat to teach the masses gathered on the shore. There is actually a place on the Sea of Galilee near Capernaum known as the "Bay of Parables." Because the land gently slopes down to the bay, sound can transmit beautifully, and it would have been possible for Jesus to preach to thousands of people there. Verse 2 states that Jesus taught many things in parables. Remember that a parable is used for comparison. The one using the parable will illustrate an unfamiliar truth by comparing it to a known truth. Jesus began his Parable of the Soils with the charge to "Listen!" He exhorted the crowd to both hear and think about what he taught. He told them about a farmer who scattered seed along a path on ground with rocks, on ground with thorns, and finally, on good soil. The farmer in Jesus' parable wanted to get every possible square inch of area covered by seed in hopes that some would yield plants that produced a harvest. Jesus' audience was quite familiar with farming, and these illustrations should have made sense to them.

The farmer in Jesus' parable did whatever he could to help the seed to find good soil. He was willing to scatter seed wherever possible. It could seem discouraging that only a quarter of the seed actually fell on soil that produced a harvest. But at the same time, to the farmer, the fruit that resulted was worth all the effort. What a blessing for the farmer to enjoy the abundance of thirty, sixty, and one hundred-fold return on the seed that landed in the right place. What about you? Do you "withhold" seed from ground that you perceive can't be productive? Or do you scatter seed wherever you can? Let's make sure we are like the farmer in this parable, willing to do whatever we can to get as much seed out as possible for the joy of harvest time. With whom have you been reluctant to share the gospel? Do what you can to pray for and get time with that person, and then scatter seed. You never know what kind of soil God is preparing under the surface.

april
TWENTY-SEVEN

MARK 4:10-20

The disciples asked Jesus about his parables, specifically the Parable of the Soils. In verse 11, Jesus makes a clear distinction between "to you" and "to those." Jesus said, "to you" has been given the secret, but "to those" everything is in parables. The parables reveal truth about God and his kingdom to those who follow him, and hide truth from those who are opposed to him. A clear difference in Mark's Gospel emerges between the insiders and the outsiders, and the division is determined by who is and isn't willing to do things God's way. In verse 13, Jesus basically says, "Wow, if the Parable of the Soils was hard for you, the rest will be even harder," and he went on to explain the parable to them. The sower or farmer is Jesus. The seed is the word of God or the gospel. The birds represent Satan. The rocky ground is the heart of the person who refuses obedience as a result of hardship. The thorns signify the heart of the person who is all about this life. The good soil symbolizes the heart of the genuine follower. Those who are on the inside, the "to you" group, are represented by the good soil. They will bear fruit. Even though the fruit will be different depending on each plant, they will still bear fruit that lasts.

Jesus taught that people will "try God," yet not be genuine followers. The second and third soils, or the rocky and thorny grounds, represent such people. In verse 16, Jesus says the rocky ground receives the word with joy. They shout, "Praise God!" and "Hallelujah!" one day, but as time goes on, the difficulty of doing things God's way becomes too much. The hot sun of self-denial is too much for them. These people were never really saved. In verses 17 and 18, the thorny ground looks good for a while as well, but the thought of letting go of certain "pleasures" stumbles these people. They want this life and not the life to come. These people were never really saved either. What about you? When did God create "good soil" in your heart? When did you let go of living for self and this life and begin to bear fruit for him? Real followers of Jesus hear, and by the grace of God they believe and bear fruit.

april
TWENTY-EIGHT

MARK 4:21-34

Mark lists many of the parables Jesus taught, showing the reader that Jesus expected his audience to ponder and respond to these comparisons. In verses 26-29, Jesus gives another parable about a man scattering seed on the ground. Interestingly, Mark is the only Gospel writer who records this particular parable. Jesus described what happened after the man, or the farmer, scattered his seed and went on with regular life. Things proceeded normally for him. He slept night after night, he rose day after day, and even though the farmer did no actual "work" after scattering the seed, somehow the seed sprouted up and grew. The honest farmer admitted that he didn't even know how this all happened. Jesus taught that the "earth produces by itself" (v. 28). The Greek word translated "by itself" is actually the word that the English "automatic" comes from. So Jesus taught the earth produces "automatically." The seed has power in itself, and it grows in a way consistent with its design. First the blade appears, then the ear, and finally, the full grain arrives. Again, the seed has everything it needs to bring forth the harvest. After the seed, or the gospel, is sown, it is a matter of time before God makes the seed grow and bring forth his harvest. When the harvest is ready, the farmer brings out his sickle to reap in the wheat.

Jesus used this parable to teach that the final harvest would come, but it wouldn't come as suddenly as his followers hoped. The disciples were called to do what God asked them to do while waiting patiently for his timing. We can become overly discouraged as we look around at the world and see no sign of God's coming. He allows things to continue as usual, and it often seems like bad becomes worse, while God remains out of sight. But just as a planted seed will grow and bear fruit, what God has promised will come to pass. Soon, God's sickle will emerge, and the last judgment will arrive. As the patient farmer sleeps and wakes without anxiety, so too the Christian should do as God has commanded her, knowing he will accomplish all that he intends when everything is just right. If you are anxious about God's timing today, be patient. God keeps his promises. He knows "what" is right, and he knows "when" is right too.

april
TWENTY-NINE

MARK 4:35-41

At the end of the day, after Jesus taught the crowd, he wanted to cross over to the other side of the Sea of Galilee. He took the disciples with him, and they all got into a boat. Many of the disciples were professional fishermen, so for them, a trip across the Sea of Galilee was a very ordinary activity. These experienced fishermen took charge of the boat, wanting to give Jesus the break he needed, possibly lifting him directly out of the boat he was teaching from and into theirs. Verse 37 states that a furious storm suddenly broke out on the sea, and the waves were actually crashing into the boat and filling it with water. The disciples, though experienced mariners, were totally stressed out. They woke Jesus up and told him they were all going to die (v. 38). During the commotion, they probably wondered, "How in the world is Jesus sleeping through all of this? Is he totally disconnected from reality?" Jesus must have really been tired! He passed out on a sailor's cushion in the stern of the boat. When the disciples woke him up, he rebuked the wind and ordered the sea to be still. Can you imagine what this was like for the disciples? Surely their jaws all dropped. Then Jesus turned to them and asked, "Why are you so afraid?"

The disciples didn't realize yet that Jesus was God. They were beginning to get the picture, and after this incident they all asked each other, "Who then is this, that even the wind and the sea obey him?" They should have answered their own question, "This is God." Even though we know who Jesus is, we can become afraid like the disciples in the storm. We know that as Christians, Jesus is with us, but we can begin to panic when it looks like the storms God allows in our life are out of control. We must remember that just as he calmed the roaring sea, Jesus has the ability to rebuke the trials and struggles we are going through as well. In difficult and scary situations, let's continue to trust in him. After we ask Jesus for help, let's be confident that he is able to do whatever is best for us. We don't want him to ask us, "Have you still no faith?"

april
THIRTY

MARK 5:1-9

After Jesus and his disciples made it safely across the Sea of Galilee, they came to the country of the Gerasenes. Most who lived in this region were not Jewish but Gentiles. Jesus even went into areas that could be considered "unclean," bringing the good news to a variety of people groups. Verse 2 states that right when Jesus stepped out of the boat he met this demon-possessed man. The possessed man came from the tombs, which were caves in the rocks used to bury the dead. This is where the man with the evil spirit lived. Because he was possessed, he was totally out of control. No chain was strong enough to bind him, and no one could calm him down. In fact, he would scream and "cut himself" with sharp stones. When the demon-possessed man saw Jesus coming, he ran and fell down on the ground before him. The evil spirit that lived in the man begged Jesus not to "torment him." He literally yelled, "Swear to God that you will not torture me!" After Jesus asked, the demon stated that his name was "Legion." In the Roman army, a legion was a troop that consisted of almost six thousand men. This demon, who spoke for the many demons who were in the man, revealed the power and strength of the evil forces that controlled the human.

While the disciples were just beginning to understand who Jesus was, this demon knew exactly whom he was dealing with. The demon acknowledged Jesus as the Son of the Most High and as the one with authority to torment him. Yet even though the demon knew and agreed to facts about Jesus, he was ultimately condemned. Let's not miss the lesson found here. God isn't looking for people or beings who merely believe truths about Jesus. Some may say, "Jesus is God, he died on the cross for sins, and he is coming again." But at that point, they really have said as much as an evil spirit may confess. What about you? Do you have saving faith or do you have demon faith? How can you tell? We all must agree to the facts about who Christ is, but God will move his people past the point of only believing facts to the place of willingness to do things his way. If we honestly believe, our trust will impact our behavior.

may ONE

MARK 5:10-20

The account of the demon-possessed man whom Jesus and his disciples met after crossing the Sea of Galilee continues in today's text. When the representative demon realized Jesus was going to command him and the other evil spirits to leave the man, he begged Jesus to allow them to move into a nearby herd of pigs. Jesus permitted it. Then the entire herd, two thousand pigs, rushed down to the sea and drowned themselves, one by one. The people who owned the pigs were not too thrilled with Jesus at this point. Though they could have rejoiced that the man was in his right mind and delivered from the evil spirits that inhabited him (v. 15), instead they were angry about their monetary loss. The townspeople knew who this demon-possessed man was. They also heard about what happened to him and to the pigs, but they had to see with their own eyes. They met the man in his right mind, saw the drowned pigs, and were stunned. Then they begged Jesus to leave that area. They were afraid of what he might do next! But the formerly possessed man responded differently. He actually asked to go with Jesus. Jesus told him to go back to his friends and family and tell them and others about the mercy God had shown him and about all that happened.

It's interesting to compare the different ways this miracle of Jesus was received. The townspeople saw what Jesus had done and they were literally awestruck. Yet, they implored Jesus to leave their area. They wanted him away from them because he had caused them great financial loss. The demon-possessed man, however, approached Jesus and begged to go with him. This man was under the power of the evil one, yet Jesus freed him, and he became a model of the miracle of a converted life. Because Christians continue to struggle with sin, it's easy to dismiss the supernatural change that takes place when one is born again, or transferred from the kingdom of darkness to the kingdom of light. Just like the demoniac, saved people are changed from the inside out and long to follow Christ. If you are a Christian, thank the Lord for interrupting your life and for the miracle he has worked in you, causing you to become a new creation in Christ Jesus. The old is gone; the new has come! Praise the Lord!

may
TWO

MARK 5:21-34

Jesus and the disciples went back to their home region, and again, a crowd gathered around them. A leader (like a president) of the synagogue approached Jesus. He desperately begged Jesus for his help because his daughter was on the verge of death. So Jesus went with him. While Jesus moved through the crowd around him, a woman who had hemorrhaged for twelve years made her way to him and touched him. She was convinced that if she were able to touch his clothes, she would be healed of her bleeding. She went to many doctors, spent all her money trying to get well, but only got worse for 12 years. What a burden! The Old Testament said that a woman was "unclean" for a week after her menstrual period due to the blood, so this woman lived in a continual state of "uncleanness." Verse 27 describes what she did: she heard about Jesus, she approached him, and she touched him. After she touched Jesus, she was immediately and completely restored. Jesus knew that healing power had left him. He asked, "Who touched me?" The disciples thought, *What in the world? What a ridiculous question!* And they responded to Jesus, "How could we know who touched you? We are in a massive crowd!" But the woman knew Jesus was talking about her, and she confessed.

This woman persisted in making her way through the crowd to Jesus. In the same way, Jesus persisted in looking around to discover who touched him. Before she confessed, the woman fell at Jesus' feet in fear. But Jesus didn't scold her for touching him, even though she was unclean. Instead, he let her know she was healed both physically and spiritually. Jesus responded to her with kindness, calling her "Daughter." She was now a part of his family! It was her faith that healed her body, and more importantly, her soul. Like the woman, we have heard about Jesus. Have we longed to touch him the way she did, knowing that he can make us well? If you are burdened by sin in your life today, do what you can to get to Jesus. Don't put it off any longer. Just as Jesus waited until the woman revealed herself to him, he waits for us too. Stop now and talk to him. Confess and tell the truth, and then trust Jesus to restore you.

may
THREE

MARK 5:35-43

While Jesus was talking to the woman with the bleeding problem he just healed, some from the synagogue ruler's household interrupted them and told the ruler not to bother with Jesus anymore. The man's daughter had died, and there was no point in dragging Jesus to the house. It was too late for the little girl. Remember, Jesus was initially traveling with his disciples to the home of the synagogue ruler. The ruler had expressed to Jesus that his daughter was dying, and he trusted that Jesus could heal her. If Jesus hadn't "wasted time" with the bleeding woman, maybe he would have made it there before the little girl passed away. But Jesus basically ignored the report and spoke directly to the ruler. Jesus encouraged him, "Do not fear, only believe" (v. 36). That must have been tough. He had just learned his twelve-year old daughter had died, and Jesus commanded him to not be afraid. Jesus also told him to continue believing. He trusted that Jesus could keep her alive before death. Now his faith was tested even further. Could Jesus do anything after she was dead? Professional mourners were already at the home, making a scene, as was the custom when someone passed away. Jesus told them to stop because she wasn't dead but asleep. They all laughed like Jesus was out of his mind. Jesus went into her room with her parents, bringing Peter, James, and John, and he spoke to her. He directed her, "Little girl, I say to you, arise," and she did. The others in the room were absolutely astonished.

Wow! What a challenge this process must have been for the ruler of the synagogue. He was probably stressing out, wondering when Jesus was going to move away from the bleeding woman and to his own daughter. He must have thought, "Come on, Jesus! Hurry up!" The professional mourners mocked Jesus when he said the girl wasn't dead. They were experts in death. It was their job. They knew she wasn't "sleeping." Jesus wanted the ruler to trust in him, even though the circumstances radically challenged his faith. In what situation is Jesus asking you to trust and not to fear today? Choose to put your focus on him and believe that he can do whatever he wants. If it is for your best and his glory, he will make it happen.

may
FOUR

MARK 6:1-13

Jesus and his disciples traveled back to his hometown, the city of Nazareth, located in Galilee. Nazareth was primarily Gentile in population. It was a very small city, and historians say only about five hundred people lived there (at the most). When he arrived in Nazareth, as was his pattern, Jesus went to the synagogue and taught on the Sabbath. Many of those who heard him were amazed. They wondered how he had become so wise and where his ability to accomplish such extraordinary works came from. Their amazement wasn't one of awe and respect though. Instead, their astonishment led to disdain. Why did they respond this way? It was because the people of Nazareth knew Jesus. They knew his family. As far as they were concerned, he was the local carpenter, Mary's son, the oldest of four other brothers and at least two sisters. There was nothing special about Jesus in their minds. And so, verse 3 says, they "took offense at him." The word for "offense" means they "refused to believe," or they were "repelled by him." Jesus, knowing what they thought about, responded, "A prophet is not without honor, except in his hometown and among his relatives and in his own household." His own people should have been the first to embrace Jesus, getting behind him and his teaching. Instead, those from his community and his family rejected him.

Jesus was simply too ordinary for the people of Nazareth. This must have been really painful for him. We all know the hurt of rejection from those we know and love. Verse 6 says that Jesus marveled because of their unbelief. We realize that Jesus was the sinless Son of God. He preached and taught perfectly, he never did anything wrong, and he worked wonders. Yet these people were offended by him. Even his own family didn't understand who he was. If you ever feel frustrated that those around you don't get the gospel, know that Jesus felt the same way. We must remember that those who embrace the gospel do so by faith, and that faith is a gift from God. Stop and pray for the ones you know and love who don't see Jesus as they should. Pray that God would make them willing to follow what may seem to our culture like "ordinary" instead of "special" teaching.

may
FIVE

MARK 6:14-29

Many people heard of Jesus and the supernatural works he did. Even Herod Antipas I, the ruler of Galilee and the son of Herod the Great, heard about Jesus. Despite the rejection Jesus received from those in his hometown, his reputation continued to grow. Now, Herod Antipas I was married when he fell in love with his half-niece Herodias, who happened to be married to Herod's half-brother, Philip. Herodias and Philip had a daughter named Salome. Herod Antipas I and Herodias were determined to be together, so Herodias divorced Philip and Herod divorced his wife. Herod and Herodias then married each other. Wow, what a mess! Rightfully, John the Baptist came along and denounced this relationship. He told Herod that his marriage to Herodias was unlawful and wrong, and as a result, Herodias was furious. She wanted John dead for speaking against her. So on one occasion, when Salome, the daughter of Herodias, danced before Herod and his guests, he was so pleased and pompous that he offered her whatever she wanted, up to "half of his kingdom," as a reward. She quickly consulted with her mother, who told her to ask for the head of John the Baptist on a platter. Herod did as Salome wished and ordered John beheaded. John's head was given to Salome on a platter, and Salome presented it to her mother, Herodias.

Herod knew that John was a man of God, and he and Herodias were both tormented by John's message and teaching. Herod's guilty conscience continued to plague him, even after John's death. In his paranoia, Herod believed that John rose from the dead and worked through Jesus (v. 14). Often, those who reject God feel that if they could only rid themselves of the followers of Jesus, then the conviction of the Holy Spirit would leave too. But that's never the case. God's Spirit continues to testify to human hearts, convicting them concerning sin and righteousness and judgment. If you are standing up for Jesus today and experiencing rejection, don't grow weary. May we be emboldened by the courage of John to speak the truth in love and trust the Spirit of God to have his way with whomever he chooses. Like John the Baptist, don't fear what men can do. Instead, be faithful to proclaim the gospel to a lost world.

may
SIX

MARK 6:30-35

As we saw in verse 12, Jesus sent the twelve disciples out in pairs to preach repentance. By verse 30, they have returned to report all they taught and did. Mark refers to the twelve here as the "apostles." The word "apostle" literally means "sent one" and indicates someone commissioned for a specific purpose. It is interesting to look at how Mark explains the account of Jesus sending the apostles out (vv. 7-12), then shifts gears to describe John the Baptist's execution by Herod Antipas (vv. 13-29), and then picks the story of the apostles back up here. Why would Mark insert John's execution right after the apostles' departure to do as Jesus commanded them? Mark uses this structure to show that martyrdom may result from obedience, as it did for John. After the twelve returned, Jesus asked them to come away and get some rest. The apostles were so busy that they didn't even get time to eat. But the crowd wouldn't leave them alone. When the people saw Jesus and the disciples getting into a boat, they ran to the other side to be there when the boat landed. The people were determined to see Jesus. Although Jesus and his friends were tired and hungry, Jesus still had compassion on them (v. 34) because they "were like sheep without a shepherd." He wasn't annoyed or irritated with them. Jesus knew these people needed both a leader and direction. The crowd remained with Jesus, even when it got late.

Jesus called the disciples to come away from all the busyness of working for and serving Jesus to be with him by themselves. It is easy to forget that Jesus' followers are called to get solitary time with him. It has been said that the busier we are, the more time we should spend alone with Jesus. What about you? In the midst of your fast-paced schedule, do you get time with Jesus away from the crowds? If not, you need to actually schedule times with God. Get out your calendar and make some non-negotiable appointments with the Lord. We can get so busy working for Jesus that we forget that the purpose of working for Jesus is to lead others to a relationship with him. If we want others to know and spend time with God, we need to be doing it ourselves.

may
SEVEN

MARK 6:35-44

Great crowds of people followed Jesus and his disciples, headed them off, and were there to meet them when the boat landed on shore. Although Jesus and his friends were exhausted and hungry, Jesus had compassion on the people, so he remained with them and taught them until late afternoon. The disciples grew concerned. They told Jesus to dismiss the crowds to the neighboring villages so they could buy some food and eat. By now, everyone was pretty hungry. The disciples must have been totally caught off guard when Jesus said to them, "You give them something to eat." Ha! Where would they get that much food? Did Jesus expect them to go the neighboring villages and buy bread and bring it back? That would cost far more money than they had. Maybe Jesus was so overtired that he was losing his mind. But Jesus continued to press his apostles, asking how much food they had with them. They let him know that they had a total of five loaves of bread and two fish. This was good enough for Jesus. So Jesus had everyone sit down in groups, took the five loaves and the two fish, thanked God for the food, and had the disciples pass it out. When they were done, five thousand men, not including women and children, had eaten and were no longer hungry. And there were twelve baskets full of leftovers, one for each apostle. This was nothing short of a miracle!

The disciples must have watched in astonishment while Jesus supernaturally fed the large mass of people with the little they brought. Initially, the disciples were discouraged, as they considered only what they didn't have. Literally thousands of people had come, and they had no food or money. And everyone was hungry! Unlike the disciples, Jesus focused on what they did have. He asked them how much food they could collect. For Jesus, five loaves and two fish were plenty. In the same way, we often place too much emphasis on what we need or what we lack when it comes to serving or working for Jesus. Instead of being discouraged by our lack, let's focus on what we do have. God can do whatever he wants with what we offer. Our job is to simply bring him all we've got.

may
EIGHT

MARK 6:45-56

As soon as the crowd finished eating, Jesus rushed his disciples into a boat to cross over the sea. He had the disciples set sail while he dismissed the crowd. After Jesus fed the five thousand men plus women and children, people must have been pretty excited to follow him, but Jesus always wanted to make sure people followed for the right reason. So when the disciples were gone and the crowd had taken off, Jesus drew apart to pray. Even after it was dark and the disciples were well out at sea, Jesus remained alone on land, talking to his Father, God. Jesus saw from the shore that the boat was fighting against a strong wind and wasn't going in the direction its crew intended. The disciples rowed and rowed, struggling against the severe weather. They must have been totally exhausted from rowing all through the night. Without the wind, it wouldn't have normally taken long to cross. About the fourth watch of the night (v. 48), anywhere from 3 a.m. to 6 a.m., Jesus decided to go out to the boat. Can you imagine the disciples screaming as they looked out on the sea and saw Jesus standing there? They were horrified! They thought it was his ghost. Jesus looked at them and said, "Take heart; it is I. Do not be afraid." Then Jesus walked to the boat and climbed in with them. After he got in the boat, the wind stopped. As the passage says, "they were utterly astounded." The Greek word translated "astounded" can mean "out of their minds or senses."

When Jesus was with the disciples, they would usually act in faith. But when Jesus wasn't physically near them, they would often panic once things got rough. Jesus used this opportunity to demonstrate that he was God over creation by walking on water. Because he is God, he is always with us. Earlier, Jesus showed compassion on the hungry crowd, and now he showed compassion on his tired and frightened disciples. We may wrongly think that Jesus' compassion is limited, and he can only dispense it in measured amounts. We think it can "run dry," but that's not true! We can never exhaust the supply of God's compassion. If you are tired or afraid, call out to Jesus, ask him for his kindness, and trust that he will meet you, even in the middle of the storm.

may
NINE

MARK 7:1-13

Jesus had an interesting encounter with the religious leaders. They asked why he allowed his followers to eat with unwashed or defiled hands. Mark's readers were primarily Gentile and so not completely familiar with Jewish customs. So verses 4 and 5 provide a parenthesis for the non-Jewish reader to explain the hand-washing custom. These customs were not found in the Old Testament, but were part of Jewish tradition and considered by most to be as mandatory as God's law. Since the Jewish people had to deal with Gentiles, they would wash their hands before they ate so that whatever went into their bodies was not "contaminated" by their contact with outsiders. This hand-washing wasn't to prevent germs, but to prevent interaction with people considered beneath them. Jesus responded to the religious leaders' question about his disciples' neglect of hand-washing with an answer they weren't expecting. In fact, he didn't even talk about his disciples' hand-washing practice. Instead, he rebuked them for not obeying God's laws so they could hold on to man-made regulations. He illustrated this by going to the Law of Moses, which commands that parents be honored. This honor would naturally include financial support of elderly parents. But the religious leaders got out of taking care of their parents by saying their money was "*Corban*" or "dedicated to God." In other words, they said, "Oops, Mom and Dad! Sorry you need my help, but I've already dedicated all my money to God. After I die, it goes to the temple. Bummer! I really wanted to make it happen, but I can't." Jesus said this practice violated God's plan for the family and actually reversed God's law.

Ugh. What a mess. Jesus ended with the words, "And many such things you do." Think about it. Do we hold fast to man-made customs, traditions, and regulations and end up breaking the law of God as a result? Jesus came for people. God loves people, and Christ died to redeem people. Search your heart today. Are you missing an opportunity to love and serve people because you want to hold on to doing things your way? If so, stop. Let's make sure that we are honest, humble, and right with God on the "inside" rather than focusing so much on the "outside." If the inside is right, the outside will fall into place.

may
TEN

MARK 7:14-23

Jesus now answered the question the religious leaders posed about why his disciples ate with unwashed or defiled hands. He called the crowd to gather around him and explained that the soul of a person cannot be defiled by food. Food prepared on Gentile surfaces, touched by Gentile hands, or even considered unclean, was not the real issue before God. Neither foods nor their preparation harm the inner man. Jesus wasn't talking about germs and proper food handling techniques for the sake of health. Instead, he was talking about morality and sin. The disciples still didn't get it. Food laws were an important part of their religious system. So Jesus gave them further explanation. He went on to discuss what does defile the soul of a person. The things in a person's "heart" are what have the potential to cause moral harm. Jesus taught that one could "wash" her hands perfectly and practice all the ceremonial traditions, yet remain unclean before God because her heart is full of evil. Such evil includes the many sinful acts and attitudes that Jesus lists in verses 21-22. Moral contamination doesn't come from the outside, but from the inside.

When we talk to people, we find many honestly think they naturally have "good" hearts. They assume they will be okay with God at the judgment and reason that "God knows my heart." But based on what Jesus said, the fact that God knows the natural human heart should be a cause for terror and not hope. Whose heart hasn't engaged in some, if not many, of the things on Jesus' list? Who can say she has never coveted, or been envious, prideful, or even foolish? According to Jesus, these are the things that defile a human. And yet somehow, many think God is "okay" with it all. Jesus worked hard to help those around him understand that all people, even the religious leaders of the day, have sinned and fallen short of the righteousness that God requires. But there is hope! When we turn from our sin and trust in Christ, God promises to remove our heart of stone and give us a brand new heart of flesh. Praise the Lord for the heart surgery that only God can perform! If you are a Christian today, thank God that he has made your heart right before him.

may
ELEVEN

MARK 7:24-37

Jesus traveled into the regions of Tyre and Sidon, which lay northwest of Capernaum. Tyre and Sidon were not inhabited by many Jews and would have been considered "Gentile territory." Jesus wanted to spend some time alone with his disciples, teaching them. But the fact that Jesus was in town, even in a Gentile area, didn't go unnoticed. As soon as a Syrophoenician Gentile woman heard, she set off to beg Jesus for relief. Her daughter was demon-possessed, and she knew that Jesus had the power to help. When she asked Jesus for assistance, he let her know that he was there for the purpose of teaching his disciples (the children). There just wasn't enough time to feed the "pets" (dogs) too. This wasn't quite as derogatory as it sounds. Jesus was simply stating to her, in a way she would understand, that his agenda with his own followers didn't allow time for her daughter. She wasn't offended, and replied to Jesus with "Yes, Lord; yet even the dogs under the table eat the children's crumbs." She affirmed to Jesus that he didn't need to interrupt his plans because even a "crumb" of his grace was enough for her daughter's healing. Jesus was impressed. He told the woman her daughter was delivered.

Can you imagine a demon possessing your child? How painful it must have been for this woman to watch her daughter, day after day, tormented by an unclean spirit. Surely, she called out to God for deliverance. At the same time, what would Jesus, a Jewish man, have to do with a Gentile woman? The rabbis of the day would never converse with a woman like her. Jesus reveals through this encounter that gender and ethnicity are not barriers to him. The woman simply expressed her desire and her full confidence in the fact that Jesus could deliver. His grace could meet the needs of his disciples and her need at the same time. What great faith! Do you ever limit what God can do? Do you look at situations or people and think, "No way. God can't help there." That's not true! Jesus is fully capable of meeting all needs. Think "outside the box" today and begin to imagine how God could change the lives and circumstances of those around you. Then ask him in faith to make those changes. And if you don't have faith, ask for that too!

may
TWELVE

MARK 8:1-10

Jesus continued to travel and teach others, and he ended up on the east side of the Sea of Galilee. He was in Gentile territory again. The crowd with him had followed him for days! They were hungry and weak. Jesus felt sorry for them and didn't want to send them home with no food. What if they fainted on their way back? So, it was time to feed another crowd, although this time the crowd was made of up Gentiles. Again, the disciples wondered how Jesus would provide for so many people in such a desolate place. Where would they get bread or fish for such a large crowd? Jesus asked his disciples how many loaves they had. They had collected seven loves and a few small fish. Jesus took the food, thanked God for it, and had the people sit down. God miraculously multiplied the bread and the fish so that all who were present ate and were full. Plus, seven large baskets of food were left over. Right after they finished, Jesus and the disciples got into a boat and made their way back to the west side of the Sea of Galilee.

Mark had just recorded the feeding of the five thousand (6:36-44). Now he records the feeding of the seven thousand. In both stories, large crowds gathered, Jesus had compassion upon the people, the disciples didn't know how Jesus would feed so many, the people sat down, Jesus gave thanks for the food, they ate bread and fish, all were full, and there was food left over. Whew! That seems like the same incident, doesn't it? Why would Jesus repeat and Mark record such similar episodes? Well, the disciples weren't "getting it" regarding who Jesus was and what he expected from them (6:52). He was patient though, and continued to teach, illustrate, and even prove the truths he wanted them to learn. Think about yourself. Does Jesus keep "revisiting" some area in your life? Maybe some unique circumstance happens over and over again. Perhaps you fail to respond in faith when it comes to a certain situation. Or maybe you are just continually convicted about something you need to change, but haven't done so yet. If so, ask Jesus for faith to learn and properly respond to what he's trying to teach you. Don't let any more time go by. Instead, do what Jesus is calling you to do today!

may
THIRTEEN

MARK 8:11-21

When Jesus and his disciples landed in the district of Dalmanutha, the Pharisees, hoping to debate with him, asked him for a "sign." When they demanded this sign, Jesus sighed deeply. The Greek word translated as "sighed deeply" is only used here in the New Testament and not very often in Greek literature either. It means "to inwardly groan," not in pain or anger, but in discouragement. The people of Israel refused to embrace Jesus for who he was, and their rejection caused him to feel despair. Jesus got back in the boat and moved on. No signs were given for the stubborn Pharisees in Dalmanutha. Those with Jesus got back into the boat too. Then Jesus warned them about the "leaven" of the Pharisees and Herod Antipas. Leaven means yeast, which is an important ingredient in bread. Yeast works by spreading throughout the bread dough, causing it to rise. Jesus tried to teach them that the critical and hostile attitude of the Pharisees and Antipas had affected the entire nation. As Jesus was working to instruct them, the disciples thought he used the word "leaven" because they had rushed off and forgotten to bring more bread into the boat. Jesus felt further discouraged. Didn't the disciples get it yet? Jesus had just fed the five thousand men and then the four thousand. He wasn't worried about bread.

Jesus was exasperated. The Pharisees demanded a sign, and the disciples still didn't get it. Jesus asks his disciples a series of questions in verses 17 and 18: "Do you not yet perceive or understand? Are your hearts hardened? Having eyes do you not see, and having ears do you not hear? And do you not remember?" Try to gain a sense of the exhaustion he must have felt as he asked these questions. He concludes with, "Do you not yet understand?" (v. 21). Sometimes, we can adopt kind of a "been there and done that" attitude when we are looking for something more from God. If you are a follower of Christ today, beware of the leaven of the Pharisees and Antipas. Make sure you aren't depending upon the new and spectacular to fuel your trust in Jesus. Instead, remember who he is and where he has brought you so far. If your faith is small, ask him to increase it. He didn't give up on the disciples, and he won't give up on us either.

may
FOURTEEN

MARK 8:22-30

Jesus and his disciples moved from the district of Dalmanutha to Bethsaida, on the north shore of the Sea of Galilee. Some people in Bethsaida had heard of or knew about Jesus, and they brought a blind man to him. They begged Jesus to touch the blind man, confident that he could restore the man's sight. Verse 23 says that Jesus physically took the blind man by his hand and led him out of the village. Jesus preferred to be alone with the man. Jesus then spit on the man's eyes and touched them. He asked the man if he saw anything. The blind man said he saw people who looked like trees, walking. Most believe he saw the disciples, standing and moving around Jesus. So at this point, the blind man could see, but only partially. Then Jesus touched the man's eyes again, and his vision was completely restored. Why the touch? What difference did it make, if any? In the Old Testament, sin was symbolically transmitted from the priest to the sacrificial animal when the priest placed his hands on the creature. Scholars say that in this case a reverse effect occurred, and sin moved from the blind man to Jesus, at which time the man was healed. The blind man could see clearly now. Many note that seeing is often associated with spiritual insight. Jesus ordered the man not to go back to the village of Bethsaida, but to go home instead.

Mark recorded this fascinating account of the blind man's "two stage" miraculous healing to demonstrate a point. The events concerning the blind man modeled the slowness of the disciples to understand. Just as the blind man could see, but his sight was fuzzy, the disciples were "getting it" about Jesus, but not completely. Jesus asked the man, "Do you see anything?" (v. 23). Previously, Jesus had asked his disciples, "Do you not yet understand?" (8:21). Jesus touched the blind man a second time, and he saw clearly. Jesus made sure the blind man's sight was fully restored, and he would make sure his disciples' spiritual understanding was complete as well. Jesus will do the same for us too. The ability to spiritually see or understand is always a gift from God. If you struggle with understanding and spiritual "sight," ask Jesus for his touch today. He wants us to "get it" more than we can imagine.

may
FIFTEEN

MARK 8:31-9:1

Jesus taught his disciples that he would suffer and be rejected. He told them he would be killed, and yet rise again on the third day. He spoke openly and plainly about what came next. This must have confused the disciples, especially Peter. Just before this teaching, Peter boldly announced that Jesus was the Messiah. In Peter's mind, the Messiah's plan should have been to set up his messianic kingdom and rule in Israel as quickly as possible. Now Jesus told his disciples he would die. What? This made no sense! Peter wasn't happy with any of this suffering and rejection talk coming from Jesus. So in his passion, Peter took Jesus aside and rebuked him. The word "rebuke" literally means "to express strong disapproval." Peter tried to warn Jesus about the error of his thinking and correct what he was saying. But Jesus saw behind the rebuke to the real power driving Peter's push for Jesus to focus on self-preservation. Jesus turned the rebuke on Peter and said, "Get behind me, Satan! For you are not setting your mind on the things of God, but on the things of man." Then Jesus gathered the disciples and the crowd around him and taught them that to follow him means to embrace a life of self-denial and suffering.

How bizarre to think that God allowed himself to be rejected by the men he created. As Christians, we must be ready to face rejection as well. We will run across people who say they are disciples of Jesus, but refuse to suffer for the sake of the gospel. Jesus clearly declared that all who desire to follow him must be willing to deny themselves and take up their crosses as well. What a strange concept! Our sinful nature hates the thought of rejection and suffering. Yet Jesus became a human ultimately to suffer and die. Could it be that when we hide from suffering and run from rejection, we miss knowing an aspect of God that can only be discovered through pain and difficulty? That's actually what Jesus taught those around him. He added, "Whoever loses his life for my sake and the gospel's will save it." The road Jesus traveled was one of self-denial. Let's make sure we are always open to whatever God is asking us to do, even if it doesn't feel good in the moment.

may
SIXTEEN

MARK 9:2-13

Jesus said some were present with him "Who will not taste death until they see the kingdom of God after it has come with power" (9:1). Six days after that declaration, Jesus took Peter, James, and John with him to a high mountain. When the four of them were alone, Jesus was transfigured in their presence. We get the English word "metamorphosis" from the Greek word translated here as "transfigured." Jesus was changed in a way outwardly visible to Peter, James, and John, and even his clothes took on a new nature. No wonder the three disciples with Jesus were terrified. To top that off, Moses and Elijah appeared with Jesus. In the Old Testament, God revealed himself to both Moses and Elijah on a mountain. So, the two men to whom God previously revealed himself on a mountain were now present and talking to Jesus. Poor Peter didn't know what to do. He suggested they make tents to hang out in. Peter probably thought Jesus decided to set up his kingdom right then and that Moses and Elijah were staying. God interrupted Peter and declared from heaven, "This is my beloved Son; listen to him." God set Jesus apart from Moses and Elijah and proclaimed to the disciples that Jesus is above those two great men.

God said, "This is my beloved Son; listen to him." The word translated as "listen" is worth noting because of its verb tense. It is an imperative, which is a command. God said to Peter, James, and John, "Be obedient to Jesus. Do what he says." Jesus, not Moses and not Elijah, was God's definitive representative, because he was God in human flesh. The disciples and all who follow Jesus after them must heed God's announcement. We are to do what Jesus says. This seems so simple, yet we can make it so confusing. None of us is saved by works or by doing anything. Not one human has the ability to earn her salvation. But if we are followers of Christ and enjoy a relationship with him through repentance and faith, then we need to do what he said. Take some time to really search your heart today. Are you doing things or failing to do things that conflict with what Jesus commands his people? If so, confess, repent, and do things his way. You will never regret your decision to "listen to Jesus."

may
SEVENTEEN

MARK 9:14-29

Jesus, along with Peter, James, and John, came down from the mountain where he had been transfigured and spoke with Moses and Elijah. When they returned, they saw a large crowd of people plus some of the religious leaders surrounding the disciples who didn't go up with Jesus. The nine who stayed back weren't idle. They had been at work attempting to do what Jesus taught and commanded them. But because of their lack of apparent success, the disciples and the religious leaders were now disputing and fighting with one another. Suddenly, they noticed Jesus had returned! The crowd ran up to him and greeted him. Jesus asked what they were arguing about. A father replied by telling him that his son was demon-possessed. The father asked the disciples to cast the evil spirit out, but they weren't able to. Jesus then spoke to the crowd and his followers, saying, "O faithless generation, how long am I to be with you? How long am I to bear with you?" The disciples couldn't cast the demon out because of their unbelief. Jesus asked the father what the problem was with his son, and after the father described what the demon did, he added, "If you can do anything, have compassion on us and help us." The father witnessed the failure of the disciples. Maybe Jesus would fail too. Jesus exclaimed, "If!" And then he added, "All things are possible for one who believes."

The lesson Jesus taught was clear: true faith doesn't put a limit on what God can do. Our question should never be "Can God do it?" Instead, our question should be "Is it God's will to do it?" When the father approached Jesus, he asked for compassion from God (v. 22). Now Jesus asked him for faith. The lonely and desperate father faced a tough challenge from Jesus. Did the father have faith? In broken humility, the father cried out to Jesus, "I believe; help my unbelief!" (v. 24). What a beautiful request. The father knew his weakness. He brilliantly acknowledged that Jesus was both the object and the source of his faith. Without God, none of us can believe the way God calls us to believe. In what area do you doubt God's ability to move? Respond as the father did. Cry out to Jesus today, "I believe; help my unbelief!"

may
EIGHTEEN

MARK 9:30-32

Jesus and the disciples passed through Galilee. This was where Jesus grew up and spent most of his life, but now they passed through quickly without letting anyone know they were there. Jesus knew his time was short, so his heart and mind remained fixed on Jerusalem and the cross. Jesus announced three things to his disciples: 1. He would be rejected ("delivered into the hands of men"), 2. He would be executed ("they will kill him"), and 3. He would rise from the dead ("after three days he will rise"). Jesus carried the pain of knowing the humanity he created would soon treat him with absolute cruelty. And there was no way out for him, since it was God's plan. The disciples didn't get what Jesus was talking about. Just think, even the twelve closest to Jesus were partially blinded to what he taught. It didn't make sense to them, and they were afraid to ask what he meant. They may not have wanted the explanation. They tried to hold on to their hopes for their Messiah, but were perplexed about how such hopes could fit in with the information Jesus gave them about approaching events.

Jesus again reminded the disciples of the rejection, suffering, and death he was about to experience. He knew exactly what would happen. And yet, he had to move forward. The disciples didn't realize that Jesus was establishing a pattern for them to follow as well. We all must admit that this life includes various degrees of rejection, suffering, and death. And it's hard to suffer and die. It's hard to let go of things that are pleasurable and joyful and embrace the way of the cross instead. But we must move forward too. We can either humbly open our hands to God now and learn to follow in the footsteps of Jesus, or we can hold tight and have a difficult time when it's our turn to die to whatever the Lord is asking us to let go of. If you are struggling with your willingness to let go of whatever he is asking from you, pray for courage and strength. Jesus endured the cross for the joy set before him. Like Jesus, may we be confident that God has great things ahead for all who put their trust in him.

may
NINETEEN

MARK 9:33-41

Jesus heard his disciples arguing while they were traveling back to Capernaum. He asked them what all the fuss was about. They didn't want to answer because they were embarrassed and felt ashamed. They had been fighting about which one of them was the greatest and would be most honored in the future kingdom. Peter, James, and John were selected by Jesus to witness the transfiguration. Perhaps that meant they were the greatest. But Peter spoke openly and boldly about Jesus being the Messiah, so maybe he would be the most honored. But then again, Peter said some foolish things too and was publicly rebuked by the Lord. Who was the greatest of the disciples? Clearly, they still didn't comprehend the truths Jesus taught about suffering and sacrifice. Jesus then sat down and called all twelve disciples to gather around him. In the posture of a rabbi, he taught them if one really wanted to be the greatest, then he must humble himself and choose to serve. Jesus didn't tell them they were incorrect in wanting to be first, but he did define greatness in a new way. Jesus brought a little child into their midst. The child must have been very young, since Jesus held him in his arms. He said, "Whoever receives one such child in my name receives me, and whoever receives me, receives not me but him who sent me" (v. 37). In other words, if we want to serve Jesus and even the Father, we need to pay attention to the needs of those who might be considered insignificant. Children were considered the least important members of Greek and Jewish societies.

What is greatness in God's eyes? We can forget that God may not view the qualities we admire in others the same way we do. We often esteem the powerful, rich, intelligent, and beautiful among us. But God considers the one who freely and humbly puts the interests of others before her own interests as "first." And that's exactly what Jesus did. He humbled himself, and was found in appearance as a human. He went all the way down the social ladder, even to the point of enduring a slave's execution of death on a cross. In serving one another, we display the love of Jesus to a dying world. If you want to be great in God's kingdom, then follow Jesus' example and embrace the lowly in your midst today.

may
TWENTY

MARK 9:42-50

Jesus firmly declared that all his followers must guard themselves against causing someone else's sin. In fact, it would be wiser for a woman to get a great round millstone, which was used for grinding wheat and could weigh over a thousand pounds, put it around her own neck, and then toss herself overboard from a ship than to spiritually mislead one of Jesus' followers. Jumping into the sea with a millstone attached to the neck would ensure a trip to the bottom of the ocean. It is important that we exercise extreme care when interfacing with others. We never want to be the reason for another's stumble, downfall, or departure from the faith. Jesus graphically illustrated to the disciples that if their hand should cause them to fall away, then they should cut it off. If the foot should cause them to fall away, cut it off. The same was true of the eye; so even if their precious eye should cause them to fall away, get rid of it. One would be better off having no hand, no foot, and no eye but entering the kingdom of God than going to hell with her body parts intact. The point was clear. Those who desire to follow Jesus must be willing to do whatever it takes to deal with sin.

We have to be super cautious when it comes to condoning or lowering the bar concerning others' sins. When we relax about iniquity and wrongdoing as representatives of Christ, we act as if God doesn't really care about sin that much. When we say, "Who cares? Relax!" and "Don't worry about it!" instead of giving helpful advice about how to battle iniquity, we misrepresent Jesus. If an area of our life causes us to stumble or fall, let's exercise radical amputation, doing whatever we can to cut it off at the source, not excusing and overlooking it. You won't find Jesus telling anyone to "relax" when it comes to her struggle with sin. Let's make sure we have the same attitude toward wickedness that Jesus had. May these truths drive us to the cross, and cause us to cling to the mercy of God again today.

may
TWENTY-ONE

MARK 10:1-12

Jesus traveled through Judea, slowly making his way toward Jerusalem. Again, the Pharisees tried to trap him. This time, they questioned him about marriage and asked about the legality of a man seeking a divorce from his wife. The two main groups among the rabbis of the day were divided on the issue of divorce. One group said a man could divorce his wife, but only if she were unfaithful. The other group said a man could divorce his wife for any reason. The Pharisees hoped that Jesus would offend at least one of the groups and thereby lose some of his popularity. But Jesus turned their question back on them and responded with a question: "What did Moses command you?" Well, they answered that according to Deuteronomy 24, if a man wanted to divorce his wife he needed to give her a certificate. Jesus explained that Moses allowed the certificate to protect women who were victims of men demanding an unjust divorce. A woman with the certificate was free to marry another man and at least retain some social dignity. The men who wanted to "put away their wives" without valid reason often didn't care what happened to women after they'd been discarded. That's why Jesus said Moses allowed it due to the hardness of their hearts (v. 5). Then Jesus added, "What therefore God has joined together, let not man separate."

Jesus declared that in God's design for marriage, a man should leave even his parents and be joined to his own wife. Then he continued, "And the two shall become one flesh" (from Genesis). Marriage is a lifelong covenant of unity that models the loving bond between Christ and the church. Genuine Christians are in a permanent relationship with God and cannot be separated from the love of Christ. As Jesus said, in the end, it is God who has joined the husband and wife together, so unjust divorce is a sin against him. If you are married today, put the concept of divorce out of your mind. Don't ever threaten your husband with divorce. And if you are not married, make sure you look for a spouse who agrees with God about divorce. We are to view marriage as highly as God does. Jesus saw marriage as the most important human relationship; his followers should value it in the same way.

may
TWENTY-TWO

MARK 10:13-16

All sorts of people were bringing their children to Jesus, hoping he would touch them and bless them. But the disciples weren't happy about this. In fact, they rebuked those who brought their kids to Jesus. Children were not seen as important, so the disciples must have thought this was a waste of Jesus' time. Yet verse 14 says that when Jesus saw what was happening, he was indignant. Jesus was filled with anger at the unjust actions of his disciples. He spoke clearly to them and said, "Let the children come to me; do not hinder them." Then Jesus explained why the disciples were to let the kids come to him by adding, "To such belongs the kingdom of God." Jesus went on to say, "Whoever does not receive the kingdom of God like a child shall not enter it." These children didn't feel entitled to Jesus or his time. In humility, they approached him, having been brought to him by others. We too must come to Jesus as these children did. We must be totally dependent upon the grace of God and not presume that we have anything to offer him beside our sin. Only then can we fully trust in God's provision for our moral failure through the person and work of Christ, resting in the blamelessness that he provides for us. None of us has earned our relationship with or right to God.

Jesus' attitude toward children was not normal in the first century. This is hard for us to picture, as our culture loves babies and children. But again, this wasn't the way people viewed young ones in the time of Christ. Children were seen as a drag, and boys were prized above girls. We can easily overlook the radical way Jesus responded to people whom his society frowned upon. Whether they were Gentiles, women, or even kids, Jesus valued all human life and even took time from the "religious leaders" to invest in the outcasts and unwanted. What people are you neglecting to spend time with because you don't honestly feel they are all that valuable? Every human has tremendous worth in God's sight, from the greatest to the least. If you want to be like Jesus today, take time out of your busy schedule to invest in someone "less desirable." In doing so, you will be living according to the pattern Jesus set for his disciples.

may
TWENTY-THREE

MARK 10:17-31

As Jesus left the house, a man ran up to him and fell at his feet. This man was passionate and basically asked, "What can I do to be saved?" He addressed Jesus as "Good Teacher." Jesus turned his question back into another and said, "Why do you call me good? No one is good except God alone." Jesus showed this man that no one is truly "good" except God. Not one person has met God's perfect standard of righteousness, except Jesus. Every single human who stands before God without Christ in the judgment will be found guilty. Jesus wanted the man to understand that no matter how many moral things he had done or would do, he would never be saved by his own "goodness." Jesus then listed some of the Ten Commandments, and the man proclaimed he had obeyed all of these his entire life. We can think about how self-righteous the man was to declare he had always kept the law. But in verse 21, we see a different response from Jesus, who looked at him and loved him. Jesus saw a man who bore the image of God desperately seeking advice, and Jesus felt compassion for him. So Jesus told the man to give his possessions to the poor and follow him. But the man went away sad. Jesus knew this man loved wealth more than God, and Jesus' request revealed the man's heart.

It is strange that Jesus didn't run after the man and say, "It's okay. You're fine. We can work on full surrender later." Instead, Jesus told his disciples it would be easier for a huge camel to go through the tiny eye of a sewing needle than for a rich man like this one to enter the kingdom of heaven. We too must recognize that we have not met God's righteous requirement for human life. And we too must turn from living for ourselves to following Jesus. The man was "disheartened" (v. 22), which means he was saddened or even shocked. He wasn't ready to make Jesus the source of his trust instead of his wealth. What about you? Is your confidence in your possessions, or in Jesus? If your response isn't "Jesus," then turn to him with an open heart and open hands today. If you are afraid, ask him for help. All things are possible with God.

may
TWENTY-FOUR

MARK 10:32-45

James and John approached Jesus privately to ask for the highest places of honor and authority in his coming kingdom. One brother wanted to sit at his right, and one wanted to sit at his left. Jesus asked if they were able to drink the cup of suffering and be baptized with the agony he was about to be immersed in. In one sense, this was impossible. Only Jesus could satisfy the rightful wrath of God against the sins of mankind. But, a seat at his right and left is a place reserved for those who have experienced great pain as a result of obedience to God in a hostile world. They still didn't get it. In verse 39, they responded, "We are able." When the other disciples learned about this conversation, they were extremely angry at what they perceived to be a selfish request from the brothers. Clearly, they wanted the seats too! Jesus called them all together and taught them the key to greatness and honor in his kingdom. If the disciples wanted to be first in the next life, they must voluntarily and sacrificially serve other people. This was exactly what Jesus did, even dying for others. In God's kingdom, we go up when we willingly move down.

The way Mark recorded the brothers' request, it sounds bold as they said to Jesus, "We want you to do for us whatever we ask of you." But we do the same thing, don't we? We approach Jesus and ask him to do whatever we request. It's interesting that Jesus didn't correct the two brothers for their desire. In fact, Jesus responded with "What do you want me to do for you?" (v. 36). But Jesus let them know they had no idea what they were asking for. An honor like this came with a huge price tag, and James and John were clueless about what lay in store for them, or who could occupy the seats they longed for. But they thought they knew best, and so claimed they were able to do whatever was necessary to get those spots. Has God seemed to answer "no" to any of your requests? If so, don't get discouraged. Instead, thank Jesus for not always giving you what you want. He knows what we can and can't handle.

may
TWENTY-FIVE

MARK 10:46-52

Jesus and his disciples came to Jericho. Many remember Jericho as the place where Joshua and his army marched around the city and the "wall fell down." The city Mark wrote of was the rebuilt Jericho. Located about a mile south of the original Jericho, it was reconstructed under Herod the Great. When Jesus left the city, a large crowd followed him. Despite all the commotion, a blind beggar named Bartimaeus repeatedly called out for his attention. Bartimaeus and his persistent pleading with Jesus started to annoy those around him and many rebuked him, telling him to "knock it off." But as Jesus passed, Bartimaeus became more hopeful, and he continued to cry out for mercy. Bartimaeus referred to Jesus the "Son of David," a recognized title of the Messiah, as the Jews knew he would descend from the line of David. Even though Jesus headed toward Jerusalem with a purpose, he stopped for the determined blind man. When Jesus asked for him, he eagerly sprang up and approached. Then Jesus asked, "What do you want me to do for you?" (v. 51). This was the same question Jesus had just asked James and John (10:36). Bartimaeus told Jesus he wanted to see again. With that, Jesus let him know he was healed. It was his faith in Jesus' ability to heal him that made him well.

Bartimaeus was physically blind, yet he could "see" Jesus for who he was, perhaps even better than Jesus' own disciples. He didn't see Jesus with his eyes, but he recognized Jesus was the Messiah. His spiritual sight was sharp, even though his physical eyesight was nonexistent. As soon as Bartimaeus could see, he got on the road and began to follow Jesus too. Bartimaeus models for us what a disciple looks like. He was blind and fully dependent upon Jesus for sight, he cried out for mercy in confidence that Jesus could heal him, and as soon as his sight was restored, he left his place along the road and followed the Messiah. When did Jesus open the eyes of your heart and allow you to trust in him? Did you immediately follow after him? Let's not forget that if we are asking Jesus for healing or help, we must be ready to follow him too. Real faith isn't willing to stay on the side of the road.

may
TWENTY-SIX

MARK 11:1-11

While on the road from Jericho to Jerusalem, Jesus sent two of his disciples ahead to get a young, unbroken donkey. According to Jewish tradition, a king's mount should never be ridden by anyone else. If someone were to question the disciples, Jesus instructed them to reply, "The Lord has need of it." Jesus referred to himself as "Lord," suggesting his divine authority. Some did question the two disciples. They repeated what Jesus told them, and the bystanders simply let them go. The two brought the young donkey to Jesus and threw their cloaks on its back to form a last-minute saddle. As Jesus rode into Jerusalem, many took off their cloaks and joined in the procession. But instead of throwing their cloaks on the donkey, they threw them on the road. They spread branches on the road too. Then the crowd began to call out, "Hosanna!" This word was originally used as a prayer to God and can be translated "Save, I pray." "Hosanna in the highest" meant "Save us now, O God in heaven." The crowds called for a blessing upon the one who came in the name of the Lord and upon the coming kingdom of David. Verse 11 says Jesus went into the temple and looked around to see how it was being used. Little did those around him know that the God the temple was constructed to worship stood right there in the midst of them.

Jesus knew what was coming. He gave the two disciples specific directions because he had everything prearranged. Jesus foresaw not only the plan to get the donkey and the right response to questioners, he knew everything that was coming. We wonder what it would be like to know the future, yet we forget that there are future things we know already. For example, we all know our time on earth is limited. We know we won't be here forever, but even though we know this we often try to push it out of our thinking. We somehow believe that if we don't think about it, it won't happen soon. But failure to consider our end isn't wise. Maybe we need to make some changes today in light of what we know about the future. Let's never forget that even though we don't have all the details like Jesus did, we aren't totally in the dark about what's coming, and we're responsible to live accordingly.

may
TWENTY-SEVEN

MARK 11:12-19

Jesus and his friends were leaving Bethany, a little less than two miles from Jerusalem, when they saw a fig tree and supposed they would eat the fruit. But when they got to the tree, no fruit grew on it, only leaves. Jesus cursed the tree and moved on. This account has been controversial. To some, this record of Jesus' action simply doesn't make sense. Why would Jesus curse the tree just because it bore no fruit? It wasn't even the season for figs (v. 13)! Was Jesus "venting" his frustration on the tree? Some scholars argue that Jesus should have controlled himself here. Figs were normally picked during harvest time, anywhere from late May all the way through to mid-October. When harvest time was over, undeveloped buds still remained on the trees, which became edible by the following March or April. After those buds were ready to eat, the trees produced lots of leaves. This fig tree was loaded with leaves, so Jesus expected to find the buds, but none grew there. Although it wasn't the season for full and ripe figs, something edible should have grown on that tree. In the verse before this account, Jesus was in the temple (11:11). In the verse right after, Jesus entered the temple (v. 15). This account was strategically placed between verses 11 and 15 to illustrate Jesus' frustration with the temple.

The temple was full of activity and people. Many came to worship God. The temple was full of "leaves," and Jesus expected to find "fruit" there as well. The fig tree, which created the hope of fruit yet was barren, was just like the temple. Just as Jesus should have found something edible on the fig tree, he should have found "spiritual fruit" in the temple. The fig tree's curse was actually a sign of the coming judgment upon the temple. We shouldn't miss the warning here. We too can be full of activity, or leaves, but lack real fruit. Genuine fruit comes from abiding in Jesus or being connected to him. Think about it. Are you really depending on Jesus, or are you trusting in yourself? Do you seek him in his word and talk to him in prayer? Remember that "leaves," or lots of activity, can be deceptive. Make sure you aren't so busy doing things for Jesus that you have no time for a relationship with him.

may
TWENTY-EIGHT

MARK 11:20-33

The next day, Jesus and his disciples passed by the fig tree Jesus had cursed. This time, it was withered all the way down to its roots. The Greek words used for "withered" and "roots" here are the same ones Jesus used when he taught the parable of the soils (6:4). "Wither" means "to dry up" and typically occurs when the roots of a plant are bad and don't function properly. Some believe Jesus allowed this to foreshadow the destruction of the temple. Others believe it was a picture of the failure of Israel. Peter was surprised by how quickly the fig tree dried up and remarked about it to Jesus. In response, Jesus taught his disciples about faith in God. Jesus told them that although challenges might arise in the future that would seem as large as mountains, even the Mount of Olives, faith is able to move those mountains if that faith is in God. Jesus then transitioned to the subject of prayer. He taught his followers to pray in faith, knowing that the things they asked for within God's will could be considered done. After that, he taught them to forgive one another. Those who have been forgiven by God would be foolish to come before God with unforgiveness in their hearts.

Jesus made a strong connection between faith and prayer in verses 23 and 24. Faith is a confidence in God's ability to do whatever he wants, whenever he wants, and however he wants. When we pray, if what we ask for is in line with God's desires, we will have it, even if it includes moving mountains. When we pray and ask for things that aren't in line with God's will for us, we are probably not going to get them. It's funny how we can get mad, frustrated, or even lose heart when God doesn't give us what we want. But if something is not in God's perfect will for us, why would we want it anyway? Why do we resist his will for us? Take a few minutes to pray about things that have been troubling you. Let God know that you trust in his ability to answer. Let him know that you would like to see things done as you request, but if that's not best, then you are totally content with whatever he sees fit.

may
TWENTY-NINE

MARK 12:1-12

After Jesus' encounter with the religious leaders in the temple, he told them a parable about a wealthy landowner. Surviving records from the time of Jesus describe the relationships between landowners and farmers. Landowners would lease out part of their land to farmers, who would take care of it when the owners were away on other business. When harvest time came, the farmer would pay the landowner a portion of the crop as his rent. If the owner had to be away from home during the harvest, he would send a representative to collect his share. This often led to tension between the farmer and the owner's representatives. In Jesus' parable, the landowner plants a vineyard. He goes to great lengths to put up a wall and a tower to protect his vineyard. He also digs a pit for his winepress to collect juice after the harvest. This wealthy man represents God, and the vineyard is his people, Israel. The man then goes away and leases his vineyard to tenants, signifying the religious leaders of Israel. As the parable unfolds, the tenants repeatedly mistreat the owner's representatives. Finally, the owner sends his own son to get what rightfully belongs to him, but the tenants kill the son. Jesus used this parable to show the religious leaders around him that as Israel had rejected God's prophets in the past, they were doing the same thing now, even rejecting God's own Son.

When the tenant farmers rejected the owner's representative and the owner's own son, they were actually rejecting the rightful rule of the owner himself. In the same way, when the religious leaders of Israel rejected the prophets and even God's own Son, Jesus, they too rejected God. Jesus quoted Psalm 118:23-24 to the religious leaders. The stone the builders rejected was Jesus. And as Jesus added, "This was the Lord's doing, and it is marvelous." God wasn't caught off guard by the rejection of his prophets or his Son. It was all part of his plan for the redemption of humanity. If you are faithfully telling others about Jesus, trying to live consistently with God's laws and principles in your life today, yet being rejected for the gospel, don't forget this truth. In the end, it's not you people are rejecting, but God. And ultimately, God is in control, even over the rejection we experience.

may
THIRTY

MARK 12:13-17

The religious leaders continued to pressure Jesus, hoping to trip him up and cause him to say something that would reveal him as a false teacher. They sent the Pharisees and Herodians, who approached him and actually addressed him as "teacher." Then they added that they "knew" he was honest and didn't care about what people thought as he taught the truth of God. After this, they planted the trick question on Jesus: "Is it lawful to pay taxes to Caesar, or not?" In asking, "Is it lawful," they referred to the Law of God. Did God want them to give their hard-earned money to the pagan Roman government? The goal of the question was to paint Jesus into a corner. If he said "yes," the people would be disappointed, and if he said "no," Rome would be angry. Either way, they thought Jesus would lose. Jesus asked them to bring him a coin. He noted Caesar's image on it, and basically said, "give it to the one to whom it belongs." But he added, "pay both Rome and God. Give Rome the coins it wants, and give God the worship he is due." This response silenced the opponents.

One aspect of the account that's so incredibly sad is the way the Pharisees and the Herodians used flattery in their attempt to trick Jesus. They remarked on his honesty and his concern for God's will, all in an effort to entrap him so they could discredit him. Like Jesus, we should be cautious when people flatter us. We can quickly decide that those showering us with praise love us and want the very best for us, but some use words of praise as part of a strategy to catch us off guard before they harm us. It's easy for a woman to speak wonderful things about us, but what's more important is what she ends up doing. The old saying "Actions speak louder than words" holds true in this passage, and applies to us as well. We should be careful to live "in sync" with the generous words we speak to and even pile on one another. Choose to make your goal today to keep your behavior as consistent as possible with your words. Mean what you say, and say what you mean.

may
THIRTY-ONE

MARK 12:18-27

Having passed the last test, Jesus' opponents presented him with another question. The Sadducees came to him with what they believed to be a problem concerning the resurrection. They were convinced that the soul no longer exists after death. In contrast, most Jews at the time of Jesus, including the Pharisees, believed in the afterlife. The Sadducees asked Jesus about the practice known as Levirate Marriage. According to this Old Testament principle, if a man died and his wife remained childless, the man's brother was obligated to marry the widow to keep the land and property in the family, thereby protecting the inheritance of the deceased. The Sadducees asked Jesus to suppose a woman's husband died and her brother-in-law married her. Then, what if the brother-in-law or the new husband died, and another brother married her? What if this happened so many times that she married all seven of the family brothers? Which one would be her husband when she died and went to heaven? Ha! They thought their hypothetical problem was brilliant. Clearly, their proposed dilemma disproved the resurrection. Jesus responded by saying to them, "First, you don't know your Bible," and "Second, you don't know the power of God. Just as the angels aren't married in heaven, she won't be married either, and furthermore God *does* raise the dead!"

But could Jesus prove that the dead will rise again? God spoke to Moses from the burning bush, "I am the God of Abraham, and the God of Isaac, and the God of Jacob." Jesus reminded the Sadducees that God confirmed to Moses that the prophets were still alive, even after their deaths, by using "I am" instead of "I was." Jesus told the Sadducees they were wrong about the Scripture, which would have been a huge blow to them, since they were considered the experts in the Law of God. If anyone believed in the resurrection, it was Jesus. He not only taught the resurrection, but he *was* the resurrection. The Sadducees didn't understand God's power. Every now and then, we can't fathom how God will work out the details of a certain dilemma. But let's not undermine the power of God because of our own inability to grasp how he will sort things out. Our job is to keep searching the Scripture and trusting God's ability to work out the details of his plan and program.

june
ONE

MARK 12:28-37

After Jesus responded with authority and wisdom to the Sadducees who argued about marriage and the resurrection, an individual scribe, most likely a Pharisee, questioned Jesus. This scribe was not hostile and was seeking wisdom. He asked Jesus which commandment overarched all the other commandments, a question commonly asked of well-respected rabbis. Jesus said the most important of all the commandments is to love God. And then he said the other is to love your neighbor. Jesus added, "There is no other commandment greater than these," again highlighting how important these two commandments are. The command to love God with the heart, soul, mind, and strength comes from Deuteronomy 6 and was known by the Jews as the *Shema*. The word *shema* comes from the Hebrew equivalent of "hear" in English. Deuteronomy 6:4 begins with "Hear, O Israel," and then goes on to give the command to love God. The book of Leviticus teaches that one's neighbor should be loved as much as oneself. The scribe was pleased with the answer Jesus gave. He replied by telling Jesus he was right, and he then repeated Jesus' instruction. When Jesus heard the scribe's response, he told him he wasn't far from the kingdom of God. The scribe was beginning to "get it."

The word "all" is used four times in verse 30. Jesus didn't say "Love God with some of your heart, soul, mind, and strength," or even "most of your heart, soul, mind and strength," but "You shall love God with *all* your heart, and *all* your soul, and *all* your mind, and *all* your strength." The scribe didn't ask Jesus for a second commandment, but he gave it anyway: Love your fellow humans as much as you love yourself. Although the two commands are inseparable, at the same time, Jesus didn't simply blend them into one hybrid command. We must love God first, and then we can love others the way we are called to. We can't reverse the order. We don't love others first so that we can love God. When you love God with all of your being, that love will be apparent in the way you treat others. An honest passion for God drives a sincere interest in the well-being of others. You can't have a heart for Jesus without loving others. And remember, "others" includes both those you like and those you don't.

june
TWO

MARK 12:38-13:2

Jesus was back in the temple and teaching again. He portrayed the scribes as men who wore long, white linen prayer shawls to distinguish themselves from the common people. They sat in the synagogue seats reserved for the most important in society, and they were honored at feasts with the finest treatment. When the scribes walked around in public, people gave them special greetings and even rose before them. They received income from others and depended upon their sponsors' generosity to survive. Some of the scribes took advantage of the kindness of their supporters, which is why Jesus said they "devour widow's houses." Their prayers were long and for the purpose of making impressions. Jesus warned his followers about these men. Jesus then moved into the temple's court nearest the treasury. This area was known as the Court of Women because women and children couldn't go any further than this point, although men were permitted there. The court contained thirteen receptacles or chests known as the Treasury, placed against one of the court's walls, in which worshippers would place their offerings. Most gave moderate amounts, and some even gave large amounts. But Jesus drew attention to a poor widow who gave two small copper coins, the smallest coins available. Jesus said she contributed more than all the others because she gave all she had.

From God's perspective, it isn't the value of the offering that counts, but how much the offering costs the giver that really matters. The others who made contributions that day gave a small part of their wealth. Although the widow gave basically nothing compared to everyone else, her sacrifice was tremendous in the sight of God. The scribes Jesus spoke of were interested in the approval, respect, and finances of men for themselves. The widow, although unnoticed by men, was considered exemplary by Jesus. What may look like a failure on earth could be a huge success in heaven, and conversely, what may seem outstanding on earth could be insignificant in heaven. Do you think you don't have much to offer the Lord? Even if what you have feels like little, give generously. God knows how much your gifts and offerings cost you, and he won't overlook your sacrifice. Jesus was about to lay down his life for his followers. We can lay down some of our wealth in return.

june
THREE

MARK 13:3-13

Jesus and his disciples went to the Mount of Olives and sat down opposite the temple. Peter, James, John, and Andrew, who happened to be the very first disciples Jesus called, asked him a question privately. They wanted to know when the destruction of the temple and other end times events would occur and what sign would be given before these last things take place. The disciples expected Jesus to set up his kingdom shortly. They had no idea that God would patiently allow thousands of years to pass so that as many as possible might come to Jesus through repentance and faith. Jesus answered them and warned about false christs who would come and lead many away from the truth. Then Jesus advised them not to assume the last events had arrived when they heard about battles and wars. Even though there will be much fighting and strife on earth, it doesn't necessarily signal the appearance of the end. Instead of focusing on these things, Jesus warned them to be on guard. The followers of Jesus will be persecuted for the gospel. But they are never to give up! God's will is for the good news of his Son to be preached everywhere on earth.

When Jesus cautioned his disciples to be on guard, he taught them not to be fooled into believing the Christian life will be free of difficulties. Those who follow Jesus will suffer for the sake of the truth. Yet not one of our tribulations is outside of God's sovereign design. Jesus encouraged his disciples to use their difficult circumstances as platforms for preaching the gospel (v. 11). What hardships and trials are you facing right now? Are you focused on getting out of your struggles, or on using the persecution God has allowed in your life to promote his Son? What if God told you he could lift you out of all your trials, but then he could no longer use you to build his kingdom? Would you choose to stay in your struggles and make a difference for him, or live a comfortable life? As we suffer today, let's never forget that God often reveals himself to the world through our pain. Choose to show others that not even difficulty can keep the followers of Jesus from the love of God. Instead of merely asking God to fix things for us, let's ask him to use us however he sees fit.

june
FOUR

MARK 13:14-23

Jesus continued to answer the questions his disciples asked. They wondered when the temple would be destroyed, when the other End Times events would occur, and what sign God would give before these things happened. According to Jesus, the Abomination of Desolation will be the key incident, signaling that the final things are about to take place. In the Old Testament prophecy of Daniel, the Abomination of Desolation is mentioned three times. The original event took place in 167 BC when Antiochus Epiphanies from Syria plundered the temple, then sacrificed a pig to Zeus over the altar. "Let the reader understand" is included by Mark to trigger something in the mind of those who study his gospel. An episode like the one that occurred in 167 BC was to happen again. Many believe Jesus referred to an ultimate event that hasn't taken place yet. In fact, 2 Thessalonians 2 predicts the coming of a "man of lawlessness" who will defile the temple and exalt himself as God. The man 2 Thessalonians speaks of is commonly known as the Antichrist. Jesus warned the disciples not to be caught off guard. All sorts of false christs, wonders, and signs would arise. After Jesus' death, the temple where Jesus and the disciples spent so much time was destroyed. But this was not the final event Jesus spoke of to his followers. He said the last tribulation will include more persecution than any event that has happened to date (v. 19).

Although Jesus and Mark gave us insight into the last events that will take place on our planet, we are still left with the need to be watchful. No one knows when Jesus will return. We all live and will continue to live in a subtle tension regarding the timing of the final events. The phrase translated "be on guard" is actually a command. Things will get dark, but the call and charge to the followers of Jesus is to stay awake and watchful. It has been said that the unfaithful are those who depart when the road gets dark. Let's determine to be steadfast, immovable, and faithful until the end. And to do that, we must be steadfast, immovable, and faithful in what God has called us to today. We live with a measure of uncertainty about things unknown. But we can be prepared, hopeful, and confident that God is with us.

june
FIVE

MARK 13:24-37

Jesus begins verse 24 with the word "but," shifting the direction of his teaching to the time of his return. Before Jesus comes back, strange things will take place. For example, the sun, the moon, the stars, and the powers in the heavens that Jesus refers to will be thrown "out of whack." He could have been referencing rulers, leaders, and authorities, whether seen or unseen, that will be brought down by God. Either way, darkness and chaos will break out on earth before Jesus returns. Jesus declared that after these things transpire, all people on earth will see the Son of Man coming in power and glory. The Old Testament prophet Daniel wrote about the Son of Man. In one of Daniel's prophetic visions, he saw the Son of Man with the clouds before the throne of God. Jesus was the Son of Man of whom Daniel spoke. Jesus then added that the elect will be gathered from the ends of the earth to the ends of heaven. He used this language to explain that he will have followers from people groups who dwell all over the world. And when he returns, the redeemed will gather to him, as he is the focal point of human history.

The study of what will happen in the end times is known as Eschatology. As we read about the second coming of Jesus and the events that will precede his return, we should be encouraged. One day, Jesus will come back, and everything that's currently wrong in this life will be made right. Those who love and practice evil will be judged and condemned. Those who have turned to Jesus in repentance and faith will be gathered together from all over the globe to live out eternity in a place more glorious than anything our finite minds can imagine. The disciples were going to suffer greatly for the gospel, but it would all be worth it in the end. We too must suffer for the gospel. We suffer when those who hate Christ persecute us. We also suffer when we deny the desires of our flesh, living for a kingdom that is not of this world. If you are a weary or tired follower of Jesus today, take courage. One day we will clearly see that God's long-term plan for our lives, including every aspect of our pain, was founded in nothing less than perfect wisdom and love.

june
SIX

MARK 14:1-9

Mark's biography of Jesus moves to the time of his last Passover. The Jews celebrated the Passover festival every year as they gathered in Jerusalem to remember God's deliverance of his people from slavery in Egypt. The Passover included sacrificing a spotless lamb in the temple as a substitute for the worshipper's sin. Before God's people left Egypt, they were instructed to put the blood of the sacrificed Passover lamb on their doorposts. When the angel of death saw the blood, he would "pass over" the home. Two days before this important celebration, the chief priests and scribes were plotting to arrest and kill Jesus. But now Jesus was with his friends at the home of Simon the Leper in Bethany. Mary, the sister of Martha and Lazarus, approached Jesus and anointed him with very expensive perfume. It was common to anoint the heads of guests who came for dinner, but this anointing was unusual. The perfume Mary used was worth about a year's wages. She understood much of what Jesus had previously taught about his impending death, and she was preparing him for burial. The disciples weren't happy about her wasting the costly perfume on a one-time anointing, but Jesus defended her actions.

As the religious leaders schemed to kill Jesus, a woman was giving her most treasured possession to him in an act of devotion. She took the teaching of Jesus to heart, and responded with compassion and commitment. She also responded with courage. It was not proper for a woman in the first century to interrupt male fellowship unless she was bringing them food. As a woman, Mary couldn't have held down a job to earn the kind of money necessary to buy an item of such value. The perfume could have been her entire inheritance. But she broke it open and generously poured it out upon Jesus in an act of love. The disciples accused her of doing a "wasteful thing," but Jesus commended her for doing "a beautiful thing." We live in a culture that can be very cynical about a Christian's financial generosity, especially when we give to the church or to Christian organizations.. We should be inspired by the example of Mary. She gave, and even though she was mocked as a result, Jesus honored her for her devotion. If you are a follower of Jesus, give generously to God today. Jesus is worth it!

june SEVEN

MARK 14:10-21

Mark recorded the interaction that took place between Judas Iscariot and the religious leaders of Israel. Mark put full responsibility for the betrayal of Jesus on Judas' shoulders. It was Judas who went to the chief priests and initiated the treachery. Verse 11 records that the chief priests were glad he did it. The Greek word used for "glad" literally means they "rejoiced" in response to Judas' actions. They may have thought God was granting their desires, as Judas was "moved" to seek them out and offer his services, despite the fact that they were the known enemies of Jesus. Although the betrayal of Jesus by Judas was right in line with the sovereign plan of God, Judas was fully responsible for what he did. And Jesus went on to declare that Judas would have been better off if he had never been born because of the punishment which would result from his actions. The betrayal and murder of God's Son was ordained before the world began. Yet at the same time, Judas did exactly what his own desires led him to do, and he was accountable for his great sin. It is important to remember that even though God is in control of the affairs and actions of men, all who sin do just as they long to do. No one is forced to resist the will of God.

Mark transitions the reader from the incredible sacrifice of Mary, as he recounts her anointing Jesus for burial with lavish perfume, to the plot of Judas to betray Jesus into his enemy's hands. What a contrast! Mary gave financially out of love for Jesus. Judas profited financially from Jesus out of love for himself. Judas was among Jesus' inner circle of companions. He was a chosen disciple who had been with Jesus throughout his entire ministry. How painful this rejection must have been! A friend's betrayal can be overwhelmingly discouraging. Maybe you have invested in a friendship and lived right alongside someone, only to later be rejected or deceived by her. Jesus was perfect, and he was betrayed. In fact, all of Jesus' friends ended up abandoning him. If a friend has rejected you, know that Jesus understands your pain. Like Jesus, choose to move forward, trusting in the goodness of God despite the sinfulness of man. God will make all things right in the end.

june
EIGHT

MARK 14:22-31

After Judas left, Jesus held the first Lord's Supper service with his disciples. The annual Passover meal was celebrated in remembrance of God delivering his people from slavery in Egypt. Jesus brought a new focus to the bread and the wine. Jesus took bread and gave thanks for it. Then he broke it and gave it to the eleven with him as he explained, "This is my body." Obviously, it wasn't literally his body. He was right there with them serving the bread, but it represented his body. Jesus wanted the disciples to see a close connection between the broken bread and his entire being, given up for his followers. Then Jesus took a cup of wine. Again, he gave thanks for it. He passed it to the eleven with him and after they drank, he said, "This is my blood of the covenant." The pouring of wine into the cup symbolized the blood of Jesus, which was to be poured out for the sin of mankind. God instituted the covenant with his people through Moses with the Ten Commandments, but now the sacrificial blood of God's own Son would confirm the final covenant, the full forgiveness of sins. This promise is available for all who turn to the Lord and trust in the provision of Christ.

All eleven disciples present with Jesus ate the bread and drank from the cup. And they all insisted that they would not deny Jesus. They were willing to die with him, yet Jesus let them know they were about to "be scattered." When the heat was on, the disciples caved in to fear. They didn't stand by or with Jesus. Yet as they celebrated the Passover meal together and learned about the symbols of the New Covenant, they all took the bread and the wine. What an amazing picture of the grace of God! The covenant Jesus provides for his followers is not based on or even kept by our performance. If you are discouraged by your lack of faithfulness today and you are truly a follower of Christ, then look up! Your righteousness is totally and completely a result of what Jesus did for you. You can never add to it, nor can you take from it. All each person can do is accept or reject the agreement God offers. May you be encouraged and inspired to serve him more fully today than ever before.

june
NINE

MARK 14:32-42

Jesus and the eleven disciples with him went to the Garden of Gethsemane. The word *Gethsemane* means "oil press" in Hebrew. It was a place where any of the disciples could have gone to find Jesus, because they went there together often. Jesus told his followers to wait for him while he prayed, and then he asked Peter, James, and John to personally accompany him. He explained that his soul was very sorrowful. The Greek word translated "very sorrowful" can literally mean "burdened" or "crushed with grief." He asked the three specifically to wait and watch while he prayed. The verb translated as "watch" means to "stay awake," "be on the alert," or "be ready." Jesus knew what lay around the corner, and he was alarmed. Jesus dropped to the ground and intensely prayed. He asked God if there were any other way. If it were within the will of God, could the impending doom Jesus was about to face be removed? The cup that Jesus asked God to take from him referred to the horror he would experience when the wrath of God for the sin of mankind was poured out upon him. No human has or will ever experience anything like this. Even those who will one day be sentenced to eternal hell will only experience wrath in proportion to their own sin on earth. We simply can't imagine the suffering Jesus endured so that we might be reconciled to the Father.

Jesus went to the "garden of the oil press," and his soul began to be broken. Isaiah 53:10 states, "It was the will of the Lord to crush him." We can forget that it was actually God's plan to crush Jesus. Jesus was about to face not just normal human death, but a transaction that had never before occurred and never would again. The spotless Son of God was about to provide our ransom by literally taking on the punishment we deserve, experiencing separation from God the Father as a result. If you are a Christian who is feeling insignificant, unworthy, or unloved, then remember the cross. Jesus was dejected and fearful as he walked right into the crushing God desired him to experience on your behalf. He loves you more than you could ever imagine. Jesus paid for every sin you have ever committed or will commit. May that truth inspire you to live for him today.

june
TEN

MARK 4:43-50

While Jesus was speaking to his disciples, Judas approached him with a crowd of Roman soldiers. Judas knew where they would be, as the group had gone to the Garden of Gethsemane often in the past. But the Romans soldiers with him didn't know, so they depended on Judas to lead the way. But how would they know which was one Jesus? No one wanted a commotion, especially during the Passover, so a plan was agreed upon. Judas would reveal to the Romans exactly who Jesus was with a kiss. Judas rushed right to Jesus and kissed him. That was all the Romans needed. They placed Jesus under arrest. Jesus made no attempt to free himself from the seizure. He had prayed about this hour, asking the Father for any way out, but God said "no." This was the only route by which the salvation of the human race could be accomplished. So Jesus went peaceably. He did ask about the crowd of soldiers. Jesus had been with them in their midst, teaching and leading, and he didn't try to flee from his enemies. Did they actually think he was a criminal? The crowd seemed like overkill. Yet again, Jesus knew this was what the Scripture had foretold. This was God's plan for his Son.

Judas knew exactly what he was doing. His kiss wasn't a small or insignificant act. The Greek word used for "kiss" implies intensity. It is the type of kiss one would give someone for whom she cared deeply. He also addressed Jesus as "rabbi." This meant not only teacher, but was an honorary title for an outstanding teacher, even a master. Judas had been taught and trained to lead others to Jesus that they might have eternal life. Now he was leading others to Jesus that they might execute God's only Son. Judas knew he wasn't really "on the same page" with Jesus and the disciples, but he pretended to be. Judas was the ultimate hypocrite. People will say they don't follow Jesus because there are too many hypocrites in the church. Do hypocrites exist in the church? Yes. They always have and they always will. But when an individual stands before the throne of God to face judgment, the "too many hypocrites" excuse will be useless. Don't let the hypocrisy of others keep *you* from doing what God expects of you. And make sure, in the end, that you aren't the hypocrite.

june
ELEVEN

MARK 14:51-65

Many commentators believe the "young man" mentioned in verses 51 and 52 to be Mark himself. This hypothesis argues that Mark's father owned the house where Jesus celebrated the Passover. After Jesus and the eleven left for Gethsemane, Mark took his cloak off, wrapped himself in a linen cloth, and went to bed. Judas and the crowd may have initially returned to the house to look for Jesus before they moved on to the Garden. The servants who worked for Mark's father may have woken Mark up after Judas left. Then, maybe Mark ran to Gethsemane to warn Jesus, but by the time he got there, it was too late! The disciples fled, and so did Mark. The accusers tried to seize Mark, possibly as a witness, but he got away, leaving his linen cloth in their hands. We don't know for sure, but we can be certain Jesus was taken to the residence of the high priest, Caiaphas. Peter courageously followed, waiting to find out what would happen. The chief priests sought to put Jesus to death, but the religious leaders couldn't get the agreement between witnesses that the law required for a conviction. So Caiaphas asked Jesus directly, "Aren't you going to say anything in your defense?" Jesus remained silent. Then Caiaphas asked, "Are you the Christ, the Son of the Blessed?" Jesus replied, "I am" and added, "You will see the Son of Man seated at the right hand of Power, and coming with the clouds of heaven." That was it! Caiaphas tore his clothes, expressing horror over Jesus' words. Jesus claimed to be God.

If anyone ever tells you that Jesus never said he was God, just point her to Mark 14:62. The claims Jesus made about himself were so radical that the high priest tore his clothes in shock. Jesus said, "I am the Christ" or the Messiah. He didn't have to, but he went on to say that he was the Son of Man, referring back to Daniel's prophecy in Daniel 7:13. And he added that he would be "coming with the clouds." This was a way of stating he would be coming back in judgment. Jesus stood trial before the men he created, but one day they will stand trial before him! Now is the time to get your life right with God. Confess your sins and follow him today. Keep your eyes on the clouds, because Jesus is coming back soon.

june
TWELVE

MARK 14:66-72

Mark brings us back to Peter and the courtyard of the high priest. First century Mediterranean homes often had large courtyards, and most of the rooms offered a view of the enclosure. In large homes, both upstairs and downstairs rooms faced the courtyards. Jesus was probably upstairs, which is why Peter was referred to as "below" (v. 66). The courtyards of the wealthy would often be adorned with lavish plants and even fountains. The high priest's courtyard had some type of fireplace. A servant girl was in the courtyard too and may have watched the door, allowing people to go in and out. She saw Peter warming himself by the fire. She studied his face, illuminated by the fire, and exclaimed, "Hey, you were with Jesus!" Peter did something quite out of character in response: he denied that he was with Jesus. In fact, he told the servant girl that he didn't know what she was talking about. Peter moved further away from where Jesus was and went to the entryway. He was headed for the front door! The rooster crowed once. The servant girl saw him again, and began to tell others that Peter was one of Jesus' followers. Peter denied it again! Finally, the bystanders told Peter there was no use hiding it. They could tell who he was by his Galilean accent. Peter cursed. He was so scared and frustrated that he insisted he didn't know "this man of whom you speak" (v. 71). He couldn't even say the name of Jesus anymore.

When the rooster crowed the second time, Peter broke down and started weeping (v. 72). Jesus stood on trial and boldly declared his identity to Caiaphas. But Peter buckled under the questioning of an ordinary servant girl. What a warning to the followers of Christ! We must always be on guard against the temptation to deny Jesus, whether by our actions or our words. We will all encounter situations in which acknowledging what we really believe as followers of Christ will result in rejection and even persecution. Sometimes we want to be "undercover Christians," but a lack of courage never defeats fear. If we are truly followers of Christ, the world just won't fully embrace us, but it is far better to be rejected by the world than to suffer the misery Peter experienced when he compromised who he was and what he believed.

june
THIRTEEN

MARK 15:1-5

Pilate was the Roman high official over Judea, the region in which Jerusalem was located, at the time of Jesus' trial. The ancient Jewish historian Josephus recorded that when Pilate first took his post in Judea, he brought political banners with Caesar's image into Jerusalem. The Jews were livid and protested for days. Later, Pilate took money from the Jewish temple to pay for an aqueduct. The Jews were again enraged, and many protesters died at the hands of Pilate's troops. Pilate was eventually removed and replaced because of the violence in Samaria that resulted from his leadership decisions. So Pilate was considered a harsh ruler, and he disdained the Jews. He normally didn't live in Jerusalem, but he would go there to keep order during large events like the Passover. Now the chief priests brought Jesus across town to Pilate as soon it was morning because the Romans usually did their legal business as early as possible, taking the afternoons off. Pilate, the final authority when it came to sentencing a criminal in Jerusalem, wanted to hear what Jesus had to say about all this. He asked him, "Are you the King of the Jews?" If Jesus tried to rule as the King of the Jews, this would create problems for Rome. But Jesus never sought to overthrow the government. His kingdom is not of this world. Jesus replied, "You have said so." The response of Jesus was so vague that Pilate stood amazed. Why wouldn't Jesus try to defend himself? His life was on the line!

The Greek word used for "amazed" means to be "extraordinarily impressed" or "disturbed" by something. Pilate just couldn't understand why Jesus would remain silent. This was Jesus' chance to defend himself. Little did Pilate know, Jesus could have called down legions of angels, or done whatever he wanted, even destroyed Pilate and all of Rome in an instant. But he endured the persecution and suffering that God willed for him so that we might be redeemed. Have you been slandered, wrongly accused, or charged with something falsely? There is a time to speak up, and a time to stay silent. Like Jesus, we must always consider the greater good. When persecuted, will God be most glorified by our words, or by our silence? As redeemed people, we are called to imitate Jesus. Following Jesus may be hard some of the time, but it is right all of the time.

june
FOURTEEN

MARK 15:6-15

    Legally, Pilate had the authority to pardon whomever he chose, whenever he wanted. But rulers would often offer the release of a prisoner during festive occasions to curry favor with the masses. The crowd asked Pilate to act according to this custom and release a prisoner in honor of the Passover festival. So Pilate allowed the crowd to decide whom they wanted released in this gesture of goodwill. Pilate asked them if he should let Jesus go. Contrary to Pilate's expectations, the crowd begged for the release of Barabbas instead. Barabbas was a robber and murderer who was part of an uprising; he probably sought to stir up trouble for Rome. The crowd begged for the this criminal's freedom and for the execution of the Son of God. Now Pilate realized something was fishy about all of this. Verse 10 says Pilate "perceived that it was out of envy that the chief priests had delivered him up." The word used for "envy" can also be translated as "jealousy." The chief priests didn't like that Jesus had won the honor and favor of the people. They wanted the praise Jesus received to go to themselves. Pilate recognized that they didn't bring Jesus before him because Jesus was a threat to Rome. Instead, Jesus was a threat to the religious leaders. They wanted things to stay as they were, and they didn't want anyone, even God, to change it up.

    What's discouraging in all of this is that even though Pilate knew Jesus was innocent, he "wished to satisfy the crowd" (v. 15). Pilate ordered Jesus scourged, a hideous and horrific way of preparing a prisoner for crucifixion. The victim of a scourging was strapped down and beaten with a leather whip. These whips incorporated bits of metal and bone attached to the leather that worked to rip open the flesh of the prisoner and literally tear it apart. All of this was intended to begin the death process and possibly shorten the time of execution on the cross. Pilate allowed Jesus to suffer so that Pilate wouldn't personally face rejection from the people and even his leaders. Have you allowed another person to suffer so that you could avoid rejection or mistreatment? Followers of Christ should never compromise what they know to be true out of self-preservation. If you have dodged suffering to avoid the negative actions and attitudes of others, decide to make the necessary changes and be honest today.

june
FIFTEEN

MARK 15:16-20

After Jesus was scourged, the Roman soldiers took him to the governor's palace. This "headquarters" probably referred to Herod's palace, where one with the political status of a governor may have stayed during the Passover festival. Jewish history books describe Herod's palace as large, lush, and lavish. When Jesus arrived, a battalion of soldiers gathered together to taunt him. A battalion or cohort of soldiers was a tenth of a legion, and a legion was typically comprised of six thousand men. So this battalion could have boasted six hundred men, but most likely was made up of about two hundred to three hundred soldiers. The hundreds of Roman soldiers began to harass Jesus even further. They first put a purple robe on him, because purple was the color of royalty. Then they drove a crown of thorns into his head and mocked him as they saluted him, "Hail, King of the Jews!" The soldiers went further, until their mockery erupted in violence toward Jesus. They hit him over the head with something like a bamboo pole and spit on him while they kneeled before him, again mocking him as the "King." What a horrific scene. Jesus was bloodied, and the soldiers continued to torment him. After they finished, they took the royal purple robe off his back and put his own clothes back on his beaten body.

Jesus was betrayed by Judas, arrested by a crowd of Romans, taken away to impromptu trials, severely scourged, dressed as a king, hit over the head multiple times with a pole, mocked, and even spit upon. It should be difficult for us to think about the horrific nightmare Jesus experienced in his last hours on earth. But at the same time, if we are to see ourselves rightly, it is something we must consider every now and then. Theologian John Calvin noted that as sinful beings we deserve God's hatred, "and that all the angels should spit upon us; but Christ, in order to present us pure and unspotted in the presence of the Father, resolved to be spat upon" so that we could be seen as blameless in his sight. If you are feeling discouraged, thinking things just aren't fair in this life, you're right. It's not fair that Jesus was spit upon so that you could be reconciled to God. Remember, if God chose to treat us according to what we deserve, not even one could stand before him. Thank God for his grace today.

june
SIXTEEN

MARK 15:21-32

Mark transitions us from the beating and mocking Jesus received via the hundreds of Roman soldiers in the governor's palace right to the crucifixion. Since we are inundated with images of crosses in western culture, we can forget the horror of crucifixion as a method of execution. We find crosses on sweaters, earrings, cups, even stickers. We probably wouldn't think of putting an electric chair image on our t-shirt or necklace, but we should consider that even though it may seem absurd, the electric chair is tame compared to the cross. Even in the first century, the cross was extreme. No citizen of Rome could be sentenced to crucifixion. It was a painful, prolonged, and torturous death reserved only for slaves and those considered the dregs of society. By the time Jesus was forced to carry his cross to the crucifixion site, his body was so broken and beaten that he didn't have the strength to do it. A bystander named Simon from northern Africa was drafted to carry it instead of Jesus. Since crucifixions took place outside of the city, the soldiers drove Jesus up to Golgotha. Verse 24 begins, "And they crucified him." As Jesus hung on the cross, the taunting and the tormenting from those around him continued. It just didn't stop. Even those being crucified around him joined in the mockery (v. 32).

It has been said that Simon was the very first person to literally carry the command of Jesus to pick up the cross and follow him. Mark explains that Simon was the father of Alexander and Rufus, who were probably members of the church in Rome where the apostle Paul spent time. Some say that Simon's carrying of the cross of Christ possibly factored into the salvation of Alexander and Rufus. Simon probably had no idea how God could and would work the bizarre situation he was placed in for some benefit in his life and the lives of countless others. If Simon became a believer, then Romans 8:28 promised him, as it promises us, that all things work together for good in shaping Christians to be more like Jesus. If God is allowing some strange situation in your life today, trust him and walk through it in the way he desires. God has a purpose in every detail of what he orchestrates in the lives of those who follow Jesus.

june
SEVENTEEN

MARK 15:33-41

Mark records key events that occurred during the crucifixion of Jesus. Darkness came over the whole land from noon to 3 p.m. This darkness symbolized God's judgment upon sin, unleashed on his Son while he endured the cross. Jesus suffered the punishment humanity earned for disobedience to God, and he was judicially separated from the Father for the first (and last) time in eternity. The letter to the Galatians teaches that Jesus actually became a "curse" for us. Bearing the load of the curse, Jesus questioned, "Why have you forsaken me?" Yet even while experiencing God's wrath against human sin, Jesus remained faithful, crying, "My God, my God!" Despite the unfathomable horror he underwent, he continued to depend on the Father in total trust. Verse 37 records that Jesus died. After he took his last breath, the curtain of the temple was torn in two from top to bottom as a symbol of mankind's new direct access to God through the final and complete atonement Jesus made for our sin. Immediately following his death, a Roman officer realized the truth about Jesus. For the first time in the Gospel of Mark, a human acknowledges Jesus as the "Son of God." This officer, who probably oversaw many crucifixions, understood that Jesus was no ordinary man. Through his death, Jesus' full identity was made known to the world.

Every single human soul not covered by the righteousness of Christ remains under the curse that Jesus bore on the cross. But those of us who have repented and put our faith in Jesus are totally free from the judicial penalty of sin we have earned and even continue to earn. If you are feeling down today, discouraged or stressed out by the cares of this life, and yet you are honestly a follower of Jesus, stop and consider your position before God. Take a minute to marvel at what Jesus accomplished for you on the execution rack we call the cross. You, Christian, are considered blameless before the Almighty God of the universe. God literally gave his own Son to be punished so that you could be righteous before him. Romans 8:32 declares that since God gave us his only Son, we would be foolish to think he will withhold what's best from us now. He's already given you the most valuable gift in the universe. The rest is just like pennies to him.

june
EIGHTEEN

MARK 15:42-16:8

Jesus' lifeless body hung on the cross as the day came to an end. The Sabbath, the day on which no work could be done, began Friday evening at 6 p.m. sharp. Friday was known as the Day of Preparation because work had to be finished in preparation for the day of rest. Every Jew took the Sabbath off, and all "work" came to a 24-hour halt. Jewish law required dead bodies to be buried before sunset, so if anyone was going to get Jesus' body off the cross and properly buried, it was critical that it be done before 6 p.m. Joseph of Arimathea used his influence to intervene for the appropriate treatment of Jesus' corpse. Joseph went to Pilate and asked permission to bury Jesus. He probably did this right at around 4 p.m., since Mark records it as "when evening had come" (v. 42). Pilate was amazed to hear that Jesus was already dead. Pilate called the Roman officer who oversaw the execution to make sure of it. When Pilate learned that Jesus was in fact dead, he allowed Joseph to take the body and bury it. Maybe Pilate felt guilty about allowing Jesus to be crucified, and as a result, didn't fight Joseph's request. Joseph wrapped Jesus' mutilated corpse in a linen sheet. Jesus's body was then placed in Joseph's own personal tomb. No one today knows for certain where that tomb was located, but we do know that Jesus didn't spend a lot of time in there.

Joseph of Arimathea lived about twenty miles northwest of Jerusalem, but was present for the Passover. He was a respected member of the Jewish Sanhedrin, the highest Jewish council in the first century. Up to this point, Joseph had been a "behind the scenes" disciple, but now he took courage and acted consistently with what he believed (v. 43). Although his decision could have cost Joseph dearly, he did the right thing. Joseph became an outstanding model of Christian faith for the followers of Jesus. Remember, the eleven disciples were still hiding, yet Joseph acted boldly and at great risk to secure the body of Jesus. What are you afraid to do for Jesus today? Follow the model of Joseph of Arimathea and be courageous. Do what God is calling you to do. Your righteous action could make an impact for good that lasts for years, even decades to come.

june
NINETEEN

LUKE 1:1-4

Luke states that he was not the first to write a biography of Jesus. In fact, many others spoke and wrote about the life of Christ. Luke was a medical doctor, a Gentile, and a companion of the apostle Paul. He was a disciplined student of the life and teaching of Jesus, and his dedication to hard work was used by the Holy Spirit in writing this Gospel. The reason Luke penned this report (and its second volume, Acts) was to provide an "orderly account" for an unknown man, Theophilus, whose name literally means "loved by God." This man previously learned about Jesus, and Luke set out to prove that what Theophilus had been taught was true. Jesus made radical claims about himself, and he asked for radical behavior from his followers. If Christianity isn't absolutely true, if it just exists to help us "get through this life," then we need to be honest and stop playing the Christian game. If what Luke wrote isn't certain, we can enjoy his writing like we enjoy Shakespeare or any other timeless work of literature, but we would be foolish to base our lives on its teaching.

We live on this planet for about eighty years, on average. While we reside here, we must consider how we got here, what the difference is between right and wrong behavior, and what happens after we die. Christianity teaches that a personal God created us, and that we all have great value as a result. It also teaches that God, who is outside of time, has revealed to us what behavior is ultimately right and wrong. And finally, every individual soul will stand before God and be fairly judged based on whether she lived in line with God's perfect design for humanity. Only those who are in Christ, who have repented and placed their faith in Jesus, will be protected from the rightful punishment their sins have earned. Luke said these things are certain (v. 4). Stop and think about the end of your life today. Don't resist the Holy Spirit's witness any longer. Choose to trust in God by putting your confidence in his Son and obeying all that he taught. If you are a Christian, then decide to do what God is directing you to do as we study the Gospel of Luke. Live the rest of your life as consistently as possible with the truth.

june
TWENTY

LUKE 1:5-25

This section begins and ends with Elizabeth, the mother of John the Baptist. Elizabeth was a descendent of a priestly family, and she married a priest named Zechariah. The couple did the best they could to live according to God's laws and principles, yet Elizabeth and Zechariah had no child. Elizabeth was both old and barren. In that culture, barrenness was one of the greatest pains a woman could experience. Women married young and set out to have children right away. The more children a woman bore, the higher her status in society. In addition, children brought financial and physical security in old age. When Elizabeth's husband, Zechariah, was serving as priest, he was chosen "by lot" to offer incense before God. Because there were so many priests, this honor fell to each priest only once in his lifetime. While Zechariah was praying for the nation, an angel appeared to him and announced that he and Elizabeth would have a child. Their son would be the forerunner of the Messiah, and he would be great before God. Zechariah just didn't believe the message of the angel. No way could his wife conceive a child at their age. He asked for a "sign." And God gave him a sign, though probably not one he was hoping for. He was unable to speak until the child was born and named.

Can you imagine how many weeks, months, and years Elizabeth probably prayed, hoping God would deliver her and grace her with at least one child. But for decades, God said "no." She probably never imagined that God would grant her the honor of mothering the one who prepared God's people for the Messiah. After she conceived, she stayed in seclusion for five months—almost half a year! What pain are you enduring today? Have you struggled with the same affliction month after month, year after year, even decade after decade, only to hear a "no" from God? If so, you are in good company. Not only Elizabeth, but countless others recorded in Scripture lived with tremendous pain. All who follow Jesus can know for certain that one day our pain will come to a final end. In the meantime, we can rest assured that God allows every hardship in the lives of believers for a purpose. Let this truth motivate you to joy in the midst of your difficulties today.

june
TWENTY-ONE

LUKE 1:26-38

Six months after Zechariah was told he would father the Messiah's forerunner, God sent the same angel, Gabriel, on a mission to Nazareth. The town was so small that Luke's readers might not have known it, so Luke included its location in Galilee. Gabriel then appeared to a teenaged virgin named Mary, who was engaged, and told her that God favored her. As verse 29 says, "She was greatly troubled at the saying." The angel repeated himself and let her know this was a "good thing." He said, "Do not be afraid. You will conceive a son and you will name him Jesus." The angel added more for Mary: "About the son you will conceive, he will be the Messiah." Mary replied, "What?! Wait! I am a virgin. How can I have a son?" Gabriel explained to her that the Holy Spirit would cause a child to conceive in her womb. The child would be the offspring of both Mary and the power of the Holy Spirit, making Jesus fully man and fully God. And as a sign that all this is true, the angel went on, "Your relative Elizabeth is pregnant too!" Gabriel ended with "None of this," or "nothing" is impossible with God.

Can you imagine what this situation must have been like for Mary? She was engaged, but quite young. In the first century, most Jewish girls married at between 13 and 16 years old. Mary would not have been formally educated. She was from an unknown village, and not wealthy. Couldn't the Lord have found someone who had a better résumé? When Mary heard these things, though overwhelmed, she responded, "Behold, I am the servant of the Lord; let it be to me according to your word" (v. 38). She declared herself the servant of God, and willing to do whatever he asked of her. God isn't looking for age, education, fame, or money when selecting people to advance his agenda. No matter where you are in life at this moment, you can choose to demonstrate the same character and attitude as Mary. Does what you are intending to do (or not do) line up with humble servanthood of God? If not, move your confidence from yourself to the Lord. He can do whatever he wants with those who trust in him.

june
TWENTY-TWO

LUKE 1:39-45

Previously, Luke introduced us to Elizabeth and then to Mary. Now we read about the two together. Both Elizabeth and Mary were upright and godly. Elizabeth was an older woman, and Mary was a teenager. Both were pregnant, and both carried children whose significance to God's plan was monumental. Elizabeth's son, John, was to prepare the way for Mary's son, Jesus, whose birth was more important than anyone else's in all of human history. What an exciting moment when these two pregnant women, who were also relatives, met up! Although Elizabeth was the older and perhaps the wiser of the two, she put her focus on Mary and the child she was carrying instead of herself. She saw Mary's visit as an incredible honor. It is worth noting that John the Baptist, an unborn fetus, responded to the presence of Jesus, even though Jesus was an embryo at this stage. It would be hard for anyone who embraces the Bible as God's message to mankind to argue that God doesn't consider unborn humans to be persons. To "leap for joy" (v. 44) implies more than just life within the womb of Elizabeth. And what about Jesus? Was he not yet a person in the womb of Mary?

Elizabeth called Mary "the mother of my Lord." Elizabeth saw the bigger picture. She gave birth to and mothered John the Baptist, and in due time John left and went on to do the work that God called him to, leaving Elizabeth, in a sense, in the same place she had been before John's birth. If Elizabeth's hope and ultimate joy were in motherhood, she would have been disappointed once again. When God grants us relief from pain in this life, the deliverance we receive is never intended to remove our need for him. Maybe you have all you want, or maybe you don't have much, but wherever you are today, know that in the end all that matters is whether or not you are going to live with God in eternity. If you find yourself holding too tightly to the things God has graced you with, even allowing them to take his rightful place, ask him to help you keep your hands open. May God allow us gratitude and true enjoyment of the blessings he's given us, alongside willingness to give them back if he asks.

june
TWENTY-THREE

LUKE 1:46-56

Luke records Mary's words after Elizabeth greeted her. When Mary and Elizabeth got together, they enjoyed rich conversation. Now, someone else was most likely around the house during the months Mary stayed with Elizabeth, but he wasn't able to join in verbal praise to God. Remember, Zechariah was made mute while he awaited the birth of John because he didn't trust the message from Gabriel. Mary, on the other hand, believed the same angel's announcement and was ready for whatever God called her to do. Mary and Elizabeth glorified God with their words, but Zechariah was temporarily "benched." Zechariah was an old man and a religious leader in Israel. Mary was a teenaged girl. It would seem their responses should have been the other way around. Even though Mary was poor, uneducated, and young, she knew the Scripture. The beautiful praise she gave to God is loaded with Old Testament quotations and references. Mary glorified God for what he appointed her to, and she drew attention to his character, pointing out that God is mighty, holy, strong, just, kind, and merciful. Mary recalled what God did for Israel in the past, and she gave thanks to him for providing for his people through the Child she carried. Mary's "magnification of God" (v. 46) revealed that her hope wasn't driven by her faithfulness, but instead resulted from her exemplary confidence in God's faithfulness.

In verse 50, we see Mary's maturity as she declares, "And his mercy is for those who fear him from generation to generation." She knew that those who fear God enjoy his mercy. The word Luke uses for "mercy" in Greek is equivalent to the Hebrew word that describes the steadfast and committed love of God for his people. She also recognized that one who fears God is willing to do what he says. Because of her reverential awe of God, she was wise. The Proverbs declare that wisdom results from a healthy fear of God. We may think, "Fear the Lord? No! I want to love him, but not fear him!" We can forget that both are necessary for the Christian. In fact, many of our problems result from our failure to fear God. The more we fear God, the more we become liberated from the fear of man. Ask God to grant you mercy and help you grow in wisdom today, increasing your fear of him.

june
TWENTY-FOUR

LUKE 1:57-66

When Elizabeth gave birth to her son, friends and family gathered together to celebrate the new baby's arrival. According to Scripture, Jewish boys were circumcised on the eighth day. It was at this time that Zechariah and Elizabeth named their boy. It was traditional for a child to be named after a father or grandfather, and the elderly couple should have named him Zechariah. Those gathered together expected him to be named after his father, but Elizabeth said, "No." She announced that her son's name was John, the name God chose for this child. The crowd was totally caught off guard. Why John? So they asked Zechariah, and he wrote on a tablet, "His name is John." What a reminder to all that something was very different about this child. The moment Zechariah finished writing "His name is John," he was able to speak again. His time of discipline was over. As a religious leader in Israel, Zechariah should have responded with trust when he heard Gabriel's message. But he didn't believe, so God removed his ability to speak throughout the entire nine months of Elizabeth's pregnancy. When the nine months were up and the crowd asked Zechariah what the baby's name was, he boldly wrote "John." There was no questioning the decision. Zechariah determined to do what God wanted him to do this time. He had definitely learned his lesson. The neighbors were afraid. First the elderly couple became pregnant, then the child received an unexpected name, and finally the priest who became mute could suddenly talk again after he wrote, "His name is John." What was up with this kid?

Zechariah was a God-fearing man, and the Lord kept his promise to him. God keeps his promises to us as well. One of the wonderful privileges of following Jesus is that he loves us so much he will discipline us when we get off track. God promises to work all things together for good in the believer's life so that she will become more Christ-like. When we are fearful, unbelieving, or disobedient, God will go to great lengths to let us know we need to do things his way. God's discipline is intended to draw us closer to him. If you have resisted God's will in a certain area of your life and you sense that you have been "benched" as a result, confess, repent, get back up, and get in the game today.

june
TWENTY-FIVE

LUKE 1:67-80

Luke records what Zechariah said after he was able to speak again. Remember, Zechariah was mute for nine months because he didn't believe the angel's message from God. The people who were with Zechariah and Elizabeth at John's circumcision were afraid, wondering who this child would grow up to be because of the many unusual events surrounding his birth. So the Holy Spirit filled Zechariah, and Zechariah announced that his son, John, was the prophet spoken of in the Old Testament, the one chosen to go before Israel's Messiah. God's plan to redeem his people was moving forward. The Lord had not forgotten his children. Then, Zechariah encouraged the people around him to praise God because he had come to redeem his people. Zechariah explained how God would deliver Israel through her Messiah, who is called the "horn of salvation." In the Old Testament, the horn was a symbol of strength and power. Just as the horn of an animal served to destroy the animal's enemies while protecting its own head, the Messiah would destroy the enemies of Israel. In verses 76-79, Zechariah calls specific attention to the role of his own newborn son. As the angel Gabriel previously said, John would prepare God's people for the Messiah. John was appointed to do this by proclaiming to the nation a message about sin and salvation.

As John grew up, he became strong in his spirit. He secluded himself in the wilderness or the desert until it was time for him to appear to the people of Israel. It is encouraging to see the physical and spiritual growth of John and the spiritual growth of Zechariah as well. God benched Zechariah for nine months because of his unbelief. But when Zechariah was called back up to the plate, he came back stronger than ever. In verse 73, Zechariah boldly proclaims that God was in the process of fulfilling the oath he made to his people, even all the way back to Abraham. Zechariah learned, without a doubt, that God keeps his promises. If you have suffered a spiritual setback, don't despair. Instead, use the season of discipline to grow even more confident of God's hand on your life and the lives of his people. God doesn't allow any circumstance in our walk with him to be wasted. Even in the "down time," he is doing a work in the hearts of those who follow Jesus.

june
TWENTY-SIX

LUKE 2:1-7

Luke transitions the reader from the birth of John the Baptist to the birth of Jesus. The events surrounding the birth of John the Baptist were unusual, but the events surrounding the birth of Jesus were nothing less than extraordinary. Right before Mary was to deliver her son, Caesar Augustus decided it was time for a registration. Augustus decreed that people must return to the city of their ancestors to register so they could properly pay the taxes owed to Rome. Joseph and Mary must have thought, *Are you kidding me? We have to travel 85 miles from Nazareth to Bethlehem right now? Ugh. What is God doing?* It had to have been a real drag for the heavily pregnant Mary to ride on a donkey all the way to Bethlehem. And to make matters even worse, when Joseph and Mary arrived, there was no place for them to stay. Can you imagine being ready to bear your first child and being denied a place to rest your head? Again, what was God doing? Mary went into labor and gave birth to Jesus in Bethlehem, and she was forced to put her newborn boy in a place where animals were kept. In fact, they placed him in a manger or a feeding trough because they simply couldn't afford to rent a place under a proper roof (v. 7).

Micah 5:2, written four hundred years before the birth of Jesus, declares the Messiah would be born in Bethlehem. Joseph and Mary were from Nazareth, not Bethlehem. How could God get Joseph and Mary to move almost one hundred miles south? Mary would be out of her mind to travel during the last days of her pregnancy unless she had no choice. God orchestrated the circumstances by prompting Caesar Augustus to issue the decree. This truth should cause us to stop and bow in humble submission before the Lord. God uses situations, people, and even great world rulers to carry out his purposes. What is happening in your life right now that seems absurd for God to allow? Mary had no idea why God let her undergo these strange circumstances right as she was to give birth. And Caesar Augustus had no idea how God was using him to fulfill Old Testament prophecy. Even when things seem tough or unreasonable, the Christian can trust in God's ability to manage both the big picture and the little details of her life.

june
TWENTY-SEVEN

LUKE 2:8-21

When Jesus was born, shepherds were working at night in the field near Bethlehem. An angel appeared to the shepherds and announced that in Bethlehem, the City of David, the Messiah of Israel had arrived! The shepherds were afraid, but they chose to go to Bethlehem to see what had happened. In the first century, working as a shepherd was not an esteemed occupation, so normally only lower class persons ended up in this role. Jesus' transition from the womb of the teenaged Mary to our world was steeped in humility. The local hotel rejected him and his family, they landed in an animal barn, Jesus ended up in a feeding trough, and he was visited by shepherds, who were considered the lowly of society. And yet, through all of this, God was with Jesus and his family. After the shepherds saw the newborn Jesus, they spread the news about what they experienced and heard to those with whom they crossed paths. They were the first men to preach the gospel or the "good news" about Jesus to others. These things amazed those to whom they spoke. Mary, however, heard what the shepherds said about the angels' visit, and, as verse 19 says, "treasured up all these things, pondering them in her heart." She didn't simply marvel, like the others, but embraced the testimony of the shepherds.

Jesus' birth wasn't spectacular or grandiose by the world's standards, yet it was the reason for the angels' rejoicing and praising of God. The view from heaven is not the same as the view from earth. Psalm 15 says the one "on the same page" with God rejects the unrighteous but honors those who fear the Lord. When the prophet Samuel anointed David as the King of Israel, though David was young and didn't seem like the best candidate for the job, God said, "Man looks on the outward appearance, but the Lord looks on the heart." Are you trying desperately to fit in with the cool crowd, to be embraced by the world while longing to be right with God? If so, realize that the followers of Jesus are called to live differently than the ungodly around them. Choose today to stop trying to gain acceptance from man, and instead humbly embrace the approval that comes from God, even if you become the laughingstock of the world.

june
TWENTY-EIGHT

LUKE 2:22-38

After Jesus was circumcised, Joseph and Mary traveled to the temple in Jerusalem to offer a sacrifice for purification. The Law required a lamb for a burnt offering and a pigeon or a turtledove for a sin offering. If the woman gave birth to a son, this purification was to occur forty days after delivery. The Law made provision for those who couldn't afford a lamb. A pair of pigeons or turtle doves satisfied the burnt and sin offering requirement for the poor, so Mary and Joseph offered the pair of birds without the lamb. Although Joseph was a carpenter who earned his living working with his hands, the young family did not have much money. When they arrived in the temple, they met an old man named Simeon, who was waiting for the coming of the One promised to redeem Israel. The Holy Spirit revealed to Simeon that he would not die until after he actually saw the Messiah. When Simeon saw Joseph, Mary, and Jesus, he recognized Jesus as the Christ. He took the baby into his arms, praised God, and prophesied over him. Simeon declared by the Spirit that Jesus was a light not only to Israel, but to the Gentiles too. This amazed his parents. God provided Jesus for the salvation of all people groups.

Through the prophecy of Simeon, the Holy Spirit told Mary that Jesus would be opposed, and a sword would pierce her own soul. Not all would embrace the truth Jesus was born to bring. The word Simeon used for "sword" described a large and broad sword used by Gentiles, representative of great pain or anguish. Jesus' ministry included choices that were hard for Mary to bear. It can be difficult for women to let go of their children, or to hand them to the world to be salt and light after training them up in the way of the Lord. We often hold onto things we love rather than allowing God to take them from us for his glory. If you are struggling to give over to God any person or thing in your life right now, let go today. The pain we endure now in doing things God's way will one day yield much more fruit than if we had insisted on getting our own way. His way is always best in the end.

june
TWENTY-NINE

LUKE 2:39-40

In these two simple verses, Luke moves the reader away from Jesus as a baby and briefly focuses on Jesus in his teenaged years. Joseph and Mary returned home to Nazareth in Galilee. Luke says that during this time Jesus grew and became strong. The Greek word for "grew" basically means "to increase in size." So the growth Luke speaks of refers to Jesus growing from a baby into a young man. The word for "became strong," on the other hand, usually refers to spiritual strength. Luke adds that Jesus was "filled with wisdom." This phrase draws attention to the fact that Jesus grew in spiritual wisdom or the wisdom of the Father. It is easy to forget that Jesus had to grow both physically and spiritually. Although he was fully God, he voluntarily chose to limit himself and live as a genuine human. He didn't stop being God for one single moment, but throughout the majority of his day-to-day life, he embraced his full humanity by choosing not to exercise his divine right, unless it was the will of the Father and for the good of God for him to do so. Jesus grew spiritually by reading and studying the Scripture and relying on the Holy Spirit to impart to him wisdom and understanding of the depths of God's word.

As the one and only Son of God, Jesus was the object of God's special favor. And yet, he voluntarily limited himself and was "found in human form" (Philippians 2:8). He had to grow the same way we grow, both physically and spiritually. It's amazing to think that we actually have the same Scripture and the same Holy Spirit available to us as Christians that Jesus had. He totally depended on God's Spirit and God's word to live in complete obedience to the Father. And he did it perfectly! Though we can never live flawlessly the way Jesus did, we can still make use of the resources he accessed, and we too can become spiritually strong, increasing in the wisdom of the Lord. Let's choose to follow Jesus' example today by determining to learn God's word and rely on the Spirit for insight. May we be able to look back at this time right now in a year, five years, even ten years and see how we have moved upward on our own spiritual growth charts.

june
THIRTY

LUKE 2:41-52

Luke continues the account of Jesus' early years. Mary and Joseph were godly parents who obeyed the Law by going to Jerusalem to celebrate the annual Passover. The Passover itself lasted a day, and the Feast of Unleavened Bread, which lasted for seven more days, followed it. Often, the entire eight day period was referred to as the Passover. So according to the account, when Jesus was twelve years old, he and his family journeyed with a group to Jerusalem, participated in the Passover festivities, and began their return home, as was their custom. One day into the trip back to Nazareth, Joseph and Mary realized Jesus was missing from their large group. This must have been totally out of character for Jesus, who clearly always did everything right. His parents were "in great distress." It took Joseph and Mary a day to return to Jerusalem. They must have been nervous and even panicked, wondering what could have happened to Jesus. After another day of scouring Jerusalem for him, they finally found him. He was in the temple, asking the teachers questions and listening to their answers. His parents were astonished, literally "struck out of their senses" (v. 48). What was he doing? Mary asked him why he had treated them so thoughtlessly. Jesus replied by asking Mary, "Did you not know that I must be in my Father's house?" Jesus suggested they should have known his whereabouts.

This can seem like a particularly strange story. It can seem as if the flawless God-man acted selfishly and disrespectfully toward his loving parents. But that's not the case. Evidently, by the age of twelve, Jesus understood the identity of his true Father and his true purpose. When they returned home, Jesus remained obedient to the parenting of Joseph and Mary as he continued to grow in favor not only with man, but with God. At twelve years old, Jesus passionately longed to learn about God and the things of God. He knew God was his Father, and he wanted to know his Father as intimately as possible. If we are followers of Jesus, then God is our Father too. Do you long to know God like Jesus did? Set aside extra time this week to read and study the Scripture. You'll never regret the time you spend getting to know more about your God.

july
ONE

LUKE 3:1-10

Luke's account transitions the reader back to the story of John the Baptist. When we last heard about John (1:80), Luke recorded that he grew and became strong, and he lived in the desert until his public appearance. Luke begins his biography by reminding the reader that his account is set in the context of history. It was critical that Theophilus (1:4) know for certain that the things he had been taught were accurate, so Luke continually lists people, places, and dates as reference points. Now, John didn't sugar-coat his message from the Lord one bit. In verse 3, we read the summary of John's teaching: repentance for the forgiveness of sins. God was going to come, and his coming would involve judgment. It isn't enough to be a Jew by birth, a descendent of Abraham. It doesn't matter what your father or your grandfather did for Jesus. It doesn't matter what church you attend or who your neighbors are. On Judgment Day, God will treat people as individuals. God must personally adopt a woman's soul in order to release her from the punishment her sins have earned. This adoption takes place when she repents and places her trust in Jesus.

John used some harsh language when he addressed those who came out to hear him. He called them "sons of snakes." They were priding themselves in being sons of Abraham or the chosen people. John said that God didn't see them as sons of Abraham but as sons of the devil (snakes). In the wilderness where John preached, when a fire broke out in the brush, nearby snakes would flee from the heat. Were these people ready to run from their holes like the snakes to get their lives right with God? Time would tell. We can get comfortable in our little holes too. We can begin to embrace sin and rationalize it by reminding ourselves that we are Christians, so we are fine with God no matter what. It is true that if we are honestly followers of Jesus, our salvation is assured. But at the same time, it's clear that God will judge sin. So why would Christians cling to things that God hates? Prayerfully consider what you are tolerating in your life today. What behaviors do you know you should turn from but fear to release? Ask the Lord for help. He wants you to get it right, and he will come alongside you all the way.

july
TWO

LUKE 3:10-22

John preached to the crowds who came to hear him in the wilderness. The message was simple: repent so that your sins might be forgiven. John told those who listened that it wasn't enough simply to be born a Jew. Those who are right with the Lord through repentance will seek to live consistently with the character of God. Some present were convicted and wanted to make changes in their behavior. They wondered what a repentant life looked like and responded with "What then shall we do?" John gave them specific application, explaining how they could live more consistently with God's design for people. One fruit of repentance John listed sharing with those in need. Those who came to John wondered if he were the Christ. John said, "No. No." John explained that he baptized with water, but one far mightier than him was coming. This one, the Messiah, would baptize with the Holy Spirit and with fire. He would be greater than John. In fact, John said he wasn't even worthy to untie the sandal of the one for whom he prepared the way. It was the duty of a servant to untie the sandal of his master, but this was considered a degrading act. In fact, in the first century, a Hebrew slave was not supposed to untie a sandal because it was considered a dishonorable job fit only for the lowest. John said he wasn't worthy of being Jesus' lowly servant! What humility John possessed!

John shamelessly announced that compared to Jesus, he was nothing. And he was right. When the disciples of John heard later that people were following Jesus instead of John, they ran to let him know what was up. John's response to his disciples was "He must increase, and I must decrease." John knew that he did his job, and that the focus in this life and the life to come is to be on Jesus, not oneself. Later, when Jesus described John, he called him "the greatest of all men born among women." What a tribute! Like John, we need to remember that this life isn't about us. It's about Jesus. We wonder what Jesus can do for us or what his plan is for us. Instead, we should wonder what we can do for him and how we can be useful in his plan. Like John, we need to move the spotlight away from ourselves and onto Jesus.

july
THREE

LUKE 3:23-38

Luke provides the genealogy of Jesus and traces his ancestry all the way back to Adam. Luke begins with Joseph, Jesus' supposed father (v. 23). The reader knows the Holy Spirit conceived Jesus, making Joseph Jesus' actual stepfather. Jesus' brothers and sisters were half-siblings. Mary was the mother of them all, but Jesus had a different father. The genealogy makes its way back to King David in verse 31. It was promised to David in the Old Testament that the Messiah would come from his descendants and sit upon his throne. In verses 32 to 34, Luke goes even further back, this time to Abraham. God promised Abraham in Genesis 12 that the whole earth would be blessed through his offspring. In the very beginning of the book of beginnings, Genesis, God revealed a plan for all people groups of the world. Finally, Luke ends the genealogy in verse 38 with Adam. In tracing the genealogy of Jesus all the way back to Adam, Luke shows that Jesus fully identified with the human race. Luke called Adam the "son of God." This doesn't mean Adam was the one and only Son of God in the same sense that Jesus was, but it does mean that as a human being, Adam was created in God's image.

Sin came into the world through one man, Adam, and death came through sin. We may question the fairness of Adam's rebellion against God placing all under sin, but it's even more unfair that Jesus paid sin's penalty. Adam was created, he broke God's rule, and we all suffer as a result. Jesus had to put on human flesh, live the perfect life, be rejected by those he longed to redeem, and absorb the wrath of God to undo what Adam did. When we recognize that things in this life just aren't the way they should be, let's also remember the extreme lengths God went to in order to fix the problem. Not only has Christ solved our sin issue, but he will restore things to the way they would have been before the fall of Adam. Those who follow Jesus will receive a new body that won't even have the ability to sin anymore. If you are tired or weary today, keep doing the right thing. Soon, you won't ever desire the wrong.

july
FOUR

LUKE 4:1-13

Jesus was filled with and led by the Holy Spirit into the wilderness, where he faced Satan himself. Luke emphasizes the Holy Spirit twice in the same sentence. Clearly, this trial wasn't a result of any defect in Jesus; God desired him to take this route. Jesus came to live the perfect human life, enduring and withstanding all temptations to sin and undoing the spiritual mess our forefather Adam created for the human race. Jesus was weak, having fasted from food for forty days, and it was an opportune time for the enemy to try to break him. Satan tempted Jesus in three ways. The first seemed to fit the circumstance well. Jesus was tired and hungry, and Satan tempted him to create his own bread from rock. Instead of supernaturally providing for himself, Jesus trusted in God's ability to bring food. He quoted Deuteronomy, saying, "Man shall not live by bread alone." Then Satan tempted Jesus to worship him. If Jesus agreed, Satan would give him the entire world. Again, Jesus quoted Deuteronomy: "You shall worship the Lord your God, and him only shall you serve." Finally, Satan tempted Jesus to test God's ability to protect him. It's as if Satan said "Prove it! Let's see if God will take care of you!" Jesus quoted Deuteronomy again, saying, "You shall not put the Lord your God to the test." In all three instances, Jesus stood on the authority of recorded Scripture.

As fully God and yet fully man, Jesus resisted the natural wish to assert his human will and chose God's way instead. He resisted Satan, and Satan left for a time. Satan declared to Jesus that all the kingdoms of the world had been given over to him, and he had the authority to give them to whomever he chose. This world is under the realm of Satan. In fact, Peter stated that Satan walks around like a lion looking for someone to devour. Satan wasn't able to overcome Jesus, but he would love to destroy those who follow the Lord. He wants us to fall so that the testimony of Christ will be marred. He knows exactly where your weaknesses lie and will go straight to the area of vulnerability in your life. Like Jesus, when you are tempted, stand on the authority of Scripture. Just say "no" to the devil, and he will leave you, for a time.

july
FIVE

LUKE 4:14-21

Jesus traveled from the wilderness back to Galilee and finally to Nazareth where he was brought up. He did what he usually did: he went to the local synagogue on the Sabbath. While teaching there, Jesus selected a particular Old Testament text from Isaiah and read it aloud, as was the custom. Those who were students of the Prophets knew this particular passage ultimately described the work of the Messiah. They were curious. Some may have even started to wonder, *What is he going to say about these words from Isaiah?* Jesus rolled up the scroll, gave it back to the synagogue attendant, and sat down to continue teaching. All eyes were fixed on Jesus now (v. 20). The word translated "fixed" is from a Greek word meaning "to look intently at" or "to stare at." Everyone present anticipated the next words of Jesus. What would come from his mouth? Then Jesus clearly stated, "Today this Scripture has been fulfilled in your hearing." Jesus boldly and truthfully addressed these people with whom he had grown up, "to all those who have been waiting for deliverance from God, it's now the time, and it is found in me." Can you imagine what the people of Nazareth must have thought? *Found in you? Jesus? We imagined someone very different for our Messiah. What is Jesus thinking?*

When Jesus set out to tell those in his hometown that he was their promised Deliverer, he read from Isaiah. How interesting to consider that Jesus could have used whatever means he wanted to reveal his identity to his neighbors, but he made the choice to use Scripture. He wanted them to ponder what God said long ago about their promised Messiah. We still need to know what God declared long ago about important topics. We can forget that we have a written record of what God thinks about all sorts of things preserved in a book known as the Bible. In fact, the Bible is the resource we use to discover the unchanging mind and will of God, and it's the tool we use to show others their Creator and their Savior. Make sure you are spending time in God's word on a daily basis. Through consistent time in the Scripture, we become healthy spiritually and ready to undertake whatever God may set before us.

july
SIX

LUKE 4:22-30

The crowd responded both positively and negatively to Jesus' teaching in the synagogue. His declaration impressed them, and they were amazed by his words of grace, but at the same time, they questioned, "Hey, this is Joseph's son. How could the local carpenter's boy claim to be our Messiah?" Jesus was aware of their desire for signs and additional proof that he was the Promised One. He reminded them that their ancestors previously rejected the prophets, and he was prepared for dismissal by his hometown as well. Jesus went on to cite examples from the history of Israel to demonstrate how even in the past God's people refused to believe. Jesus first mentioned the account of the widow of Zarephath for whom Elijah supernaturally provided food during a time of famine. Many widows lived and struggled in Israel during this famine, but not a single one was blessed by the prophet except for the widow of Zarephath, and her blessing was because of her faith. Then Jesus mentioned a leper, Naaman the Syrian. He used Naaman to prove the same principle. Many lepers also lived and struggled in Israel, but only Naaman was healed. So why did this make the crowd so mad (v. 28)? Both the widow of Zarephath and Naaman the Syrian were Gentiles, not Jews! Why did the prophets of Israel bless the Gentiles? These specific Gentiles believed the word of God, while Israel didn't.

Jesus used accounts from the nation's history to reveal that the majority of those who would ultimately trust in him would come from outside the nation of Israel. The crowd in Nazareth did not like what Jesus was saying. *Outsiders blessed? Insiders left out?* They were ready to execute him. Jesus declared an often-repeated truth: "No prophet is acceptable in his hometown." Those who knew Jesus best couldn't get past his ordinariness, and as a result, they would not believe the message he brought. Our neighbors can do the same thing, refusing to listen to the good news we bring because we are just regular people. If you feel downcast because you are trying to do things God's way and are continually spurned by those closest to you, know that you are in good company. Don't get discouraged! Keep doing what God has called you to, even when you don't get the support you hope for. Though many may refuse the Lord, God's purpose cannot be thwarted. His desire will be accomplished.

july
SEVEN

LUKE 4:31-37

While Jesus was in his hometown of Nazareth, he taught in the local synagogue, and when he traveled to Capernaum he did the same thing. Luke recorded that Jesus' teaching struck the Jews in Capernaum out of their senses, just like it did the Jews in Nazareth, because of its authority. When Jesus spoke, he didn't rely upon the traditions of men to support what he said, but depended only upon the Scripture and his own understanding of the text. This was different from the typical sermons the scribes delivered in the synagogues. In this particular Capernaum synagogue, Jesus encountered a demon-possessed man. While Jesus was speaking, the demon cried out to him, asking, "What do you have to do with us? I know you are the Holy One of God." The presence of Jesus threatened the demons. Jesus simply rebuked the evil spirit and commanded, "Be quiet, and come out of the man." The demon threw the man down on the ground and came out again. Everyone there was absolutely amazed. They recognized that the authority of Jesus was unlike any they had ever seen before, as demonstrated in his words and actions.

One of the demon's most interesting questions was "Have you come to destroy us?" The spirit was unclean, and Jesus was the Holy One. When Jesus stood before the demon, the forces of evil literally met the Force of good. Jesus' power horrified the evil spirit (v. 34). But when Jesus faced off with the demon, no big battle was necessary. Jesus spoke, the demon left, and the man emerged from it all entirely safe. Jesus had the power to remove the demon while keeping the health and integrity of the man intact because Jesus was and is in control. Although it can feel eerie to think about unseen powers around us, there is something within the human soul that senses the reality of spiritual battle. We know innately that good and evil exist. Soon, the forces of light and darkness will come to a final face-off. If you are a Christian today, no matter how the armies of wickedness press in on you, be encouraged, because you are on the winning side. For now, God's children are called to resist darkness. Ask the Lord for help to make the best choices. Jesus is holy, and he desires that his followers be holy as well.

july
EIGHT

LUKE 4:38-44

Jesus left the synagogue at Capernaum and went to Simon's house. Although Simon was his birth name, Jesus renamed him Peter. Simon's nickname, Peter, is used most often (159 times) in the New Testament. When Jesus entered the house, he found Peter's mother-in-law quite sick with a high fever. Her condition was more life-threatening and dangerous than it sounds. Because no effective fever-reducing medicines or even antibiotics were readily available and in the first century, people died far more easily than they do in the western world today. So those in Peter's home appealed to Jesus on behalf of the woman. It's worth noting that Peter was clearly married. In fact, according to church history, Peter had children, and his wife was very involved in women's ministry. Jesus stood over Peter's mother-in-law and rebuked the fever. The Greek word translated as "rebuke" literally means "to express strong disapproval." Jesus let the fever know it wasn't welcome in her body. Immediately, Peter's mother-in-law got up and began to serve Jesus and those in the home. She was instantaneously healed. Jesus then went on to heal any who were sick or suffered from various diseases.

Jesus could have said to Peter's mother-in-law, "Hey, this life is temporary. Get it together. You'll be dead soon." But he didn't. Instead, he had compassion on her, along with all those who were brought to him, and he healed every one of them. The physical healing Jesus brought reflected the spiritual healing that all desperately need. Have you been healed by Jesus? Was there a time when he rebuked the sin in your life, declaring that you are a new creation and from his perspective entirely whole again? Has he snatched you from the dominion of death and darkness and placed you into his righteousness? If so, then like Peter's mother-in-law, you should get up and serve Jesus too. Do we serve the Lord to earn our salvation? No! That would be impossible. No one can earn her way to perfection. Instead, we serve Jesus because we are grateful for the healing he has imparted to us. If you are a Christian, make sure you are serving Jesus by taking on some role in your church. As we serve in our church, we display our gratitude to Jesus, who delivered us from darkness. We long to serve him because we realize we would be dead without him.

july
NINE

LUKE 5:1-11

Jesus' popularity was increasing, and the people "checking him out" began to press in on him to hear what he had to say. So Jesus taught from Peter's boat to avoid being crushed by the multitude. This teaching occurred at the Lake of Gennesaret, also known as the Sea of Galilee. Calling the Sea of Galilee a lake seems appropriate, as it is only thirteen miles long by eight miles wide. Though it is the largest freshwater lake in Israel, it doesn't match the picture one might imagine of a "sea." Jesus hopped into Peter's boat while Peter washed his nets on shore. When Jesus finished teaching, he told Peter to get the boat into deep water and let down his nets. Strangely, the carpenter's son gave fishing advice to the fisherman. Peter must have thought, *Are you kidding me? We just washed the nets. Besides, the best fishing occurs at night.* But in faith, Peter did what Jesus asked and caught so many fish that the nets were tearing. Peter's fishing partners came and helped him haul in the catch. The two boats threatened to sink from all the weight.

When Jesus told Peter to get back out on the lake and start fishing again, the request must have sounded absurd. But Peter responded in obedience to Jesus and said, "At your word I will let down the nets" (v. 5). What a picture of total trust! This whole proposal made no sense to Peter, but he was willing to do things God's way instead of his own way. When Jesus led Peter to the fish, Peter responded, "Depart from me, for I am a sinful man, O Lord." Peter realized the enormous difference between himself and Jesus, and he fell to his knees. Let's never forget that Jesus knows what we need, and he knows how to give it to us, even when things don't make sense in our minds. What is Jesus asking you to entrust to him right now? Does he want you to hang in there with a tough relationship? Or trust him to provide what you need financially? Or press on in an area of service? Even though you may feel weary like Peter, thinking, *I've been at this all night*, be ready to say, "At your word, I will let down the nets." Jesus knows what he is doing.

july
TEN

LUKE 5:12-16

While Jesus was in Galilee, a man covered in leprosy approached him. This skin disease was absolutely horrible for the person who contracted it. This leper suffered an advanced, "stage four" case. Because of his condition, he was considered unclean and cut off from the community. In desperation, he fell down before Jesus, begging him to remove the disease. Although the leper looked to Jesus as his only hope, he sought help with a respectful attitude towards Jesus' authority. Jesus agreed to heal the man, and immediately the leprosy was gone. When the leper next appeared before the priest to make an offering for his cleansing, the religious leaders would be shocked, and the news would quickly spread. Now, Jesus didn't have to heal this man. If Jesus chose to walk away, nothing "unfair" would have occurred. The leper approached Jesus in humility, aware that Jesus didn't owe him anything. There were many sick and hurting people around Jesus during his ministry, and he passed a lot of them by without helping them. Was Jesus in error? Did he miss the mark regarding what God called him to do? Not at all! In fact, Jesus actually came to his Father with the same reverential attitude. At the moment of his greatest crisis in the Garden of Gethsemane before the cross, Jesus said to his Father, in essence, "This is what I want, but I am willing to be in alignment with whatever you want for me." When the Father rejected Jesus' desire for a way out, it was for the greater good, and Jesus embraced that truth.

What are you praying for today? Are you coming before God with the same attitude of deference towards the Lord and his will? Don't stop asking him for your desires. But remember that if he doesn't give you what you want, no injustice has occurred. And yet, God promises, "If we confess our sins, he is faithful and just to forgive us our sins and to cleanse us from all unrighteousness" (1 John 1:9). That answer is certain. God promises to receive us every single time we come to him in repentance and faith. That should blow us away! We should never tire of confidently asking God to restore our intimacy with him and draw us closer to his side. And we should continue to ask him for everything else, mindful of his loving wisdom, even when the answer is not what we hoped for.

july
ELEVEN

LUKE 5:17-32

Again, Jesus taught. This time, all sorts of religious officials were present. Some came from Galilee, some from Judea, and the most prominent came from Jerusalem. On this occasion, the house Jesus was teaching from was so crowded it became almost impossible to get to him. So some very determined men scaled the walls, climbed on the roof, shuffled around a few tiles, and lowered their paralyzed friend on a mat right in front of Jesus. What faith! Jesus looked at the paralyzed man and forgave his sins. The religious leaders were outraged! *Who did Jesus think he was? Forgiving sins? Did he think he was God?* Knowing what was in their hearts, Jesus cured the man, proving he had the authority to heal the physically and the spiritually sick. Those who witnessed the event were awestruck. Luke transitions to Levi in verse 27. Although he was a tax collector, Jesus singled him out. Tax collectors were quite unpopular with the Jewish community, yet Jesus specifically called Levi to come with him. Levi dropped everything to follow, willing to make Jesus his number one priority in life. Then Levi prepared a great feast in Jesus' honor, and many other tax collectors showed up. He couldn't wait for his friends to get to know Jesus. The religious leaders were not "cool" with this at all. No Pharisee would be caught dead eating with such spiritual "losers." Again, what was Jesus doing?

Jesus responded to those who grumbled against him for eating with "sinners" by saying, "Those who are well have no need of a physician, but those who are sick. I have not come to call the righteous but sinners to repentance." The religious leaders saw themselves as spiritually healthy with no need for the healing of Jesus. But the religious leaders were blinded by self-righteousness. No person can come to Jesus unless she sees her spiritual lack. Many are like the Pharisees and scribes, who didn't see their need for a Savior. They wrongly think that if they end up standing before the throne of God, they will be allowed entrance into his Kingdom because they are "good" people. If you recognize that you are not good and have placed your trust in Jesus, realize that you have been chosen, just like Levi. If you are a follower of Jesus, he specifically asked you to come with him. What an honor and a reason for rejoicing today!

july
TWELVE

LUKE 5:33-39

Fasting was an important component of first century Judaism. The Old Testament made many references to fasting as a way to set aside physical needs and focus on the spiritual. Prayer and fasting are often mentioned together, as the purpose of both was to spend more time with God. In Jesus' culture, those who were seen as very zealous for the Lord fasted two times a week, every Monday and Thursday. The followers of the Pharisees and the followers of John the Baptist practiced routine fasting. On national fast days, the whole community of God's people would fast together. So the curious crowd approached Jesus and asked him why their practices were different. Why weren't the followers of Jesus fasting? Jesus replied to their question with another question. He asked them if the friends of the groom fast at the groom's wedding. Of course not! The groom's friends are present for the purpose of rejoicing together. When the wedding is over, the same people will fast. Jesus, the bridegroom, was physically present with his followers. Very soon, he would leave, and he would not be physically with them again until the next life. During his absence, it would be appropriate to fast.

We hear a lot about fasting in our body-conscious culture. Although many fast, they don't necessarily do it "for God." There is nothing necessarily wrong with fasting for health reasons, but we shouldn't confuse this with fasting for spiritual purposes. When tragedy strikes our lives, we may become so involved in the problem that we neglect to eat. Since our focus is on the issue at hand rather than food, we end up fasting. In the same way, when we choose to focus so intently on God that we neglect things that are important to us, we engage in a spiritual fast. We may purposely plan to abstain from eating, watching TV, or engaging with social media, and instead redirect our energy to God and prayer, seeking him for wisdom and guidance. We should all fast every now and then. But when we fast, let's keep in mind that the day is coming when we will no longer need to abstain from things to focus on God. When we are face to face with Jesus, our bridegroom, everything will be made right. Our problems will be gone, and fasting will be a thing of the past.

july
THIRTEEN

LUKE 6:1-11

Jesus and his followers walked through a field of grain on the Sabbath. They were hungry, so they picked kernels of wheat and ate them. In doing this, the Pharisees said they had violated the Sabbath. On another Sabbath, a man with a shriveled hand entered the synagogue where Jesus taught. The Pharisees suspected that Jesus might try to heal him, and he did. In both cases, the Pharisees were keeping a close eye on Jesus in an effort to catch him in some sort of error (v. 7). The Hebrew word *Sabbath* literally means "rest." God used the word **Sabbath** for the first time when the Israelites were on their way to the Promised Land. They had no food, and they depended upon God to provide them with something to eat. God gave them daily manna from heaven, but every Saturday they were to take the day off and rest from collecting the food, "working" for six days and taking the seventh off. The Sabbath became a sign of the covenant relationship between God and his people, reminding Israel of the future and permanent "rest" to come. Although the Pharisees, who held spiritual authority, accused Jesus and his disciples of breaking the Sabbath, Jesus knew what was pleasing to God. He wasn't breaking the Law by eating grain, nor was he violating God's design by healing. The problem didn't lie with Jesus but with the religious leaders. Jesus declared, "The Son of Man is lord of the Sabbath."

Like Jesus, we will hear countless opinions telling us what is and isn't pleasing to God. How do we know which voices are correct? Jesus knew the Scripture, and he knew exactly what God was looking for in human behavior. Let's not forget that we have access to God's word too! There's an interesting verse in Acts 17:11, which mentions a group of people from a town called Berea. The apostle Paul praises them for eagerly searching the Scripture to make sure the things they were learning from him were true. As you listen to the sea of voices in this life trying to tell you what God's will is, don't rely on others, or even your own feelings for truth. Examine the Bible to make sure that what you hear is correct. If it's not, toss it and move on. If it is, hold on to it, apply it, and become more like the woman God desires you to be.

july
FOURTEEN

LUKE 6:12-19

Before Jesus chose his twelve disciples, he spent the entire night in prayer. Jesus moved away from the crowds and the busyness of life and went to a mountain to be alone with God. The next day, he handpicked those called to be his team. In verse 13, the phrase "chose from them" is used. Others followed Christ, but Jesus picked a core team to invest in and train to continue his work. Jesus carefully sought the wisdom of God before he made this decision. Luke calls these twelve disciples "the apostles." Apostle literally means "sent one." These twelve apostles were commissioned by Jesus to represent him and carry the good news out from Israel and into the world. The list of the twelve begins in verse 14 with Peter. Andrew and Peter were brothers. James and John were brothers. And they were all four fishermen. James and John were actually cousins of Jesus. Philip and Nathaniel (Bartholomew) were friends. Matthew (Levi) was a tax collector, which wasn't a popular occupation. Thomas was the famous "doubter." A younger James (son of Alphaeus), Simon the political radical, and Thaddeus (Judas, son of James) rounded out the list. Oh, and we can't forget Judas Iscariot, the one who betrayed Jesus.

What an interesting group of men Jesus chose: fishermen, a hated tax collector, a man who had to "see things with his own eyes," and a political radical. Did Jesus make mistakes with this group of twelve? Not at all! These men were the specific ones whom God hand-selected and commissioned to carry out his work on earth. Jesus really prayed hard before he called these guys. It is astonishing to consider that God led Jesus to even include Judas Iscariot in this group of twelve. Although Judas was never saved, the other eleven sure were. Have you ever felt like you're not smart enough or beautiful enough or witty enough to really make a difference for God and his kingdom? Those thoughts just aren't true! God masterfully uses the foolish things of the world to confound the wise. And when he does his amazing works through the weaker among us, his power and glory are magnified. Instead of focusing on past failures, look forward and let God work in and through you today. Jesus can change the world through a surrendered life and a trusting heart.

july
FIFTEEN

LUKE 6:20-26

It was common in the ancient world to pronounce blessings. In its literal sense, "blessed" means "happy," describing the person who encounters good fortune from God. Jesus goes on to state what makes a happy person. The first happy people are the poor. *What?! The poor?!* The poor see their need and are driven to God in desperation. Jesus said the next group of happy people is the hungry. Sound just as strange? These are the people who long for God's kingdom. They are hungry for righteousness and know real satisfaction can only be found in the Lord. The third group Jesus describes as happy seems even more odd. He said those who weep or cry are blessed. That seems like a contradiction, unless they are weeping tears of joy. But Jesus wasn't talking about "happy tears" here. He truly meant that those who sorrow are blessed. When we take an honest look at the world around us and even our own choices, we see sin and failure. The one who is broken and sad about things not being the way they should be is blessed. Finally, the happy people are those who are persecuted. Those who are hated, left off the party invitation lists, and mocked are blessed. This doesn't mean it's good when others hate us for treating them like jerks, but when we gently and respectfully stand up for God and his word and are despised as a result, we will receive God's good fortune, reward in the life to come.

Jesus described four parallel reasons to grieve. The woes were a pronouncement of displeasure. According to Jesus, those who are rich, full, laughing, and popular have cause for concern. These are the ones "enjoying" this life so much that they dread the thought of letting it go. They see no need for repentance. In fact, real repentance may include giving up some of the pleasurable things they love and enjoy, so they avoid it. Jesus says to these people, "Woe!" As we pray for our families, our children, our friends, and even ourselves today, let's remember to keep our view of life consistent with God's. Maybe we should pray less for money, good times, and popularity, and pray a little more for a deep recognition of our spiritual need, a longing for things to be done God's way, a hatred of sin, and a commitment to stand for truth, no matter the cost.

july
SIXTEEN

LUKE 6:27-36

Jesus expects his disciples to love in a way consistent with those who have experienced the total forgiveness of God. The Greek verb used here for "love" is *agapao*, and its noun form is the commonly known *agape*. This love often describes the love of a higher for a lower. It is not a natural love, based on feelings, emotions, or what those around us "deserve," but a supernatural, others-oriented love that seeks to do and respond to others in a way that is best for them and their spiritual growth. In these verses, we see seven general exhortations. The first is to love our enemies (v. 27). The Christian is called to go above and beyond what is considered normal. Second, Jesus calls us to do good to those who hate us (v. 27). Even when people stand against us, we are called to help them be reconciled to God. Third, Jesus commands us to "bless" or speak well of those who don't speak so well of us (v. 27). Fourth, Jesus asks us to pray for those who give us a hard time. Fifth, verse 29 says we are not to retaliate. We let God settle things in his timing. Sixth, we are to be generous with others (vv. 29-30). And seventh, we should treat other people the way we want to be treated (v. 31). We usually don't have a hard time dealing graciously with ourselves. We understand why we messed up, and we let ourselves off the hook. God is "over the top" generous with his kids, and he expects us to extend his kindness to others (v. 35).

Jesus declared (John 13:35) that the world has the right to judge whether you are following him based on the way you love others. This is not an optional or selective love. If you have been totally pardoned from all of your wrongdoing by a flawless and almighty God, then you must love. If you don't love the way Jesus called you to, then either you don't really know him or you are forgetting the incredible mercy he has showered upon you (v. 36). Be honest. To whom in your life are you failing to show supernatural love? If you really want to be a "godly woman" by being like your Father, then choose to love that person. Display the mercy you have received from God by extending it to others.

july
SEVENTEEN

LUKE 6:37-45

Jesus switched the topic of his teaching from loving to judging. Most see 6:31, "Be merciful, even as your Father is merciful," as a hinge verse that transitions the reader from the love section to the judgment section. Many of those with Jesus may have objected to his charge to love even their enemies. They must have wondered, *But where does judging wrong behavior fit into all of this?* Jesus reminded his audience that the recipients of God's great mercy are called to extend that same mercy to others. It only makes sense. But are there times when the follower of Jesus needs to correct wrongdoing in others? Absolutely! Jesus never said we aren't called to judge, but he is concerned with the way we do it. Jesus wanted to make certain his disciples knew that the way they treated others would end up reflected in the way others treated them. If they wanted justice, they would get it! Those who were merciful would receive mercy. Those who were judgmental and condemning would end up judged and condemned, and those who were forgiving and generous would receive the same from others. This passage is not saying that we are not to make any moral evaluations. But it is warning us that we are never to do so with a harsh, unforgiving attitude that expects failure in others. We are not to look at anyone as if she is "too far gone" for God. That is something only God can determine.

Although he lived in a dark world, Jesus maintained a perfect attitude. He didn't grow cynical or sarcastic. Jesus was never mean, hypercritical, or overly harsh. He hoped for the best in people, and he even felt compassion towards those who failed to respond rightly. In Mark 10:21, when the rich young man walked away from Jesus' difficult teaching unrepentant, Jesus still "loved him." Those who follow him should have the same encouraging, optimistic attitude, knowing that God is able to reach down to the darkest depths of humanity and redeem whomever he pleases. Let's stand up for what's right, making proper judgments when necessary, but also making sure we aren't miserable in the process. Jesus kept the right balance. Ask him for help today! We will never be able to communicate the mercy and forgiveness we have received from God if we aren't willing to extend mercy and forgiveness to anyone else.

july
EIGHTEEN

LUKE 6:46-7:10

Jesus wrapped up his challenging sermon with a powerful conclusion. Jesus taught that people's words should be consistent with who they really are. Yet in the end, it's not what we say that matters as much as what we do. He asked his hearers, "Why do you call me 'Lord, Lord,' and not do what I tell you?" The professor of faith didn't only say, "Lord," but "Lord, Lord" with passion and emotion. Jesus added, "If you view me like this, why won't you follow my commands?" No matter how emotional the confession of faith, if one's actions don't follow her words, she didn't honestly consider her statement about Jesus. The one who hears and puts into practice what Jesus said is wise. This person is like one who dug deep into the soil to lay a strong foundation before building her house. When the flood came, her house remained. Another was foolish. She heard and may have even agreed enthusiastically to what Jesus said, but she didn't put his words into practice. Since she didn't do anything about it, her house had no foundation. When the flood came, her house washed away. What is the flood? It could be the trials and difficulties of life, or it could even be the last judgment of God. Either way, the point is clear: if you believe, then do what Jesus says.

Why do we find ourselves gushing over how much we love and prize Jesus, yet not doing as Jesus commands? He wasn't referring to the tripping up we experience as we walk through the world, but to the deliberate attitude that knows what he wants and nevertheless says, "No. I am going to do things my way." Are you willfully disobedient to the teaching of Jesus in any area of your life? Maybe you are planning to pursue an unbiblical divorce. Perhaps you don't want to live without a favorite habit or addiction in which you find pleasure, yet you know it is inconsistent with God's design for life. Or it could simply be that you refuse to attend or serve in a church. If you know that you are living in willful disobedience to the commands of Christ, choose to repent today. Ask Jesus to turn your disobedience into a desire for obedience. Instead of "I will not," say, "I am struggling. Help me to get it right."

july
NINETEEN

LUKE 7:11-17

As Jesus came near the gate surrounding the city of Nain, he encountered a funeral procession. During these types of funerals, corpses were taken outside the city walls and placed in a family plot. This time, the deceased was the only son of a widow. Her husband was dead, and now her child was gone too. A large crowd came with her as those who loved this broken widow grieved together with her. When Jesus saw her, he had compassion on her. The dead body of her son would have been visible, although covered by a cloth. Jesus touched the plank that carried the corpse and spoke to the dead man! What in the world was Jesus doing talking to a dead body? Jesus said, "Young man, I say to you, arise." The dead man sat up, he spoke, and Jesus presented the son, alive, to his mother. The frenzied spectators were afraid, and they gave glory to God. We may forget that Jesus wasn't a fan of death. It actually wasn't in God's original design for humanity. When Adam and Eve disobeyed God's command, sin entered into the world and the process of death began. Jesus didn't say death was great, a "part of life," or that we should learn to love it. On the contrary, death is a termination of this life.

Even though Jesus graciously brought the widow's son back to life, the man would go on to die again. We will all die too. As time proceeds, either you will attend the funeral of a loved one, or you will be dead yourself. In Psalm 90, Moses prayed for God's people, asking God to help us number our days so that we might get a heart of wisdom. If we are willing to continually remember that this day may be our last, it will change the decisions we make. What if you knew this day would be your very last? What would you do? Would you make a phone call to tell someone how much you love him? Would you do whatever it takes to fix a broken relationship? Would you communicate the gospel to as many as you possibly could? Or would you fully surrender your life to Jesus in repentance and faith? May God answer the prayer of Moses in our lives. Let's determine to finish without regrets, and live each day as if it were our last one on earth.

july
TWENTY

LUKE 7:18-35

Luke picks up the account of John the Baptist. John was imprisoned as a result of rebuking Herod for his adulterous relationship with his brother's wife, Herodias. John was discouraged. He believed Jesus was the Messiah, but things weren't panning out the way he hoped. He was sure the Scripture taught that the coming One would set up the Kingdom. What was taking so long? Didn't Jesus know John was in prison? At the same time, reports of all that Jesus was doing got back to John. He was confused, so he sent two of his followers to Jesus to ask on his behalf. Should they be looking and waiting for someone else? Jesus responded to the disciples of John with Scripture. Quoting from Isaiah, Jesus asked them to tell John, "the blind receive their sight, the lame walk, lepers are cleansed, and the deaf hear, the dead are raised up, the poor have good news preached to them." The answer was "no." They should not be looking for someone else. Jesus threw in an extra sentence, "And blessed is the one who is not offended by me." The word translated as "offended" is the Greek word *skandalizo*. We get our English word "scandalize" from this Greek word, and it means "to suffer a lapse of faith as a result of someone else's behavior." John was stumbled by the fact that Jesus hadn't yet established his kingdom.

Jesus will set up his kingdom. Soon we will be together with him in a place so amazing it is beyond our ability to conceive. But until then, God has us here for a reason. And his plan for us will include hardship and difficulty, even times of doubt. Jesus said of John the Baptist, "Among those born of women none is greater than John." What a compliment! And yet, even though John was so incredibly esteemed by God, he suffered greatly, even to death. Are you experiencing troubles and trials in your life? Do you ever feel like you just aren't that important to him? Don't let your circumstances shape your sense of worth before God. If you are a follower of Jesus, you are so important to him that he gave his life for you. And according to Jesus, every single Christian under the New Covenant is greater than John. Wow! May we never allow discouragement to cause us to forget how valuable we are to the Lord!

july
TWENTY-ONE

LUKE 7:36-50

A Pharisee named Simon invited Jesus to dinner. A woman heard that Jesus would be there, and even though she wasn't on the guest list, she showed up. Often, when a rabbi was invited to an event in someone's home, uninvited people came to listen to the guest teach. The woman brought an expensive jar of perfume in case she could get near Jesus. And she was able! As she approached him, she began to cry, and as she cried, she wet Jesus' feet with her tears. She wiped her tears off his feet with her hair, she kissed his feet repeatedly, and then she anointed them with her perfume. What she did was a sign of utmost respect. The price of the perfume was something that she probably couldn't "afford" to pour out, but she did so anyway. Everyone present at the meal saw this. The wiping, kissing, and anointing went on for some time. Simon looked at Jesus with disappointment. If Jesus were any type of prophet, he would have known a sinner was touching him. This woman had a bad reputation. In fact, she was probably a prostitute who had come to Jesus for forgiveness. Simon assumed Jesus was clueless. But Jesus knew exactly what Simon was thinking. He asked Simon in a parable which debtor would love a lender more, one released from a small debt or one released from a large debt. Simon answered, "the large debtor," and his answer was right.

The problem with Simon and the rest of the Pharisees was that they honestly believed they were not sinners. They compared themselves with other people instead of with God, and because of this, they felt superior. If God were going to let anyone into his kingdom, surely it would be them. They failed to realize that God never asks us to compare ourselves with ourselves. We are to compare ourselves with God. And when that evaluation takes place, we all fall short. No one ends up judged "good." Simon needed the forgiveness of God just as much as the woman did. Her faith saved her, and she loved much as a result. If you are forgiven, think of a way to express your gratitude to Jesus today. Try to spend an extra ten minutes thanking him and praising him for all that he has done for you.

july
TWENTY-TWO

LUKE 8:1-8

Jesus traveled to all sorts of places teaching others about the kingdom of God. His disciples followed him, and so did a group of women. Many of these women had been delivered from illnesses or evil spirits. Not only did the women go with Jesus on his travels, but they also helped support him financially. It was common for a rabbi to travel as he taught and to be followed by his disciples, but it was rare to be followed by women. Jesus continually challenged the social norms to prove that all types of people are included in God's plan of salvation. Luke points out three specific women: Mary Magdalene, Joanna, and Susanna. Mary Magdalene was delivered from seven demons. She was present at his crucifixion, anointing his body for burial after he died. She was at his tomb when and she met the angel who announced that Jesus had risen from the dead. Joanna the wife of Chuza is also mentioned. Chuza is named because he was an official in Herod's court. Joanna was with Mary Magdalene when the angel appeared at Jesus' grave. These women were faithful to Jesus, and their generosity extended to his whole group (v. 3).

Just as the sinful woman loved much, these women loved Jesus much as well. They demonstrated their love through generosity. Jesus and the disciples were called to preach the gospel to the Jews first and then to the Gentiles. In order to do this, they needed the financial support of others. In the same way, God has designed the church to be made up of people with different talents. The apostle Paul compared these gifts to different parts of a body, stressing the oneness of the whole body. Are you fulfilling your role so that your church can function the way God designed it to? If not, decide now to bless and serve your church by using your unique gifts. If you are, be encouraged! The effort and energy that you invest into your church allows it to function and thrive the way God designed it to. Mary Magdalene, Joanna, and Susanna may not be well known by men, but God will never forget their generosity. Everything you do for Jesus will be remembered too as you store up treasure where moth and rust don't destroy, and thieves can't break in and steal.

july
TWENTY-THREE

LUKE 8:9-15

Jesus told the crowd who had gathered around him a parable about a farmer who went out to sow his seed. The disciples had been around Jesus long enough to realize that he wasn't giving them a lesson in agriculture. After he finished, they asked him what it meant. He told them that the purpose of parables is to reveal secrets about the kingdom of God. But their meanings are hidden to "the others" who don't really care about the pursuit of truth. The points of the parables actually testify against such people. The parable of the sower illustrates the different ways people respond to the word of God, or the "seed" the farmer sows. All four groups receive the same seed. The first soil the seed falls on is hardened ground. Satan, who doesn't want people transferred from darkness to light, snatches the seed that falls on this path. He and his demons are still actively seeking to keep people from being saved. The second and third "soils" are interesting because they apparently profess some form of faith. The second seed falls on ground filled with rocks. This seed dies shortly after it springs up because it can't take root. The hardships associated with following Jesus are too much. This "soil" doesn't follow through. Thorns, or the love of money and the pleasures of this life, choke out the seed in the third soil. To trust exclusively in Jesus is too great a leap of faith for those represented by this soil. Even though these people are really interested in Jesus, their passion for material things takes over in the end.

The fourth soil, the good soil, represents the person who hears the word, holds fast to it, and bears fruit. The key to identifying the fourth soil isn't the absence of obstacles, but the presence of fruit. In a sense, we all have a few rocks and thorns to deal with as the word of God works itself out in our lives. According to this parable, only the fourth soil was actually born again. Though there may be rocks and thorns to deal with in the believer's life, those things can't permanently hinder the good soil from bearing fruit. If you are an honest follower of Jesus, you have been created for good works. You may hit a few rocks and thorns along the way, but you will bear fruit. It's guaranteed!

july
TWENTY-FOUR

LUKE 8:16-25

Luke records that Jesus' mother and his brothers came to him. The crowd surrounding him was so thick that his family couldn't reach him. Someone there reported the situation to Jesus, and he was told that his mother, Mary, and his brothers were outside, desiring to see him. Jesus used this opportunity to teach a critical lesson to those with him. He said his mother and brothers were those who hear the word of God and respond to it with action. Jesus referred to them as those who "hear the word and do it." Following Jesus isn't simple as hearing facts concerning God, holiness, human nature, sin, judgment, grace, mercy, and forgiveness and then saying, "Oh, yes! I agree to all of that." Of course, those who follow him must concur with what he taught. But throughout the Gospels, we see that we must also respond rightly to these truths. We are saved by faith. Salvation is not something we work up ourselves. Instead, it has been granted to us from above. Yet, saving faith includes a supernatural rewiring. God reworks those whom he has graced with salvation so that they will not only believe, but "do" something about that belief as well. If you hear the word of God and do it, in the end you will discover that it was God who graced you with both the hearing and the doing. He gives us the package deal. How humbling is that?

Jesus said his mother and brothers are those who hear the word and do it. In other words, those who obey God's word are Jesus' family. They are the ones he wants to be intimate with. Just as Jesus' closest relationships were with those who obey the word, our closest relationships should be with those who obey the word as well. Stop and think for a minute. Whom would you call your top three best friends? Do they obey the word of God? Would Jesus call them his mother and his brothers? If not, maybe it's time to invest into some new friendships. If so, then let those friends know how much you appreciate them. Remind them that they are like family to you. As the proverb says, "There is a friend who sticks closer than a brother." Do something special for a sister in Christ today!

july
TWENTY-FIVE

LUKE 8:26-39

Jesus and his disciples sailed to Gentile territory, and after they stepped out on land, they were met by a demon-possessed man. This man was living in hideous conditions because of his demon possession. In verse 27, the word for "demon" is plural, so he was actually possessed by more than one, even many demons. He didn't wear clothes, and he didn't live in the city with others, but he lived in the tombs alone. He had been bound in the past, but his demonic strength allowed him to break the chains (v. 29). What a tormented, desperate, and lonely life this man lived. When the man saw Jesus, he cried out and fell down before him. This falling down was not in worship, but in recognition and acknowledgement of his authority. The man spoke, yet it wasn't actually the man who conversed with Jesus. It was one of the demons in him. Jesus asked the representative demon what his name was. He called himself "Legion," and said there were many of them in this man. The demons then begged Jesus to allow them to relocate from the man into a nearby herd of pigs. Jesus agreed, and the entire herd drowned. Those who witnessed the event told others, and they all asked Jesus to leave. They were afraid of Jesus. But the formerly possessed man, now in his right mind and even clothed, asked to go with Jesus. Jesus asked him instead to go back home and tell others about what God had done for him.

It is strange to think about demons falling down before Jesus. They know who he is, and they must show him the respect he is due, yet at the same time, they are at war with him. They know their time is limited, and they ask him not to torment them. What a bizarre picture! The demons went with Satan, who wanted to be like God, and they were doomed as a result. They were never offered redemption after their rebellion. We have no idea how incredibly gracious God's offer of eternal life is to fallen man. He could have been through with us the moment we disobeyed and been totally fair in doing so. If you are a follower of Jesus, then fall down before him today, because of his authority, but also in worship. If you are in Christ, you are a friend of God. Unbelievable mercy!

july
TWENTY-SIX

L U K E   8 : 4 0 - 4 8

Jesus returned to Galilee and was met by a very eager crowd. One person in this particular crowd was a man named Jairus, a leader and possibly even the primary ruler of the local synagogue. His daughter was seriously ill and about to die. Jairus heard about what Jesus did and humbly fell before him in a posture of respect. He begged Jesus to come to his house and heal his only daughter before she left this life. Although Jairus was a respected community leader, he didn't let his social status keep him from honoring Jesus. Time was short though! The girl was near death (v. 42), and they needed to move quickly. A great crowd was pushing in on, even crushing Jesus. Suddenly, Jesus stopped and asked, "Who touched me?" Those with him must have thought he was losing his mind. *Who touched him? Umm...many people "touched" him.* But this "touch" was different. Power left him. The person he referred to was a woman who realized he was no ordinary human. She knew that if she could even touch him, or the hem of his garment, she could be healed. She had been sick for twelve years with a bleeding condition that made her unclean. When she touched him, she was healed immediately. But why was Jesus calling her out? Maybe he was angry because an unclean person touched him. Although she was scared, the woman had to confess. Jesus knew what happened, but he wanted to see the woman face to face.

After the woman made herself known, Jesus graciously addressed her as "Daughter" (v. 48). Jesus was probably younger than this woman, but he called her daughter to emphasize the close relationship with those who trust in him. He also told her she was made well because of her faith. Both her physical and spiritual healing were the direct result of her faith. What is faith? A good replacement word for "faith" would be "trust." Faith is trust in who God says he is, what God says about humanity, and what Jesus has done to reconcile us to the Father. Faith believes that God can and will do whatever he wants. If what he wants doesn't line up with what we want, we trust that his will is better in the end. Even though we don't know what will happen tomorrow, God does. We can trust him with the future.

july
TWENTY-SEVEN

LUKE 8:49-56

It appeared that Jesus' conversation with the woman he just healed (Luke 8:47) was a bad decision. While Jesus was chit-chatting with her, someone from Jairus's house let Jairus know it was too late. His daughter was dead. Jairus must have been crushed. Because Jesus "stopped everything" to wait for this woman to confess, the twelve-year-old girl died. If only Jesus had taken the crisis seriously and moved quickly, maybe he would have saved her young life. There was no point in Jesus coming now. Jesus overheard all this, and said, "Do not fear; only believe." So they made their way to Jairus's home. Despite the crowd, Jesus only asked Peter, James, John, and the girl's parents to come with him. The neighbors knew the girl had died, and they had gathered to mourn with her family. Jesus told them to stop weeping, because she was asleep. They mourners laughed at this. They had seen death many times. There was no hope for this girl. But Jesus took the girl's hand and told her to get up, as if he were waking her up from sleep. Immediately, she rose up and ate. Her parents were in awe, obviously.

Have you ever felt like Jairus must have felt that day, like Jesus either doesn't care or doesn't have the ability or desire to do anything about your crisis? At times, we can feel like God "dropped the ball" with respect to a tragedy that he allowed or didn't fix. What about those in the crowd who didn't go back to Jairus's house? They probably assumed that Jesus' choice to hang out with the woman who had been healed from bleeding was unwise. Sometimes Jesus allows us to see his power, and sometimes we don't get to see the big picture. Either way, we are called by Jesus to trust him. If he has removed the blinders from your eyes and allowed you to place your faith in him, turning from your sin, then you have been saved from real death. May we be encouraged by Jesus' ability to raise Jairus' daughter from the dead, but may we also be awed by Jesus' ability to keep us from the second death, the only death that really matters. Nothing in this created universe can thwart God's plan for his children. Rejoice in that truth, no matter what you face today.

july
TWENTY-EIGHT

LUKE 9:1-9

Jesus called together his core team of disciples, and he gave them power and authority over sickness and demons. "Power" means "the ability to do something," and "authority" has to do with the right to use that power. They were sent to preach the coming of God's kingdom and to heal the sick. Jesus told them to pack lightly for their journey and not to bring a staff, a bag, bread, money, or an extra shirt. Why shouldn't they bring these things? What would be wrong with packing a little cash for the road trip? Jesus wanted his disciples to depend upon others' generosity, as those they met would be prompted by God to help them out. They weren't to worry about their personal comfort. He was also building their trust in God. When they entered a city, they were to find a place to stay and remain in that home while they worked in that city. If no one took them in, they were called to "shake the dust off their feet." This was a symbolic action against the inhabitants there. The Jews would shake their feet off when they returned from traveling through Gentile territory. So shaking their feet in this case would proclaim that the unreceptive Jews were acting like Gentiles in rejecting the kingdom and the Messiah. Luke adds that even Herod the tetrarch (the one who beheaded John the Baptist) heard about Jesus and his apostles (v. 7). The message about the coming kingdom was going out to many places and up the social ladder.

As followers of Christ, we have the same commission. We have been given the Holy Spirit and the gospel. Jesus has charged all of his followers to bring his message to as many people as possible and make more disciples. As we do this, some will receive the message, but many, if not most, will not be interested. But Jesus takes the rejection of his followers personally. When he confronted the apostle Paul, who was called Saul, he asked, "Why do you persecute me?" Paul terrorized Christians, not Jesus directly, yet according to Jesus, Paul was persecuting Jesus nonetheless. As it would have been ridiculous for the apostles to be sent out by Jesus and not preach his message, it is just as silly for us as his followers not to communicate what he wants to say to others. Keep proclaiming the good news to as many as you can. It's your job.

july
TWENTY-NINE

LUKE 9:10-17

The apostles returned to Jesus and told him about all that their mission had accomplished. So Jesus took them to a town called Bethsaida, near the Sea of Galilee, to get some rest. When the word got out that Jesus was going there, the crowds followed. Jesus received them favorably, healing the sick and teaching about the kingdom. As the day went on and on, finally the disciples stepped in and said, "Listen, Jesus. You have to send these people away now. We are in a remote place. There's nothing here to eat, and we are all getting really hungry." But Jesus directed them, "You give them something to eat." What? How were they going to do that? The disciples didn't have enough food themselves to share with over five thousand men, not including women and children, and they couldn't just walk to the nearest town and carry back that much food. What was Jesus thinking? Was he exhausted and talking nonsense? Then Jesus told them to have the five thousand men sit in one hundred groups of fifty. Jesus took the five loaves and two fish the disciples had gathered between themselves, thanked God for the food, and then gave it to them to distribute. Everyone who was there ate and was satisfied, and strangely enough twelve baskets were left over, which was more food than they began with. This clearly was a supernatural event.

When Jesus told the disciples to give the people food, they only thought of two possible options: either share what they had or get to a nearby town and buy stuff. But they didn't think of asking Jesus to provide more food himself. The disciples were called to serve food, but Jesus was the source of the food. In what area has Jesus called you to serve others? Are you asking him to provide for those to whom you minister, or are you trying to provide yourself? When it comes to spiritual matters, Jesus is the only source that can satisfy hunger. Whether you are preaching the gospel, attending to the needs of children, washing dishes, folding laundry, or entering data into a computer, ask Jesus to meet the needs of those you love and serve. Jesus wanted his disciples to have a dependent attitude, and he desires the same for us. In whatever he has called you to do today, ask him to give abundantly through your energy and effort. And after he does, make sure he gets the glory.

july
THIRTY

LUKE 9:18-27

The disciples were alone with Jesus. They had traveled a great distance, met many people, healed the sick, cast out demons, and taught about God and his kingdom. What were the crowds saying about Jesus now? The disciples must have heard something, so Jesus asked them. Some said Jesus was John the Baptist. Since both Jesus and John preached repentance, these people believed that after Herod ordered John beheaded, John's spirit continued on in Jesus. Others said Jesus was Elijah. The prophet Malachi said Elijah would be sent before the Day of the Lord. And still others said he was a different prophet who had returned to speak to their generation. All three categories recognized that the message Jesus taught was from God, but they didn't grasp who he actually was. Jesus then asked the disciples, "Who do you say I am?" Peter answered with four simple but profound and powerful words: "The Christ of God." "The Christ" is the Greek way of saying "the Messiah" or "the Anointed One." Jesus was the expected and anticipated deliverer of Israel, the Promised One who was to come and save the people. But the disciples didn't realize how the ministry of the Messiah would play out. First, Jesus would suffer. Then, at a later time, his reign as King would commence. Jesus let the disciples know that just as he would be rejected and suffer, so too those who follow him then and now will be rejected and suffer (vv. 23-25).

Jesus let his disciples know that neither his path nor theirs would be easy. Following Jesus requires that we let go of the things of this world that keep us from obedience to Christ. Jesus called this self-denial, "taking up the cross daily," a willingness to "lose one's life," and an absence of shame in him. And yet, when we get to the end, all the rejection and suffering that accompanies following Jesus will be worth it. Though we will never be truly accepted by the world, Almighty God accepts us. If you are tired or disheartened today, take courage! Jesus will take his rightful place as King, and we will be with him. It has been rightfully said that if you are a Christian, you have royal blood in your veins.

july
THIRTY-ONE

LUKE 9:28-36

Jesus took Peter, James, and John with him to pray up on a mountain. As Jesus prayed, he physically changed. He grew radiant, and even the clothes he wore dazzled with light. Then suddenly, out of nowhere, Moses and Elijah showed up and talked to Jesus. The three of them discussed what the future held, as Moses and Elijah looked forward to all that Jesus would fulfill in Jerusalem. When Peter, James, and John listened to Jesus pray, they grew weary and fell asleep, yet when they realized Jesus had changed and was conversing with Moses and Elijah, they jolted wide awake. Can you imagine how Peter, James, and John must have felt? They had no idea what was happening or going to happen. When Moses and Elijah began to leave, Peter said, "Wait! Let's set up some tents so that you guys can stay longer." In other words, "Don't go yet!" While Peter was talking, a cloud came, and God spoke from it. God's focus wasn't on Elijah or Moses, but on Jesus, his Son. In Deuteronomy, God said he would raise up another prophet, and the people were to listen to him. Moses had set the standard, but now someone even greater than Moses was present. God told Peter, James, and John that they were to listen to the ultimate Prophet, Jesus.

Peter had just confessed that he and the other disciples believed Jesus was the Messiah. God added to their knowledge of Jesus' identity by revealing that Jesus was the ultimate Prophet, greater than any of the prophets who had gone before him, even Moses. Although some of the things Jesus taught were not what the disciples expected from their Messiah, Jesus was the Son of God and the One who ushered in the New Covenant. As we read through the Gospels, it can be hard for us to embrace all that Jesus taught. We are overwhelmed with gratitude when we consider what he went through to provide for our sin problem. We are awestruck when we ponder his amazing love for us. But it is still difficult to consider that he desires us to follow in his footsteps in willingness to do things God's way instead of our own. May we have a renewed passion to listen to Jesus today, and may we be determined to meditate on and put into practice all that he said and did.

august
ONE

LUKE 9:37-48

Luke records an argument that erupted among the disciples. Jesus had just boldly told them in verse 44, "Let these words sink into your ears: The Son of Man is about to be delivered into the hands of men." But they still didn't get it. And they broke out into an argument over which one of them was the greatest. Wow! What a contrast. Jesus told them about his coming death, and they focused on which amongst them was the best. In anticipation of what Jesus would do, they began fighting over who deserved what title and position in God's coming Kingdom. Jesus corrected their thinking by pulling a child over. In first century Judaism, a child wasn't taught the Scripture until age twelve, and it was considered a waste of time to hang out with kids. Jesus turned that thinking upside down and used the child to show them what greatness is. Jesus said, "Whoever receives this child in my name receives me, and whoever receives me receives him who sent me." In other words, if you receive even someone as "lowly" as this child, then you are actually receiving me and receiving God who sent me. Then Jesus added, "For he who is least among you all is the one who is great." Greatness results from a relationship with Jesus. Even the least of those who follow Jesus is great. All people count in God's eyes.

It can be hard for us to picture the disciples arguing with each other. Even though they had the incarnate God right there with them, they still thought about themselves and fought to get the recognition and titles they felt they deserved. But Jesus taught them that their greatness is actually a result of their relationship with him. We can feel like we aren't so great in the eyes of the world. And sometimes the choices we make to do things God's way lower us further in the sight of men. But if you are a follower of Jesus, God sees you as great. The disciples had a lot to learn about God and his kingdom, and we do too. No matter how others may perceive you today, know with confidence that because you are in Christ you are honored. May that truth motivate you to love, serve, and honor others, even those considered "lowly," in our midst.

august
TWO

LUKE 9:49-62

Jesus set his face toward Jerusalem. He was absolutely determined to do the will of God and accomplish what he was sent to do on earth. After he left Galilee, he traveled through Samaria, which was on the way. Now, the Jews didn't like the Samaritans. They considered them compromisers since they were only half Jewish, and so not full-blooded. The Samaritans believed the first five books of the Bible alone were authoritative, and they set up their own worship center on Mount Gerizim. Although the shortest route from Galilee to Judea and Jerusalem ran through Samaria, Jews would travel out of their way to avoid crossing this region. But not Jesus. He sent disciples ahead of him to prepare for his arrival at a Samaritan village. Jesus tried to reach out to these people, but they weren't interested in him. It wasn't only the Jewish people who rejected Jesus. All sorts of ethnic groups snubbed him. James and John were fed up. Attempting to follow in the footsteps of Elijah, they asked Jesus if they should call down fire from heaven and destroy the ungrateful Samaritans. Jesus responded with a rebuke. "No! God will judge when he is ready." He directed them simply to move on.

Even though the Samaritans' rejection of Jesus was wrong, it wasn't time for their judgment. James and John were called to preach the gospel to the Samaritans, but they weren't permitted to call down the fire of God. There will come a time when God does judge based on how each individual responded to Jesus, but until then God continues to offer grace. Just consider the ramifications if God's judgment had come earlier! What if he had wrapped things up ten or twenty years ago, or even thirty or forty? How many of us would have been excluded from his kingdom eternally as a result? Judgment hasn't arrived yet, but it will. God is not overlooking sin. God's kindness continues so that as many as possible will come to repentance. He desires people to turn to him. If you are a follower of Jesus today, thank him for his patience with humanity. Pray that like him, you would control your will in the face of frustration. May the patience you extend to those around you draw others to God, the author and source of all longsuffering.

august
THREE

LUKE 10:1-12

Jesus traveled toward Jerusalem to complete what God ordained for him. With the goal of getting the message of God's kingdom out to as many as possible, Jesus appointed more than the twelve to prepare people for his ministry. Time was short, and there was much to do, so he selected seventy-two individuals as his representatives. They were told to go without money, suitcases, or extra shoes, and to stay away from small talk on the road. The work of the seventy-two was urgent because time was short and their mission was dangerous. There was no room for messing around. They were called to depend on the hospitality of those they met. The seventy-two did the Lord's work, and the Lord provided for them. When they came across a town that welcomed them, they were to stay there. And when they came across a town that rejected them, it would be as if the town had rejected the Lord himself. The seventy-two were to tell all who would hear that the kingdom of God was near. The Messiah was around the corner. But the cities that rejected this message were in for big trouble. Judgment was coming, and even the most notoriously wicked cities of Sodom and Gomorrah will fare better than these in the judgment.

Jesus expanded the group of those he sent out from the twelve to seventy-two. And he charged the seventy-two to pray passionately that God would raise up even more workers, because the harvest was plentiful. Jesus never intended ministry to belong to a select few. Instead, all who follow him are called to his service. Just as the harvest was plentiful then, it is plentiful now. Masses of people today need to sit down with a cup of coffee or tea and listen to an intelligent argument for the existence of God, the sinfulness of man, and the need for reconciliation through Jesus Christ. When was the last time you did this kind of work? The seventy-two prayed earnestly for more workers in the ultimate harvest. Maybe they even prayed for you! Who lives near you or crosses paths with you and needs to hear the gospel? Why don't you ask her to lunch or coffee, or even just sit down together with a glass of cold water? Then let her know you are here to help her discover Jesus. Your friend's life may never be the same, and yours won't either!

august
FOUR

LUKE 10:13-24

The seventy-two returned from the mission Jesus sent them on, and they were thrilled. They let Jesus know that the demons were subject to them! The seventy-two were conduits of the authority Jesus exercised as they operated in his name. They made sure to acknowledge that their ability was a result of their relationship to Jesus. They had no innate power in themselves, but because they were sent out as representatives of Christ, the demons reacted to them the same way they reacted to Jesus. What an honor and a privilege for these seventy-two disciples! They were literally full of joy. Then Jesus explained to the disciples that the cause of their authority over the demons was Satan's defeat. If the demons were subject to the seventy-two, then Satan's time was limited. When Jesus said he watched Satan fall, he was referring back to when God cast Satan from heaven. Jesus added even more. He told the seventy-two that they had authority over the forces hostile to God, and because they were followers of Christ, they could and would overcome the enemy. Wow! The seventy-two must have been incredibly encouraged. Yet, Jesus taught them not to rejoice in that truth. *What? Don't rejoice in this? Why not?* From the disciples' perspective, this kind of authority and protection was certainly a cause for joy.

Jesus taught the disciples not to rejoice "that the spirits are subject to you, but rejoice that your names are written in heaven" (v. 20). The latter happiness surpassed their authority over evil and darkness. Their lasting joy came from their right standing with God. Their names were written in heaven. And no power of hell could erase those names from God's books! Double wow! Talk about real confidence! For those who are truly followers of Jesus, our position is secure before God. How amazing is that? The disciples rejoiced in their successes, but Jesus said their joy should come from their eternal relationship with him. Like the disciples, we can become so preoccupied with our spiritual successes that we forget that the root of our joy is in our reconciliation and peace with God. No matter how difficult, tough, or even overwhelming life's circumstances are for you today, if you are a Christian, you have the greatest reason in the universe to rejoice.

august
FIVE

LUKE 10:25-37

An expert in the Jewish law tried to test Jesus. He asked Jesus what he would have to do to share in the resurrection at the end of the age. In other words, how can one be sure he is saved? Jesus responded by asking the lawyer about what he had learned from studying God's revealed will for humanity. Think about that! The lawyer asked Jesus what he must do to be saved, and Jesus responded by asking the lawyer what the Scripture said he must do to be saved. The lawyer ended up answering his own question, even though it was originally intended to trick Jesus. The lawyer responded by citing Deuteronomy 6:5, "You must love God with all your heart, soul, strength, and mind." And as Leviticus 19:18 declares, love for God implies love for our fellow humans. Jesus said the lawyer answered correctly and then added, "Do this, and you will live." Well, that's easier said than done! Was Jesus saying works can save us? Not at all! Who can say she has perfectly loved God and loved others? Clearly no one, not even the lawyer, has lived consistently with God's law. Sensing this, the lawyer hoped to tone God's demand down a notch, and so tried to justify himself by asking who his neighbor was. Jesus showed him through the Parable of the Good Samaritan that all people should be considered neighbors.

It's amazing how Jesus turned the tables on the lawyer in this conversation. The lawyer was looking for the bottom line. What was the minimum he could do and still be sure of his salvation? Jesus showed him the minimum requirement was nothing less than total and complete devotion to God and the rest of mankind. No one can do this without fail. We have all sinned and we all need Jesus to stand in the gap between God and us. And yet, if we are Christians, we can ask the Spirit of God to help us live more closely to his design for our lives. The world pushes us to "find ourselves" and take care of our own needs, yet Jesus calls us to prioritize God and our fellow humans. If Jesus loves us, let's be satisfied in his love and respond by devoting ourselves to him and to those around us. Seek to lose yourself by loving God and meeting the needs of others.

august
SIX

LUKE 10:38-42

Jesus and his disciples continued their journey toward Jerusalem. On their way, they stopped off in Bethany and dropped into the home of Jesus' close friends, Martha and Mary. Martha did exactly what was proper when a home received guests. She worked hard to honor Jesus and his friends by serving what was probably an extravagant meal. As Martha labored in the kitchen, she was pulled by all that needed her attention. What should have been a blessing became a burden, and she ended up troubled. Martha needed a major attitude adjustment. As Martha stewed in the kitchen, she noticed her sister, Mary, just sitting at the feet of Jesus, learning from him as if she were a disciple. What was Mary thinking? Clearly, she should have been helping Martha in the kitchen where she belonged. Martha couldn't take it anymore. She burst in on Jesus and the others who were learning from him, asking Jesus if he even cared about the fact that her sister was trying to get out of her share of the work. Martha "rebuked" Jesus, and let him know he needed to tell Mary to get up and get to work. Jesus kindly warned Martha that her anxiety was sinful, and in fact, her sister Mary had made the better choice. Mary didn't need to go anywhere.

We can miss how countercultural this scene was. In the first century, women were not treated the same as men. One leading rabbi of the first century said it would be better to burn the Torah (the first five books of the Bible) than to teach it to a woman. Wow! Martha really believed Mary was in the wrong, but Jesus absolutely endorsed Mary's decision. What a testimony to God's love for all people, Jew or Greek, slave or free, male or female. He calls all to know him and "sit at his feet." Mary never said a word in own her defense, but Jesus vindicated her. Both men and women are important to Jesus, and both men and women are called to learn and even devour his word. If you aren't in a Bible study that meets at your church, sign up for one today! And if you are, good work! You won't regret the extra time spent listening to Jesus as you pour over his word, and what you learn will never be taken from you.

august
SEVEN

LUKE 11:1-13

When Jesus finished praying, one of his disciples asked if he would teach them to pray too. In verses 2 through 4, Jesus responded by providing a template for prayer that they could all follow. Jesus never intended this prayer to be recited word for word as a substitute for genuine connection with God. Rather, he provided themes for organizing his disciples' thoughts directed toward God. The prayer begins with an address to God the Father. The word "Father" implies both authority and intimacy. What an honor to know that the follower of Jesus can address God as her Father in prayer. The prayer has five basic components after the address:

1. "Hallowed be your name" requests that God and his name be treated as holy.
2. "Your kingdom come" asks that righteousness be manifest on earth.
(These first two petitions establish an attitude of worship and admiration.)
3. "Give us each day our daily bread" asks for God's provision of life's basic needs.
4. "Forgive us our sins as we forgive others" reminds us of our need for reconciliation with God with the implication that we will surely reconcile with those who have wronged us as a result.
5. "Lead us not into temptation" asks that God help the believer to live in alignment with God's character.
(These last three petitions demonstrate an attitude of total reliance upon our Father.)

What a wonderful resource this template for prayer is for all followers of Jesus! We can feel like God is too important or too busy to listen to our requests and petitions, but when Jesus taught the disciples to address God as their Father, he reminded them of the familial love that exists between God and his children. He taught us to be concerned with our Father's reputation and accomplishing his will, along with our need for provision, forgiveness, and protection. Most of us know this prayer as the "Lord's Prayer," but it should be called the "Disciples' Prayer" because Jesus, the sinless one, had no need to ask for forgiveness. May we all be challenged to pray more. And when we pray, let's communicate with the Lord in a way that is balanced, not merely focusing on daily needs, but with an attitude of reverence and respect. May our prayer time always include the confession that we are wholly dependent upon the Lord for everything pertaining to life and godliness. Make sure you set aside some time to talk to God today.

august EIGHT

LUKE 11:14-23

Jesus exorcised a demon from a man who couldn't speak. This man's inability to talk was a result of evil activity. The demon left the man, the man spoke, and the people marveled. Simple enough, right? The word translated as "marvel" is a Greek word that literally means "to be extraordinarily impressed or disturbed by something." These people knew there was something undoubtedly legitimate about Jesus and what he did. So what happened? Did they fall down in repentance and faith? Nope. Although the crowd was amazed by Jesus' actions, they still didn't believe. Some said he cast out the demon by the power of hell, and others tried to test him. They wanted more signs. Jesus knew exactly what they thought. He responded by explaining that Satan would not work against himself. That would be counterproductive. The crowd was just pushing for a reason not to believe.

Clearly, the supernatural was involved in Jesus' work, so some attributed it to Satan. If they said it was the Lord, then they would have to line up under his authority. They didn't want that. Others said, "That's fine, but we want even more signs." What kind of signs? What would be enough? People around us often respond the same way. Many agree that there's something unique about Jesus, but they don't want to concede that he is the only way to the Father. Others will say, "sure, I can go along with that if…" and they require even more proof. How much proof? If someone you know is demanding more, ask this simple question: "If I were to answer all the questions you have about Christianity in an intelligent and logical way, would you become a follower of Jesus?" Many times the answer will be "No." Just like Jesus' first century audience, our problem with God is usually a problem of our will. No one wants to come under the authority of God. But when the Lord removes the blinders, we not only want to believe, but we also desire to do things God's way. If you are a believer today, thank Jesus for changing your desires. And keep praying that God would create a willingness to follow Jesus in those around you as well.

august
NINE

LUKE 11:24-32

In verses 24 through 26, Jesus explains the need to respond rightly to the work God accomplished through him. Jesus had been teaching, healing, and delivering from demons as he traveled with his disciples. So he commented on exorcism in general. Jesus described an unclean spirit that was forced to leave a person. Perhaps he referred to the man he had just delivered from the presence of darkness. Whether it was that man or another, the person became an object lesson to all who were listening. One may be delivered from the power of darkness, but after the evil has departed, she still must respond rightly to Jesus. If a person doesn't respond to Jesus in repentance and faith and receive the indwelling presence of the Holy Spirit, when the demon comes back looking for a place to "live," nothing will prevent that same demon from returning. If the demon were to return, the potential damage could be worse than the original problem. If the one who was delivered continues to live in an "empty house," devoid of God's Spirit, more spirits may take up residence in her, and it would end up harder to deliver her from darkness than if she had never started the whole process.

Jesus used this thought-provoking illustration to show what it could be like for one who experiences an act of God but does nothing about it. We can't just remain neutral about Jesus. We must do something as a result of what he has demonstrated about himself to us. If you have called out to God and cried, "God, please save me, or help me, or get me out of this" and he has, you have got to make up your mind about him. If you have been rescued from Satan's grip, you must make a decision. If you try to stay "on the fence" about following Jesus, you will end up worse off than before you began. Your conscience may become hardened, and you might lose sensitivity to the Spirit, until one day you aren't even able to repent. Don't play games with God. If he has revealed himself to you, turn to Jesus in honest and humble faith. If you have experienced the grace of the Lord, you should be following him today as a result.

august
TEN

LUKE 11:33-36

Jesus had just taught the growing crowd around him that their continual need for another sign was evil. He reminded them that they had received the same message Jonah brought to the ungodly people of Ninevah, which was the call to repent. And the Ninevites obeyed! The record of those in the Old Testament who positively responded to God's messengers was a sign against this crowd's continued unbelief. Then Jesus added that no one lights a lamp and puts it in a place where the light cannot be seen. Light symbolizes illumination and guidance. The psalmist refers to God's word as "a lamp to his feet" and "a light to his path." In this section of Luke, Jesus repeatedly taught the crowd that they needed not only to hear but also respond to his teaching. The teaching and preaching of Jesus created the light to which he referred. It was not hidden. On the contrary, his work was done in the open, and his message proclaimed in public. If one failed to respond properly, it certainly wasn't because he had no access to the light. And if an individual's eye were healthy, he would take the light in and process it rightly. If the eye were bad or marred by evil, he would not respond rightly to the light. It's interesting that Jesus didn't suggest we have any "inner light." Instead, he is the ultimate source of light for the world.

Jesus warned those around him to "be careful lest the light in you be darkness." They were to confirm that they were taking in the light of truth and not the darkness of false teaching, so that they would be spiritually healthy. Jesus concluded by saying that if one has responded properly to the light and is spiritually healthy, she becomes a reflection of his light for others. The disciple is not the source of light, but she allows the light of Christ to work through her. When we respond rightly to the light of Jesus' teaching, it demonstrates that our spiritual eyes are healthy, and we have his revelation to help us make day-to-day decisions in life. At the same time, we can be light to others and help them also to respond rightly to the true light of God's word. Let's determine today to obey the teaching of Jesus and reject any messages that contradict what he has revealed in his word.

august
ELEVEN

LUKE 11:37-54

Jesus accepted an invitation to dine with one of the Pharisees. Others were also present at the meal. The Pharisee was shocked when he saw that Jesus didn't wash before the meal, since washing was a sign of purity to the religious community. But Jesus rebuked the Pharisees for making such a fuss about the outside of things while tolerating ugly or unclean attitudes in their hearts. He then pronounced "woes" upon them. The first was for focusing on minor issues while ignoring the call to practice justice and love. The second was for desiring attention in their pride, and the third was for contaminating those who followed their false teaching. Then one of the lawyers present told Jesus he had insulted the law professionals. So Jesus pronounced three more woes upon the experts in the law or the scribes. First, he said they placed enormous burdens on others, yet gave them no help in carrying those loads. Like the Pharisees, they too were hypocrites. Next, they rejected God's messengers, the prophets, and finally, as they weren't following the path of true knowledge, they were keeping others from finding it as well. Clearly, the Pharisees and scribes were not happy with that lunch conversation. After this, they began to go all-out in their attempt to entrap him into saying something wrong. They couldn't wait for him to mess up.

Jesus came down hard on the religious leaders for their hypocrisy. Without repentance, they were destined for judgment. Sadly, they didn't listen to the tough but loving words of Jesus. Instead, they grew even more calloused and hardened against him and his teaching. As verse 40 records, Jesus illustrated the foolishness of the two-faced lives they were leading. He asked rhetorically, "Did not he who made the outside make the inside also?" In other words, we may feel like we can divide our lives into inner and outer or private and public, but this is insulting to the character of God, who sees both. If you are a follower of Jesus today, check your heart. Are you living one way before man and another way when no one is watching? If so, ask God to make you as sincere as possible. Though others may focus on our outward behavior, God looks at our hearts. Ask the Holy Spirit to cleanse you today from the inside out.

august TWELVE

LUKE 12:1-12

The multitude around Jesus continued to grow. Thousands came to hear him. The crowd actually grew so large that people climbed over one another to listen to him teach. But this didn't change Jesus. He continued to do what he was called to do, knowing that soon his "popularity" would end. He spoke to his disciples and exhorted them to guard against hypocrisy. Then Jesus let his followers know that in time all would be revealed before God. The Lord sees everything that is done, whether out in the open or hidden in secret. He knows not only what we do, but why we do it. And at the judgment, people will have to account for both. Then Jesus added the statement, "Whatever you have said in the dark shall be heard in the light, and what you have whispered in private rooms shall be proclaimed on the housetops." Jesus explained the foolishness of hypocrisy. Why live a double life? The day is coming when even the most private or secret conversations will be brought out into the open. This is good news for the one who has lived a life of integrity, but for the one who has lived hypocritically, more concerned about how he appears before his fellow-man than before God, this will not be a happy experience.

Jesus followed this by warning the disciples again not to live before man or to fear man, but instead to fear God. How foolish we must appear before heaven when we chase after the approval and respect of man, who has no real authority compared to God. We often dismiss what we know we should do before the Lord, because we want the people around us to think well of us. And besides all this, Jesus added even another reason to live without hypocrisy. God cares very much for his children. Sparrows were the cheapest item in the marketplace at this time, yet not one sparrow is beneath God's attention (v. 6). If God cares about sparrows, you have nothing to worry about. As his adopted child, you are well taken care of. Don't be afraid, but instead live before God and not man. Whose approval are we looking for? Is it the approval of man or the approval of the Lord? God will work everything out in the end. Fearlessly do things God's way today.

august
THIRTEEN

LUKE 12:13-21

An unknown man approached Jesus and asked him for help in settling a family dispute about an inheritance. Instead of getting involved, Jesus warned the man about the danger of greed, the insatiable desire to have more. He told the man to watch out for covetousness because life was never meant to be about possessions. Then he gave the crowd a parable to illustrate the concept. The parable describes an extremely wealthy man whose crops were particularly productive for an entire year. His peers would have seen him as quite blessed. Because of his great financial success, the man realized he didn't even have enough rooms to store all of his crops. So, acting in a way our society would consider wise, he constructed new and bigger buildings to store his grain and all his stuff. He was set for life. He planned to retire and enjoy all his things. As verse 19 says, he planned to "relax, eat, drink, be merry." There was one glaring problem though. The man had made everything about himself. He never even thought about using his great wealth to be generous toward God and others. God wasn't impressed with his decision. Instead, the Lord called him a fool.

Just when he was preparing to kick back and enjoy the good life, God said the man's time was up. In his pursuit of financial freedom, the man made everything about himself and didn't invest into others. In the parable, we see his self-focus as he emphasizes, "*My* crops, *my* barns, *my* grain and *my* goods." Jesus never condemned having money. There is nothing inherently evil about it. The problem emerges when we become selfish with the resources God has graced us with and forget that in the end it all belongs to the Lord. We may be surprised when we carefully consider how many of the disputes, conflicts, battles, and even wars in this world are driven by a desire for money. Though money can provide us with stuff in this life, it will be of no benefit to us in the life to come unless we manage it in a way that honors God. How generous are you? Are you using some of the wealth God has given you to invest into your church, advance the gospel, and help others? Remember, we wouldn't even be saved if God hadn't "given" us his only Son. Open your hands, your heart, and your wallet, and be generous today.

august
FOURTEEN

LUKE 12:22-34

Jesus had just explained to the crowd around him the folly, even sin, of putting their confidence in their possessions. He continued his sermon by teaching the disciples where they should put their trust as he described how to respond to anxiety. He began by explaining to them that they shouldn't be anxious about food or clothing because these aren't the ends of life. Just as God takes care of the birds, he will take care of us. Of course, this doesn't mean that we stop working. The birds continue to work for food, but they don't worry that it won't be there. Jesus added that worry is useless and helps nothing. He reminded them of how God beautifully clothes the flowers. He is in control of even the grass! He will take care of us too. In verse 29, Jesus tells his followers not to worry about food or clothing for a second time. The word for "worried" in verse 29 is an interesting one in the Greek. It isn't used anywhere else in the New Testament. It literally means "to hover between hope and fear." The word pictures the woman who goes from one extreme to the other. We need to stop. Let's not act like those who don't have a God in the heavens watching out for them. That's what Jesus said (v. 30). Instead, we are to keep seeking God's kingdom. He will bring us the security and freedom from anxiety that we long for.

Jesus ended by teaching the disciples how they could gain riches and treasure that would never go away. When we use our resources to benefit others, we are storing up eternal wealth. He closed with a statement defining priorities. Jesus said, "Where your treasure is, there will your heart be also." Who we are and what we think is reflected by what we do with our time, our money, and the extent to which we "stress out" about things. As followers of Jesus, we are to battle against our tendency to worry, because worry reveals a distrust in God's ability to provide and care for us. Anxiety reflects a self-focus, while generosity reflects a focus on God and others. If you are battling spiritual anxiety today, stop and ask God to help you trust him more than ever before, even in the midst of circumstances that may be telling you the opposite.

august
FIFTEEN

LUKE 12:35-48

Jesus went on to teach the disciples always to be prepared. Staying "dressed for action" meant tucking their long robes up so they would be ready to go at any time. Keeping the "lamps burning" meant they were set for whatever they were called to do, even at a moment's notice. Jesus said they were to be like men who waited up all hours of the night for their master to return from a wedding party, which could have lasted for days. Those who follow Jesus are to live expecting his return. Peter asked, "Wait, are you saying this to *us*?" Jesus answered him with another parable about a faithful and wise manager. A manager or a steward was a particular slave left in charge of his master's house. He was responsible to take care of the other slaves, including the distribution of food. The manager who does his job well will be blessed and given even more opportunity for service. But the servant who takes advantage of the responsibility entrusted to him, living the "good life" by eating and drinking to excess, will be strictly judged. The servant rejected by Jesus could represent someone like Judas or the religious leaders of the day. The servant who knows what to do but is lazy will be severely disciplined, but apparently not rejected. And the servant who is truly ignorant of what he was supposed to do will be punished, but less harshly.

The bottom line is that all of Jesus' followers are given a responsibility to serve him. Jesus' second parable includes four types of servants. Three are disobedient and only one does well. Regarding the three who were unfaithful, their punishments mirrored their varying degrees of disobedience. The one who did well was entrusted with more authority. As we face choices every day, our desires can fluctuate between wanting to do things God's way and wanting to yield to our own sinful desires. But disobedience comes at a high price. Are you serving Jesus by investing in your home church and putting the needs of others above your own? If not, today is the day to get this right. We all want Jesus to see us as the faithful stewards. The great news is that if he finds us doing as he asked, we will be rewarded in a way that is beyond our imagination.

august
SIXTEEN

LUKE 12:49-53

Jesus spoke to his disciples about what his mission and ministry would bring. He used the word "fire" to highlight the division that will result when his judgment comes. Reconciliation with God often results in divided relationships. He longed to complete the redemptive work God ordained for him to do. Then Jesus made a statement that may seem odd to some. He declared that he did not come to bring peace on earth, but rather division. What? We may think, *Well, that's not the Jesus I know.* But it is the Jesus of the Bible! He then illustrates what this division might look like. Maybe a father and son relationship will be strained. Perhaps a mother and daughter could end up responding differently to Jesus. He even brought the in-laws into the picture. The point is that the gospel can divide people, all the way down to what we would consider the most intimate relationships. Jesus says "mother against daughter" and "daughter against mother" to show that hostility will run both ways. Jesus' teaching was intense. He taught about judgment and God's anger toward sin. He taught about the need to give up our lives to gain his. And he instructed his disciples to follow him at all costs. These compulsory and powerful responses to his word are sure to create tension and drama in our relationships.

We don't like to think about this, but Jesus taught that problems would and will result for his disciples. He even went so far as to say that the gospel creates division rather than peace. Why would division result? Because some would embrace his message and others would reject it. Even those who live under the same roof may end up on opposite sides of the spectrum about who Jesus was. But the honest disciple will be willing to endure the rifts that come from living according to God's law and principle. Have you experienced trouble in relationships as a result of your alliance with Jesus? If so, be encouraged. This is exactly what Jesus said would happen. But never forget that the Christian is called to communicate the challenging truths of the gospel with gentleness and respect. When others are offended, make sure they are dividing with you over the truth, not over the way you communicated it. Pray that God would keep those who are hostile to him from stumbling over you, the messenger, even when they stumble over his message.

august
SEVENTEEN

LUKE 12:54-59

Jesus admonished the crowd for failing to interpret the spiritual signs around them. They could determine when it was going to rain by looking at the clouds. When they felt a warm desert wind coming from the south, they knew the heat was coming. They were great at discerning the physical signs, but clueless when it came to the things of God. How foolish they were! The Christ was right there in their midst, yet they couldn't see him. Jesus was so upset that he called them "hypocrites." Then he called the people in the crowd to judge for themselves. The spiritual signs were in front of them. What would they do? Would they concede that Jesus was the key to the kingdom of God? Jesus warned them about making the wrong judgment with a scenario from a court of law. If a woman knew she would be found guilty before the judge, she would be wise to try to "settle out of court" before she was forced to go to jail.

In the ancient world, one who owed a debt was at the mercy of her debtor. When payment was delayed, the debtor would take the borrower to court and hand her over to the legal system. In Jesus' parable, the debtor summoned the borrower to court. The borrower had a short window of time to make things right before she would stand in front of the judge and it would be too late. She would be thrown into prison until she paid the last penny. The word for "last penny" is the Greek word *lepton*, a smallest value coin, worth about an eighth of a cent. Once in prison, the debtor wasn't getting out of anything. Eventually, every person who has lived on this planet will have to stand before God. If we end up in the court Jesus referred to, we will be found guilty. But we can settle accounts with God today! We can turn to Jesus in repentance and faith. If you have put off your need to get things right with God, don't wait any longer. You never know when you will be called to face the Judge. If you have already responded rightly to Jesus' offer of "debt forgiveness," then fully enjoy this day with the sense of rest that can only come from knowing that you have been freed from the penalty of your sin. What a great cause for rejoicing!

august
EIGHTEEN

LUKE 13:1-9

Some who were present while Jesus taught asked him about a recent event when Galileans were murdered as they prepared to offer their sacrifices. Apparently, these Galileans were approaching the temple and getting ready to make their offerings to the Lord when Pilate attacked them, and they died. Their blood was mingled with the blood of their sacrifices. Those who asked may have wondered what Jesus thought about the incident or even questioned what he planned to do about it. Instead of giving a social and political message, Jesus used their interest in the event to turn their thoughts to God and their own relationships with him. Jesus responded to their question with another question. He asked them if they thought this happened to the Galileans because they deserved it. Maybe those present thought God was getting even with those Galileans for some hidden sin, which was a common belief in the time of Jesus. Before they could answer, Jesus responded by clarifying that the Galileans were not "worse sinners" than other Galileans. Jesus then explained that their untimely deaths should have reminded the audience that not only the Galileans but any of them could die at any time. Jesus asked those present about their own personal status before God. Had they repented? The response to Jesus that keeps anyone from the second death must include repentance and faith.

Jesus mentioned another example that they didn't bring up. He asked about the eighteen who died when a tower collapsed at Siloam. Were they "worse sinners"? Again, they were not. But those eighteen should have been a continual reminder to all of the certainty of death. No one needs to worry about death if she has repented. Only those who have not placed their trust in Christ should be concerned about eternal death. Those present with Jesus needed to turn to him while there was still time. And the same is true for us. We all must repent and put our trust in Jesus. If we leave this planet without getting right with Jesus, nothing is left for us but eternal rejection. Stop and pray that God would use local, national, and even world tragedies to open the eyes of those around you to their need for repentance. May God redeem the many awful things that take place on our planet and use them to lead others to reconciliation with him.

august
NINETEEN

LUKE 13:10-21

Jesus taught in the synagogue on the Sabbath again. This is actually the last time Luke records him teaching in the synagogue. Jesus saw a woman who was bent over and couldn't stand up straight. He called her to himself and healed her so that she could stand upright. She immediately began to praise God for her healing. This woman became a picture of the Jewish nation. Its people were spiritually bent and couldn't stand up straight, but sadly, they didn't see their need to be straightened up and healed. Instead of giving glory to God along with the woman, the ruler of the synagogue was furious. He asked why Jesus chose to heal on the Sabbath, reminding him he could have healed on any of the six other days. Why did he have to do it on that day? Jesus responded to the attack by showing the ruler what a hypocrite he was. The ruler, along with the other Jewish leaders, had no problem helping their animals on the Sabbath. They would untie oxen or donkeys and lead them to food and then to water without breaking the Sabbath. Was not this woman more important than an animal? How frustrated Jesus must have been as they showed compassion to animals but not to humans. The strange thing is that many still today give more care and attention to animals than they do to people.

Jesus continued to provide evidence to the Jewish people around him. In verse 17, we see his adversaries put to shame by his logic and reasoning, along with his supernatural power. But not all rejected him. Some around him rejoiced at what God was doing. Jesus polarized people into two distinct groups. One side rejected him and his call to repentance, and the other side followed him and gave glory to God for what he did. It's the same today. There are really only two responses available when it comes to making a decision about Jesus: rejection or repentance. When we choose to repent and follow the Lord, he makes us straight too. We will be able to stand spiritually free from the influences that cripple and bow us. If you are a follower of Jesus today, ask him to free you from whatever is keeping you bent low. He is able to deliver us. And when he does, don't forget to praise and glorify God for all he has done.

august
TWENTY

LUKE 13:22-30

A person traveling with Jesus was surprised that the nation didn't embrace Jesus' ministry. This person asked, "Lord, will those who are saved be few?" So Jesus told the story about a man who gave a feast. When the party arrival time had passed, the man got up and shut the door. No one else could enter. If the guests weren't in, they were permanently out. Those who came late tried to persuade the master of the house to open the door for them. They reminded him that they had eaten and drunk in his presence while he taught in the streets. Jesus referred here to the Jews who didn't respond to his teaching. Soon it would be too late. Despite their pleas, the master of the house told them to go. They were workers of evil and refused to obey prior to the door shutting. Jesus added that there would be weeping and gnashing of teeth, or intense emotional and physical grief, resulting from of the anger of those who were shut out. But the faithful men of the past, such as Abraham, Isaac, Jacob, and the prophets, would be in the kingdom. The religious leaders would have been furious. They assumed that because they were children of Israel, God accepted them.

Then Jesus really shook things up. He added that there would be people from east, west, north, and south in God's kingdom. *What?* The unbelieving Jews would have burned with anger. These four corners symbolized people from all ethnic groups. Jesus said the Gentiles would be accepted, but not these Jews. The Jews at that time believed Gentiles were inferior. Jesus let them know that although they considered themselves the first, they would be the very last, while the Gentiles, those they considered last, would end up first. What a blessing to know that God has opened the door to people from all ethnic groups. It doesn't matter if you are a Jew or Gentile, rich or poor, man or woman. As long as the door is still open, you can enter God's kingdom. If you are a follower of Jesus today, rejoice that you got in before the door shut! Ask the Lord for another opportunity to share truth with that friend or family member who hasn't yet surrendered to Christ. As long as the door remains open, there's still hope! God can save anyone!

august
TWENTY-ONE

LUKE 13:31-35

While Jesus warned those around him about being shut out of the kingdom, some Pharisees approached him. They let Jesus know that Herod wished to kill him. This Herod was Herod Antipas. The Herod family ruled Palestine in the first century. This Herod didn't want any problems, and apparently he thought Jesus posed a threat to the peace of his domain. Jesus' message back to Herod was that he would continue his ministry and mission. The goal of Jesus was Jerusalem. He came to finish what God sent him to do. Jesus had his course mapped out, and he was right on track. He had nothing to fear from Herod, as he already knew he would meet death in Jerusalem. Jesus then lamented, "Jerusalem, Jerusalem," using a double address to show compassion and care. He spoke to the nation as her prophet, even calling himself a prophet. Jesus said he longed to gather the nation together as a hen gathers her chicks under the protection of her wings. What a beautiful picture of the love and compassion God feels toward his people.

The people of Israel would not see Jesus until the time when they would say he was the blessed one who came in the name of the Lord. The crowd would quote this phrase in the near future when Jesus entered Jerusalem, and one day, when Jesus comes back to Jerusalem, "Blessed is he who comes in the name of the Lord!" will be boldly proclaimed yet again. But for now, instead of being gathered under the wings of the Lord, the city of Jerusalem would be like an empty house. It is encouraging to see how Jesus wasn't afraid of Herod. He knew that God had marked a day and time that he would die, and that point had not arrived yet. For each of us, God has determined the exact hour and moment we will leave this planet. One preacher of the past, Charles Spurgeon, wisely said, "I am immortal till my work is done. Till the Lord wills it, no vault can close upon me." If you are anxious or troubled today, be encouraged by this truth. God knows exactly when your time will be up. Until then, press on for Jesus! No one can get in the way of God's plan for your life and ministry.

august
TWENTY-TWO

LUKE 14:1-11

Jesus ate dinner in the home of a ruler of the Pharisees on the Sabbath. Present at the meal was a man who had dropsy, a disease which would have caused his body to swell. Those with dropsy were traditionally seen as unclean. The Pharisees closely watched Jesus, probably staging everything to "catch" Jesus doing good deeds on the Sabbath. But Jesus chose to heal the man, and before the accusations began to fly, Jesus simply asked them if their own children or oxen fell into a well, would they leave the children or animals there because it was the Sabbath? The critics could say nothing. The tables turned, and instead of Jesus being watched by them, he observed those present. He noticed how they ran for the best spots at the table. At that time, the tables were U-shaped, and the host would sit at the bottom of the U. The seats to the right and the left of the host were considered the most honored. Jesus instructed them not to rush to the honored spots. How awkward if someone more honored showed up later, and the host told those seated to get up and sit somewhere else! By that time, they would be stuck with the worst seats in the house. Instead, they should begin by taking the worst seats. Most likely, the host would spot this and suggest they move up. They would be honored in the presence of all the guests and not shamed by needing to move down.

Though the parable can seem strange, the point is clear: it is wise to be humble. It is better for another to recognize your worth than to assume your own worth and be embarrassed when others don't agree with your self-estimation. Jesus ended by saying, "For everyone who exalts himself will be humbled, and he who humbles himself will be exalted." This is also true in our relationship with God. We are to come before him in humility, recognizing that even the least honorable spots are more than we deserve. Jesus humbly entered, humbly lived in, and humbly left our world. He asks us to follow in his footsteps. One day, Jesus will publicly get the seat of honor, and he will bring his followers to the table with him. Choose to humble yourself before God today, giving attention to him and to others.

august
TWENTY-THREE

LUKE 14:12-24

Jesus continued teaching those in the Pharisee ruler's home. He instructed his host about the next time he invited others to a meal. Jesus said it would please God if he were to invite those less fortunate than he, people with no means to pay him back. The poor, the crippled, the lame, and the blind were often excluded from society and normal community functions. If invited, they had no way to return the favor. Such a host would be rewarded for generosity and kindness. When we extend generosity to the less fortunate among us, not merely focusing on our own friends and relatives, God sees and will bless us in return. One of the guests at the dinner pronounced a blessing, assuming everyone there would enter into the kingdom of God. Jesus used a parable to show the guests that many present would in fact not take part in God's kingdom. The host in his parable invites specific people to his banquet. But as the arrival time approaches, one by one, they begin giving apparently valid excuses for why they just weren't going to be able to make it. They had other, more important things to do. But the host has a banquet ready, and his agenda isn't going to be thwarted because of their disregard. So the host invites the less fortunate to attend. And when still more room remains, he invites foreigners or Gentiles to come.

Jesus challenged the religious leaders' belief that they were secure before God because of who they were and the apparent blessings of God on their lives. They made the choice not to follow him, and the result would be eternal. Have you ever planned a party, and at the last minute those who promised to come said they just couldn't make it? Maybe you went to great lengths to make things nice for them, and it upset you when they bailed out. When it comes to God's program, those who don't show up to follow Jesus will regret that choice for eternity. What on earth could possibly be worth exclusion from the kingdom of God? At the same time, Jesus also revealed again that many included in the kingdom of God were considered less fortunate in life or from outside the Jewish nation. Why not invite someone to your church today? You never know who will repent and follow Jesus.

august
TWENTY-FOUR

LUKE 14:25-35

Great crowds followed Jesus. He knew that some didn't understand what it really meant to follow him, so he gave a strong exhortation about what a real disciple looks like. During Jesus' lifetime, the word "Christian" didn't exist. In fact, the term wasn't coined until years later to describe a group of believers that met in Antioch. The most common words for followers of Jesus were "brothers," "disciples," or "believers." So Jesus stopped the crowd and explained anyone who doesn't hate his closest relatives or even his very own life cannot be his disciple. What did he mean? Does he want us to hate others and even our own life? No! He was expressing to the crowd that their relationship with him had to be top priority. So much so, that the other relationships in life might feel like hate at times in comparison. Then Jesus said the Christian or the disciple must be willing to pick up her cross and follow after him. Under Roman rule, when a convicted criminal carried his cross, it was supposed to be a sign of admission to the charges against him. Jesus' followers had to be ready to admit he was right and express their willingness to follow him, even if the path led to suffering or to death. Jesus illustrated these principles with two examples explaining the potential disciples' need to consider the cost associated with their choice to follow him.

Jesus closed by saying, "Any one of you who does not renounce all that he has cannot be my disciple." Wow! That was quite a charge. But that is what Jesus said. Jesus must be the disciple's first love and first priority, even if hardship and suffering should result. In the first century when Jesus spoke these words, a commitment to him could result in rejection from one's own family or even one's entire community. Although it's tough to stand up for Jesus today, it's still far more acceptable than it was when he gave this command. For thousands of years, believers have embraced all sorts of hardships to stay loyal to Christ. Jesus said no one should make the decision to follow him lightly. Either we are all in or all out. If you are compromising your allegiance to Jesus in any area of your life, put an end to it today. If his first followers could do it, then so can we—with his help!

august
TWENTY-FIVE

LUKE 15:1-10

The Jewish religious leaders were not happy with Jesus because he ate with those considered morally worthless. The irony was that these "worthless" people drew near to Jesus instead of the nation's religious élite. In the first century, eating together was a symbol of fellowship and acceptance. Jesus' association with sinners was intolerable in the eyes of the Pharisees and scribes. In response to their grumbling, Jesus told them three parables to illustrate the same truth: God came to save sinners, and his followers should be thrilled when those who are lost come to repentance. The first parable Jesus gave was the Parable of the Lost Sheep. The parable centers on a modest shepherd with a flock of one hundred sheep. When the shepherd counts his flock one evening, he discovers that one sheep is missing. He immediately leaves the ninety-nine who are safe, and goes out after the lost one. When the shepherd finds the straggler, he carefully picks it up, puts it on his shoulders, and carries it back safely. He later goes on to call his friends and neighbors to celebrate with him. Who knew what could have happened to that lost sheep?! But it didn't matter anymore. The sheep was found, and it was a time for celebration.

In the second parable, the Parable of the Lost Coin, Jesus spoke about a woman who loses one of her ten coins. She sweeps and searches, and when she finds that lost coin she too rejoices, even calling her girlfriends and the neighborhood women to celebrate with her. Again, joy came when something lost was found. In both parables, the friends and the neighbors rejoice in the discovery of the sheep or the coin. And both times, Jesus stressed that there is great joy in the unseen realm when a sinner repents. Wow! If you want to be the trigger for a party in heaven, then go out and look for sinners to lead to Jesus. Pray for those who are working hard to bring the gospel the lost, and do whatever you can to team up with fellow believers who, by God's Spirit, are leading others to genuine faith. In doing so, you will bring great gladness to heaven, to the angels, and to the Lord himself. Remember, heaven rejoices when sinners repent.

august
TWENTY-SIX

LUKE 15:11-12

Using illustrations, Jesus continued to explain the joy associated with finding something previously lost. This last story begins with a father and his two sons. The younger son asks the father to give him his share of whatever he would get when his father died. It wasn't customary to distribute inheritances while the father was still alive, and some say the younger son may have proclaimed that his father was dead to him at this point. In any case, the younger son is ready to sever his relationship with his father and wants all the cash he can get. The father agrees and gives the son his share of the property. The son wastes his inheritance, chasing after the pleasures of life, and in time, he is totally broke. To top it off, a famine hits the land. He has no money and no way to make money. Eventually, he lands a job working for a Gentile by feeding pigs. Most Jews would never stoop so low. The younger son clearly hits rock bottom. At this point, even the pigs are better fed than he. Then it hits him. His father's servants are treated with much more kindness than he. He considers that even though he gave up his relationship with his father and forfeited his sonship, maybe his father will give him a job. The son lets the father know he is simply looking for a job, and he won't burden anyone.

What a beautiful picture of repentance! Initially, the son doesn't want a relationship with his father, and the father lets him go. In the same way, God allows sinners to do as they please. But when the sinner realizes that her life is awful without God and chooses to humbly ask God for his mercy and grace, God embraces her. The son probably never imagined his father would ask the servants to get out a robe, a ring, and a pair of sandals. The father restores the son to his place in the family. Then the father hosts a great feast so that all can celebrate with him. Let's stop and thank God for the unearned grace he has showered upon us as followers of Jesus. Even though we don't deserve it, he has put the robe, the ring, and sandals on us too and welcomed us into his family. What an unusually kind God we serve!

august
TWENTY-SEVEN

LUKE 15:25-32

Jesus wrapped up the Parable of the Prodigal Son by looking at the older son's response to his brother's repentance. Jesus used this parable to specifically address the attitudes of the religious leaders (see Luke 15:2). The older son comes home from working in the field and hears singing and music from the grand celebration in his home. A servant informs him that his lost brother has repented, and a party is happening as a result. Upon learning this, he becomes angry and refuses to rejoice with his family. The older brother should have rushed with excitement into the party, but now he is the one on the outside of the festivity. As the story continues, the father himself comes out to reason with the older son. The father literally asks the older son again and again to please join with them. The older son explains that he has faithfully slaved on his father's behalf for years and years, yet no one celebrated his work. The older brother is basically saying, "I am not going in there, because this is just not fair!" The older brother is so self-consumed that he can't bring himself to rejoice with the brother who practically came back to them from the dead. The older son despises the grace of his father toward one he considers unworthy. Which son is disobedient now?

In verse 30, the older brother's anger peaks. He calls his brother "this son of yours." He reminds his father what a terrible person the younger son is, and adds details to what his brother did by informing his father that his wealth was spent on prostitutes. But the father isn't shaken. He tells his older son that he always has access to all the family owned. Then the father gently reminds the older brother, "He's not only my son, but he is your brother." The parable's conclusion reminds us that God came to save sinners. To bring the gospel to sinners, we must associate with them. This doesn't mean we take part in evil activity, but we must work to build relationships with those who may be considered moral rejects in hopes that some might come to repentance and faith. If you have any of the older brother's attitude, ask God to forgive you of self-righteousness today. Then pray that he would use you as he continues his great work of bringing the spiritually dead back to life.

august
TWENTY-EIGHT

LUKE 16:1-13

Jesus taught his disciples another parable. This one focuses on a rich man and his manager. The Greek word used here for "manager" describes one who serves as an overseer or fiscal agent. According to reports brought to the rich man, the manager has been neglecting his duty, and as a result, the rich man fires him and asks him to turn in his books. The manager freaks out. He has a "white collar job" and is not about to descend to hard labor. The manager realizes that he has nowhere to go, so he works to protect his future. He goes to his master's debtors and has them declare what they owe, and then he cuts their debt down by as much as 50% so they will feel obligated to do him a favor as well. Wow! How does he manage to get away with that? The manager probably removes his commission from the debt. This would have created highly favorable circumstances for the manager as the debtors learned that he was relieving them of his personal cut, and it would also explain how the rich man could actually applaud his act. In verse 8, the parable comes to a close. The master praises the manager for his shrewdness. The master is not commending the manager for being dishonest, but stating that the manager acted perceptively, which is smart. The rich man compliments the manager for the wisdom he displayed in his forward-thinking.

Jesus went on to say that the ungodly think more about what's around the corner than believers usually do. How odd! Christians should certainly consider their future more than non-Christians. Jesus challenges us to use our money to make friends, as God rewards us when we are kind to others and our faithfulness in the "small" things leads him to entrust us with "bigger" things. We are all called to use our wealth to glorify God and not ourselves. Sadly, the more people selfishly accumulate in this life, the less they will accumulate property of true, lasting value. Service to God, according to this passage, means being generous with our resources. Every decision today holds potential for reward tomorrow. Pray that God would help you be as bold as the manager in looking out for your future. Let's view our choices in this life through the lens of blessing they will bring in the life to come.

august
TWENTY-NINE

LUKE 16:14-18

Although Jesus was speaking to his disciples, the Pharisees overheard him teaching his earlier parable and point. They didn't like being told that God wanted them to be generous with their resources and use their wealth for his glory. They ridiculed Jesus, literally scoffing at what he said. Jesus responded to them with a strong statement. He revealed that they were living to win the approval men, and their selfish attitudes were not pleasing God. They should have known that God's opinion was far more important than what people thought, but they were caught up in trying to impress others. Then Jesus declared, "For what is exalted among men is an abomination in the sight of God." Jesus taught them that God hates self-love and craving for one another's praise. People who exalt themselves are detestable to God. Jesus then announced that the Law and the Prophets closed with John. Now that Jesus was on the scene, a new era had come. Then Jesus added, "everyone forces his way into" the kingdom of God. The Greek verb translated as "forces" is in the middle or passive voice, and some suggest the phrase would be better translated as "all are strongly urged to come to." This would make sense in light of the context of Jesus' teaching. Those who heard his repeated exhortations may have thought they could take his message or leave it, but they were wrong. The need to respond to Jesus' appeal to repent and believe was quite serious and couldn't be overlooked.

The Pharisees turned up their noses at Jesus when he taught about wealth and money. Who was Jesus to talk about finances? He was a poor man surrounded by other poor men. What did he know about money? In fact, the Pharisees assumed that being blessed with much was a sign of God's favor. According to their logic, God wasn't all that thrilled with Jesus, or he would have made sure he had more "ready money." But Jesus clearly taught that God sees and knows the heart. He isn't impressed with the outward appearance of things. What is your attitude toward money? Do you feel like those with monetary wealth are better than those who struggle financially? Do you treat people differently based on the size of their bank accounts? If there's any hint of favoritism toward the rich within you, ask that God would take it away and make you more like Jesus today.

august
THIRTY

LUKE 16:19-31

Again, Jesus spoke about money. This time, he told the story of a rich man and a poor man. The rich man lived in luxury, dressing in expensive clothing and feasting continuously. The very poor man would lie down at the gate of the rich man's mansion, hoping to eat from his trash. The poor man was crippled, and others had to place him by the rich man's home. In addition, his skin was infested with boils or sores, which the local dogs licked, making him ceremonially unclean and probably infecting the sores. He was in bad shape! The rich man was unnamed, but the poor man was called by his name, Lazarus, which ironically means "God, my helper." In time, Lazarus died. Angels took him to "Abraham's bosom," or the place for those destined to blessing. The rich man died too. While in anguish, he looked up and in the distance saw Abraham and Lazarus being comforted. The rich man never bothered to help Lazarus in his poverty and sickness on earth, but now the rich man was begging for Lazarus to send him some water. How everything had changed! After both the rich man and Lazarus had died, their roles clearly reversed, but the reversal was forever. They both received the direct opposite of what they had on earth. The rich man suffered, while Lazarus was free of pain and in a place of total relief. The rich man wasn't tormented because he was rich, but because he used his wealth selfishly.

The rich man realized that his condition was hopeless. Nothing could be done to change things for him. He asked Abraham to send Lazarus to warn his living brothers so they would be spared his fate. His brothers lived the same way he did, but they could still change and be saved from eternal punishment. Abraham said the special warning wasn't needed, because the brothers had the message of the Old Testament. The rich man argued that the Scripture wasn't enough. He insisted a sign was necessary. Abraham disagreed. Even if "someone" were to rise from the dead, it wouldn't be enough for the unbelieving. Jesus' message was clear: death changes everything. If you are ignoring the Scripture or waiting for more revelation, now is the time to repent. For those of us following Jesus, even though at times it may not seem like God is helping us, our ultimate joy will come soon, and we will be forever comforted.

august
THIRTY-ONE

LUKE 17:1-10

Jesus taught his disciples about interacting with others. He began by noting that in this life all will face temptations to sin. But he cautioned that the one who leads others into sin will be held accountable. In fact, it would better for that person to experience a harsh death rather than do anything to harm another soul. The point Jesus made was that the disciples needed to be careful that they weren't bringing spiritual harm to anyone. Then Jesus exhorted them, "Pay attention to yourselves!" His followers must be continually on guard against saying or teaching anything that would lead someone else into sin. Just think of how many people throughout the ages have driven others to follow a false gospel. They should not expect God to treat their crimes lightly. Jesus continues in verse 3 by instructing his disciples that if one of them sinned, the other must confront him. And if the sinner repented, the other must forgive him. The disciples were to be "team players" in the arenas of rebuke and restoration. In order to keep the Christian community upright and holy, sometimes correction would be necessary. And to keep the Christian community whole and unified, sometimes restoration would be necessary. The disciples needed to watch out for one another without destroying their relationships with each other.

So how do we watch out for one another without wrecking our Christian community? In verse 4, Jesus says, "if he sins against you." So when a believer wrongs another believer, the offended party is to correct the one who sinned against her. She is not to call a friend or two, but she is to go directly to the one who sinned against her and seek the offender's repentance. If the offender is sorry and wishes to stop her sinful behavior, then the offended person must forgive and move past the transgression. Our willingness to reprove and our desire to restore will be required again and again in our Christian relationships. Even if the sinner responds with brokenness and asks for forgiveness seven times in one day, Jesus said she is to be restored. Has a fellow believer sinned against you, and have you broken your relationship with her? If so, be willing to confront her about her wrong behavior and forgive her when she is sorry. Remember, Jesus said you must forgive.

september
ONE

LUKE 17:11-19

While Jesus was traveling, ultimately heading to Jerusalem and the cross, he came to a village where ten lepers called to him from a distance. The lepers were forbidden to come near Jesus because of their horrible disease, but they had heard of the wonderful things he did, so they cried out to him in desperation. Raising their voices, they begged Jesus to have mercy on them. Before Jesus did anything, he told them to go present themselves to the priests, who would pronounce them clean and able to work normally in society again. The lepers did as Jesus instructed them, and as they began their journey to see the priests, they were totally healed. One of the ten, thrilled and grateful, praised God in a loud voice and went back to see Jesus. He fell at Jesus' feet and gave him thanks for the healing. Before the healing, he could only yell to Jesus from a distance, but now he was clean and able to approach Jesus to personally and humbly thank him. The funny thing was that the leper who returned was a Samaritan, a foreigner. The other nine were probably Jewish. Jesus then asked three questions. First he asked, "Were not ten cleansed?" Then he asked, "Where are the nine?" And finally, "Was no one giving praise to God but the foreigner?" In asking these questions, Jesus implied that all who were healed should have returned to give him thanks. After the Samaritan leper was cleansed and gave thanks to God, Jesus told him his faith had healed him. The Samaritan was now both physically and spiritually healed.

God graces both believers and unbelievers with his mercy. His kindness should lead all to repentance and faith. But most of the time, the nine will walk away unappreciative. It's funny how people often shake their fists at God when things go wrong, yet fail to give him thanks when things go right. Real faith is demonstrated through thankfulness. A thankless attitude reflects a faithless heart. God continually does so much for us that we can grow numb to his favor and feel as if we have earned our blessings, sometimes even demanding more. Let us never forget that all good things come directly from him. If God has done anything for you, fall at his feet and give him thanks today.

september
TWO

LUKE 17:20-37

Since Jesus taught often about the kingdom of God, the Pharisees asked him when the kingdom was coming. Jesus responded that they would not find it through specific signs, or even by hunting for it, because the kingdom was right in their midst. If the Pharisees really wanted the kingdom, they only needed to acknowledge that Jesus was the promised Messiah. The way to God's kingdom lay through his Son, Jesus. Imagine Jesus standing right there with the Pharisees, explaining these truths, and the Pharisees just not getting it. Then he spoke to his disciples. In verses 22 through 25, he gives them three facts about the coming kingdom. First, although they would desire to see him set up his rule as Messiah, it wouldn't occur in their lifetime. Second, when the kingdom does come, it will be evident to all. And third, Jesus said he must suffer before he is properly recognized as the rightful King. This must have disappointed the disciples, who were ready to go forward. So Jesus warned them not to follow any false Christ who may come, saying "now is the time." Then he compared his return to the days of Noah and the days of Sodom and Gomorrah. Just as people weren't ready for either of those two past events, they would not be prepared for Jesus either. When Jesus returns to judge the world, many will be caught off guard.

In the days of Noah, people ate, drank, and married. In the days of Sodom, people ate, drank, bought, and sold. Neither group was expecting the radical destruction they experienced. Eating and drinking, marrying, buying, and selling aren't bad things, but they are wrongfully enjoyed when they cause people to ignore God. Jesus exhorted his disciples to remember Lot's wife (v. 32). She provided a typical portrait of an unbeliever, because she just couldn't let go of the things of this world. Jesus added, "if anyone else wants to hold on to her life, she will lose it." Jesus never promised us protection from harm and suffering during our stay on earth. But he does offer us eternal life in his presence. No matter how hard things get, remember that if you are a follower of Jesus, you have an amazing future ahead of you. The suffering we experience in this life is as bad as it will ever get for those who know God.

september
THREE

LUKE 18:1-8

Jesus taught his disciples an important lesson about their need to continue in prayer by using another parable. He began with a merciless judge, a man not driven by kindness or pity towards those who came to him. In Jesus' parable, a widow comes to this judge. He should protect her, as God's law taught that widows were to be cared for. She is probably in financial need, and possibly being ripped off. Though the judge is unrighteous, he still has the power to help, so she begs him again and again for justice. The widow's persistence begins to annoy the judge, and to avoid her continued bugging, the judge agrees to help her out. In verses 6 through 8, Jesus compares and contrasts the judge and God. Both God and the judge have the power and authority to make a difference for those who come to them for justice, but unlike the judge, God is kind and compassionate. Jesus encouraged his disciples' persistence in prayer. God will vindicate his children, and we are never to stop asking for his will to be done on earth as it is in heaven. Jesus desires to find faith on earth. His followers are to wait and pray for his return without growing weary. His question is intended to encourage our steadfastness in prayer.

The widow is a picture of the believer in great need. As we live out our Christianity in a world that opposes God, we too are in great need of God's mercy and compassion. As Jesus taught, since the ungodly judge responded to the widow's cries for help, how much more will our loving and holy Father respond to the cries of his children? Jesus used this parable to make his point clear: in the midst of suffering, his followers are to pray again and again for his justice. If you have lost heart or grown tired of prayer, be encouraged by Jesus' parable today. Have some of your closest loved ones not yet surrendered to Jesus? Are people or circumstances making it hard for you to stand up for the gospel? Do you struggle with sins that you need God's power to overcome? Ask him for help! Don't stop praying! If you are a child of God, he loves you, and he is listening.

september
FOUR

LUKE 18:9-17

Jesus taught another parable. This time, he directed the parable towards the self-righteous. By "self-righteous," Jesus meant those who trusted in themselves and thought their admirable works were good enough for God. They didn't need a savior because they believed they were righteous, and God was therefore obligated to accept them into his kingdom. Jewish men in the time of Jesus commonly thanked God in prayer that they were not someone of lesser status. Such men were actually alienated from God, even though they didn't realize it. They disdained those they considered lower than themselves. In Jesus' parable, two men went to the temple. These men were complete opposites of one another and from totally different spheres of life. The Pharisee was a religious elite, whereas the tax collector was a social reject, hated because of his profession. The Pharisee prayed, thanking God that he was so wonderful, even listing his own righteous acts for God. The tax collector, on the other hand, stood far off. He didn't compare himself to anyone. He was only able to call out to God for mercy.

The audience must have been caught off guard when Jesus said it was the tax collector who went away justified, not the Pharisee. The parable clearly taught that no one is able to come to God on the basis of her own righteousness. No matter how good we believe we are, not one of us meets God's perfect standard. God never calls us to compare ourselves with ourselves; instead, we are to compare ourselves with the requirement of his Law. When we do that, not one of us can say she has no need for a savior. And when we truly look into the mirror of God's word, we see the ugliness of our sin and realize we too should stand far off from God like the tax collector. The cry of all humanity should be "God, have mercy on me!" True repentance, like the repentance of the tax collector, is demonstrated not by a sinless life, but by turning from sin to Jesus. Is there a broken tax collector in your life today? If so, let her know that you were there too, and that God will hear her cry for mercy, gracing her with the desire to do things his way and freeing her from bondage to sin and death. What a savior is Jesus!

september
FIVE

LUKE 18:18-30

A prominent young man in the community asked Jesus what he needed to do to inherit eternal life. This was the same question previously asked by the lawyer who tried to trick Jesus, but the young man added the adjective "good" to his inquiry. Jesus asked the man why he addressed him as "good." He wanted to shock the man into recognizing that no one is "good enough" for God. Jesus then recited part of the Law, and the man declared that he had kept those rules. Clearly, this guy thought God would accept him into the kingdom based on his own righteousness. The commands Jesus listed actually focus on how to treat others. Verse 23 adds that this man was extremely rich. Often, those who are financially blessed use their wealth for self-indulgence and not generosity. So Jesus asked him to sell what he had and use it to help the poor. The man would lose his earthly wealth, but he would have treasure in heaven as a result. And he could follow after Jesus. This sounds pretty radical. Does a person actually have to get rid of her money to be saved? Jesus knew that this particular rich man trusted in his resources and saw them as a sign of God's favor, so Jesus asked the man to let go of the false security he clung to and fully trust God by following him. The man was sad because he couldn't do as Jesus asked.

The rich young man was given an option. He could follow Jesus or follow money. The man chose money. Jesus then stated, "It is easier for a camel to go through the eye of a needle than for a rich person to enter the kingdom of God." This was again to shock the audience. These people assumed the Lord favored wealthy people. Those present questioned, "Who can be saved? Is there any hope for anyone?" Not if people are left to themselves. But as Jesus taught, God can save. Whatever is taking the place of God in your life has to be removed from the spotlight in your heart. Is anything competing with your trust in Christ? If so, don't walk away sad. Ask God to help you put that thing in its proper place. God is in the business of making the impossible possible.

september
SIX

LUKE 18:31-43

Luke records the account of another man who crossed paths with Jesus. Unlike the rich young ruler in verses 18-23, this time Jesus met a poor, blind beggar. These men were complete opposites of one another. The rich and powerful man was dependent upon no one and trusted only in his wealth for security. The poor and destitute man lived his life dependent upon others and couldn't survive without help. The blind man heard the noise of the crowd that accompanied Jesus, and he asked those near him what was going on. They told him Jesus was passing. When the blind man heard this, he began to shout out to Jesus, "Jesus, Son of David, have mercy on me!" Although he was blind, he "saw" what so many others missed. Jesus was the Son of David, the promised Messiah of Israel. Many of those present told the blind man to be quiet after he cried out to Jesus for help. But that didn't stop him. Instead, he went on to shout even more, again calling out to Jesus as the "Son of David" for mercy. This guy didn't care what anyone else thought. Jesus was passing by, and the man was determined to get his attention. He was successful! Jesus ordered that the man be brought to him. Then he asked the blind beggar what he wanted Jesus to do. The blind man replied that he wanted to see. Jesus healed him, publicly noting that his faith had made him well.

After the blind man was healed, he went on to follow Jesus and give glory to God. The poor, sightless beggar ended up seeing, praising God, and gaining riches in the life to come. Jesus is not looking for health or wealth or social status in those he calls to be his disciples. Instead, he is looking for people who recognize their need for God's mercy and humbly respond to who he is in faith. It is interesting to see how those who realize their inability to save or help themselves are the ones who end up seeing Jesus, while those who think they have everything in and through themselves end up blind to the Lord. If you are a follower of Jesus today, your spiritual sight proves you have an inheritance that will never be taken from you. The Christian has everything she needs in Jesus. What a reason for rejoicing!

september
SEVEN

LUKE 19:1-10

Luke introduces the reader to a hated tax collector named Zacchaeus. Tax collectors worked with the Romans to raise government monies, and they took an extra (and often large) cut from the people for themselves. The Jews hated the tax collectors because they were representatives of the government that oppressed and abused them, and because they personally profited from dishonest gain. Zacchaeus was actually a chief tax collector, and though he was Jewish, he sold his own people out to Romans while making a very large income. At the same time, Zacchaeus was curious about Jesus, and since he wasn't tall enough to see over the crowd, Zacchaeus climbed up a sycamore tree to get a view from the top. As Jesus passed by, he stopped right in front of the tree. Can you imagine how nervous Zacchaeus must have been? Jesus called out, "Zacchaeus!" Jesus was about to demonstrate to his followers how God could make a camel go through the eye of a needle, since this rich man was about to enter the kingdom of heaven. Zacchaeus flew down the tree and welcomed Jesus into his home. The crowd must have been amazed. Zacchaeus declared that he would return up to four times what he had cheated others out of, and he would give half of his money to the poor. Remember the rich young ruler (Luke 18:18-23)? He wouldn't part with his wealth. Jesus declared that salvation had come to the house of Zacchaeus, who was born again and now a true son of Abraham.

Was Zacchaeus saved because he gave away half of his money and repaid those he had wronged? No. He was saved by faith in Jesus. And yet, with trust in Jesus comes a desire to obey God. If we are followers of Jesus, we too should be willing to make restitution to those we have wronged. Have you stolen from others? Have you broken your promises? Have you damaged someone else's reputation? If so, be like Zacchaeus and seek to make amends for your sin. Repay what you took. Be faithful to the one you let down. And do whatever you can to build up the reputation of the one you slandered. If we have been called by Jesus to come down from our tree and into a relationship with him, let's demonstrate our salvation by living in a way that honors the Lord. Even though it can be humiliating, choose today to make right the wrongs you have done.

september
EIGHT

LUKE 19:11-27

Jesus' disciples still didn't understand that his rejection was necessary before his return to rule, so he used a parable to explain what his people were to do in the time between his crucifixion and his return. He spoke of a ruler who leaves to get his kingship. But before he leaves, he calls his servants to himself and gives them each a sum of his money (about four months' wages), asking them to use it to make more money for him while he is gone. The citizens under this man's authority hate him, and they don't want his authority over their lives. When he returns, he checks in with his servants to see how much they had earned in his absence. The first servant earned a one thousand percent profit. This servant did a great job and is entrusted with real authority as a result. The second servant earned a five hundred percent profit. He too is entrusted with much in return for his obedience. The third servant did not earn anything for the ruler. He stored the money away in a handkerchief. He actually thought poorly of his master and believed he was too hard on the servants. He decided that to work hard for the master was a waste of energy. His money is taken from him and given to the first servant. The third man ends up with no reward.

Every single follower of Jesus has been given the gospel. And every single follower of Jesus is expected to use the gospel to build the kingdom in Jesus' absence. The ruler in Jesus' parable commands his servants to "engage in business until I come," and he has asked us to do the same. Remember, we are saved by faith alone, and yet Jesus clearly taught that eternal rewards will result from our obedience to him. As a Christian, what are you doing with the gospel you have been given? Are you working hard to build God's kingdom? Or do you think God is asking too much from you and so keeping the good news to yourself instead? We don't want to "drop the ball" on this. Choose to invest your time, money, and resources into Kingdom work now. Living for a reward in the life to come reflects a heart that loves and believes in Jesus today.

september
NINE

LUKE 19:28-40

When Jesus arrived at the Mount of Olives, he instructed two of his disciples to go to a chosen village, get a specific colt that no one had ever ridden, and bring it back. The Greek word translated "colt" simply means a "young animal." Jesus also knew that someone would approach the two disciples and ask them what they were doing. He instructed them to respond, "The Lord needs it." Jesus told the two disciples exactly what would happen, and everything occurred just as he said it would. Luke emphasized the omniscience, or ability to know all, that Jesus possessed. When they brought the colt to Jesus, the two disciples threw their outer garments over it, creating a makeshift saddle. The other disciples joined in the procession, and they threw their cloaks on the road ahead of Jesus and the colt's path. They were "rolling out the red carpet" for Jesus as he prepared to enter Jerusalem. Jesus didn't stop them, but instead rode from the Mount of Olives toward the city. The disciples recognized who Jesus was, and shouted, "Blessed is the King who comes in the name of the Lord! Peace in heaven and glory in the highest!" Jesus presented himself to the city as their King. The Pharisees saw all this and demanded that Jesus get his followers to stop. Jesus responded by saying that if his followers were silent, then the rocks would cry out.

Though the Pharisees and the bulk of Jerusalem's inhabitants failed to see Jesus as the King, creation knew what was happening. A lifeless rock could testify to Jesus' identity, but most of the living were unable to see what was right in front of them. As Jesus approached the great city, he came not as a warrior but in humility. Though the disciples present tossed their cloaks ahead of Jesus, even most of their allegiance was short-lived. The time soon came for those who cried "Hosanna!" to put their words into actions, but they were nowhere to be found. It's easy to say great things about Jesus, even speaking of his glory and majesty, but it takes the work of the Holy Spirit to move a soul to the place of putting her profession into practice. Are you merely saying wonderful things about Jesus, or are you allowing him to be the King of your life? The crowd had no idea what lay around the corner, but Jesus did.

september
TEN

LUKE 19:41-44

Jesus drew near to Jerusalem, and when he saw the city, he wept. He knew what was going to happen, and he knew that the people of this great city had already rejected him. The word used for "wept" is the Greek word *klaio*, which is not a sniffling but an intense sobbing. Jesus was absolutely heartbroken over the fact that God's people missed this great hour of salvation. Then Jesus prophesied over the city. He stated that because they rejected their Messiah, their opportunity for redemption had passed. They could have experienced God's peace, but instead they would experience darkness and destruction. Those who reject the kindness and mercy of God fail to realize the great weight of their decision. As a result, the enemies of Israel would take the city. Historians record that in 70 AD, shortly after Jesus' prophecy, the nation of Rome attacked Jerusalem and the temple and brought the city and house of God to ruins. Jerusalem has never been the same since. Jesus said earlier that even the stones would cry out "Hosanna!" if necessary, to acknowledge his entry into the city as King. Now Jesus said that those same stones would be a witness of the nation's judgment.

Have you ever wept bitterly over the foolish or sinful decisions of someone you love? Have you longed to help her "get it" regarding the consequences of her wrongful actions, but she refused to listen to you? The pain you experienced at that time was a taste of what Jesus felt as he broke down in sorrow over the blindness of Israel. Although God is all-powerful and able to do whatever he pleases, he doesn't take pleasure in the death of the wicked. If someone in your life is currently making poor choices, call out to Jesus. He is not happy with her sin either. In some mysterious way, God has ordained things so that he responds to the prayers of his people. He can do whatever he wants, yet he wants us to ask that his will be done on earth and in the lives of those he has placed around us. Take a minute to pray for the unbelievers in your life today. Even break down with sorrow. Be encouraged! As your pour your soul out to the Lord on behalf of others, you are following in the footsteps of Jesus.

september
ELEVEN

LUKE 19:45-48

When Jesus entered his Father's house, he cleaned it up. In an area of the temple called the "Court of the Gentiles," animals were purchased for sacrifice and currency was changed to pay the temple tax. Those who sold the sacrificial animals and proper currency made a substantial profit and used the vulnerability of people coming to worship God for their own personal gain. When Jesus entered the temple and saw this abuse going on, it greatly upset him. Other biographies of Jesus record that he actually flipped over the tables of those who exploited the worshippers. Can you imagine what this event must have been like for the witness? Wow. The crashing tables had to have made quite a scene! Those present must have been stunned. Jesus quoted Isaiah 56:7, "My house shall be called a house of prayer for all peoples." This should have been a place where people of all ethnicities could come to worship God, but it had become a place where the foreigner would be discouraged from seeking the Lord. Jesus also quoted Jeremiah 7:11 when he said, "You have made it a den of robbers." The temple had become a place for greedy and selfish "thieves" to gather and plan to rip off the naïve who came to make a sacrifice. The nation of Israel was a mess. Not only had most of the people missed their Messiah, but God was dishonored even in the very temple.

After Jesus cleansed the temple, he taught there daily. The religious leaders attempted to trap him or trip him up in his words, but they were unsuccessful. Instead, as verse 48 describes, "All the people were hanging on his words." The scribes, the Pharisees, and the chief priests were more interested in money and commercialism than in helping others get right with the Lord. As Christians, we no longer make sacrifices in the temple, because when we turn to Jesus in repentance and faith our own bodies become temples of the Lord. The Holy Spirit of God takes residence in us, and we are called to glorify him in our bodies. So if we are Christians, we have the Holy Spirit. How encouraging is that? The Holy Spirit will help us to glorify God by living in a way consistent with his design for a redeemed life as we too hang on Jesus' words.

september
TWELVE

LUKE 20:1-8

When Jesus spoke and taught, he did so with authority. Other Jewish teachers would defer to the customs established by rabbis who went before them. They supported their teaching with statements like "Rabbi This said…" or "Rabbi That said…." But Jesus didn't quote other rabbis because he *was* the authority, and he taught directly from God. The leaders of Israel approached Jesus to challenge him on where he got his authority to teach in the temple. They prodded him to uncover why he thought he was equipped to teach without leaning upon the traditions of men. Instead of answering them directly, Jesus asked the religious leaders a question in return: was John's baptism "from heaven or from man"? They knew the Jews respected John as a man who spoke for God. John had even baptized many of the crowd. The Pharisees couldn't possibly say that John's authority didn't come from heaven. But if it did come from heaven, why weren't they baptized too? In addition, John declared that Jesus was the Lamb of God who takes away the sins of the world. They discussed these things and decided that they had better not answer him. So they replied, "We don't know." Jesus told them they weren't getting any more of an answer from him either. The religious leaders rejected Jesus just like they rejected John.

When we read this account, we want to shout to the religious leaders, "What? You have an opinion, so just say it!" But this same type of thinking and deceptive speech goes on today. What about Jesus? Was he from heaven or man? Was he a phony who lied about his identity to deceive people? Or was he delusional and did he therefore wrongfully believe he was the promised Messiah? The questions Jesus asked are the same questions we should ask those around us today. If those we dialogue with say Jesus was from man, then they must concede that either he was dishonest or a nutcase. And if either one of these is true, then they should never quote him or say he was a good guy. If they confess he was from heaven, then why aren't they following him? Stop and pray for the opportunity to engage in thought-provoking discussion with those who are blind to the truth for now. Pray that the Holy Spirit would remove the veil from their eyes, just as he did from yours.

september
THIRTEEN

LUKE 20:9-18

Jesus told a parable to explain how God felt about the religious leaders' rejection of him and his authority. He began by saying that a man planted a vineyard. The nation of Israel was often pictured as a vineyard by the Old Testament prophets. For example, Isaiah 5:7 states, "The vineyard of the Lord of hosts is the house of Israel." The Pharisees, scribes, elders, and even the people knew exactly whom Jesus was talking about. The vineyard was Israel, the man was God the Father, the servants were the prophets, the son was Jesus, and the tenants, who were supposed to take care of the vineyard or the nation, were the religious leaders of Israel. When the prophets were sent to the nation, they were rejected. They were beaten, treated shamefully, wounded, and cast out by Israel. The nation's leaders didn't want God's authority over them, and they didn't want anyone telling them to do things differently. So in the parable, the man sends his son, but he too is thrown out of the vineyard and even killed. The tenants are afraid that the son will try to take his father's rightful place of authority. Jesus told the religious leaders exactly what they were going to do to him. He also explained that "tenants" who abuse the master's servants and his son will be destroyed. What did the religious leaders say in response? "Surely not."

What a picture of God's kindness and mercy. The man in the story is patient with his tenants when they beat and reject his servants. He even goes so far as to send his own son to reason with the tenants. But in the same way the tenants killed the son, the nation of Israel killed her Messiah, God's Son, Jesus. The religious leaders had grown so comfortable with "calling the shots," they didn't really think God was going to do anything about the state of the nation. "Surely not," they declared to Jesus. Many people are saying the same thing today. God's people try to warn others that judgment is coming, and the unbelievers respond with "surely not." They don't think that God is ever going to interrupt their way of life and call them to give an account for what they have or have not done with Jesus. God's patience exists so that as many as possible might come to repentance. If you are tolerating sin or disobedience to Jesus in any area of your life, repent today.

september
FOURTEEN

LUKE 20:19-26

The religious leaders were "fed up" with Jesus. They were tired of him speaking against them and were ready to be rid of him. But there was a problem. The people around Jesus listened to him and followed him; they weren't yet ready to let him go. So the religious leaders schemed together to trap Jesus by using flattery. Most men and women are easily manipulated when they receive praise from others, but not Jesus. He didn't fall for their set-up because he didn't live for the approval of men. The scribes and chief priests sent spies who tried to catch Jesus off guard by calling him "teacher," saying they knew that he spoke and taught rightly. They added that he didn't show favoritism to anyone but instead professed what was honest before God. They thought they had him in the palm of their hands when they asked, "Is it lawful for us to give tribute to Caesar, or not?" They assumed he would say "no." Then the Romans could arrest him as a rebel. But if Jesus said "yes," the Jews around him would be furious because they thought it was wrong to give financially to a pagan and oppressive government. Either way, Jesus would be ruined. But Jesus knew what they were doing. He asked to see a small silver coin that was used to pay tax, and he questioned whose image it bore. They said it was Caesar's. Jesus said, "Then give it to Caesar. And give God what he is due too." The spies were speechless.

We gossip when we say something behind someone's back we would never say to her face, but we flatter when we say something to someone's face we would never say behind her back. The religious leaders didn't like or approve of Jesus at all, yet they went so far as to say that he accurately spoke the way of God, that he wasn't afraid of what anyone thought, and that his words about the way of the Lord were true. They were priming Jesus, hoping he would use their "encouragement" to speak against the Romans. Like Jesus, we must always beware of flattery. Men and women often use praise to get others to do what they want. And we must also be careful to steer clear of using flattery to get what we want. As followers of Jesus, let's make sure we avoid flattery at all costs.

september
FIFTEEN

LUKE 20:27-40

The Sadducees were wealthy, well-respected men in the Jewish community who only embraced the Torah, the first five books of the Old Testament written by Moses, as God's word. They insisted that Moses made no references to afterlife and didn't believe in heaven or hell, eternal rewards, or judgment. They asked Jesus a "trick question" to stump him, addressing the Old Testament custom of Levirate marriage, which protected a man who died without offspring. The dead man's brother had to marry his brother's widow to make sure that the family name would continue. The Sadducees fabricated a hypothetical situation in which a childless but married man died and his brother took the widow. What if this happened seven times over so that seven brothers ended up married to the woman? When the woman died, which brother would be her husband in heaven? Clearly, they thought Jesus' concept of the afterlife was nonsense. But instead, Jesus told them that *their* idea of the afterlife was foolish. In heaven, marriage does not exist, because death does not exist. Without death, there is no need to repopulate, and so no need for the union between a man and a woman. Jesus went on to explain that in the Torah, God declares, "I am the God of Abraham, the God of Isaac, and the God of Jacob" (Ex 3:6), all of whom were dead at the time. Saying "I am" the God of Abraham, Isaac, and Jacob made no sense if the men were not alive. If they were truly dead, God would have said, "I was," but instead he declared, "I am." Abraham, Isaac, and Jacob were (and are!) alive in the next age, according to God.

Jesus clearly taught that the afterlife is real. What takes place in this life will impact what happens to us in the life to come. Those who do not trust in the person and work of Jesus will be found guilty and end up separated from the Lord eternally in a miserable existence. But those who follow Jesus will experience more wonderful joy when all failure is done away with than our minds can yet comprehend or imagine. If you feel discouraged, thank God that one day you will be totally liberated from sin. You won't want to live selfishly, you won't struggle with making decisions, and you will be free to love and serve God without any hindrance. And best of all, you will be with Jesus forever. Look forward to heaven.

september
SIXTEEN

LUKE 20:41-47

Jesus publicly condemned the scribes, who loved to be identified by their religious role. So that all would know who they were, they wore long white robes with fringe at the bottom that touched their feet. They were considered above the common people. They were looked up to and greeted as they went through their cities. When the scribes entered their synagogues, they took special seats from which they looked out upon the audience, reminding all of how "important" they were. When large feasts or parties were given, it was a symbol of honor to have a scribe there, so they were given the best seats. Even worse than their desire for recognition, the scribes abused their religious authority for selfish purposes. The scribes managed the property of widows who dedicated their assets to the Lord. When they oversaw these widows' finances, they made sure to take a generous cut for themselves. The widows were often some of the poorest in the community, but the scribes profited even from their willingness to give. The scribes made long prayers while they lived selfishly. Their prayers should have called on God to show mercy upon their own sinful behavior, and to help them live according to the justice and kindness of the Lord. Instead, they used lengthy supplications for their own glorification, defeating the purpose of prayer.

Not only did Jesus say that these scribes would give an account for what they did, but he added, "They will receive the greater condemnation." All sin separates us from God, but some will incur more wrath than others because of the heinousness of the sins and the disobedience of the sinner. When we sin willfully, or when we cause others to stumble while we are in a position of spiritual leadership over them, our sins are weightier than the same sins committed by those with less understanding. Romans 2:5 declares that wrath can be "stored up" for the day of wrath. Think about whether you are willfully disobeying the Lord right now in any area. Choose to see your sin more seriously than you have, and ask God to help you turn from disobedience. He longs to help us get this right. For those who follow Jesus, there is no condemnation, but we should long to live in a way that pleases the One who paid our debt with his blood.

september
SEVENTEEN

LUKE 21:1-9

In the temple, Jesus was people-watching. One area of the temple, called the treasury, was located in the Court of Women. Now the Court of Women did not get its name because only women were allowed there. Instead, it meant that women could go no further into the temple than the borders of this court. The treasury contained thirteen "trumpets," or receptacles that looked like trumpets with narrow mouths fanning out to wide bases. Worshippers of God put their offerings into specifically marked trumpets. It was Passover time, so the temple was swollen with visitors. A poor widow approached the treasury. She probably wore tattered clothes. She put two small coins, *lepta*, into an offering box. A *lepton* was a tiny, thin coin worth about an eighth of a cent. So the widow gave less than a penny. Can you imagine what you would think if someone put a penny into the offering bag at church? Why bother? Anyone who noticed what the widow did may have laughed. Her offering was a joke. When the rich dropped their large offerings into the trumpets, others could see that they gave "generously." No praise was given when the widow's coins fell in. She didn't give very much, but it was literally all that she had. And though no one else was impressed by her two small coins, God was. In fact, Jesus said she gave more than the others.

Jesus wasn't only watching the widow's actions, but he was watching her motives as well. He knew the coins were all she had. In the same way, God watches not only what we do, but why we do it. Do we pray, serve, go to church, or even give financially to be seen by others? Or are we faithful and generous because we want to please to God? This examination will drive the honest heart to brokenness and repentance as we ponder how selfish many of our motives are, even for our good deeds. Thank Jesus for his mercy upon our sinful intentions! But let us also remember that just as Jesus observed the honest sacrifice of the widow, God sees our proper motives too. Determine today to be driven by the desire to do what is right in the sight of the Lord, even if it feels like what you have to offer isn't much.

september
EIGHTEEN

LUKE 21:10-19

Jesus described what would take place before the destruction of the temple. He said that false christs would attempt to deceive or mislead, wars would break out, and physical disasters would take place on earth. The world would be in a state of chaos. In addition, Jesus declared that his disciples would be severely persecuted. This persecution would even cause his followers to end up before government leaders, which would provide them with the opportunity to testify to their faith in him. What should the disciples do to plan for this coming persecution? Jesus let them know that they were not to waste their time preparing what to say. They had followed Jesus, they knew him, and God would give them the words to speak when their time was up. He went on to warn them that some would die for their faith. He cautioned that their own family members would be among those who oppressed them. If the disciples didn't realize it before, it became clear at this point: the call to follow Jesus definitely has a price associated with it. Jesus heightened the tension by stating that for his name's sake, all types of people would hate his followers. And yet, through all of this, they would find great hope in the truth that no matter what physically happened to the followers of Jesus, they were spiritually safe.

In 70 AD, the Romans demolished the Jewish temple, but the signs didn't end with that terrible event. The chaos will worsen until Jesus comes back at the end. The events of 70 AD were a sign themselves, even a foreshadowing, of what the real end will be like when Jesus returns. In laying out what would happen before the temple's destruction, Jesus demonstrated that everything took place according to God's knowledge, plan, and exact timetable. Not one thing that occurs in the universe is outside of God's awareness. Do you feel like circumstances are tough in your life right now? Does it seem like certain areas are out of control? Know that difficult circumstances don't indicate God's absence. Though things have been difficult for many of God's people in the past, he has remained with them. Those who follow Jesus can rest assured that no matter how crazy things get in this life, no one or nothing can mess up God's ultimate plan for his kids, either now or in the future.

september
NINETEEN

LUKE 21:20-28

Jesus warned his disciples about the coming fall of Jerusalem. According to Jewish history, the desolation of Jerusalem and the temple in 70 AD was horrific. Over one million Jews were killed. The suffering that took place was awful. Many even starved to death as a result of the siege. Sadly, these terrors were the result of the nation's rejection of her Messiah. No wonder Jesus was so heartbroken over his people's failure to embrace him as their Savior. Jesus didn't want these things to catch his followers by surprise, so he exhorted them to leave the city when they saw her desolation coming near. Clearly, it would not be wise to live in Jerusalem when this judgment came. This judgment upon the city prefigured the last judgment, which is yet to come. Final relief will come with the return of Christ and in the new Jerusalem, just as relief came after the destruction of this Jerusalem. Jesus shifted his focus to the end. The created world will soon signal the final judgment of God, and those still here will feel helpless when many natural disasters strike. The prophet Daniel spoke about this time over 2500 years ago, but when Jesus referred to the Son of Man, he was speaking of himself. He will come back and bring relief to his followers. What a time of joy this will be for the disciples of Christ, yet what a time of grief for those who have rejected him.

The fall of Jerusalem was horrible, but it was only a foreshadowing of the time to come before the return of Christ. Most mind-blowing of all is that the enemies of Jesus who will witness his return won't cry out to him in repentance and faith. They will acknowledge who he is and they will have no choice but to confess that he is Lord, but they will remain hard-hearted and still refuse to do things his way. This truth reminds us that even seeing Jesus in the clouds will not be enough for those who reject him. At the end, many will remain unwilling to line up under the authority of Christ. God gives the faith to be saved. If you are a follower of Jesus, then straighten up and raise your head! God has chosen you, and your ultimate redemption is near.

september
TWENTY

LUKE 21:29-38

Jesus told his disciples a parable, illustrating their need to be ready for his return. He asked them to think about the fig tree and really all trees in general. He explained that leaves forming on the branches indicate that summer is near and winter has passed. Jesus taught them that the signs he previously described were like leaves. When those things came to pass, they would know the kingdom of God was coming soon. Then Jesus added the interesting phrase "This generation will not pass away until all has taken place." What did he mean? Was Jesus saying the people around him would not die until he returned? That wouldn't make sense. A helpful explanation states that Jesus meant many of "the generation" of people who will be alive when the end times come will also be alive when he returns and wraps things up. In other words, the end times events will occur quickly and be completed (start to finish) within a generation. To keep the disciples from thinking they had time before the kingdom of God was fully established and could take it easy, he warned them to watch themselves. Followers of Jesus are not to get drunk and pursue the sinful pleasures this world may offer. His return will come unexpectedly for those who are not prepared. When Jesus comes back, everyone will know it. The disciples are to remain always alert and on guard, watching for these things. Jesus' followers are to pray continually for God's strength to be obedient and endure.

What about us? What should we do? We should do the same things that Jesus asked his disciples to do almost two thousand years ago. We must always remain ready for his return and expect him to come back at any time. We should rely on God through prayer and depend upon his strength to live in a way that brings him glory and honor. Even if the end doesn't come for another hundred or a thousand years, your own personal end could come tonight. If this day were your last, what would you do? With what would you be concerned? What would you let go of? Let's say mindful of the tension that Jesus asks us to live with. Let's work hard and make good choices for the future, yet continually remember that this night could be our very last.

september
TWENTY-ONE

LUKE 22:1-13

The Feast of Unleavened Bread and the Passover were two occasions often treated as one. The feast lasted for seven days, and the Passover immediately followed. Both remembered the deliverance of God's people from bondage in Egypt. During these celebratory times, Jerusalem and the temple swelled with visitors. The religious leaders were concerned about the crowd's potentially protective response to Jesus. Nevertheless, they were constantly looking for an opportunity to kill him. To help the enemies of Jesus in their execution scheme, Satan got involved. The devil entered into one of Jesus' own disciples, Judas Iscariot, and prompted him to deliver Jesus over to the leaders. Judas actually sought out the enemies of Jesus, and the religious leaders were thrilled with the offer of Judas's help. In verse 5, the phrase "they were glad" is a translation of the Greek verb *chairo*, most often translated as "rejoice." They finally had a solution to their dilemma of how to get Jesus out of the public eye. Jesus' own disciple was going to hand him over to death. After the financial arrangement was made, Judas went on the lookout for the perfect time to turn Jesus in.

Judas had traveled with Jesus for three years. He saw Jesus heal the sick and heard him preach the gospel. Judas witnessed the kindness and compassion of Jesus toward those who were like sheep without a shepherd, and he watched Jesus pronounce judgment on the hypocrites who lived for the approval of man and not God. What in the world happened to Judas? Some think he was disappointed that Jesus didn't establish his kingdom immediately. Others say Judas may have wanted money. It's hard to be sure, as the biographies of Jesus don't reveal Judas' motive. We can forget that physical closeness to Jesus will not save. What more did Judas need to experience to truly believe? The account of Judas reveals that the enemy of God will use people to hinder the Lord's work from moving forward on earth. Even though the powers of hell may seem victorious for a short time, we will discover that God uses dark forces for his own glory. Don't become overly discouraged by temporary defeats, but know in your heart that God can and will overcome the schemes of the devil in the lives of those who follow his Son.

september
TWENTY-TWO

LUKE 22:14-23

The time came for Jesus to eat his final meal with his disciples. The Passover's elements reminded the Israelites of God's passing over his people when the Angel of Death went through the land of Egypt. The death of the firstborn son was the last of the ten plagues God allowed the Egyptians to experience when the Lord brought judgment on Pharaoh. To keep the angel from killing the firstborn sons in the Israelites' homes, God instructed his people to sacrifice an unblemished male lamb and paint its blood on the doorposts of their homes. Exodus 12:13 states, "And when I see the blood, I will pass over you." The Angel of Death would literally pass over these homes because the blood was present. Jesus taught his disciples during this meal, giving the components of the Passover new meaning. He taught that the bread now represents his body, which would be offered for his followers. The cup now represents his blood, to be poured out on their behalf. The bread and the cup are symbols of what Jesus did on the cross to usher in the new covenant. No longer would the blood of sacrificed animals need to be offered again and again for forgiveness. The payment Jesus would provide to the Father through his blood and body would completely atone for the sins of the world.

How strange it must have felt to Jesus as he ate and celebrated the Passover with his disciples, knowing that he was about to literally become the ultimate Passover lamb. Just as the blood on the doorpost of the Israelite home signaled to the Angel of Death to bypass that house, the application of Jesus' blood to our lives signals the fact that those who trust in the Lord will not experience the second death. In verse 15, Jesus added the phrase "before I suffer." He knew exactly what he was getting into, but he did so willingly. Jesus told his followers to take the bread and the cup when they celebrate the Lord's Supper in remembrance of him. As we look backward, we are called to look forward too. One day, we will celebrate a meal with Jesus himself present at the table. The greatest meal of all time is yet to come for those who are followers of Christ.

september
TWENTY-THREE

LUKE 22:24-34

In verse 31, Jesus addressed Peter personally. He used Peter's name twice, saying, "Simon, Simon." Addressing someone like this can either express deep emotion, seriousness, or both. Jesus warned Peter that he was about to become the object of Satanic attack. The original Greek text is interesting in these verses. In verse 31, the word used for "you" is plural. Jesus let Peter know that the devil demanded permission to plunder the apostles. In English, it may look like he was saying Satan had demanded to have "you all" to sift as wheat. But in verse 32, we see that Jesus spoke specifically to Peter. He told Peter that he had prayed "that your faith may not fail." In this statement, the "you" is no longer plural but singular. Jesus was saying, "Peter, I have prayed for you specifically." Why would Jesus say this to Peter? Jesus knew that Peter was right around the corner from one of the biggest spiritual failures of his life. But Jesus had prayed for him. Though Peter sinned, his failure was not permanent. Jesus encouraged Peter to strengthen others after he repented and got back on track. God could and would use Peter's failure to influence those around him, and to influence many future believers, to steadfast hope in and obedience to Jesus.

When Jesus used the phrase "sift as wheat," he was using an agricultural metaphor. To "sift" something like wheat meant "to shake it apart." This was actually a violent process. Farmers would shake the edible part of the wheat away from the stalk and the chaff, which were useless. For the glory of God, Jesus allowed the enemy to have his way with Peter, but this testing and Peter's failure were only temporary. What an incredible picture of the total and complete forgiveness that God extends to the followers of Christ. Jesus knows ahead of time when, how, and to what extent we will disobey. And Jesus generously gives grace and mercy to his repentant disciples. Do you feel like you have been sifted or shaken apart by the powers of hell? Are you discouraged and on the verge of giving up? Know that Jesus is right there to restore you to fellowship with him and fruitfulness in his kingdom. Call out to him, and ask him to cleanse and forgive you from your sins. May Christians never forget that our Savior's compassion will always triumph over the temporary advances of our enemy.

september
TWENTY-FOUR

LUKE 22:35-46

Jesus asked his disciples to think back to when he sent them out before him. He asked them whether they lacked anything during that time, although they went with minimal resources. They replied, "No. We didn't lack anything at all." Jesus then let his disciples know it was time to change the way they did things. Now they needed to take their own money bags and knapsacks with them. They were going to have to provide for themselves. Oh, and if they didn't have a sword, they should sell their coats and get one ASAP. The world was about to reject Jesus, and his disciples needed to be ready to experience rejection too. No longer would others reach out to help them. They were going out as lights into a dark and hostile world. Then Jesus quoted from Isaiah 53:12. The Old Testament prophet, about seven hundred years earlier and speaking of the coming Messiah, said that he "was numbered with the transgressors; yet he bore the sin of many, and makes intercession for the transgressors." Jesus showed his followers that Isaiah was actually speaking about Jesus. Jesus warned his disciples that he was about to die an appalling death alongside the wicked. The disciples still didn't really "get it." They eagerly let Jesus know that they had two swords. Jesus' reply of "It is enough" probably meant something like "Forget it. You guys aren't getting what I am talking about."

How amazing to think that God spoke through the prophet Isaiah seven hundred years before this event to bear witness to his predetermined plan concerning the life and death of the Messiah! Jesus cautioned his disciples that the climate was about to change, and those who may have embraced them before would now reject them. But just as God had all the details of Jesus' life mapped out, he had the details of the disciples' lives planned out. God is in control of the details of your life too. We may be facing suffering and rejection right now because of our stand for Jesus or our desire to live according to God's law and principle, but not one moment of our pain is wasted. God knows exactly what is going on, and he is able to work it all together for good. Thank God today that he sees, knows, and is in control of the future! What an amazing God we love and serve!

september
TWENTY-FIVE

LUKE 22:47-53

Jesus was speaking to his disciples when the crowd, led by Judas, approached him. Judas planned to reveal which man was Jesus by greeting him with a kiss. Jesus questioned, "Really, Judas? You are going to betray me by kissing me?" What level of hypocrisy had Judas plunged to? The disciples realized that the crowd was going to take Jesus away, even by force. So they asked Jesus whether they should resist or fight back. Before Jesus answered their question, a sword came out. One of the disciples, who happened to be Peter, struck the high priest's servant, cutting his ear right off. Jesus told the disciples to stop. This was not what he wanted from them. The suffering that Jesus was about to face was not to be shirked or avoided. Jesus would willingly be taken to his execution. No force was necessary. Jesus stopped to heal the ear of the high priest's servant, further demonstrating his total control of everything happening. None of this caught Jesus by surprise. Jesus then addressed the religious and political leaders, who had gathered to arrest him. He asked them why they treated him like a criminal when they had access to him every day as he taught in the temple.

Jesus then declared to those who came to take him away, "This is your hour, and the power of darkness." What did he mean by that? This was the hour of evil. Darkness had come upon the world. It was physically dark, as in nighttime. And it was spiritually dark, as the powers of hell thought they had overcome God's Messiah. How ironic! The religious leaders of Israel couldn't wait to destroy the light God had sent them. This was truly the "hour when darkness reigned." Judas had given himself over to Satan and betrayed the Savior of the world, using hypocrisy. The leaders of Israel secretly arrested the Light of the World. And the disciples began to take things into their own hands instead of following Jesus' lead. Though the religious leaders thought they were doing as they desired, they were actually pawns of the powers of hell. It is easy for us to forget that we battle not against flesh and blood. Satan often uses humans to wage his war against the people of God. May you stand firm and, like Jesus, be ready to show compassion, even to your enemies.

september
TWENTY-SIX

LUKE 22:54-65

Peter was probably the most "confident" of the twelve apostles. He made declarations like "Though they all (the other disciples) fall away because of you, I will never fall away" (Matthew 26:33). Peter also declared himself ready to go to prison and even death with Jesus (22:33). Peter was ready to fight. He was the one who pulled out his sword and cut off the high priest's servant's ear. Peter loved Jesus, and he was certain that he would follow the Lord at all costs. When Jesus was taken to the high priest's house, it was Peter who followed at a distance. He entered the enemy's territory because he wanted to stay with Jesus until the end. As he was warming his hands by the courtyard fire, a woman recognized Peter. She said he was with Jesus. But Peter reacted, "What? I don't know him!" Someone else saw him and charged Peter with being a follower of Jesus. Again, Peter declared, "No." An hour later, another said that Peter was a Galilean. Of course he was with Jesus! Peter responded, "What are you talking about? I don't know that Jesus guy!" Then the rooster crowed. Wherever Jesus was, he was able to make eye contact with Peter at that very moment. Peter began to break down and sob.

Can you imagine how horrible Peter must have felt? Not only had Jesus been betrayed, not only was he about to be executed, but Peter denied him three times before his death! Ugh! When we see someone before she dies, we want our final words to affirm our love for her and let her know how important she has been to us. Peter's final words were "I don't know who Jesus is." He must have been truly tormented. As Jesus had predicted, Satan sifted Peter like wheat (22:31). But thankfully, Jesus had prayed for Peter (22:32). May you never forget how critical it is to ask God to deliver you from evil. And may we continually pray for one another. God only knows how many times good has come from darkness as a result of prayer. Take a few minutes to pray for yourself, a family member, and someone at your church. Pray that the Holy Spirit would grace us with the strength we need to get up quickly after we fall.

september
TWENTY-SEVEN

LUKE 22:66-23:5

When the elders of the people, including the chief priests and the scribes, questioned Jesus, the first thing they asked him was whether he was the Christ. In the beginning of this Gospel, Luke states many times that Jesus is the Christ, but the leaders wanted to hear Jesus say so himself in order to implicate him. Jesus told them their questioning was useless. They had made up their minds. Jesus added, "And if I asked you who you think I am, you won't answer either." Jesus also declared he would be seated at the right hand of God, referring to himself as the Son of Man. Jesus would soon take the place of honor, not them. Jesus quoted from Psalm 110:1, "The Lord says to my Lord: sit at my right hand, until I make your enemies your footstool." The right hand of God symbolizes the position of ultimate authority or rule. Though the religious leaders thought they were judging Jesus, in reality, he was the one judging them. The religious leaders considered his statement blasphemous. It would take one equal to God to sit at his right hand. They realized the significance of Jesus' claim.

Their last question to Jesus was essentially "So are you the Son of God?" They weren't seeking truth; they just wanted him to say enough to condemn himself so that they could proceed with his execution as quickly as possible. "That's what you are saying," Jesus replied. This was enough for the religious leaders. Jesus was as good as dead. Luke leaves the reader with a choice: Which judge would you prefer, the religious leaders of the day, or Jesus at the right hand of God? Though it may be hard to live with the mocking, scorning, and rejection that come from being "judged" by the world as too radical and over the top for the gospel, a day will come when scoffers will be rejected and Christ-followers ushered into a rich reward. Jesus remained calm on the precipice of the greatest suffering any human has ever endured. Jesus was the Christ, the Son of Man and the Son of God. When it comes to following Jesus, let's make sure we live before the heavenly court. May we never cower before the opinions of man.

september
TWENTY-EIGHT

LUKE 23:6-16

We meet Herod Antipas again, an outrageously immoral man. He was the one who had John the Baptist executed for speaking out against his "marriage" to Herodias, his half-brother's daughter and the wife of another one of his half-brothers. (So Herodias was his niece and his sister-in-law.) Herod persuaded her to leave his half-brother and marry him. He clearly didn't live according to the Law of God. Just as he heard about John the Baptist and wanted to check him out, Herod heard about Jesus and wanted to see him as well. Herod was probably in Jerusalem celebrating the Passover. At last, he was finally able to meet Jesus. He was hoping maybe Jesus would perform a sign for him. Herod actually spent a long time questioning Jesus, who knew that Herod wasn't interested in anything spiritual, but instead wanted to see a "magic show." So Jesus didn't respond. Had there been any honest desire on the part of Herod to seek or know truth, Jesus would have spoken with him. But conversation was useless. Even though Herod stood face-to-face with the Son of God, his conscience was seared. He went on to have Jesus dressed in a robe and mocked. How scary to think that this man was able to look right at and even question Jesus for hours, yet remain clueless about who he really was. It is dangerous thing to look long at God and make no change.

Herod and Pilate were on opposite ends of the political spectrum. Herod represented Jewish interests and Pilate represented Roman interests, but they both agreed to put Jesus to death, though they could find no fault in him. Verse 12 is strange and declares, "Herod and Pilate became friends with each other that very day." There's an old saying that states, "The enemy of my enemy is my friend," meaning when two people at odds share a common enemy, they "suddenly" become friends on that basis. Mankind's primary enemy, the devil, was behind these two political leaders, using them to carry out his purposes. Jesus kept quiet and focused. Stop and pray that God would open your eyes to see the way Satan may be manipulating people and circumstances in your life to get you off track. At the same time, God won't let his kids wander too far. Thank God that he is sovereign over the schemes of darkness.

september
TWENTY-NINE

LUKE 23:18-25

Both Pilate and Herod concluded that Jesus was innocent, and neither wanted anything more to do with him. Pilate was a powerful man in Jerusalem representing Roman rule, so he decided to have Jesus beaten and then released. Pilate was known to do whatever he could to enforce his authority over the people. He knew that Jesus had done no wrong. In addition, Pilate's wife warned him about Jesus. In a dream, she "suffered much" because of Jesus and let Pilate know that it would be a big mistake to put him to death. To top that off, Pilate heard that Jesus claimed to be the Son of God. Pilate was stressed out. Yet by now, things had intensified. It was no longer only the religious leaders who wanted to get rid of Jesus. The crowd joined in too, chanting together, "Crucify him!" They demanded the release of a murderer named Barabbas instead of Jesus. Again, Pilate said to the crowd, "This is crazy. Let Jesus go." But the crowd would not relent. This truly was the hour when darkness reigned. Although Pilate wanted to release Jesus, he yielded to the demand of the people. He released Barabbas and gave Jesus over to the Jews to do as they pleased. In an odd way, this transaction acted out the gospel: the exchange of guilty life for innocent life.

How could Pilate have done this? He knew that Jesus was innocent and even publicly declared him so. Yet, he allowed him to be executed. What did his wife say to him when he came home for dinner that night? The ancient Roman historian Eusebius records that Pilate ended up committing suicide. Other sources say he became a Christian. Either way, he was partly responsible for Jesus' death because he had the power to intervene and didn't use it. Pilate lost his seat of office a few years later anyway. People reject Jesus by either openly professing that they are not his followers or by failing to identify with him at all. As it becomes more and more difficult to stand up for Jesus in a world that's growing increasingly hostile to Christianity, make sure that you don't shrink back from what God has called you to. Better to stand up for Jesus and be rejected by man than be ashamed of Jesus and rejected by man anyway.

september
THIRTY

LUKE 23:26-31

Crucifixion was a horrible form of execution used by 1st century Romans. Yet it was the form of death that God had ordained. Jesus was led to the place of execution, forced to carry his own cross. It wasn't actually the entire cross that Jesus carried, but the crossbeam that would attach horizontally onto the pole that would stand in the ground. This crossbeam could have weighed up to one hundred pounds. Since Jesus was a carpenter and a thirty-year-old man, it would not have been difficult for him to carry this piece of wood a short distance. But Jesus had been so badly beaten and tortured that he just didn't have the strength to carry the crossbeam. Just when it appeared there might be a problem, a North African man from the city of Cyrene "happened" to walk up. His name was Simon. He was an answer to the Romans' dilemma of what to do with Jesus' cross. The Romans would never have picked up a cross and been identified with that type of shame. So Simon was seized and forced to carry Jesus' cross. It all must have happened so quickly. Simon was minding his own business one minute, and before he could blink, he was carrying the heavy crossbeam for a condemned criminal. Little did Simon know he was modeling what it was like to be Jesus' disciple. Like Simon, followers of Jesus must also "take up their crosses" and follow after him.

Then Jesus made an interesting statement to the women present, weeping and mourning for him. He said, "Do not weep for me, but weep for yourselves and your children." They would soon suffer greatly during the coming destruction of Jerusalem and the temple by the Romans, so they should mourn for themselves. But what happened to Simon? In the Gospel of Mark, Simon's sons are mentioned by name: Alexander and Rufus (Mark 15:21). How did Mark know Simon's sons? Many believe that Simon actually became a follower of Jesus! How amazing! God uses even unexpected circumstances for our good. Simon must have regularly thanked God for selecting him to pick up that crossbeam and follow Jesus. If God is allowing you to live with an odd situation right now, be encouraged. You never know! You may end up thanking him for it later.

october
ONE

LUKE 23:32-43

Jesus did not die alone. Two criminals were executed with him. Although Jesus had been severely beaten and was in utter agony, he still thought about others. He asked God to forgive his enemies, since they did not know what they were doing. It wasn't that the religious leaders didn't have enough signs, but they were blind to Jesus' identity because of their false expectations for the King of the Jews. The rulers admitted that Jesus saved others. They taunted him with "He saved others; let him save himself." Jesus hung on the cross, the lowest a human could go. In their minds, no way could this be the Messiah. The Roman soldiers mocked Jesus too, while they gambled for his clothing. Like the religious leaders, the soldiers jeered, "If you are the King of the Jews, save yourself!" Even one of the men crucified with Jesus ridiculed him, also mocking, "Save yourself!" So the religious leaders, the Roman soldiers, and the crucified criminal next to Jesus all mocked him because he "couldn't" save himself. But the other criminal spoke a different message. He rebuked the criminal who mocked Jesus, asking him what he was doing. Jesus was innocent, and his punishment was unjust. They got what they deserved, but not Jesus.

Then the believing criminal asked if Jesus would remember him when Jesus was exalted as the King of the Jews. Jesus let him know that he wouldn't have to wait until the kingdom of God was fully established, because that very day they would be in Paradise together. In Jewish thought, Paradise was the home of the righteous in heaven. The criminal would be in heaven shortly. Death is merely a passageway to a place more amazing than one could ever imagine. The religious leaders, the soldiers, and one criminal mocked Jesus for his inability to save, *yet he did save*! Jesus saved a man right then and there on the cross. When one honestly turns to Christ in repentance and faith, she is immediately delivered from death to life. What a compassionate Savior we have! Even into his final moments, Jesus focused on others and not himself. May we follow the example Jesus left for us as we also love, serve, and know that God is in control of all the details along the way.

october
TWO

LUKE 23:44-49

Although it was the sixth hour, high noon, darkness came over the entire land for three full hours. Who knows what tool God used to bring that darkness. Whether it was fog, clouds, or something else, it symbolized what was happening on the cross. Darkness depicted either mourning, evil, God's judgment upon sin, or all three. During this time, the sin of humanity was poured out upon the soul of Jesus. God laid upon his Son the iniquity of us all. As Jesus previously said to the religious leaders, "This is your hour, and the power of darkness" (Luke 22:53). We cannot begin to imagine the pain that Jesus felt. The physical pain was horrific, but the spiritual pain would have been even worse. During this darkness, the curtain of the temple ripped in two from top to bottom. This was the curtain between the Most Holy Place and the Holy Place, designed to keep people away from the Ark of the Covenant and the mercy seat where God's presence dwelled. General humanity was not allowed to enter this place. Only one man could access this room one time each year. But now, all who followed Christ could directly stand before God without a human priest or an animal sacrifice. Jesus became both the ultimate Priest and fulfilled the sacrifice. This tearing of the curtain demonstrated the end of the temple as the center of God's activity.

In verse 46, Jesus cried out with a loud voice, "Father, into your hands I commit my spirit!" He quoted from Psalm 31:5: "Into your hand I commit my spirit; you have redeemed me, O Lord, faithful God." Jesus called upon God as his Father with a statement steeped in surrendered trust. He believed that the Father would take care of him. Then he died. The centurion, a Roman soldier who oversaw one hundred soldiers, declared, "This man was innocent." Even though Jesus became a curse for the sin of humanity, he continued to trust in God's good plan. Do you feel you are suffering unjustly in some area of life? Will you trust God in the midst of what seems unfair? Jesus, fully man though also fully God, chose to do things God's way to the very end. Let's pray that the Spirit of Holiness would strengthen us to do things God's way to the end.

october
THREE

LUKE 23:50-56

This Joseph, known as Joseph of Arimathea, was not in agreement with the religious leaders' decision to crucify Jesus. He was a wealthy man, and though he lived about five miles north, he owned a tomb in Jerusalem. Although Joseph was a member of the religious council known as the Sanhedrin, he believed in Jesus, trusting that Jesus would eventually establish the kingdom of God. Joseph, along with others, recognized that Jesus was the promised Messiah, but because these men feared the reaction of the leading Jews, they kept their faith hidden. Many who professed belief in Christ during this time suffered greatly at the hands of the Jews. They were excommunicated from the synagogues they attended, kept from participation in the local the marketplaces, and even cast out of their own families. It's possible that Joseph wasn't present when the Sanhedrin voted to execute Jesus, but once he became aware of all that transpired, his status shifted from a secret disciple to an open one. He boldly went to Pilate, got Jesus' body, quickly wrapped it, and placed it in his tomb. The female disciples present at Christ's execution were relieved to see Jesus' body taken down from the cross and treated with proper respect. But because of the approaching Sabbath, Joseph had to rush. No work could be done on the day of rest. So although Jesus' body was secured in the tomb, he didn't receive a proper burial. The women who followed Jesus planned to return after the Sabbath to anoint his corpse. The Jews didn't embalm their dead, but they did anoint them in spices to cover the smell of decay. These women were fully expecting to find Jesus' body where it was left in Joseph's tomb.

Verse 50 calls Joseph of Arimathea a "good and righteous" man. Though he was a sinner and needed the atoning work of Christ credited to his account, God saw him as upright. It is important to remember that we can be pleasing to God. No one can be saved or reconciled to God apart from Christ, but those who have trusted in Jesus and turned from their sins can make good decisions and, like Joseph, long for God's kingdom. May we always remember that even though we can never earn our position in God's family, we can make choices that glorify the Lord. May God find us righteous people today as we live in a way that brings honor to Jesus.

october
FOUR

LUKE 24:1-12

After the Sabbath, the women present at Jesus' crucifixion went out to anoint his body in the spices they had prepared. They probably hadn't slept well for a couple of days. The one in whom they had put all their trust was dead, and their hope of his kingdom coming in the way they expected was over. Nevertheless, they loved Jesus and wanted to show him as much respect as possible, treating his corpse with all the care they could. When they got to Joseph of Arimathea's tomb where Jesus' body was placed, the stone that secured the tomb and guarded the body was displaced. When they went in, his body was gone! Who took Jesus' body? How could anyone have managed that with guards stationed there? The women were exhausted, discouraged, and now Jesus' body was gone. They must have felt really confused. Then two "men," actually angels who radiated the glory of God, appeared before them. The women collapsed, overcome with fear. The angels asked why they looked for "the living" among "the dead" and reminded the women of what Jesus declared: he would be delivered to sinful men, crucified, and rise again. Could Jesus have really risen from the dead? The women rushed back to the eleven apostles and reported all that they saw and heard, but the eleven thought they were losing it. They must have assumed the poor women were just drained. So Peter went to check things out.

How would you feel if you took flowers to the cemetery where a loved one was buried, and found the grave empty? The last thing you would think is that the person rose from the dead. You would be upset. You would call the owner of the cemetery and probably even the police. The women didn't remember what Jesus told them, and the circumstances were about as bad as they could get. The last thing they could imagine was that Jesus rose from the dead, even though he declared that he would. How often do we do the same thing? When the circumstances around us get really dark, do we forget the words of Jesus? By his resurrection, Jesus proved his identity and the truth of his words. We need to read, study, meditate on, and believe all that Jesus spoke and taught. Choose to make a new commitment to embrace the words of Jesus today. His truth will remain forever.

october
FIVE

LUKE 24:13-24

Jesus was sentenced to death by the Jewish religious leaders, handed over to the Romans for crucifixion, and then executed. His corpse was placed in a tomb, which was then sealed with a stone. Everyone in Jerusalem knew what had happened. The hopes of those who followed Jesus were shattered. Now what would they do? Go home? Jesus' disciples left the cross and the Passover festivities that year absolutely broken. They really thought he was the One. A pair of Jesus' followers returned to their hometown of Emmaus, a small and obscure village. As they walked, they questioned everything that happened. None of it made sense in their minds. They just weren't able to connect the dots. One of these men was Cleopas, while the other was unnamed. As they mentally wrestled through all that transpired, someone joined them along their way. Luke reveals to the reader that it was actually the resurrected Jesus, but the two disciples remained clueless. Jesus blinded them to who he was and asked them, "Why the intense conversation? What's up?" Cleopas and his friend literally stopped dead in their tracks. They couldn't hide their sorrow. Cleopas asked, "Seriously? Are you a visitor here? Haven't you heard?" Jesus played along. "Heard about what?" Cleopas responded, "Heard about Jesus, who was a prophet. Our religious leaders crucified him. We really thought he was the Messiah." They accused Jesus of not "knowing" what happened, but in reality, they were the ones "clueless," as Jesus would soon reveal.

Jesus specifically met up with Cleopas and his companion. He knew what they were thinking. He knew how broken and discouraged they felt. Emmaus wasn't a significant village, yet these two disciples from a trivial community were very important to Jesus. Do you ever feel unimportant and obscure? If you are a follower of Jesus, you are just as important to him as an entire multitude. Even though you may be insignificant in the eyes of man, you are priceless in the eyes of the Lord. If you feel downcast or distressed, be encouraged today! Jesus knows exactly where you are. Think about his teaching and his words. Believe all that he said and taught. Those who trust in Jesus will never be put to shame. He has conquered death, overcome the world, and is able to strengthen you for all that he has called you to endure too.

october
SIX

LUKE 24:25-35

Cleopas and the other disciple were both deeply discouraged as they went back to their hometown of Emmaus. They truly thought that Jesus was the one who would restore the kingdom to Israel. But Jesus had been crucified, and so their hope of deliverance was gone. The news of Jesus' empty tomb depressed them even further. The possibility of Jesus' resurrection, which should have been a ray of light, only created additional confusion. They were blind to what Jesus had promised he would do. As they told Jesus what happened, they included the fact that it had been three days since these things occurred. If only they had been open to what Jesus had predicted. Jesus spoke firmly as he observed, "How foolish you are! And you are slow of heart to believe!" These two disciples knew the Old Testament. They connected the scriptural dots concerning who Jesus was when he healed the sick, delivered the demonized, and preached the good news of God, but they missed the parts about the suffering Messiah, who would be rejected and take on the sin of the world. Those were the portions of Scripture they weren't holding on to. Jesus explained to them that all of the Old Testament pointed to him. It must have been absolutely fascinating to listen to Jesus explain those things! Suffering and death were not a problem for Jesus. In fact, they were predetermined components of God's eternal decree.

Like Cleopas and the other disciple, we too can be selective regarding which parts of the Bible we hold on to. We may pick the verses that encourage us or comfort us, or memorize the Scriptures that contain guarantees of goodness and deliverance in our lives. But how often do we cling to the passages that teach about the suffering promised to those who follow Jesus? As honest Christians, we need to be ready to embrace the full counsel of God. We must give attention to the "happy texts" and the "not-so-happy ones" if we are to think and live consistently with all God has called his followers to. We are spared much grief when we live prepared for the difficulties about which God has forewarned us. Remember that our time on earth provides our only opportunity to share in the sufferings of Christ. When we get to heaven, the pain will be gone. Let's make sure that we learn from the trials God has sovereignly allowed in our lives today.

october
SEVEN

LUKE 24:36-53

Cleopas and his companion rushed back to Jerusalem to tell the others what had happened. The women claimed they saw Jesus, and Peter did too. Things were moving quickly, but the disciples were still confused. Suddenly, Jesus stood among them and explained, "Peace to you!" They were baffled. They thought Jesus was a ghost. Jesus showed them his nail-pierced hands and feet. Still stunned, they couldn't believe Jesus was actually there, yet they disbelieved "for joy." If it were true, then Jesus really was the Lord of all heaven and earth and held the keys to life and death. Jesus asked them if they had anything to eat, and he took some fish and enjoyed it in their presence. Then they knew it was him! Can you imagine how the disciples must have felt? They were more than ready to listen to whatever he said. He reminded them that none of this should have caught them off guard. He taught them again that all of it was foretold in the Old Testament. Jesus explained his death and resurrection in the Law, the Prophets, and the Psalms. Even after his crucifixion and resurrection, Jesus still placed highest priority on the record of Scripture. The Old Testament is loaded with accounts of people and places, offerings and festivals, and predictions and prophecies that point to Jesus as the promised Messiah of Israel. God's word and his promises were there the whole time. The disciples were caught off guard because the circumstances contradicted their understanding of the Old Testament.

We must continue to remind ourselves that God has communicated through the Scripture. The risen Lord Jesus Christ stood right in the midst of his apostles and referred back to what was written. The disciples were confused because what they experienced didn't line up with what they believed about the coming kingdom of God. They lost courage when the circumstances seemed to indicate that Jesus was not who they hoped he was. Has God allowed circumstances in your life today that are creating confusion and doubt? We may not see or understand the way he is weaving all together in his master plan, but we can know for certain that not one molecule is outside of his control. Let's trust him again today. May we never take from or add to what God has revealed to us as recorded in the Scriptures. All will come to pass, just as written.

october
EIGHT

JOHN 1:1-8

"In the beginning" echoes Genesis 1:1, which reads, "In the beginning, God created the heavens and the earth." John began by tracing the gospel all the way back to before the earth or even the universe was formed. What did John mean by the "Word"? The "Word" in English is translated from the Greek *logos*. In the simplest sense, *logos* or "Word" is defined as "the independent personified expression of God" (Bauer). We see this in Genesis 1:3, which records, "And God said, 'Let there be light,' and there was light." God, or the Word, said, and everything came into existence. *Logos* was also a common term used in Greek philosophical thought, so John addressed the minds of both Jewish and Greek readers. The Word was the agent through whom everything was created. The Word was also "life" and "light." Both created life and the light dispensed to humanity were from the Word. Out of nothing, darkness, the light shone. In verse 5, John alludes to the presence of evil by using the word "darkness." Darkness has not overcome the light. Ultimately, the light will overpower the darkness. God sent a man, John, as a prophet to point people to the Light who had come into the world.

John clearly set the stage by beginning with the "beginning" and taking the reader all the way back to the time when nothing existed but God. The Word, Jesus, created everything. God is the only being who was never created but always existed. According to this passage, God includes the Word, who came into the world in the person of Jesus. If the Word existed with God before creation and everything was created through the Word, then it would be illogical to say that the Word was a created being. The Word, Jesus, is and always has been God. To declare anything less is to deny the testimony of the New Testament. May we be awed by God and humbled by our fragility as we read these eight verses. The God of the universe existed before anything was created, and by his Word he brought all into being. At the same time, may we be overwhelmed with gratitude as we consider the power of our sovereign God and our relationship to him. Choose to clear your heart of any idols today. God alone is worthy of our worship.

october
NINE

JOHN 1:9-18

John's biography of Jesus is different from the biographies of Matthew, Mark, and Luke. In fact, Matthew, Mark, and Luke are called the "synoptic" Gospels because they are very similar. "Syn" means "together with," and "optic" means "seeing," so "synoptic" means "seeing together." John focuses more on the themes of life, light, and the Holy Spirit. The Word, the Creator, or the Light came into the world. Even though he was the one who made the world and gave life to all who inhabit it, the world rejected him. And worse, his own people, the nation of Israel, rejected him too. Yet some received him. Not only did they receive him, but also they believed in his name. They embraced who the Word was as a person, his message, and who he claimed to be. These people were given the right to be the children of God. Only those who have trusted in Christ and turned from their sin are adopted into the family of God. And that privilege actually results from an act of God. Verse 14 is astonishing. "The Word became flesh" and lived with humans. The second person of the triune God put on flesh and became a human being. And John, along with the other apostles, beheld his glory as he lived, taught, and worked miracles among them.

Verse 18 declares that "No one has ever seen God; the only God, who is at the Father's side, he has made him known." The Word of God who took on flesh, Jesus, who was at the side of and co-equal with the Father as a member of the triune Godhead, broke through the wall between God and man by becoming one of us. In an Old Testament encounter with God, even though his glory was veiled, there was a terror associated with viewing his splendor. But God has made himself known to us in Jesus. The Greek verb used for "made known" is *exegeomai*, from which we get "exegete." Jesus has revealed the Father to us. Don't let anyone ever convince you that the Son is not equal to the Father. If you want to see the Father, then look at the Son. If you want to please the Father, then please the Son. If you want to be like the Father, then be like the Son.

october
TEN

JOHN 1:19-28

John the Baptist was approached by Jewish priests and Levites sent by the religious leaders to discover his identity. When asked, John emphatically said he was not the Messiah. So they questioned him to see if he was Elijah. Or was he the Prophet who was to come? The one who would be like Moses? He said he wasn't Elijah or the Prophet. The priests and Levites had to come back with some answer from John. John quoted the prophet Isaiah and identified himself as the voice from the wilderness that cries, "Make straight the way of the Lord." John said he was not Elijah, but he was the one about whom Isaiah spoke. What did he mean by "Make straight the way of the Lord?" When Isaiah proclaimed this (Isaiah 40:3), he was referring to the time when the exiled Israelites would return to the land. Isaiah spoke of a leveling of the land so that the roads would be clear for God's returning people. Now John declared the same thing Isaiah had declared. John's message was one that should have cleared the roads for God's people to return to the Lord. So the Pharisees wondered, "If John isn't the Messiah, or Elijah, or the Prophet, then why does he have the authority to baptize?" The response John gave was powerful. He said he baptized with water, but one was coming who was so much greater than John that John wasn't even worthy to untie his sandal.

In the first century, untying a sandal was a slave's job. But John said he wasn't even qualified to do that! What humility and deference John gave to Jesus! When John pointed to Jesus, he didn't see Jesus as his equal. He didn't even see himself as lower than Jesus. Instead, he said he didn't even qualify to take a slave's role with respect to Jesus. The same is true for us. We don't deserve the love and acceptance Jesus offers us. If the righteous man John recognized his place before Jesus, may we do the same. In the end, we bring nothing to our salvation. Yet Jesus lifts us up and places us in his own robes of righteousness. Let us remember today that the path to greatness lies on the road to humility. When we humble ourselves, God himself will exalt us.

october
ELEVEN

JOHN 1:29-42

Jesus approached John the Baptist, and John declared, "Look! It is the Lamb of God who takes away the sins of the world." The Holy Spirit used John to declare a truth he was probably incapable of fully understanding at that time. Then John explained that he didn't know who Jesus was until he personally baptized him. God previously revealed to John that the Holy Spirit would visibly descend upon his Son, which happened when John baptized Jesus. At that time, John knew Jesus was the promised Son of God. And Jesus brought a new baptism, in the Holy Spirit. Under the Old Covenant, the Spirit would come and go, but now, as the Spirit descended and remained upon Jesus, the Spirit would soon remain on all who turn to Christ in repentance and faith. Why is it important that Jesus was called the "Son of God"? Aren't all God's children called "sons"? At times, both angels and humans were referred to as the "sons of God" in the Old Testament, but the "Son of God" was a title reserved for the Messiah. Later in John's Gospel, we will see Jesus debating with the Jews, who wanted to stone him. When Jesus asked them why they wanted him dead, he questioned, "Is it because I said I am the Son of God?" Clearly, John's audience knew what this title meant.

John distinguished between Jesus and the rest of humanity by referring to him as "the Son of God." When John said Jesus would take away the sins of the world, he probably didn't realize that Jesus would not only judge, but he himself would be judged by the Father for the sins of the world. The Father would allow the Son to suffer the wrath that our evils have earned. Nowhere in John's Gospel does the author call disciples the "sons of God." But he does call them the "children of God." Those who follow Jesus are now God's own children and have been adopted into God's family. And once we are truly in the family, he will never cast us out. Are you discouraged or afraid today? Remember that followers of Jesus have access to the most powerful Father in the universe. He will do whatever it takes to make sure that our circumstances work together for good, moving his children exactly where he wants us to be.

october
TWELVE

JOHN 1:43-51

While in Galilee, Jesus asked Philip follow him. Philip was from Bethsaida, where Peter and Andrew grew up. Philip then went to Nathanael, who was also a Galilean. Nathanael was from Cana, and questioned whether anything "good" could come from Nazareth. Philip responded, "Come and see!" Jesus called his early team together as he sovereignly prompted those who were following him to invite others to come too. Although Nathanael and Jesus were both from Galilee, even the Galileans like Nathanael thought Nazareth was a bust. When Jesus saw Nathanael approaching, he declared him to be a man without deceit. Nathanael was truly ready to check out the claims made about Jesus. He asked Jesus how he knew him, Jesus replied, "Before Philip called you, when you were under the fig tree, I saw you." That shocked Nathanael. How could Jesus have seen him? Clearly, Jesus had supernatural knowledge that belonged to God. Nathanael then declared Jesus to be the Messiah. Jesus told him that he would do much more. In the past, Jacob saw angels on a ladder going back and forth between heaven and earth. But now, Jesus himself was the ultimate connection between heaven and earth.

Jesus called Philip and Nathanael to himself. If we are followers of Jesus today, he has called us to follow too. Philip left Bethsaida in Galilee and went with Jesus. He left the comforts of his hometown, his business, and his family to do what Jesus asked. He even called others to come and join him! In the same way, we leave our old lives and take up something new when we follow after Jesus. We live in a place and time where we are free to follow Christ. It wasn't quite as easy for Philip and the first disciples. Many of the early Christians were killed for their allegiance to Jesus. What are you giving up to follow Jesus today? Popularity? Pleasures? Let's get our priorities right as we remember that following Jesus has always come at a cost. But in the end, the things we give up to follow him are of no lasting value. God isn't keeping anything truly good from us. If you have reached a decision point today in choosing which path to take, know that you will never regret your decision to do things God's way.

october
THIRTEEN

JOHN 2:1-12

Three days after the discussion with Philip and Nathanael, Jesus, along with his first disciples and his mother, were at a wedding in Cana, Nathanael's home city. The wedding was probably for a close friend of Jesus' family, since both he and his mother attended. It must have been large, and often such wedding celebrations continued for up to a week. Some have proposed that Mary may have had a role in catering at the wedding, since she felt responsible for the wine. In this culture, the groom was liable for the wedding costs, and to run out of wine would have been a huge embarrassment for him. The bride's family could have become angry and sued him as a result. Was Mary expecting Jesus to work a miracle? Probably not. Mary was potentially a widow at this point and probably used to depending on Jesus to get things done. Jesus responded to Mary with an interesting remark: "Woman, what does this have to do with me? My hour has not yet come." The statement sounds a bit rude. But Jesus was probably letting Mary know that since he was entering the period of his three-year ministry, his agenda would no longer be subject to her desires. Jesus' ultimate Father had a plan for his life, and that program would dictate the decisions Jesus made from then on. It can be easy to forget, but even Mary, Jesus' mother, needed to come to him for salvation.

Nevertheless, Jesus provided wine for the wedding guests. He asked the servants to fill with water the nearby large stone jars used for ceremonial washing. When the servants drew the "water" out, it was wine. And it was not only wine, but good wine. Why did Jesus perform this sign? The miracle symbolized the new covenant he brought. The old ceremonial system of washing in water was coming to a close, and the new covenant had begun. What Jesus brought, the wine, was superior to the old ways, symbolized by the water. When Jesus told his mother that she wasn't to interfere with his ministry, she responded with a fascinating statement. She said to the servants in verse 5, "Do whatever he tells you." Mary recognized Jesus' authority. What is Jesus telling you to do? To trust him? To turn to him? Follow the servants' example by doing what Jesus tells you to do today.

october
FOURTEEN

JOHN 2:13-22

The Passover required that the worshippers sacrifice an animal and pay a temple tax. Many people traveled for long distances to attend this event. It would have been inconvenient and difficult to travel with the animals to be used for sacrifice, so booths were set up where the worshippers could buy animals instead. In addition, the temple tax had to be paid with a certain coin that contained a high silver content. When Jesus saw what was taking place in the temple, he became angry. He used a whip to drive the animals out of the temple, and he threw the money changers' tables over. Jesus was not angry about the purchase of animals or the exchange of money, but he was upset that it was all taking place in the temple. Jesus was passionate about the "house" that God had set up for worship. People were to pray and connect with God on the sacred temple grounds, but the place set aside for the purpose of worship had become a mess. The Jews asked Jesus what authority he had to do what he did. On what ground could he claim to be the Son? Jesus told them that if they tore the temple down, in three days he would build it again. Later, his disciples understood what Jesus was talking about. Jesus meant the temple of his body. Three days after his crucifixion, he rose from the dead. His resurrection was the ultimate "sign."

In a short amount of time, the tables were back up, and the money changers and those who sold animals were in business again. They didn't heed the message Jesus brought. It was time to turn off the "noise" and focus on the Lord, but they continued with business as usual. What about you? It is important that we too make time for God. Do you set aside time in your busy week to simply worship the Lord? Do you pray with distractions around you, or do you get legitimate "quiet time"? When you are in church, are you thinking about other things, checking your text messages, wondering what's next? It is difficult in our fast-paced, rapidly moving culture to carve out time to simply worship Jesus. But it is necessary. Determine today to get time alone with God. And make sure it's time during which outside "noise" is off, even in your mind.

october
FIFTEEN

JOHN 2:23-25

While Jesus was in Jerusalem at the Passover, many people believed because of the signs that he gave, such as clearing the temple of the money changers and animal vendors. He performed other signs that John didn't record. But sadly, the faith of those who believed because of the signs was not legitimate and only short-lived. Although they "trusted" in him, it was only for a season. Their apparent trust wasn't genuine saving faith, resulting in a changed life. So Jesus chose not to entrust himself to them. In verses 23 and 24, the same Greek verb is used twice, though it is hard to see in English. In verse 23, many believed "when they saw the signs." The word "believed" is from the Greek verb *pisteuo*, which means "trust." In verse 24, Jesus did not "entrust" himself to these people. The word "entrust" is also from the Greek verb *pisteuo*. So they trusted in him, but he did not entrust himself to them. Why? Again, because he knew their "belief" would only be short-lived. Maybe they trusted that Jesus was the promised Messiah, until things didn't pan out the way they had hoped, and their trust came to an end. Jesus could not be flattered or tricked by any phony allegiance, because he knew all things.

Jesus sees things that we cannot. We can't see into another person's heart, but he can. At times, we struggle even to see into our own hearts, but he knows all. We should continually ask him for help to see our own motives clearly so we can live more closely in step with his desire for our lives, doing the right things for the right reasons. In addition, the all-knowing, or omniscient, nature of God should be a source of great comfort to those who follow Jesus. When we pray, we can be confident that God sees the beginning as clearly as he sees the end. We cannot begin to imagine his view of eternity. Spend a few minutes talking to God today. All things, including the details, are open and laid bare before him. Let him know about your plans, your desires, and your goals, and then ask him to work everything together for good according to what he knows will be best. And thank him too, because as a legitimate follower, Jesus has "entrusted" himself to you.

october
SIXTEEN

JOHN 3:1-15

John had just stated that Jesus knew what was in a man. In verse 1, John adds, "Now there was a man." Jesus knew what was in this man too. His name was Nicodemus, and he came to Jesus under the cover of night. He was a member of the ruling group of the Jews known as the Pharisees. He was probably concerned about his reputation since Jesus wasn't popular among the Jewish leaders. Nicodemus interestingly admitted, "We know that you are a teacher come from God." The Pharisees recognized Jesus' uniqueness because of the signs that he performed. Jesus could not do what he did unless God was with him. Jesus, knowing what was needed in Nicodemus, responded to his profession with "Truly, truly." In other words, "Listen! This is the truth!" And then he continued, "Unless one is born again, he cannot see the kingdom of God." Nicodemus was confused. How could he be born again? Jesus explained, "Unless one is born of water and the Spirit, he cannot enter the kingdom of God." Although there are many opinions about what "water and Spirit" refer to, it seems they are to be taken together as a unit. To be born again means to be born of water and Spirit. To the Jew, water symbolized purification or cleansing, and the Spirit symbolized being raised from death to newness of life with the power to obey God's law (Ezekiel 36:25-27).

Have you ever referred to yourself as a "born again" Christian? You may not realize that the statement is redundant. Using the term "born again Christian" is like saying "Christian Christian." According to Jesus, if one is not born again, she is not a Christian. Jesus clearly taught that no one is physically born as a Christian. In verse 6, Jesus added, "That which is born of the flesh is flesh, and that which is born of the Spirit is spirit." This should not have surprised Nicodemus, and it should not surprise us either. When were you born again? How has your life changed since? If you were cleansed and empowered to walk in the Spirit, have you stayed on track? If not, ask God to help you walk consistently with who you are as a born again person. If you are a follower of Jesus, God's Holy Spirit has brought you to life twice, both physically and spiritually. You are truly alive!

october
SEVENTEEN

JOHN 3:13-21

The conversation between Jesus and Nicodemus continued, as Jesus provided further explanation about heavenly things. Jesus took Nicodemus back to an interesting point in Israel's history. The account is recorded in Numbers 21:4-9. When the people of God were wandering in the wilderness, they criticized both God and his servant Moses' leadership. Because the people weren't happy with their circumstances, God sent serpents among them to deliver venomous and deadly bites. Even though the people spoke against Moses, he cried out to God on behalf of the nation and asked God to forgive them. In response, God told Moses to make a bronze serpent and put it on a pole. Then Moses was to lift the serpent up on the pole. The people who looked at the serpent on the pole were saved. Jesus taught Nicodemus that in the same way he himself would be lifted up, so that whoever looked at or trusted in him would be saved. What did Jesus mean by the phrase "lifted up"? John actually used this phrase four times in his Gospel to mean "lifted up" on the cross. Nicodemus had no clue about Jesus' future, but Nicodemus would have understood the account of the serpent in the wilderness. It is interesting to consider whether Nicodemus remembered this conversation when he saw Jesus on the cross.

Nicodemus, like the rest of humanity, needed to turn to Jesus as his only hope for life. In the Numbers account, not all of the people were saved. Some refused to look at the serpent on the pole that Moses set up. Why would they not look? Stubbornness? Pride? Did they feel they didn't need God's help? Who knows! In the same way, some will refuse to trust in Jesus. Why? Stubbornness? Pride? Maybe they feel they don't need God's help. But for those of us who have looked to Jesus or trusted in Jesus, what a relief to know that we have been healed of the venomous effects of our sin! And we aren't merely preserved in this life, but we have eternal life that no one can take away from us. Is it because we were good? No. We are saved simply because we have turned to Jesus as our only hope. God sent his Son to save the world. Pray that those you know and love would be graced with the faith necessary to turn their eyes upon Jesus and be saved.

october
EIGHTEEN

JOHN 3:22-36

After Jesus' conversation with Nicodemus, he and his disciples traveled into the region of Judea. Although Jerusalem is in Judea, they left the city and went into the country. While in Judea, Jesus and his disciples gained a following, and Jesus oversaw the baptisms his disciples performed. Some of John the Baptist's disciples didn't understand why people were going to Jesus instead of their leader, John. They wondered, "Why are his disciples baptizing too? We thought people were supposed to come to us for baptism. What is going on?" John responded to his own disciples by explaining, "A person cannot receive even one thing unless it is given him from heaven." John clearly understood that God is the one who calls a person to her job, position, or status. John realized he was there to bring glory to God. He was in no way envious of what God had given to Jesus. In fact, he rejoiced when he saw that others were leaving him and following the Lord. John knew he was not the bridegroom, but the friend of the bridegroom. At a wedding, the attention is rightly fixed on the bride and the groom, not the wedding party. In fact, the wedding party is called to serve the bride and the groom. John was thrilled that others were turning to Jesus.

John adds an incredibly profound statement in verse 30. He declares, "He must increase, but I must decrease." He didn't say he *may* increase, or I *hope* he increases, but he *must* increase. We can forget that this life and the life to come are about God and his glory. He embraces us, cleanses us, adopts us, and uses us in his program, but the goal of all of this is to point back to him. Those who don't understand the nature and grandeur of God may think, "How narcissistic of God!" Well, sure, if God weren't really God, then he would seem overly self-involved. But let us never forget that he is God! The reality is that all exists because of him and all exists for him. Of course he should increase! May we stop and consider God today. Are your daily choices bringing glory to God? If so, then let us go on to rejoice, remembering that Jesus is the bridegroom, and he has made us his bride! Things don't get better than that!

october
NINETEEN

JOHN 4:1-11

The third chapter of John began with an exciting conversation between Jesus and Nicodemus, a Pharisee or a ruler of the Jewish people. Now John records a conversation between Jesus and a woman who was not only a despised Samaritan, but an adulterer. Nicodemus sought Jesus, but Jesus approached the Samaritan woman. Nicodemus and the Samaritan woman were polar opposites, and yet Jesus met with, spent time with, taught, and invested in both souls. Although they were incredibly different, they were equally important to him. It was noon (the sixth hour), the hottest time of the day. Jesus was tired, hungry, and thirsty. The disciples went to town to buy food, and Jesus waited for them by the well that Jacob gave Joseph about two thousand years earlier. While there, a woman came to draw her day's supply of water. Women usually came to draw water either early in the morning or late in the afternoon, and they also came in groups. So why did this particular woman come to the well in the heat of the day all by herself to get water? She was a social outcast, and no one wanted to be seen with her, no one except Jesus, that is. Jesus said to her, "Give me a drink." The woman was surprised and caught off guard. She asked Jesus, "Why would you, a Jewish man, ask me, a Samaritan woman, for a drink?" No Jewish rabbi would have asked her for a drink, no matter how thirsty he was.

The phrase used in verse nine, "For Jews have no dealings with Samaritans," probably referred to the fact that the Jews did not use dishes that Samaritans had used. A first century rabbinic law said that all Samaritan women were unclean. Though Jesus was parched and thirsty, his desire wasn't to get water as much as it was to meet her spiritual need. He told her that he could give her living water. Like this woman, have you ever felt like an outcast? If so, be encouraged by this account. Jesus sought her out. He asked her for a drink. He offered her living water. If you are a follower of Jesus, he has done the same for you. He bore your disgrace on the cross and set you free to live boldly for his glory. Pursue Christ without any shame or reservation today.

october
TWENTY

JOHN 4:12-26

The dialogue continued between Jesus and the Samaritan woman. Jesus told her that if she knew who he was, she would have asked him for living water. What was he talking about? Typically, when people traveled from city to city, they would take some type of canteen with them to draw their own water. He didn't have a bucket or any receptacle. How would he give her this "living water"? Then she asked Jesus, "Are you greater than our father Jacob?" Jesus answered her, "Whoever drinks of the water I give will never thirst. It will well up to eternal life." She replied, "Give me this water!" Jesus was physically thirsty, but he knew this woman was spiritually thirsty. And only he could provide what she needed. So he asked her to get her husband and come back. She told Jesus she didn't have a husband, which he already knew. In fact, he told her she had tried to satisfy her spiritual thirst with five husbands, and she wasn't even married to the man with whom she was currently living. She was empty and lonely, trying to get whatever she could to satisfy her soul. She was broken and an outcast in her community. She was so far down in the dumps that she didn't see any way out. When Jesus told her what he knew about her, she was shocked! She said, "Um. I think you are a prophet." Then she changed the subject and began to talk about the proper place to worship.

No matter what we do or how hard we try, none of us can make ourselves whole before God. We all need Jesus. Our souls long for meaning and purpose. We can numb ourselves to those inner desires by telling ourselves that we are the center of the universe, yet something gnaws at our inner man and declares that's just not true. The woman told Jesus that she knew the Messiah, or someone like Moses, would come and explain all things. Jesus revealed to her that he was the Messiah. What compassion Jesus had upon this broken woman! Though God graces us with his goodness through creation, nothing will ever satisfy like Jesus. The world will bombard us with messages that tell us we need other things or people to satisfy us and that we are missing out. Anything we look to for satisfaction outside of Jesus will leave us dry and needing more. May we determine never to turn from the living water back to empty wells.

october
TWENTY-ONE

JOHN 4:27-36

After Jesus revealed to the Samaritan woman that he was the Messiah, his disciples returned. The disciples were in shock. They wondered why Jesus wasted his time talking to a woman, and a Samaritan woman at that! Many rabbis of the day taught that it was not only useless, but also wrong to teach the Scripture to women. Some believed it was better for a man to instruct his daughters to be sinners than to dialogue with them about the word of God. And others even went so far as to say that speaking to his wife was not a wise use of a man's time. Jesus made it clear that both men and women have equal value before God, and both should be students of his word. The woman went back to town and bore witness to the people who lived there about her encounter with Jesus. She asked them to consider, "Can this be the Christ?" The people of the town decided to check it out for themselves. Something had clearly changed in this woman who was known for her sin. She wasn't hiding in shame anymore. As the townspeople were coming out to see Jesus, he told his disciples to look up. The "fields were white for harvest."

In verse 28, John mentions that the woman left her water jar and went back to town. Why did she leave her water jar? Did she allow it to remain there so Jesus and his disciples could drink? It has been suggested that John included this phrase as a symbol of what happened in this woman's soul. She had come face to face with and honestly trusted in the claim Jesus made about himself. She was now one of his followers, and the "old" water was no longer important. The woman went back to town, having experienced the living water. She would never thirst in the same way again. The natural result of a transformation like this is a desire to tell others. Those who have experienced living water don't want to keep it to themselves. Even though the world may not be interested, the joy of salvation is one that followers of Jesus have a hard time keeping undercover. Pray for an opportunity to tell someone about Jesus today. Let that person know how trusting Jesus transferred you from the realm of guilt and shame to a life of confidence and satisfaction in the Lord.

october
TWENTY-TWO

JOHN 4:39-45

The Samaritan woman with whom Jesus conversed went back to tell everyone in town that she had possibly found the Messiah. Jesus then told his disciples that the fields were ready for harvest. Verse 36 records that he said the reaper "is receiving wages." In other words, the one who reaps, or brings in the harvest, was already at work and receiving payment. The harvest, or the fruit the reaper brought in, was made up of the souls in Samaria who turned to Jesus in repentance and faith. Verse 36 tells us Jesus explained to the disciples that the sower and the reaper work together. The Samaritans believed in Jesus, and they even asked him, a Jewish teacher, to stay with them. Things were changing, and Jesus began to break down walls of animosity that had been established generations ago. Many from the town professed that Jesus was the Savior of not just the Jews or the Samaritans, but of people from all nations of the world. Two days after this encounter, Jesus and his disciples traveled into Galilee, where he was accepted, although not fully embraced in the same way he was by the Samaritans.

Jesus taught that one sows and another reaps. One plants the seeds and the other secures the harvest. Again, the harvest Jesus referred to was one of human souls. Jesus clearly taught that we all play different roles in the process of evangelism. Some sow the word of God in human hearts by conversation and discussion, and others direct those souls to Jesus when the time is right. Both the sowing and the reaping are important to Jesus. Have you ever felt discouraged because it doesn't seem like you are the one reaping the harvest of many souls? Maybe you have tried to engage in conversation about God, Jesus, heaven and hell, but few have come to the place of repentance and faith. Be encouraged still! You never know how many of those people have been or will be born again and what your part in the process was along the way. Keep talking to others about Jesus. Be prepared to step into whatever role the Lord wants you to play as he unfolds his grand design before the watching universe.

october
TWENTY-THREE

JOHN 4:46-54

Jesus went to Cana of Galilee, where he had made the water into wine. The people of Galilee wanted to see the signs Jesus performed, but they didn't receive him as the Messiah like the Samaritans did. Jesus went to a town called Capernaum, where an official sought Jesus because he had heard about his supernatural activity. The official's son was dying, and he was absolutely desperate. He was a wealthy man and had access to many resources, but nothing helped his son to get better. When the official heard that Jesus was in town, he requested that Jesus come and heal his son. Jesus responded, "Unless you see signs and wonders you will not believe" (v. 48). He was speaking indirectly to all the Galileans. The official pleaded, "Sir, please. Let's not waste time. Just come and help my son." But Jesus refused his request. Yet he told the official to go home because his son would not die. Clearly, the official believed Jesus, because he did exactly as Jesus said. The official trusted in what Jesus declared. And his trust did not fail him. The official's servants met him as he traveled home and told him his son was recovering. He asked them when his son began to feel better. When they told him the exact time, the official realized it was the very same hour when Jesus told him his son would not die. His son was saved physically and spiritually.

How often do people "come to Jesus" for the wrong reasons? Like the residents of Galilee, many today seek Jesus because they believe he will fix something that's wrong with their lives. They hope Jesus will heal them, improve their relationships, give them money, or just make them happier. But they aren't really interested in obeying the teachings of Jesus or coming under his authority as their Lord. The official at Capernaum did end up believing when he discovered that Jesus had healed his son. In fact, his whole household believed. Jesus broke natural law so that people would repent. If God has done anything for you, healing you or helping you or gracing you with happiness, make sure you respond rightly to those blessings by obeying Jesus. If you are a follower of Jesus today, then celebrate all he has done for your soul.

october
TWENTY-FOUR

JOHN 5:1-18

Jesus went to Jerusalem to celebrate one of the feasts. In the northern section of Jerusalem, two pools lay near a small gate known as the Sheep Gate. These pools were surrounded by colonnades, which supported a roof to enclose the pools. Sick people would gather around the pools, believing that the water could heal them. These pools were probably fed by natural springs, and often the water would "stir." The popular conviction was that when the water stirred, an "angel" moved it, and so the sick rushed into the water, thinking the first one in would be cured. One man who waited to get into the pool's stirred water had been an invalid for 38 years! He was probably paralyzed and depended upon others to carry him whenever the water was expected to move. Jesus approached him and asked him if he wanted to be healed. The man said he did, but explained to Jesus that he didn't have any friends who could rush him down to the water when it stirred. He was waiting, but never able to get to the water first. Jesus told him to get up and walk. He was immediately healed.

The mat on which the man rested was made of straw. After the man was healed, he rolled it, picked it up, and walked. This all took place on the Sabbath. The Jews said it was illegal for the man to carry his mat on that day. Instead of rejoicing and praising God for the healing, the Jews were angry that the man carried a mat on the Sabbath. They asked him to reveal who healed him. He said he didn't know. But when Jesus later told him to repent of his sin, he ran and told the Jews that it was Jesus who healed him and instructed him to carry his mat. This man was not interested in the Lord. Now that he had what he wanted, he saw no need for Jesus. Some will always engage with Jesus simply for what they can get. And often, after they have received from his hand, such people have no further use for him. What if Jesus allowed you to struggle with your current difficulties for the rest of your life? Would you still love him? Be faithful to Jesus because of his great love for you today.

october
TWENTY-FIVE

JOHN 5:19-29

The Jews were angry because Jesus told the man he healed to pick up his mat and go. According to their rules, it was wrong to move possessions on the Sabbath, so they accused Jesus of advocating the breaking of the law. Jesus said some remarkable things in response to their accusations. He declared that neither the Father nor the Son have stopped working. If God were to cease from activity, the universe would implode. Jesus stated that just as God works, so does he. Jesus does exactly what God wants him to do. In fact, the unique relationship between Jesus and the Father made it impossible for Jesus to do anything contrary to the will of the Father. Whatever the Father does, the Son does. The Father gives life, and so does the Son. The Son gives both physical life and, more importantly, eternal life. The Son will judge the earth and all its inhabitants. If the Son is the one who will judge all, then there is no way for that person to be right with God but not right with the Son. Jesus is God, and whatever he does is a perfect reflection of the Father's will.

In verse 23, Jesus said, "Whoever does not honor the Son does not honor the Father who sent him." Many have pointed out the truth to which C. S. Lewis drew attention: Jesus was either lying, or he was a lunatic, or he truly was who he claimed to be, the Lord of all heaven and earth. The statement "Whoever does not honor me does not honor the Father" leaves no room for exceptions. The only way to the Father is by trusting in Jesus. We can easily overlook the fact that not only Jesus believed this to be true, but so did John, the author! So John too was either lying, mad, or telling the truth. John was an eyewitness to the life and ministry of Jesus. The claims made here are so radical that no middle ground can exist. If you are not an honest follower of Jesus today, let this be your turning point. If you are a follower of Jesus, be encouraged! Your Savior has covered all your sin and shame on the cross. Keep clinging to that truth. Soon, our confidence in Christ will be vindicated.

october
TWENTY-SIX

JOHN 5:30-38

Jesus continued his discourse with those who were angry with him. Not only were they enraged, but they were also seeking to kill him because he broke the Sabbath and because he made himself equal with God. Jesus let them know that he only did what the Father wanted him to do. To reject Jesus was to reject the Father. He declared, "If I alone bear witness about myself, my testimony is not true," addressing the Jews through legal terms and concepts. He brought in additional witnesses, as a lawyer would have done in a court. First, Jesus brought in John the Baptist as a witness. John was well-known and actually revered by many of the Jewish people. He came on the scene in a prophet-like manner, and he testified that Jesus was the Lamb sent to take away the sin of the world. Second, Jesus said that even greater than the witness of John the Baptist were the miracles he performed. Miracles were signs authenticating that Jesus was who he claimed to be. Finally, Jesus brought the ultimate witness into court: the Father. The Father spoke at Jesus' baptism, testifying that Jesus truly was the Son of God. The message from the Father was "Listen to the Son!"

We have the testimony of Jesus, the witness of John the Baptist, the signs he performed, the voice of the Father, and the view of the author. All declare that Jesus is who he said he was. He is the second person of the Triune God. Those who reject Jesus reject God. In our culture, people can justify bearing false witness in a court of law. They lie about what they did or didn't do, what they did or didn't experience, or they refrain from giving all the information about which they are questioned. But God considers bearing false witness a very serious crime. Do you believe the testimony of Jesus and his witnesses? If so, then choose again this day to live your life according to his words. Anyone and everyone who chooses to follow Jesus, trusting in his righteousness and not their own, will never regret that decision. Jesus is true, and so is his teaching. As the old hymn says, "Trust and obey, for there's no other way to be happy in Jesus, but to trust and obey."

october
TWENTY-SEVEN

JOHN 5:39-47

The Jews were diligent students of Scripture and believed that their intense study of the Old Testament would add to their acceptance by God. Although they steeped themselves in their Bibles, they missed the fact that those very writings bore witness to their need for Jesus. Messianic Old Testament prophecy pointed to Jesus, and many of the people and events in the Scripture foreshadowed Jesus. In fact, the entire Old Testament sacrificial system awaited its final fulfillment in Jesus. The Scripture was another witness Jesus brought into "court," but the people didn't get the intent of the documents they so passionately embraced. Even Moses, the author of the Torah, would charge them as guilty for missing the mark when it came to the purpose of the Bible. The aim of Jesus was to please the Father, even if that meant displeasing men. Jesus asked them, "How can you believe, when you receive glory from one another and do not seek the glory that comes from the only God?" The people Jesus addressed sought the praise that came from one another, not the praise that comes from God. They were willing to follow those who bore messages they wanted to hear, messages that appealed to their desires, but they rejected both God's message and his Son. They simply didn't want to do things God's way.

All of humanity possesses some form of a conscience and an awareness of right and wrong behavior that comes from God. Yet if we concede that he exists and has given us this knowledge, then we must admit that he is the Creator. And if he is the Creator, it is critical that we line ourselves up under his will, even when it contradicts our own will. Jesus taught that no one is qualified to stand before God by herself. No one can meet his standard. The Scriptures show that all humanity has failed to live according to God's plan and design. The Jews with whom Jesus spoke needed his provision for their sin. In the same way, our friends and neighbors, no matter how nice or kind or moral they are, need the righteousness of Jesus. Each must see her hopeless state before she can cry out to God for deliverance. Stop and pray that those you love would clearly see their desperate and immediate need for salvation through the only one qualified to make them acceptable to the Lord. If God can save us, he can save them too!

october
TWENTY-EIGHT

JOHN 6:1-15

The "Feeding of the Five Thousand" is the only miracle recorded in all four Gospels, Matthew, Mark, Luke, and John. Many people were following Jesus because they heard about his miracles. When Jesus saw a massive crowd coming to him, he asked Philip, "How can we feed all these people?" Philip lived nearby and would know where to get food. Philip replied, "Even if we had two hundred days' worth of wages (or about eight months of pay) we couldn't feed them all." Andrew chimed in and told Jesus of a boy present who had five loaves and two fish. But Andrew said that wouldn't be of much help. John is the only Gospel author who mentions that the loaves were barley. What difference would that make? Barley was the lowest and cheapest form of grain available. Barley loaves were the food of the poor. The fish were also small and simply served to add flavor to the low-grade bread. John also records the abundance of grass. This lets the reader know it was springtime (Passover). Verse 10 states that five thousand men were present. That means the total would have been thousands and thousands more if the women and children who ate were added in, and many scholars suggest fifteen to twenty thousand were actually present.

The people hoped that Jesus would be a king who would continually provide them with food, eliminating their physical hunger. But Jesus came to satisfy a much deeper need: their spiritual hunger. The miracle of physical provision was to teach them about Jesus' ability to satisfy the hunger of their souls. Verse 15 states, "Perceiving then that they were about to come and take him by force to make him king, Jesus withdrew again to the mountain by himself." He knew there would be no kingdom established before he met the cross. The feeding of the five thousand or the fifteen thousand was a miracle. If you are feeling discouraged, like you only have a few barley loaves and a couple of sardines to offer, remember that Jesus is the one who can and will abundantly fill you. And he will fill you so that it will seem as if baskets full are leftover. Ask Jesus to satisfy the longings of your soul today, and expect him to do it.

october
TWENTY-NINE

JOHN 6:16-21

After feeding the five thousand men, plus women and children, the crowds wanted to forcefully make Jesus king. He knew their motives were wrong, and he left them so that he could be alone. His disciples went ahead of him down to a boat on the Sea of Galilee. They wanted to get to Capernaum. It was dark, so they got into a boat and headed out. Well into their journey, when they were close to halfway across the lake, the wind grew strong, and the sea grew rough. Because the Sea of Galilee is located significantly below sea level (six hundred feet), it is not unusual for cool winds to rush down upon the warm air sitting right above the water, creating sudden and even violent weather. The disciples continued to row, struggling to get across the lake. Then they looked up and were horrified. They saw a person walking across the water right toward them. They were certain it was a ghost! But Jesus literally said to them, "I am," or "It is I." Then he exhorted them to be not afraid. They eagerly welcomed him into the boat, and suddenly they reached their destination. Symbolically, in the Old Testament, the sea often represents chaos and destruction. Jesus calmed and brought order to the disciples' confusion and trouble. The presence of Jesus in the boat brought them to the other side.

When Jesus walked to the disciples, it was dark, and the storm was raging. The disciples, many of whom were professional fisherman, really struggled to get the boat across the lake. Yet as soon as they took Jesus into their boat, the fierce sea was calmed. Clearly, Jesus was no ordinary man! Not only could he defy the law of nature by walking on water as if it were dry land, but he had the authority to calm the storm when he wished. Jesus had this kind of power and authority before his death and resurrection, and he has it now as he sits at the right hand of the Father. Do you feel like your life is entering an hour or season of darkness? Are your current circumstances stormy? If so, call upon Jesus. Just as he was able to control the storm on the Sea of Galilee, he is able to control the difficulties in your life. Jesus will get all who follow him safely to the other side.

october
THIRTY

J O H N   6 : 2 2 - 2 7

The thousands of men, women, and children whom Jesus fed wanted to make him king. This was the kind of leader they were looking for, one who would produce bread and fish as needed. After the miraculous feeding of the massive crowd, darkness fell, and the disciples left to cross the Sea of Galilee. But Jesus wasn't with them. He had gone off by himself. The next day, the people thought, "Hmm. There was one boat. The disciples are gone. So where is Jesus? Is he still in the area?" They looked, but he was nowhere to be found. Other boats then pulled up to the crowd's location, and the people decided to travel back with them across the lake. When they finally found Jesus, they asked him, "When did you come here?" But Jesus didn't respond to their question. Jesus knew that the crowd had missed the significance of his miracles. Jesus' supernatural provision for their physical hunger should have caused them to see that he was able to provide for their spiritual hunger. They saw the signs, but they were really only interested in another meal. They lacked much more than they realized, and Jesus was right there to fill them, but they failed to recognize their true need. It's easy to think that if you were a participant in something as spectacular as Jesus' multiplication of bread and fish that you would "get it" and be "good to go." Clearly, witnessing miracles doesn't always lead to conversion.

Verse 27 records that Jesus said, "Do not work for the food that perishes, but for the food that endures to eternal life, which the Son of Man will give to you." There's nothing wrong with working at our jobs, and we need to do what God has called us to with excellence. But life is not about simply working to exist. Jesus warned the crowd not to spend their lives pursuing only things that have no eternal value. Let's stop and refocus today. Ask God to help you follow the advice of Jesus and work for things of eternal value. God set his seal on Jesus. The Father authenticated the Son as legitimate. If you want to know what God wants you to do today, listen to his Son and invest in the life to come.

october
THIRTY-ONE

JOHN 6:28-34

Jesus had told the crowd they should not only work for the bread that perishes, but for things of eternal value. The crowd didn't get what he meant, so they asked what they needed to do. They were basically saying, "Tell us what God wants from us, and we will do it." Jesus responded that the "work" God wanted from them was to believe. But they weren't to believe in just anyone or anything, because the work of God was to believe specifically in Jesus. The crowd then requested that he perform another sign. If he made the food again, then they would believe. Actually, if he continued to provide them with food, like Moses did with the manna in the wilderness, then they would follow. Jesus told them it wasn't Moses who gave them manna to eat, but God. In fact, God gives true bread from heaven. The true bread that came from heaven was Jesus himself. Manna fed and sustained the body, but Jesus feeds and sustains the soul. "Hmm," the people thought, "true bread?" Then they asked him to give them this true bread, not just today but always. The people were still focused on the here and now.

This crowd may frustrate us. We can think, "Seriously? Jesus just fed your crowd of possibly fifteen thousand or more with a young kid's snack. But that wasn't enough? You want more signs to believe?" In verse 30, they asked Jesus, "What will you do?" They wanted him to go above and beyond what Moses did if he was who he claimed to be. Let's not forget that we can sometimes act and think as oddly as this crowd did. Jesus answers our prayers, yet we soon grow frustrated by what he doesn't do. Jesus rescues or delivers us from trouble, and we say we aren't whether it really was him. Jesus saves our souls and graces us with his righteousness, and we feel like things aren't fair and we aren't getting all that we deserve. Who knows how strange we might appear to the multitude watching from above. Choose today to focus on what you have, rather than thinking about what you don't have. To begin, if you are a follower of Jesus, then you have the true bread from heaven.

november
ONE

JOHN 6:35-44

After being supernaturally fed, the crowd around Jesus said they wanted the true bread from heaven. Jesus clarified that when he spoke of true bread, he was referring to himself, not physical bread. True bread was the remedy for humanity's spiritual hunger. The bread that Jesus provided didn't have to be given again and again. Once one becomes a follower of Jesus, her soul is continually satisfied. And Jesus quenches spiritual thirst too. In the first of Jesus' seven "I am" statements recorded in John, Jesus declared, "I am the bread of life." Although the crowd saw Jesus, they still didn't believe. Jesus next declared, "All that the Father gives me will come to me, and whoever comes to me I will never cast out." Jesus wasn't worried that his life and work would be fruitless. Then and now, God has ordained souls who come to him. The focus of Jesus' life was to do the will of the Father. And the focus of our lives should be to look on and trust in the Son. The Jews present weren't happy with the statements Jesus made. Wasn't he the son of Joseph and Mary? They knew his parents! How could he say he "came from heaven"? Jesus told them to stop grumbling. They couldn't come to him without God's intervention anyway. They were trapped by their own unbelief.

Jesus stated some fantastic truths in this passage. He said those who are his followers have been given to him by the Father. Wow! Before even time began, God planned to save all sorts of people through Christ's provision for sin on the cross. And those people are the Father's gift to the Son. If you are a believer, God has played a bigger part in your redemption than you may ever have realized. Even your faith is not from yourself. God has chosen you to be a part of his eternal family. And Jesus will raise you up on the last day. If you have been born again, your eternity is absolutely secure because it is based on Jesus' work, not your own. Christian, if you are discouraged about anything right now, lift your head. You are the bride of Jesus, and he will never stop loving you or break his commitment to you. You are in the most secure place in the universe! What a reason for joy today!

november
TWO

JOHN 6:45-59

Jesus referred to Isaiah the prophet's teaching and added that all who hear and learn from God will come to Jesus as a result of the internal illumination the Holy Spirit gives. Jesus continued to emphasize that if one truly trusts in him, she has eternal life, and the credit even for her trust belongs to God. Again, Jesus proclaimed himself to be the bread of life. Then Jesus took them back to the manna that God gave their ancestors in the wilderness. Even after eating the manna, they still died. But those who "eat" of him will never die. When Jesus talked about "eating" his flesh, he wasn't speaking about the Lord's Supper or Communion, because he didn't institute that until a year later. John began this Gospel by stating that the Word became flesh (1:14). Eating his flesh meant putting one's full hope, trust, and confidence in the work that he came to do. Only by turning to him can anyone ever gratify the longings of her restless heart. Of course, the Jews were quite puzzled and even offended by all this, wondering how Jesus could give his flesh for food. Jesus said, "unless you eat the flesh of the Son of Man and drink his blood, you have no life in you." The things he referred to were necessary for salvation. But drinking blood was forbidden! What was he talking about?

In saying his flesh and blood must be consumed, Jesus meant that one must ingest or feed upon him to be saved, describing total dependence on Jesus and his teachings. It isn't enough to be familiar with Jesus. Instead, we must be nourished by him as if he were our very food. We must realize that we cannot survive without him. Was this a hard teaching? Yes! In fact, many left after Jesus spoke these words. But followers of Jesus understand what he meant. We recognize that we have no source of life outside of him. Jesus is our everything. When we eat food, we are strengthened to do what the day requires. In the same way, when we turn to Jesus as our sustenance, he provides us with everything we need to live and act as God desires. May we never neglect the true bread who satisfies and strengthens the souls of his people.

november
THREE

JOHN 6:60-71

Jesus' teachings were hard. They were so hard that not only the hostile audience, but many who said they believed began to grumble. This wasn't what they were looking for. What Jesus taught was difficult to understand, and it seemed harsh too. Jesus asked his disciples whether they took offense at what he said. They were upset, but certainly not because Jesus didn't communicate with gentleness and respect. He asked them, "What if you should see the Son of Man ascending to where he was before?" For some, this was only the beginning of what would offend them, and for others these things would prove true when Jesus was vindicated. Jesus added that it is the Spirit who gives life. Our flesh profits nothing. Those who were not stumbled by the teaching of Jesus were actually enlightened by the Spirit. We simply can't embrace the teaching of Jesus without the work of the Spirit. Jesus again said, "This is why I told you that no one can come to me unless it is granted him by the Father." Humbling as it may be, according to Jesus, the ability to truly trust in him is an act of God. No one can work up saving faith by herself. It is impossible. So that was the end of the line for many. They were just done with Jesus.

What about you? Would you be offended by this teaching? Many of God's truths are difficult. As Jesus watched people walk off, he turned to his twelve disciples and asked them, "Will you leave too?" Who knows whether an awkward silence followed or the twelve looked down in embarrassment. Peter asked, "Where else can we go?" What other religious teaching will satisfy our soul? For the Christian, there is nowhere else to go. We have been changed from the inside out and made brand new by the Holy Spirit. Even if we battle with the hard teachings of Jesus, we can't leave him. Are you struggling with obedience to a challenging teaching of Jesus today? If so, be encouraged. Though things may seem hard, if you are his follower, he will give you what you need to do what he asks. His Spirit has rewired you, and his Spirit will be right there with you as you journey through even hard days and difficult nights to come.

november
FOUR

JOHN 7:1-11

After Jesus' difficult teachings about being the bread from heaven, he didn't want to remain in Judea, the region in which Jerusalem lay, because the religious leaders there sought to kill him. Now the Feast of Booths, one of the three most significant Jewish feasts, drew near. This was a time of abundant celebration of thanks to God for the year's harvest. Jesus' brothers urged him to go to Jerusalem and make himself known. They didn't understand why he wasn't doing more in public. No one who wants to gain a following does so much in secret. They thought if he really were the Messiah, he needed to work harder to gain a following. The Feast of Booths would be the perfect time for him to make himself known as the King of the Jews. Then the nation could finally experience the political deliverance she desperately longed for. Like the crowds who were fed by Jesus, his brothers were looking to him for what they could get. Previously in John's Gospel, Jesus' mother wanted him to make wine at a wedding to save the bridegroom from embarrassment. Jesus asked why she bothered him with the issue, but then he took care of it. The same thing happened here. He told his brothers it wasn't the right time, but then he secretly went to the Feast on his own. All the Jews watched for him, but all were afraid to admit it.

Verse 5 reads, "For not even his brothers believed in him." His brothers grew up in the same home with him, but they were not saved until after Jesus' resurrection. They saw him as a political deliverer, not the One who came to take away the sin of the world. Unlike Jesus' brothers, we must recognize that our problem with God is due to our sin, and trust in Jesus as our only hope. But we can't follow a Jesus that we create to satisfy what we want. He doesn't help us work our way to God or give us assistance when we need it. We are totally unable to get to heaven without his provision for our sin, and we can add nothing more to the righteousness he gives us. Let's determine anew to believe what the Bible proclaims about Jesus instead of what the world or even our own imaginations suggest about him. Jesus is our Savior, and he is our only hope.

november
FIVE

JOHN 7:14-24

Halfway through the Feast of Booths, Jesus went to the temple, which would have been swollen with crowds, including people visiting Jerusalem. Jesus began to teach, and the Jews who heard him were astonished. They wondered how Jesus, an unschooled and untrained man, had so much "learning." He didn't go to the notable rabbis of the day for his education. How was he able to handle the Scriptures so masterfully? Those trained by the leading religious experts deferred to the opinions and decisions of past rabbis. But Jesus was different because he only taught what was from God. The people actually challenged Jesus' credentials. How ironic! God took on flesh, and the people wondered what qualified him to teach! Jesus explained that he wasn't self-taught. Instead, God taught him. Now, does this mean that Jesus "just knew" everything because he was God? Not really. As a human, he chose to limit himself and only exercise his divinity when it was to the glory of the Father. When he took on flesh, he played by the rules of humanity, suffering and learning in the same way we do. But he did it all perfectly, without any error or even slight deviation from the will of the Father.

Jesus added, "If anyone's will is to do God's will, he will know whether the teaching is from God or whether I am speaking on my own authority." The crowd listened to Jesus perfectly communicate the desire of God to humanity, but they didn't believe him. Their unbelief had nothing to do with Jesus' education, presentation, or explanation of eternal truths. Those who rejected him did so because they didn't want to turn from their own ways and do what God asked. So too today, people will hear the word of God, yet walk away unchanged. It's not the fault of the Scripture when God's message makes no impact, but the fault of the hearer who honestly isn't willing to do things God's way. When God moves a soul to desire obedience to Jesus, that person knows the teaching of Jesus is from God. If you are struggling today, ask God to make you willing to do his will. He wants you to want what he wants. Stop and ask him to help you do what is right.

november
SIX

JOHN 7:25-31

The people from the crowds in Jerusalem realized that something was amiss. They knew the religious leaders were plotting to execute Jesus, but they didn't do anything about it when he taught openly. The people asked one another, "Do you think the religious leaders know he is the Messiah?" Maybe the authorities sat down and realized Jesus was who he claimed to be. The duplicity demonstrated by the religious leaders of Israel confused the people. If Jesus was a liar or a lunatic, then get rid of him. But if he really was the Christ, then they needed to listen to him. But almost as quickly as they proposed the notion that Jesus actually was the Messiah, they shut the suggestion back down. They reminded themselves that when the Christ appeared none would know where he came from. Where did they get that idea? Rabbis taught that when the Messiah would come, he would basically appear out of nowhere. He would arrive suddenly to deliver the nation from bondage. So Jesus couldn't be the Messiah, because they knew Jesus was from Nazareth. It's funny, but the reader of John's Gospel knows the truth behind Jesus' origins. He was in the beginning with God. Jesus didn't begin his public ministry until his last three years of life. The people missed what was right in front of them.

Jesus responded by literally crying out and exposing their foolishness. They thought they knew him and where he came from, but they had no idea what they were talking about and no clue about who sent him. Not only did they fail to recognize that Jesus was sent from God, but missing Jesus the Christ evidenced that they didn't know God at all. This all must have been exhausting for Jesus! It's frustrating just to read about it. Nevertheless, he continued to work with them. As we see in verse 31, suddenly, many did end up "getting it," and they believed. How thankful we should be for the great patience of our God! Where would you be if Jesus hadn't intervened in your life by removing the blinders from your eyes and allowing you to see? If someone you love just isn't getting it, hang in there. Keep praying for her and talking to her about Jesus. You never know when she too might "suddenly" believe.

november
SEVEN

JOHN 7:32-39

As far as the religious leaders were concerned, it was time to get rid of Jesus, so a formal arrest warrant was issued. But Jesus let them know that though they were ready, God wasn't. Jesus would be arrested, but not yet. In fact, where he would ultimately go, they wouldn't be able to find him. The Jews listening wondered what in the world he was talking about. Was he going to go after the Greek-speaking Jews who had moved out of Israel and get involved in foreign lands? Not yet. Not until his followers took the gospel to the ends of the world. For now, he meant he would ascend to heaven, where the Father was, very soon, and the leaders would not be able to come after him. Many were in Jerusalem during the Feast of the Tabernacles, a celebration of the provision and the presence of God. A water-pouring ceremony occurred throughout the feast, in which the people would express their thankfulness for the provision of water. On the last day, they would go around and around the pool and cry out, "Please bring salvation now! Lord, save us!" On the last day of the feast, Jesus made an astounding statement. He boldly proclaimed that only he could satisfy spiritual thirst. Jesus actually declared that they should come to him and drink.

What did John mean when he wrote that the Holy Spirit had not yet been given? Were believers at this time saved without the Spirit? Did they live without the help of God? No. In many Old Testament incidents, the Holy Spirit illuminated, worked through, or empowered God's people to do his will. In fact, no one has ever been able to trust God for salvation apart from the Holy Spirit. Nevertheless, we should not overlook the fact that we, the church, are incredibly blessed to have the indwelling presence of the Holy Spirit upon conversion. Forgetting this great truth can cause us to live discouraged and defeated lives and not walk victoriously in the freedom with which the Lord has graced every believer. If Jesus has provided for your thirsty soul, then live consistently with the Holy Spirit with whom he has filled you. Say "no" to sin and "yes" to righteousness today.

november
EIGHT

JOHN 7:40-52

Some in the crowd, those who heard Jesus declare himself the one to whom they should come for their spiritual thirst, believed he was the Prophet or the Messiah. But others said, "No way. He can't be the Christ." They reasoned that any good student of Scripture would know the Messiah comes from Bethlehem and not Galilee. Those people had no idea that Jesus was born in Bethlehem! In fact, God moved Caesar Augustus to issue a census so that Jesus would have to be born in the city of Bethlehem. The people began to divide over who Jesus was. The soldiers sent by the Pharisees with an arrest warrant came back empty-handed, and the religious leaders demanded, "Where is Jesus? You were sent to arrest him!" The officers explained that there was no way they could arrest him. The crowd would have been in an uproar. Right in the middle of the water-pouring ceremony, as the crowds were calling out to God to save them, Jesus declared himself as the solution to the thirst of humanity. The Pharisees were furious and wondered if the officers believed in Jesus. Then they boasted that none of the religious leaders among them believed in him.

At this point, Nicodemus, who had secretly approached Jesus at night, spoke up. He asked the Pharisees, the experts in the law, "Since when do we condemn a man without investigating his claims first?" The Pharisees accused Nicodemus, a member of the ruling class, of ignorance. They told Nicodemus to read the Scripture. The Messiah doesn't come from Galilee. They thought they were superior to these "common people." In all the commotion, Jesus didn't end up getting arrested as the Pharisees planned, and Nicodemus displayed great courage. He was one of them, but he stepped out from them and stated that he wasn't buying into their logic. It is hard to identify with Christ, especially when the élite among us see us as idiots. And yet, our belief in Jesus means that we can and will stand up for him. If you are mocked for your confidence in Christ, remember the many who have walked this path before you. Be encouraged! Your hope in Jesus will be vindicated in the end.

november
NINE

J O H N   7 : 5 3 - 8 : 1 1

    This is an unusual passage because the oldest surviving manuscripts of John's Gospel don't contain the account. Although it is debatable whether this was part of John's original Gospel, little else falls into the "maybe" category when it comes to passages of the Bible. There are many surviving New Testament documents, and scholars have a tremendous number of texts from which to work. The majority of scholars believe this account actually occurred, although it wasn't part of John's biography. Either way, including or omitting it doesn't alter Christian theology. According to the story, while Jesus was teaching, the religious leaders drug a woman before him who had been caught in the act of adultery. They reminded him that Moses commanded stoning for this offense and asked Jesus what he thought should happen to her. They weren't really interested in Jesus' opinion, but they thought this would be a great way to entrap him. The scribes and Pharisees wanted to execute her, but because they were under Roman rule, they didn't have the authority to do so. If Jesus said she should be stoned, he would be "in trouble" with the Romans. If he said she shouldn't be stoned, then he would be "in trouble" with Moses. He didn't speak at all, but instead wrote something in the dirt. He told those who were without sin to stone the woman. One by one, they walked away.

    Many women throughout the world, in the past and even now, have been executed because of a manipulative mob. In today's text, the mob claimed that this woman was caught in the act of adultery. If that were true, then what happened to the man? Why was he released while she was condemned? The religious leaders used this woman to entrap Jesus. But Jesus saw through their deceit. He defended the woman without condoning her sin. He reminded the angry mob that they were just as guilty of sin as she. People often wonder what Jesus wrote in the dirt. Many suggest he listed the sins of those present, maybe even writing the names of those with whom they were committing adultery. This would make perfect sense given his charge to the woman to "Go and sin no more." Jesus defended the woman against unjust treatment, and he spoke to her sin, saying, "Neither do I condemn you." We all deserve death and hell, but because we are in Christ there is no condemnation for us either. The mercy of Jesus should bring us to our knees in gratitude today.

november
TEN

JOHN 8:12-20

On the last day of the Feast of Tabernacles, Jesus made a profound statement about himself. He made the second of his seven "I am" statements found in the book of John when he proclaimed, "I am the light of the world." Verse 20 says that Jesus was in the treasury of the temple when he spoke these words. The treasury was the busiest place during the Feast of Tabernacles. It was located in the Court of Women and housed thirteen large "treasure chests" into which the people put their monetary offerings. Now every night during this feast, they held what was called the Illumination Ceremony. In this ceremony, the Levites, priests, and musicians with all sorts of instruments moved through the temple and sang from the psalms. Four giant candelabra in the Court of Women stood almost 75 feet high, equipped with four golden bowls, one on top of each stand. The priests made wicks from worn out garments, and during the ceremony, young men who carried ten-gallon pitchers of oil would climb ladders to fill the bowls. When the oil in those bowls was ignited, it produced beautiful fires that leapt toward the sky. One ancient book says every courtyard in Jerusalem was illuminated. Jesus stood in front of these massive candelabra and declared, "I am the light of the world." Can you imagine? Jesus declared himself to be the light of the world against the backdrop of this massive candelabra.

The giant candelabra lights in the temple were to remind the people of God's presence with them. As he was with them during their wilderness wanderings under Moses in the form of a pillar of cloud by day and a pillar of fire by night, he was with them still. No matter how difficult times were, they could rejoice, knowing that God was there. And just as God was present with his people in the days of Moses, during the time of Christ, and at all other points in history, he is present with believers right now. Even if you are feeling forgotten or left out, know that as a Christian, Jesus is with you. He is the light of the world. It is his light that has illuminated your soul. And his light will take you by the hand and guide you all the way into the next life. Christians never walk alone.

november
ELEVEN

J O H N   8 : 2 1 - 3 0

Jesus contrasted himself and the Pharisees, who were hostile towards him. He said he was going away to a place where they could not go; he was from above and he was not of this world. In contrast, they would seek him and not find him, they would die in their sins, they were from below, and they were of this world. His passion, focus, and agenda centered on the life to come. Their passion, focus, and agenda centered on this life. Jesus declared that unless they believed he is the "I am," they would die in their sins. All they could ask in response was, "Who are you?" Jesus declared he was who he said he was all along. What does it mean to die in sin? It means that when you leave your physical body, entering into the next life, you remain in your sins. Because your sins are what separate you from God, you will remain separated from God for all eternity. But we can die in faith, rather than in our sins. Jesus said, "unless you believe in me" or "unless you have faith in me," you will die in your sins. To have faith in Jesus means to trust in his provision and payment for our moral failure before a holy God. It means to receive the righteousness that he provides for those who turn to him, and it means to live life longing to do his will over our own.

Jesus said he would be "lifted up." As he told Nicodemus in chapter 3, he would be lifted up on the cross. At the same time, he would be lifted up when he conquered sin and death, exalted as the victorious one. His greatest hour of humiliation was also his greatest triumph. As we follow after Jesus, at times God will allow us to suffer and experience pain and loss. The cross was both Jesus' humiliation and his glory. Jesus asks his followers to take up their crosses as well. God allows us to die to certain hopes, dream, and aspirations so that he can free us by lifting us up as we shine the light and love of Jesus to a lost and broken world. Stop and ask God to help you magnify Jesus in the midst of your suffering. May he be more glorified through our pain than he would be without it.

november
TWELVE

JOHN 8:31-38

After Jesus' last dialogue with the Pharisees, many listeners believed in him. At the same time, those hostile to Jesus increased their determination to get rid of him. Jesus instructed those who trusted to abide in his word. Jesus knew some were genuine disciples, and others were "fair weather" disciples who walked with him only until things became difficult. So Jesus taught those with him that if they were truly his disciples, they would remain in his word. It can frustrate us to think that some who associate themselves with Jesus or enjoy the benefits of being around Jesus may not be really converted, yet we must remember that Jesus addressed this very thing. He taught those who said they believed in him that they must remain under his teaching to be set free. This tripped them up. How could they be set free? They weren't enslaved to anyone. Sure, they were under Roman rule, but they weren't slaves. And to top it off, they were the descendants of Abraham. How could Jesus say they were slaves? Jesus pointed out that all of humanity is born into a state of slavery. He used the phrase "truly, truly" to emphasize this fact. He wanted to be clear to all who heard him teach. None but Jesus himself has been able to live a life totally free from sin. It just can't be done.

Every soul is born with a wish to do things her own way instead of God's way. But when we trust in Jesus, we are liberated from our bondage to sin. Upon conversion, for the first time, we are set free so that we can live right. The indwelling power of the Holy Spirit gives us the ability to say "no" to sin and "yes" to righteousness, even though our sinful nature keeps us from living as victorious as we really are in Christ. But thank God that although we battle our sinful nature on a moment-by-moment basis, if we are honest followers of Jesus, we are truly free. One day, when we see him face to face, our old self will be forever cast off, we will want nothing but what our God desires, and we will do everything in harmony with who we are in Christ. What genuine hope the promise of freedom brings to those who believe! Praise Jesus for your freedom today!

november
THIRTEEN

JOHN 8:39-47

Jesus just explained to those who rejected him that they were slaves to sin. But they didn't see themselves as slaves. In fact, they boasted that they were descendants of Abraham. Jesus declared that if they were true descendants of Abraham, they would have received him. Abraham believed God and desired to do things the Lord's way. If they were like Abraham, they would have embraced Jesus. Jesus explained that they were children of the one they obeyed. Then they threw in a dig at Jesus by saying, "We were not born of sexual immorality," hinting that Jesus' birth was questionable. They were thinking, *Who was Jesus' father anyway? Was Joseph his father, or someone else? At least we know the identity of our fathers!* Jesus made it plain that they would have known him too if they knew the Father, as the Father and the Son are inseparable. He spelled out to them that their father was in fact the devil, which is why they wanted to follow the devil's desires. If they were children of Abraham, they would have done what Abraham did. But since they were children of the devil, they did what the devil does. What a person believes is displayed in what she does.

The Jews just couldn't understand what Jesus was talking about. Verse 43 tells us that Jesus beseeched them, "Why do you not understand what I say?" Did he mumble when he spoke? Did he have a hard time finding the right words to express what he wanted to say? No! In fact, he went on to answer his own question: "It is because you cannot bear to hear my word." Jesus' words couldn't permeate their flinty hearts. The same thing happens today. Many people hear the truth of Jesus explained in a way that is clear, articulate, and logical, and they often agree to more than a few facts about Jesus. But in the end, they just aren't willing to do God's will. But those of us who are followers of Jesus can rejoice, knowing that God himself removed our hearts of stone and replaced them with hearts of flesh. Because God has done this for us, we can be confident that we have been chosen to take part in his plan for eternal life. If you are feeling anxious and fearful about the future, remember that God will faithfully finish the work he began in you. The Christian is in good hands with Jesus!

november
FOURTEEN

JOHN 8:48-59

Jesus continued his conversation with the hostile Jews. They were not happy with him, and they didn't appreciate his statement that their father was the devil. In their minds, to say that Jews had any father apart from Abraham was nonsense. They accused Jesus of being demon-possessed. Jesus let them know that he was not possessed by a demon, but only did what the Father asked him to do, and because the crowd failed to honor Jesus, they failed to honor the Father. Emphatically, using "truly, truly," Jesus affirmed that if they kept his word, they would never see spiritual death. "Ha!" the crowd sneered, "Now we know you are demon possessed." The claims Jesus made about himself were outlandish, unless he really was God. The crowd thought Jesus had lost his mind. They questioned who he thought he was. Jesus explained that God's will was to glorify his Son. In fact, Jesus argued, they didn't know God because they didn't obey his word. If they obeyed, they would have realized that Jesus was the Son and they would not have rejected him. On the contrary, Jesus knew the Father and did exactly what the Father wanted him to do. Jesus added that he was the fulfillment of Abraham's hope. The crowd was done with him. They asked him what he was thinking. How could Abraham have seen Jesus? Abraham had been dead for a very long time. This all sounded like absolute nonsense to Jesus' audience.

Jesus wrapped the conversation up with a loaded statement. He told them to listen. "Truly, truly," he said again, "before Abraham was, I am" (v. 58). What did that mean? Jesus told them he existed before Abraham. And to top it off, Jesus declared himself to be the "I am!" He said he was God. And the Jews knew exactly what he meant, so they picked up rocks to stone him for blasphemy. As Jesus concluded this intense conversation with his opponents, one thing was clear: Jesus declared himself to be God. Because he is God, those who trust in him will live forever. Jesus diligently dialogued with his opponents so that he could communicate his identity to them and to us. He displayed great patience by becoming a human and by reasoning together with other humans. If he has persuaded you, then keep his word by paying attention to all that he taught. Live consistently with what you believe.

november
FIFTEEN

JOHN 9:1-12

Jesus and his disciples walked by a man who was born blind. As they passed him, the disciples wondered why he was born blind. Was it because he sinned, or because his parents sinned? They clearly believed that sickness, disease, and pain were a result of sin. This was known of as the Doctrine of Retribution, which held that if a person sinned, bad things would happen to her, and if a person obeyed God, good things would happen to her. The disciples should have remembered the lesson of Job. Sometimes suffering is not a direct result of sin or wrongdoing, but God allows it to occur for his own good purposes. Suffering is not always the direct result of an individual's own disobedience. Jesus responded to the disciples' question: "It was not that this man sinned, or his parents, but that the works of God might be displayed in him." Then Jesus chose to heal the man. For the first time in his life, he was able to see. Did he know that God allowed him to live his life blind so that Jesus would be glorified as a result of his supernatural healing? Some days, he probably even wondered if his own sin or his own parents' sin had caused his condition. It is easy to forget that bad things can happen to obedient people and good things can happen to disobedient people.

In one way, all suffering is the result of sin. Had no sin ever entered the world, we would still be living in perfection with no sickness, disease, or pain. Yet, many people suffer greatly as a result of something unrelated to their personal sin. The ultimate example of this is Jesus. He suffered tremendously, not for his own sin, but for the sins of others. Sometimes the Doctrine of Retribution proves true, and other times it doesn't. We like to think that if we do good, then good will happen to us, and we can live pain-free as long as we do the right thing. It often feels better to believe all is related to the Doctrine of Retribution instead of the sovereignty of God, because it keeps us in control. May the Lord help you to trust his ability to manage the affairs of your life today, rejoicing in all things as long as he is glorified.

november
SIXTEEN

JOHN 9:13-23

The Pharisees realized that Jesus performed a miracle when he restored the blind man's sight, so they asked the man how Jesus did it. The man maintained that he really didn't know. Jesus put clay on his eyes, he washed, and then he could see for the first time. When the Pharisees heard that Jesus "made clay" on the Sabbath, they called him a law-breaker. He broke their Sabbath rules when he mixed mud and water together. "How could Jesus be from God?" they reasoned, "He worked by making clay on the Sabbath. He must be a sinner." But others asked, "How could Jesus do these great signs and *not* be from God?" A division arose, and they asked the man who was healed what he thought about Jesus. He believed that Jesus was a prophet. Now, some of the Jews must have suggested that this man was never actually blind. They proposed that it was all a big hoax and got the man's parents involved. They asked the parents if the man was their son and if he was born blind. They said "yes" on both accounts. They also asked the parents how he was able to see now. They said they didn't know, which couldn't have been true. When their son came home seeing for the very first time, there's no way they didn't ask how it happened. They were silent because they feared for their safety if they mentioned Jesus. So they told the Jews to ask their son himself.

Just as Jesus healed the man born blind, God has healed his followers of many spiritual sicknesses, diseases, and infirmities as well. In fact, all those born again have been delivered from spiritual death! Sometimes critics will wonder why the Christian doesn't fear trials and tribulations the way non-believers might. The world wonders why we want to live for the life to come and not the here and now. When our spiritual opponents question us, we have to be honest and courageous. We don't want to be like the man's parents who claimed, "We don't know who opened his eyes." Let's make sure we are always prepared and ready to give an honest and intelligent defense to anyone who would ask us about the hope that is within us. Let's always do it with kindness, and let's never forget to include the truth that Jesus is the one who allowed us to see, healing us of our spiritual blindness.

november
SEVENTEEN

JOHN 9:24-34

After the Pharisees questioned the parents of the man born blind, they questioned the man himself again. They would not concede that Jesus was from God. They tried to push the man to expose some "dirt" on Jesus. "Give glory to God," they commanded. They wanted him to tell the truth about Jesus, and he did. They insisted that Jesus was a sinner. The man born blind said he didn't know whether or not Jesus was a sinner. He only knew that he was blind, and now he could see. They asked him yet again, "What did he do to you? How did he do this?" Fed up with these questions, the man boldly confronted them: "Why do you keep asking me about this? Do you want to become his disciples?" What a great response! Unfortunately, they just grew angrier and insisted they would never be disciples of Christ. They were disciples of Moses. When the religious leaders insisted that Jesus was not the Christ, they had firmly declared, "We know where this man comes from" (John 7:27). Now, suddenly, they claimed they had no idea where Jesus came from: "As for this man, we do not know where he comes from" (v. 29). The religious leaders were so bent on putting Jesus away that they were beginning to lose their minds!

Then the man whom Jesus healed grew even bolder. The spiritual blinders seemed to fall from his eyes as his interrogation proceeded. God allowed him to be born blind, and Jesus healed him. But the Pharisees could only "see" his blindness as punishment for some special level of sin. Was God now in the business of answering the prayers of sinners? Unthinkable! So they admitted he was born blind and could now see, yet they refused to consider Christ. They failed to see their own blindness and excommunicated the man from their synagogue because they decided he was now a follower of Jesus. The truth that God has made provision for humanity through Jesus alone can make people very angry. In fact, sometimes they begin to think, act, and reason in totally illogical ways. If you are a Christian today, like the healed man, be honest and kind, but don't be ashamed of drawing attention to the folly of unbelief. You may not get the response you want, but by discussing spiritual matters, your own faith often grows stronger.

november
EIGHTEEN

JOHN 9:35-41

Jesus heard about the man he had healed and his interrogation by the Pharisees. Jesus also learned that this man was cast out of the synagogue for his courageous testimony. The man had never actually seen Jesus. When Jesus put the clay on his eyes and told him to wash in the pool of Siloam, he was still blind. It wasn't until after he washed that he could see. But by then, Jesus was gone. Jesus found him and asked him if he believed in the Son of Man. The healed man asked who the Son of Man was, so that he could believe in him. Then Jesus revealed himself. Hundreds of years earlier, the prophet Daniel saw a vision of the Son of Man. The Son of Man was presented to the Ancient of Days and given an everlasting dominion and a kingdom that would never be destroyed. Daniel saw all people groups of the world serving the Son of Man. This title happened to be Jesus' favorite designation of himself. It is a unique term because it conveys Jesus' humanity along with his mission to redeem mankind. When Jesus disclosed who he was, the healed man believed and worshipped him as the Lord. Jesus then revealed that he came to pronounce judgment on the actions of the ungodly. He would cause the blind to see and the sighted to grow blind because the blind admit their need, whereas the seeing think they have no need.

Evidently, this conversation occurred in a public place, because the Pharisees asked Jesus if they were blind. Jesus answered that if they were honestly blind, they would not be guilty of rejecting him. But they had the opportunity to see, and because they didn't believe in the Son of Man, they remained guilty. The healed man faced rejection for his alliance with Jesus. His parents, concerned about what others thought, also left him on his own. Then Jesus showed up. Jesus made the first move and found this man. Jesus revealed himself so that the man could see physically and spiritually. God has promised that even if those closest to us reject us, he will never leave us. Not only does he stay with us, but he is the one who takes the initiative in seeking us out. Stop and thank Jesus for loving you first and gracing you with the faith to love him in return.

november
NINETEEN

JOHN 10:1-6

Jesus contrasted those who enter the sheepfold through the door with those who try to get in some other way. Shepherding was common in the first century, and Jesus' audience would have been quite familiar with the subject of the analogy. The sheepfold was like a gated courtyard where sheep were placed at night. Different owners would often use the same sheepfold, and a gatekeeper was hired to make sure no one unauthorized entered the pen. Jesus called those who attempted to jump the fence "thieves" because they were interested in stealing the sheep. The religious leaders of Israel were like thieves. They had just excommunicated the man born blind after he bore testimony to the fact that Jesus healed him. The religious leaders were called by God to take care of his sheep or his people. Instead, the Pharisees and other leaders abused God's flock. When a legitimate shepherd wanted to access the sheep, the gatekeeper opened the door to him. The shepherd would enter the fold and call out to his sheep, even using the personal names he had given each one. He knew exactly which sheep were his, and the sheep knew his voice too. If a stranger called, the sheep would not respond. When the shepherd collected his sheep, he went out before them, leading them, and they all followed. Many believe Jesus was showing the Pharisees how his people were leaving the religion of Israel to follow after him.

The ancient shepherd would lead the way before his sheep. He would call out to his sheep, and they would hear and follow after him. Jesus' opponents did not recognize his voice, as verse 6 makes clear. Although they should have, they simply didn't understand what he was saying. Hundreds of years earlier, in Numbers 27:15-17, Moses asked God who would go before and lead Israel like a shepherd. In the very next verse, God tolls Moses to lay his hand on Joshua, displaying to the people that Joshua would lead Israel. It is easy to miss that the Hebrew name "Joshua" is translated "Jesus" in the Greek. God's plan was always for Jesus to lead his people. If Jesus is your shepherd, your leader, make sure you are following in his footsteps. He won't let his sheep get too far off the path, and because they are his sheep, they won't even want to. Sheep want to be near the shepherd.

november
TWENTY

JOHN 10:7-21

Jesus had said he was the shepherd and his people were his sheep. He then continued to teach about himself and his relationship to his people using the analogy of shepherding, but he explained his role in a second way here. Jesus declared, "I am the door of the sheep." This was the third of the seven "I am" statements in the Gospel of John, and it meant that no one could go into the sheepfold except through Jesus. According to this illustration, the only way to become a part of God's flock is to enter through Christ. While others come, trying to win over the sheep, only Jesus promises abundant life, because he is the only provision for the sin of humanity. Then, Jesus made the fourth of the seven "I am" declarations in John's Gospel. He declared, "I am the good shepherd." What was the difference between the shepherd and the "good shepherd"? Often, shepherds would hire others to take care of their flocks. When danger came to the sheep, the hired hand wouldn't invest as much into protecting the sheep as the true or "good" shepherd did. In fact, the good shepherd was willing to risk his own life for the safety of his sheep. The hired hand would quit his job before he took a chance with his own personal peace and safety for someone else's flock. Jesus wasn't simply a shepherd, but he was the Good Shepherd.

Jesus was qualified to be the good shepherd because of his total control over all of life's circumstances. He affirmed that he would both lay down and take up his own life. No one could take it from him without his permission. Jesus was and is fully capable of taking care of each and every one of his sheep. Jesus also said that some of his sheep were *not* from Israel and not even born yet! The latter includes all of us! If you are a follower of Jesus today, you are a member of his flock. He laid down his life for you, not only to protect you from wolves, but to liberate you from the penalty of your sin. As a part of his flock, you have abundant life. Because you continue to follow his voice, your life will overflow with much to do for your shepherd. As a Christian, your life can make a difference in this world and the world to come. Now *that's* abundant living!

november
TWENTY-ONE

JOHN 10:22-30

The Feast of Dedication was not one mandated in the Old Testament. It was added to commemorate the victory of God's people over Antiochus Epiphanes, the Syrian leader who defiled and desecrated the temple in 167 BC. After this event, Judas Maccabaeus, a Jewish man, assembled an army of passionate Hebrews who became guerrilla fighters and took the temple back. The people celebrated for eight days, and according to tradition, a tiny amount of oil, only enough for one day, burned supernaturally for eight days in the sanctuary lamp that had been rededicated to the Lord. We know this event as Hanukkah, and even today Jewish families light a candle each day for eight consecutive days to remember this triumph. This festival was also known as the Feast of Lights. During this time, Jesus remained in the temple. The Colonnade of Solomon lay on the eastern side of the temple, which would have been warmer during the cold winter months. The Jews closed in on him and asked, "When are you going to tell us if you are the Christ?" They couldn't wait to hear him just say it publicly. They were hoping Jesus was another Judas Maccabaeus who would overthrow the Roman government, but that simply wasn't Jesus' mission. They still didn't recognize him because they were not his sheep. Jesus' sheep listened to him, responded to his word, and followed him. The Jews who questioned him simply wanted political deliverance.

Jesus made a most remarkable statement about the eternal security of the believer in this passage. He said no one will snatch his sheep out of his hand, and no one will snatch them out of his Father's hand either. Jesus declared that he has the Christian protected safely in his hand, and the Father has his hand over that! Those who follow Jesus are in God's double hand-clasp. One hand in the clasp belongs to Jesus, and the other hand in the clasp belongs to the Father. Who can "rip off" what belongs to God? No one! There is no way anyone can harm the soul of the one who belongs to the Lord. Though this life may be difficult and filled with ups and downs, the believer is guaranteed to arrive safely at her destination in the next life. If you are a follower of Jesus, you are in the most secure place in the universe.

november
TWENTY-TWO

JOHN 10:31-42

Jesus had just declared to the Jews around him that he and the Father were one (10:30). In response, the Jews picked up rocks to throw at him and kill him. They claimed they weren't going to stone him for what he did, but for what he said. Jesus reminded them that even in the Old Testament human beings were called "gods." In Psalm 82, God, the ultimate judge, appointed mere men to act as judges on earth, and they were termed "gods." These men were supposed to judge rightly for the Lord, but they failed. Some see the nation of Israel as a whole represented by these judges or "gods." Whether men or the nation, although none were actually God, they acted as his representatives on earth. Jesus taught that these people weren't stoned for being "gods," so again, why were the Jews so upset with him? If other people were called gods in the Scripture, why were the Jews so angry that he called himself the Son of God? The answer is that they thought Jesus was a man who made himself out to be God (v. 33). The reader of John's Gospel must realize that the converse is instead true: Jesus was and is God, who made himself a man. He wasn't an ordinary man, but truly God in the flesh. Of course he should be called God! The Jews had things reversed.

Jesus explained that if he truly was who he claimed to be, then they were the ones committing blasphemy, and they would incur the judgment of God. Jesus further explained that the Scripture cannot be broken, because it is the word of God. The Jews recognized this as true, and they were unable to argue with what the word of God declares. They understood the Scripture's inerrancy, or inability to be wrong. Even if it is difficult to understand or tough to apply, because it contains the truth that God desires to reveal to humanity about himself, us, and our relationship to him, we cannot afford to treat it lightly, cast it aside, or ignore the laws and principles it illuminates. The word of God is a lamp to our feet and a light to our paths in this dark world. Make sure you spend time daily in the Scripture. Meditate on it, memorize it, and apply it to your life. Heaven and earth will pass away, but the word of the Lord will remain forever.

november
TWENTY-THREE

JOHN 11:1-10

When Jesus was far away, his close friend Lazarus became deathly ill. The two sisters of Lazarus, Martha and Mary, sent a messenger to Jesus, letting him know that his beloved friend was quite sick. When Jesus received the message, he declared that there was a purpose for this illness. The sickness didn't come upon Lazarus so that he would die, but instead so that God would be glorified. The watching world would see the glory of God and the glory of the Son of God through this incident. Verse 5 reminds the reader that Jesus loved Lazarus and Martha and Mary, but when he heard about all that was happening down south in Bethany, he stayed where he was for two more days. Finally, after the two days, Jesus said to his disciples, "Let's go to Judea again." This was dangerous because the religious leaders in Jerusalem were ready to kill Jesus. In going back, he put his life on the line. The other disciples understood this. They advised, "The Jews want to stone you. Don't go back!" Jesus reminded them of the twelve hours in each day. At night, it is hard to work (especially without electricity). Jesus still had work to do, and the day was not done for him, although night would be coming soon. One of the things he needed to do while it was still "day" was to glorify himself and the Father through the sickness of Lazarus.

The natural response at this point, especially in light of verse 6, would be, "Wait, What? Why would Jesus stay for two more days in the far away place?" They were already about two days' journey north of Bethany. So by waiting two more days, they didn't reach Lazarus for at least four full days. And as the messenger said, Lazarus was on the verge of death. But Jesus knew exactly what he was doing, and his timing was impeccable. Are you in a crunch situation right now, and does it seem like Jesus is waiting longer than makes sense? Jesus is totally aware and in control of whatever difficulties you are currently dealing with. If it seems like he hasn't moved, don't get discouraged. Instead, decide to trust him again, even in midst of waiting for a season. In the end, the goal of all our suffering is his glory and not our own. Ask that Jesus be exalted through your weakness today.

november
TWENTY-FOUR

JOHN 11:11-22

Jesus decided to go back to Jerusalem when he heard his friend Lazarus was dying. This was risky since the religious leaders of Israel wanted Jesus dead too. Because Jesus used the term "fallen asleep" as a euphemism for the death of Lazarus, his disciples assumed that Lazarus was simply getting a good rest and would awake recovered. Jesus let those with him know that Lazarus had died, and that he was going to bring him back from the grave. Even though it would be dangerous to travel south to Bethany, Thomas said, "Let's do this." He declared his readiness to be killed with Jesus if necessary. When they arrived, Lazarus had been dead for four days. Because of the warm climate in Israel, people were buried right after death, as their bodies would begin to decompose quickly. According to Jewish tradition, a human spirit hovered over the body for three days. By the fourth day after death, all hope of resuscitation was gone. Jesus knew exactly what he was doing in the timing of all events surrounding his friend's death. God would be glorified. As soon as they arrived, Martha spoke with Jesus. She seemed to accuse, "If you had been here, my brother would not have died."

But then Martha made an interesting declaration of her faith in Jesus. She announced, "But even now, God will do whatever you ask." Even now? What did she mean by that? Martha told Jesus that even though things didn't work out as she had hoped, even though her beloved brother was dead, and even though Jesus could have kept Lazarus alive had he come earlier, she still knew that he had a supernatural relationship to God the Father, and she had not lost her conviction about who he was. What a beautiful portrait of trust in the Lord Martha provides for us! What about you? When things don't work out the way you hoped and planned, does your confidence in Jesus remain firm and steadfast? What about when Jesus clearly could fix things if he wanted to? Do you become angry, bitter, or discouraged with him? No matter what he is allowing in your life now, keep your trust in Jesus. Allow the watching world to see that your misfortunes don't keep you from the joy that can only come from knowing and being known by our Lord.

november
TWENTY-FIVE

JOHN 11:23-27

When Jesus arrived in Bethany, where Lazarus and his sisters Martha and Mary lived, it was too late to prevent Lazarus' death. Martha approached Jesus and told him that she knew he could have saved her brother if he had been there. So Jesus explained to Martha that Lazarus would rise again from the dead. Most of the Jewish people at this time believed in the resurrection of the dead at the end of all things or on the last day, and Martha affirmed that God would raise her brother to life at that time. But Jesus was not referring to the last day here. In the fifth of the seven "I am" statements in John's Gospel, Jesus declared to Martha, "I am the resurrection and the life." Jesus announced to Martha that he is the provider of eternal life. He holds the keys to life and death, and he has the power to raise dead people from the grave. If a person believes in Jesus and dies, she will live, and if she lives and believes in Jesus, she will never die. Because Jesus is the resurrection and the life, such a person "has" eternal life, and the moment she leaves her physical body, she will immediately be with the Lord. Then Jesus asked Martha if she believed this to be true about him. She affirmed that she did.

What an amazing and counter-cultural conversation Jesus engaged in with Martha! Although women were not normally educated under Jewish rabbis in the first century, Jesus nevertheless entered an incredibly theological discussion with her. He talked about deep truths, even declaring a critical "I am" statement to her. Jesus clearly demonstrated that all humans, regardless of ethnicity, social status, or gender, have great worth in the eyes of the Lord. Martha boldly professed to Jesus, "You are the Christ, the Son of God, who is coming into the world." What a wonderful declaration of faith from a broken woman. Like Jesus, may we be willing to step outside cultural conventions and value all of humanity. Engage in a conversation about Jesus and his provision for all people groups with someone new. You never know who may be surprised to learn that Jesus spent time with all types of people in an era when not all were typically seen as worth the time and effort.

november
TWENTY-SIX

JOHN 11:28-37

Jesus just finished an intense conversation with Martha, whose brother Lazarus had recently died. Though Martha was challenged, she kept her confidence in Jesus and knew that he had a unique relationship with the Father. She believed that Jesus could do whatever he wanted. She then called for her sister, Mary, who had stayed home to mourn. She told Mary that Jesus was looking for her. When Mary heard this, even though it was too late to save Lazarus, she got up quickly to meet Jesus. Those who were mourning with Mary saw her get up and leave, and they followed too. Mary also confronted Jesus about not coming sooner to save Lazarus before he died. Because he "took his time," Lazarus was dead. Hopefully, Jesus would be more prompt in the future, especially in crucial times. Verse 33 declares that Jesus was "deeply moved in his spirit and greatly troubled." The Greek word rendered as "deeply moved" is a strong verb translated elsewhere as "greatly disturbed" or even "welling up with deep anger." Why was Jesus so mad? Everyone around him was sobbing. Jesus was furious with the result of sin, which is death. If sin had never entered the world, there would be no death. Jesus came to conquer death. Death was our Lord's enemy.

Jesus did not despair, but he was angry at the pain and suffering death causes for those he loved and all of humanity. Death was not part of God's original plan. Those around them wondered why Jesus didn't do something earlier. They knew he had just healed the man born blind. Why didn't he help Lazarus since he clearly loved this family so much? How often do we respond in the same way? We want God to do what we ask of him, and we want him to do it now. We don't want to wait. In fact, we can become discouraged while waiting for God's timing without knowing the reason for his apparent delays. It can seem to us that God doesn't hear, doesn't care, or isn't able to help. But if any of those were true, then God wouldn't be the God of the Scripture. Let's trust in God's perfect timing and not accuse him of being less than he really is. Determine to keep your emotions in line with your theology. Emotions come and go, but God's character remains intact eternally.

november
TWENTY-SEVEN

JOHN 11:38-44

Jesus saw the pain and suffering that his enemy, death, created for his friends. Verse 38 declares that Jesus became angry, or deeply moved, a second time. So he went to the tomb where Lazarus lay and asked those present to take the stone away from the entrance. Martha intervened, "Umm. Wait a minute! It's been four days since my brother died, and it's going to smell really badly in there." Jesus responded, "Martha, I told you, if you would believe, you would see the glory of God." Jesus then prayed out loud to the Father for the sake of those around him. Jesus did exactly what God called him to do, but so that others would know the unique relationship between the Father and the Son, he prayed again. Then Jesus cried with a loud voice. He literally yelled out loud, "Lazarus, come out of there!!" And Lazarus came out wrapped up in his burial clothes. Those standing around must have been absolutely shocked. Jesus ordered that Lazarus be unbound and let go. Jesus called a dead body, allowed it to hear, and the corpse returned to life.

The return of Lazarus from the dead has to be one of the most dramatic of all Jesus' miracles. From the moment Jesus heard Lazarus was ill, he knew what he was going to do. He spoke with Martha and addressed her concerns. And he spoke with Mary to address her concerns as well. And he wept with those around them. The whole time, he knew what would happen next. What a portrait of the compassion and kindness of our Lord Jesus. It is really worth noting what Jesus said to Martha according to verse 40: "Did I not tell you that if you believed you would see the glory of God?" Stop and think. How many times do you think Jesus could say to us, "Did I not tell you?" He has promised us so much in and through his word, yet we doubt and don't believe. May this glimpse into the heart of Jesus cause you to turn from doubt and unbelief. Jesus told us so much. He will do as he promised. May he grace us with new trust and hope as we cling to him again today.

november
TWENTY-EIGHT

JOHN 11:45-57

Jesus asked to see the tomb where the corpse of Lazarus lay, and then he went on to call Lazarus back from the dead to life. Many of the Jews who saw all of this believed in Jesus. Others went back and told the Pharisees about all that transpired. The religious leaders of Israel, the chief priests and the Pharisees, quickly gathered for an emergency meeting. They assembled together to try to figure out how to "stop the madness." If they allowed Jesus to continue with these great signs and miracles, pretty soon all of Israel would believe in him. The high priest of Israel at the time was a man named Caiaphas. He was afraid of trouble with the Romans, so he declared that it "made more sense" to allow Jesus, one man, to die, than to allow the entire nation to be exterminated. Although Caiaphas didn't know it, he was actually prophesying on behalf of the Lord. Jesus would die. And his death would be substitutionary for all of Israel who trusted in him. The religious leaders sought to stay safe. They rejected their own Messiah because they feared the potential problems that would arise with upsetting the Romans. In the end, their plan to appease the Romans and avoid problems didn't work out anyway. A couple of decades later, the Romans decimated the temple and Jerusalem.

According to verse 48, the religious leaders agreed that if more and more began to trust in Jesus, "the Romans will come and take away both our place and our nation." Even though the Jewish leaders were oppressed by Roman rule and actually hated it, they grew comfortable with their own personal power and prestige in the community. Though times were bad, they figured it could be worse, and they didn't want Jesus "rocking the boat" politically. We live in a time when it is no longer popular to be a follower of Jesus. Our culture will tolerate us, but it certainly doesn't want us preaching the gospel and communicating God's command to all humanity to repent and believe. Let's stop and ask God for new courage today. Though we may lose popularity, a few friends, and even some extra income, let's never be like the religious leaders of Jesus' day and compromise truth for so-called peace and safety.

november
TWENTY-NINE

JOHN 12:1-11

John notes that it was six days before the Passover. Jesus' remaining time was short. He departed from Bethany after calling Lazarus back to life, and went north to Ephraim. He then returned to Bethany, where he attended a dinner in his honor. The event must have been a joyous occasion with his dear friends Mary, Martha, and Lazarus there. As the meal progressed, Mary left the room. She returned with an expensive perfume, poured it on Jesus' feet, and wiped his feet with her hair. The pure nard from which this costly ointment was made was worth about an entire year's wage. It could have represented Mary's whole "life savings." The value of the perfume was equivalent to about $50,000. Why would Mary "waste" $50,000 on Jesus' feet? Judas Iscariot objected to this apparent waste. And why was Judas so angry about it? Because he was the treasurer of the group, holding the purse for the band of disciples. He argued that the perfume could have been sold and the money given to the poor. But Judas didn't truly care about the poor. He would have kept that money for himself, which is why the expenditure upset him so much.

But was Judas wrong? $50,000 was a lot of money to spend on one sitting with Jesus. Was Mary making a bad decision? Was her gift too extravagant? Jesus had just raised her brother from the dead. So was her gift too much in comparison to what Jesus did for her family? No way. We who believe are all like Mary's brother Lazarus. We were all dead in our transgressions and sins, yet God raised us from the grave. He transferred us from the kingdom of darkness and placed us into the kingdom of his Son. Is anything we can do for or give to Jesus too much? Not at all! Jesus certainly approved of Mary's action. Judas' concern about the waste was wrong. In fact, maybe we should be doing or giving more than we are. Let's never forget what Jesus has accomplished for us, gracing us with eternal life when we deserved death. Follow the example of Mary and always give Jesus all that you can, as Jesus "paid it all" for you. It's hard to put a price tag on eternity.

november
THIRTY

JOHN 12:12-26

The assembly of the religious leaders, the Sanhedrin, planned to kill both Jesus and Lazarus, since Lazarus had come back to life from the dead, and many believed in Jesus as a result. John stated that many who were at the Passover feast heard that Jesus was coming. The Passover crowd must have been massive as every Jewish man was called to celebrate the Passover in the city of Jerusalem. The Jewish historian Josephus records that over two million Jews came at one time to celebrate. When this huge gathering of people, who had heard about Jesus and his great works, learned that he was coming to the city, they picked up palm branches and began to shout, "Blessed is he who comes in the name of the Lord!" Many palm trees grew in and around Jerusalem, but palm branches weren't traditionally picked up during the Passover feast. Between the time of the Old and New Testaments, palm branches had become a national symbol of victory. Over one hundred years before the birth of Jesus, the Jewish people drove the Syrians from Jerusalem, and their success was celebrated with music and palm branches. Would Jesus drive the Romans from Jerusalem? Was he another political deliverer? In eager anticipation, the Jews cried out, "Hosanna!" or "God, save us right now!" and they proclaimed Jesus to be the King of Israel. The crowd waited and watched for Jesus to present himself as the coming King.

But Jesus came in a way quite different from what the crowds expected. Jesus got on a donkey and rode the small, young animal into the great city. Normally, a conquering king would come into his home city riding a strong and majestic horse. But Zechariah 9:9 declares that the righteous King of Israel would come to the people of God riding on a donkey. Jesus let the onlookers know in a visual way that he wouldn't do as they wanted, but would do things God's way instead. How often do we expect and demand certain things from God? We want our relationships fixed, our financial problems solved, and our health restored. But Jesus came to do something far greater. He came to qualify those who follow him for entrance into his eternal kingdom. If Jesus doesn't seem to be "making things happen" for you, may the joy of your salvation outweigh your difficulties today.

december
ONE

JOHN 12:27-36

Throughout his ministry, Jesus repeatedly foretold that his hour was coming. Now he made clear to those in the temple with him that the hour had come for him to be glorified. Although this was exactly as God had planned before the earth was even formed, Jesus' soul grew troubled. The horrible pain and intense suffering Jesus faced was real, and no human has ever experienced such agony. The Greek word for "troubled" is a strong one and means "to cause inward turmoil, stir up, disturb, unsettle, or throw into confusion." Jesus asked himself, "What shall I say?" Then he called out to his Father in distress, exclaiming, "Father, save me from this hour!" It is impossible to imagine the anguish he felt as he prepared himself for the cross. Even before the Garden of Gethsemane, Jesus felt the weight of his impending execution and separation from his Father, yet he knew and agreed that this was exactly what he had come to earth to accomplish. In full obedience, Jesus prayed, "Father, glorify your name." God responded audibly to Jesus, "I have glorified it, and I will glorify it again." The crowd around him heard God's response too and debated the source and meaning of the voice.

Jesus declared to those discussing what they heard, "This voice has come for your sake, not mine." Some said the voice of God was like thunder. Others said it was an angel speaking. So too today, some will hear God's voice via creation, their conscience, or even the Scripture, and attribute it to "thunder" or something natural. Some will hear it, but remain unable to quite figure out what he said. It's easy to forget that if you have responded to God's call upon your life to repent and trust in Jesus for the forgiveness of your sins, that means God actually allowed you to hear his voice. God gives us the ability to understand and respond to his word. We can't see God, but he is present with us. We don't hear him audibly, but we listen to him through the pages of the Bible as he speaks to us. We embrace the hope of heaven by faith, but the life to come is real. May we remember today that much exists beyond our ability to perceive, and may we never foolishly believe that reality is limited to what we can observe.

december
TWO

JOHN 12:37-50

John's Gospel makes clear that most people did not believe in Jesus. The prophet Isaiah foretold this rejection, and John boldly declared that those who did not believe literally could not believe. They scorned Jesus, and the Lord gave them over to their hard hearts. Verse 41 says that Isaiah saw the glory of Jesus, yet in Isaiah's vision (Isaiah 6), he saw the glory of God. John uses this example to explain again that Jesus was God manifest in the flesh. Some religious leaders believed in Jesus, but they were afraid of what others would think or do, so they were not open about what they knew. Their fear of man's opinions proved more important than their faith in God. Jesus declared, "Whoever believes in me, believes not in me but in him who sent me." When a woman believes in Jesus, she believes in God. There aren't two options or two paths. Either believe in God and Jesus, or don't believe in God and Jesus. According to Jesus himself, a person can't believe in one without the other. Jesus came to save humanity from the penalty of sin, but because most rejected him, they were left unsaved and judged by their evil deeds.

If you saw a dead person come back to life at the command of Jesus, would you trust in Jesus? Most of those who witnessed the return of Lazarus from the dead still didn't believe. Jesus performed other supernatural signs, communicated the mind of God brilliantly, and lived the perfect life, but it still wasn't enough for most. Our belief is never simply a matter of intellectual agreement with the facts. The most obvious example of this is found in the devil or Satan. He sees, knows, and agrees to more about Jesus than we can imagine, but he doesn't love God. The Scripture clearly teaches that we love Jesus because he loved us first. God chose to love you and grace you with the faith necessary to believe. If you are a Christian, realize that God knew you before you were even born. He is aware of everything you have ever done and everything you ever will do, yet he is committed to you. God doesn't give up on those he loves, so let's respond by not giving up on those whom he has called us to love.

december
THREE

JOHN 13:1-11

Jesus wanted to express to his disciples how much he loved them, so after eating, he took off his outer layer of clothing and put a towel around his waist, preparing to wash their feet. In first century Israel, foot washings were common and necessary. People wore sandals without socks, and the dust from the desert ground accumulated on their feet. Washing the feet of others was considered such a low job that it was reserved for slaves. When Jesus wrapped the towel around his waist, he put on the garment of a slave. Peter felt uncomfortable. He didn't want Jesus to wash his feet. When Jesus got to him, Peter questioned, "Lord, do you wash my feet?" Peter felt like he should be washing Jesus' feet. This whole thing didn't make sense to him. Although Peter didn't get it now, Jesus assured him that he would later understand what Jesus was doing and why. Peter resisted, insisting, "No way. You will never wash my feet." Jesus responded that only those who have been washed have a relationship with him, referring to the cleansing he would provide for the sins of all of those who put their trust in him. Peter exclaimed, "Then wash my hands and my head too!"

Jesus corrected Peter again. He explained that Peter was already clean, or a believer. As a believer, he didn't need to be cleansed again. He simply needed his feet washed. Then, referring to Judas, Jesus clarified that not everyone was clean. Judas never truly trusted in Jesus and followed him for the wrong reasons. Since Peter was clean, why did he need his feet washed? As Peter walked around in life, his feet got physically dirty. The same principle applies spiritually. Peter needed to continually come to Jesus, confessing his sin, not to become a Christian, but because he was a Christian. If you are a follower of Jesus, you have been cleansed. Nevertheless, we all need to continually confess our sins to the Lord. We do this not to be saved, but because we are saved. Is there any dirt on your feet today? Do you need to confess to Jesus some sin you have entertained? If so, talk to him about what you have been doing wrong and ask him to forgive you. What a relief to know that "the one who has bathed does not need to wash, except for his feet, but is completely clean."

december
FOUR

JOHN 13:12-20

After Jesus and his disciples ate together, he took on a role fit for the lowest of slaves, removing his garments and putting on the attire of a servant. Then he washed his disciples' feet. After he was done, he got up and redressed in the clothes he wore at the dinner and asked them if they understood what he had just done. He explained that because they rightly called him their teacher and their Lord, they should follow in his footsteps and do the same. He called them to wash one another's feet. As he humbled himself before them, taking on the lowest role, looking to their interests rather than his own, he called them to do the same. Does this mean we should gather together, take out buckets of water, and wash each other's feet? Not really. For one thing, in our culture we don't commonly walk long dirt roads wearing sandals without socks. Jesus didn't establish foot washing as an ordinance, like Baptism or Communion. Instead, he addressed the need for Christians to prefer one another and look out for each other's needs. This is an issue of the heart, which should drive our actions. Jesus explained that those who live this way will be blessed.

Because Jesus is our Lord and our King, we need to do as he asked. And what a wonderful Lord and King he is! Not only does he ask from us, but he also models what our behavior should look like. He isn't a leader who demands what he would never be found doing. In fact, the opposite is true. Because of his love for us, he humbled himself and went all the way to death, even a slave's death, on a cross. As Jesus looks out for us, he commands us to look out for our fellow believers. What does your sister in Christ need today? What would benefit her as she walks through the roads of life and comes home with dusty feet? Think about a practical way you can honestly meet a legitimate need of another Christian woman, and "wash her feet" today. When you put on the garment of a servant, you will be doing exactly what Jesus called you to.

december
FIVE

JOHN 13:21-30

Jesus washed the disciples' feet and asked them to look out for the interests of one another by humbly taking on the role of servants. He mentioned that he wasn't speaking to them all, because one among them wasn't really one of them. Jesus quoted Psalm 41:9 where David wrote about a time of anguish he experienced when "Even my close friend in whom I trusted, who ate my bread, has lifted his heel against me." In Psalm 41, David grieves because of the pain his enemies created by spreading rumors about him, slandering him, and rising up against him. The breaking point comes when David reveals it was his friend who betrayed him. In the ancient near east, it was considered a horrible crime to betray a friend, even more a friend who ate with, fellowshipped with, or served with the one betrayed. Jesus was heartbroken, yet this was exactly what God had ordained. The disciples had no idea what Jesus was talking about. From their perspective, they were all "on the same page." Each one began to wonder if he could be the betrayer! They desperately wanted to know who it was, because they were honestly afraid they might be the guilty ones. So Jesus said he would give a morsel of bread to the betrayer. He gave it to Judas and told Judas to get it done quickly. After Judas left, the other disciples still didn't understand what was going on.

Verse 30 ends with "and it was night." John (the author) continues to contrast the themes of darkness and light. Jesus is the light of the world. Darkness represents sin, evil, and judgment. It truly was "night" when Judas left the table of the Last Supper and went to sell Jesus to his enemies. The Bible teaches us that we don't merely wrestle against flesh and blood, but against principalities and powers. We war against spiritual forces of darkness in the unseen realm. When Judas took the morsel Jesus used to identify him as his betrayer, Satan himself entered Judas. When we choose to sin, doing things our way instead of God's, we cooperate with darkness. God wants his children in the light. If you have embraced any sinful habits or practices and you are a child of the light, turn from the darkness now. Ask Jesus to forgive you and cleanse you from all unrighteousness. Our Father hears our cries of repentance.

december
SIX

JOHN 13:31-38

Judas left to betray Jesus, and Jesus knew that very little remained between him and the cross. Jesus would soon be reunited with the Father in the glory he had before his incarnation. Jesus addressed the disciples as if they were all family, calling them "little children." He let them know that he was going away and that they wouldn't be able to find him, as he was about to return to heaven. So he taught them how they should live together in his absence. He said, "A new commandment I give to you, that you love one another." But this really wasn't a "new commandment." In fact, Leviticus 19:18 declares that God's people are to love their neighbors as themselves. So what's so new here? Jesus added the phrase, "Just as I have loved you, you also are to love one another." This was new. How did Jesus love them? He loved them to death, which is how he asked them to love each other. Then Jesus went on to declare that the world would know they were his disciples because of their love for one another. Jesus actually taught that the world will judge whether someone is born again by the way she treats her fellow brothers and sisters.

How far have we departed from the command of Jesus? He instructed his followers to love one another. Judas had just betrayed him, and he was heartbroken. It was as if Jesus were saying, "Please don't betray one another!" We have to stick together, even when disputes, dissensions, and problems arise. This requires genuine compassion, true humility, and above all, a keen awareness of the great depths from which we as individuals have all been redeemed. Although we are born again, brand new in Christ Jesus, we still live with sin. Every Christian will make mistakes, and Christian relationships are going to be tested. Will we be obedient to our Lord, who desperately desires his children to get along? Or will we give in to our selfish and sinful flesh by fighting, warring, and severing relationships with one another? Oh, that we would be like Jesus, the one who was able to love all the way to the cross! Let's pray that we would let go of our pride and our so-called "rights" and love each other unto death. Then the world will stand back and declare, "These are the followers of Jesus."

december
SEVEN

JOHN 14:1-14

Jesus told his disciples he was going to a place where they couldn't follow. Peter wondered where he was going and insisted he would lay down his life for Jesus, but Peter would actually go on to deny him. The disciples had to be discouraged at this point. Jesus was going to a place they couldn't come, one of them was a betrayer, and Peter was going to deny him. Jesus encouraged them, "Don't let your hearts be troubled." He let them know that one of the reasons he was going back to his Father was to prepare a place for each one of them. Thomas was still confused and didn't understand what Jesus was talking about. Jesus was the Messiah, right? He hadn't set up his kingdom yet. So where could he be going? Then Jesus declared the sixth of the seven "I am" statements in the Gospel of John. Jesus said, "I am the way, and the truth, and the life." Only Jesus was God incarnate. Therefore, he was and always will be the only way to get to God. He said, "No one comes to the Father except through me." This is probably the most politically incorrect statement ever made, yet it came from the mouth of God. To deny this truth, that Jesus is the only way, is to deny Jesus.

What did Jesus mean when he said, "I am the way, the truth, and the life"? Was he speaking about three distinct and different things? Scholars say that based on the original Greek construction, Jesus meant he was the true revelation of the Father and the one with the ability to give eternal life. No human can get to God by her own effort. Everyone is separated from him because of her sin, and will remain separated from him for eternity when she dies. The only way to be reconciled to God is through the provision that Jesus made. Pray that God would have mercy on his people today and help his followers be immovable when it comes to the gospel. May we love the world enough to warn it about the tremendous consequences of living life and leaving life without Jesus.

december
EIGHT

JOHN 14:15-24

Jesus comforted his disciples by telling them he would prepare a place for each of them in heaven. He also taught them that he was the only way to be reconciled to God. Now Jesus let them know that he would not leave them alone, but the Father would send the Holy Spirit to be with them. Soon all followers of Christ would be graced with the same power Jesus had, so that they could continue the work Jesus began on earth. Jesus said the Father would send them another Helper. Like Jesus, the Holy Spirit teaches, instructs, encourages, and aids believers to do as God has called them to. The Holy Spirit is also called the "Spirit of truth," literally the Spirit of "the" truth. Remember, Jesus had just declared himself to be "the truth." The Holy Spirit bears witness to the truth of Jesus' identity. The things of Christ are veiled to the world because the world does not have the presence of the Spirit. When the Holy Spirit came, the followers of Jesus would know that he was in the Father, that they were in him, and that he was in them as well.

Because of the supernatural change that takes place when a person puts her trust in Jesus, Jesus could confidently state that whoever has and keeps his commandments is the one who loves him. Does that mean we are saved by keeping the Law? No. Instead, it means if we are saved, then we will *want* to keep the Law. When we are born again, we are given new hearts and new desires. And our new lives impact the way we live in this world. Does that mean we always and only obey after we are converted? Again, no. But it does mean that our relationship to sin has definitely changed. When we sin, we are living according to our old nature. If you find yourself a slave to anything contrary to the will of God, pray that the Holy Spirit would enable you to live consistently with who you really are: a woman set free from the law of sin and death. Just because you find yourself in sin doesn't mean you have to stay there. The Spirit empowers us to obey Jesus. Call out to God, asking his Spirit to strengthen you with courage to keep the words of our Lord today.

december
NINE

JOHN 14:25-31

Jesus continued to dialogue with his disciples. The conversations in John 13 through John 17 all occurred the night before Jesus' crucifixion, and at least part, if not all, occurred in the upper room where they ate the Passover meal together. These were Jesus' last words to his followers, and he sought to instruct and encourage them. He told them they would receive the promised Holy Spirit whom the Father would send to represent Jesus in his absence. The Holy Spirit, or the Helper, would teach them all things and bring to remembrance all that Jesus said. Although they were partially blind to many of Jesus' teachings, the Spirit would help them recall and put into context all that Jesus taught. The apostles traveled with Jesus as he journeyed around Israel preaching, teaching, and performing signs and wonders for three years. They heard volumes of Jesus' teaching. Now Jesus guaranteed that the Holy Spirit would allow them to remember everything they learned. The Spirit would make sure they got his message right. When leaving, instead of saying, "Good bye," one would say, "*Shalom.*" In Israel, the Hebrew word *shalom* means "peace." Jesus left his followers with eternal peace.

Jesus encouraged his followers not to be troubled, agitated, or stressed out. If we have his peace, we have all that we need for this life and for the life to come. Those who trust in Jesus are at peace with the Father as well. Because of sin, all outside of Christ are at war with God. Only through the cross can we have real peace. If you have been reconciled to God through faith in Jesus Christ, God will never, ever be at war with you again. If you are truly born again, you have inherited the grandest gift, the peace of God. You need not fear death or the future, because God's peace will guard your heart and your mind. No matter what you are experiencing that stresses you out right now, if you are a follower of Jesus, remember that even in tense times, Jesus left you with his peace. Pray also for those who don't have the peace of Christ, that their hearts would be troubled so they too might cling to the cross.

december
TEN

JOHN 15:1-11

Jesus stated the last of the seven "I am" statements recorded in the Gospel of John. He declared, "I am the vine." After feeding the five thousand men, Jesus declared, "I am the bread of life." At the Feast of Tabernacles, while standing near the giant candelabra in the temple, he said, "I am the light of the world." While illustrating the relationship between himself and his disciples, he said, "I am the door" to the sheepfold, and "I am the good shepherd." Right before he called his dead friend Lazarus back to life, he said, "I am the resurrection and the life." The same night that he declared, "I am the true vine," he said, "I am the way, the truth and the life." All of these powerful statements contain the Greek words *Ego eimi*, which translates "I am" and remind the listener of God's revelation of himself to Moses in the burning bush when he announced, "I am who I am" in Exodus 3:14. When Jesus declared "I am the vine," he added a second statement: "And my Father is the vinedresser." Jesus explained that his disciples were the branches. Those who tended grape vines, the vinedressers, cut the dead branches, the ones that bore no fruit, from the vine. The vinedressers trimmed the healthy and living branches so that they might bear the best fruit possible. Judas was cut from the vine, and the other disciples would be pruned.

It is the vinedresser's job to prune the vine so that the plant will bear as much healthy fruit as possible. The pruning process includes cutting back, clipping, and cleaning the healthy branches. God uses the truth of his word, painful trials, and his discipline to prune his children. But what about those branches that are cut and burned? Does that mean a believer can lose her salvation? No! It means there will always be some, like Judas, who hang around Jesus and the people of God, but aren't really genuine disciples. These people will be cut off. What is God allowing so that you might bear more fruit? If you have lost your joy, maybe you aren't being as obedient to God as you should. Ask God to help you learn from what he is showing you, making you as fruitful as he would like, as you fully trust in Jesus for everything.

december
ELEVEN

JOHN 15:12-17

As Jesus continued his farewell discourse, he commanded his disciples to love one another, adding, "as I have loved you." This was the second time in the same night that Jesus asked his followers to love each other. All believers in Christ are the children of God, making them brothers and sisters. It is incredibly discouraging to a parent when her children fight, and it would be heartbreaking to see one's own children refusing to speak to one another. Can you imagine if your children said they never wanted to see each other again? You probably wouldn't have much patience for an attitude like that. Yet we often expect God to tolerate our disdain for our spiritual siblings. We may have a rude awakening when we stand before the Lord and discover that he was not pleased with our attitude toward our fellow believers. According to Jesus, those who love God will love each other. If we don't love one another, then something is deficient in our love for God. Jesus said if we have true love we will lay down our lives for our friends. Laying down our lives means sacrificing everything we have for the sake of our brothers and sisters. We all long to have a friend who loves us so much she will lay down her life for us.

Jesus said his disciples were his friends. He was their Lord and their friend. Why were they his friends? Because he confided in them! A servant doesn't usually have an intimate relationship with a master, but Jesus' servants were intimate with him. The disciples failed to live according to God's standard of perfection, yet Jesus chose to make them his friends. We have failed to meet God's righteous standard as well, yet Jesus chose us, those who trust in him, to be his friends. This truth should motivate us to continue loving each other without giving up. Have you been at war with your sisters in Christ? If so, repent today. Be like Jesus, willing to love, even if it costs you everything. In the end, the price of restoring the relationship usually boils down to letting go of your pride. "Why should I be the first to love her?" Because Jesus chose to love you first. Go and do likewise today.

december
TWELVE

JOHN 15:18-27

Jesus explained that because he was hated, his disciples would also be hated. Jesus loved his disciples and didn't want them caught off guard. Why did the world hate Jesus? He is light, and the world is not only in darkness, but loves the darkness. The light of Christ exposes the darkness, and the world hates having its wicked works uncovered. When we are in physical darkness and the light is turned on, our eyes burn, and it hurts. In the same way, when the light of Jesus appeared in the midst of a dark and sinful world, the resulting pain was unpleasant, and many did and will do whatever they can to get rid of the light. Those in Christ no longer belong to this world. This truth provides more fuel for conflict between the world and the believer. Those of the world live for this life. They seek personal peace, and they do what they can to ensure their own security and comfort on earth. But those who follow Jesus have inherited a new and lasting home. Our hope and focus on the life to come frustrates those who see no further than what lies here under the sun.

The world hated Jesus so much that it begged to see him executed on a Roman cross. Because the followers of Jesus are empowered by his Holy Spirit and have been charged to continue to the work he began on earth, the world's hatred for Jesus is projected onto those who represent him. If you are an honest follower of Jesus and you have never been rejected by the world, you will be. It's guaranteed. If you are currently suffering because of the hostility of the culture around you that despises our God, know that you have been called to it. Never shrink back from doing what Jesus would do. Whether you are faithful or not, the world will reject you anyway. If you accurately reflect Jesus, the world will hate you. If you shrink back from the truth, they will hate you as well. Be kind, but be honest. Don't be taken by surprise when you aren't invited to the next community party. But make sure you aren't invited because of the message that you carry, not because of the method by which you carry it.

december
THIRTEEN

JOHN 16:1-4

Jesus gave his disciples another reason why they would be hated by the world in order to keep them from falling away. The Greek word translated "falling away" is *skandalizo*, the root of the English word "scandal." The Greek word means "to cause to sin." Jesus didn't want his followers discouraged when the world rejected and even cast them out of their own synagogues. Many devout Jews thought they were doing the work of the Lord by persecuting the followers of Jesus. Just as Jesus was executed for his message, so the disciples would also face execution for adhering to it. Those who despised the believers didn't know Jesus, and they didn't know the Father either. Jesus said that when these things happened, his followers would be encouraged as they remembered that he had warned them about it. They wouldn't be caught off guard, but would realize their suffering was exactly as Jesus foretold. After Jesus' departure, the world would vent its anger on his followers; because it hated Jesus, it would hate his disciples as well.

In preaching the gospel, sometimes its messengers give new converts false hope. Young believers are frequently told that by becoming Christians their lives will get easier and their general circumstances will improve. When things instead become harder, the new convert who has been given such false hope will not be prepared for reality and may become overly disheartened, "falling away" when persecution comes. How much better to be honest from the beginning! That's what Jesus did. There will be sufferings associated with turning from living life our way and embracing life God's way. Circumstances may improve for Christians as they lead lives more closely aligned with the will of God, yet the Christian's ultimate hope is in the life to come. As the brilliant author and theologian C.S. Lewis once said, "If you want a religion to make you feel really comfortable, I certainly don't recommend Christianity." If you knew you would have troubles in this life as a result of following Jesus, would you still trust in him? What if your faith meant your difficulties would not go away but instead be magnified? Would you continue to cling to Jesus? Those who are genuine believers say "Yes." We realize that the present sufferings are nothing compared to promised glory. And for the joy set before us, we press on.

december
FOURTEEN

JOHN 16:5-15

Jesus taught the disciples that it would be to their advantage for him to go to the Father. In his physical absence, he would send the Holy Spirit to be with every one of his followers. The Holy Spirit not only dwells in believers, but he also works in the world. He convicts the world concerning sin and righteousness and judgment. He is the one who reveals to humanity that God is holy and that all who are outside of Christ will be held responsible for living an imperfect life. The Holy Spirit reveals to the world that God's absolute requirement is righteousness, and the Holy Spirit puts the fear of judgment into humanity. Standing before the Lord on the last day, not one will be able to say she is without blame. The fear of the Lord that arises from this knowledge is from the Spirit of God. But it is not enough just to feel conviction. We must respond to it. If you have never turned to Jesus and trusted in him for salvation, please do so now. Ask God to forgive you and make you a brand new creation in Christ Jesus. Then you will be blameless, not because of your own perfection but because of Christ's!

How often have we read through the Gospels and thought, *If only I could have been there when Jesus ministered on earth! Then I would understand! Then I would have the courage to do what he's asking of me!* But Jesus said it is to our advantage that he has gone back to the Father. If this sounds difficult to believe, it is probably because we have forgotten the monumental benefit of having the Holy Spirit dwell in us. Those who have the Holy Spirit have him forever. We can grieve him, or bring deep pain to him, by our sinful and selfish choices, but he will never leave us nor forsake us. The Spirit wants us to live victoriously in our battle with the world, our flesh, and the enemy. If you are feeling defeated and discouraged today and you are a follower of Jesus, remember whom you have. The third person of the triune God is with you right now, and he wants you to be successful in your struggle against sin. Determine to yield to the Spirit's power, living consistently with God's will and God's desire. The Christian will never regret yielding to the Spirit's way.

december
FIFTEEN

JOHN 16:16-24

Jesus told his disciples that soon they would no longer see him, but then soon they would again. The disciples did not understand what Jesus was talking about. They kept asking one another what in the world he meant. How could they not see him and then see him in a little while? Jesus meant that he was going to die soon, within the next day, but shortly after, he would rise from the dead and appear to the disciples in his glorified body. So they would not see him, but they would see him. And all this would take place in "a little while," or the next few days. Jesus let the disciples know how they would feel by warning that they would weep and lament. They would be broken and miserable, yet the world would celebrate. What a contrast! The world could not wait for Jesus to be gone. He was the light of the world, and because the world loved the darkness, it hated his presence there. The enemies of Jesus wanted him gone quickly. Jesus warned his followers that even though they would be shattered by his death, his departure would soon become their joy. Because Jesus provided for the sins of all who trust in him, his death delivered the believer's reason for rejoicing.

The disciples would experience anguish, but not for long. It would only last "a little while." Actually, every pain we experience as Christians on this planet lasts only for "a little while." Jesus said the sorrow his disciples experienced would be like the agony of childbirth. Every mother knows how painful the birth process is, yet when it is complete the joy of new life so overpowers the pain that the discomfort is soon forgotten. In fact, most women are willing to endure pregnancy again! When we stand before the Lord in heaven, the problems of life will be like the pains of childbirth. Although the troubles we endure are real, they only remain for a night. What is your soul agonizing over right now? What is causing you great grief and sorrow? Make sure you don't waste one minute of what God has given you in this life. Use everything to point others to Jesus. Let the watching world see and be drawn to your confidence in the joy that will come in the morning.

december
SIXTEEN

JOHN 16:25-33

The disciples were puzzled by what Jesus meant when he said they would not see him in a little while but see him in a little while. These apparent contradictions seemed like a riddle. He knew they were confused, and the things concerning his death and resurrection were veiled to them. Because Christians believe in and love Jesus, the Father loves Christians. After Jesus explained himself again, the disciples responded, "Now you are speaking plainly!" They professed that Jesus came from God and knew all things. Jesus responded by asking, "Do you now believe?" It's as if he asked, "Really?" Jesus knew that within hours they would all scatter. They thought they were ready to stand by him until the end, but he knew better. Although they would all scatter from him, the Father would remain with him. It wasn't the faithfulness of his followers that led to their salvation. Instead, it was the faithfulness of Jesus and the Father who sent him. Jesus would experience excruciating agony in being made sin, and it would seem that God had left him. The Father would "abandon" the Son as he poured out his wrath toward sin on the human Jesus, yet the Father was always with him.

Those with Jesus for three years, his best friends, left him in his most difficult hour. Knowing his disciples would abandon him, Jesus gave them this word ahead of time: "take heart; I have overcome the world." Jesus has overcome the world for us too. We exist in a world hostile to Jesus and the message of Christianity. As a result, we will suffer in this life. But because Jesus was faithful and triumphed over the world, we who trust in him share in his great conquest. What is Jesus asking you to do today? Where does he want you to go? Be courageous! Jesus doesn't expect us to overcome the world. Instead, he wants us to trust in what he accomplished. Because of what he achieved, we can stand firm and endure whatever he asks us to do. In fact, the world can do nothing to us that God cannot use for his ultimate good. Even though we may not feel like overcomers, Jesus is, and he will get us safely through whatever he calls us to. We are victorious because Jesus was victorious.

december
SEVENTEEN

JOHN 17:1-11

Jesus taught and conversed with his disciples the night before he went to the cross. John devotes almost twenty-five percent of his Gospel to recording what went on during that last evening. Now John records Jesus' farewell prayer. Jesus began by addressing the Father, stating, "The hour has come." Then he prayed for himself, asking that he would be glorified so that he could glorify God. In this prayer, Jesus said he granted eternal life to all whom God had given him. Jesus clearly stated that all whom the Father gave would come to him, and those who follow Jesus are a gift to him from the Father. Jesus also said, "I am not praying for the world but for those you have given me." Jesus prayed that God would keep those whom he had called. Jesus was leaving the world, but his disciples would remain, so Jesus prayed for their protection. Those who hated Jesus would continue to be frustrated because Jesus' disciples reflected his light to the world. The animosity the world felt toward Jesus would be vented on his followers, who were no longer truly of this world. Jesus emphasized the difference between himself and the world when he referred to God as the Holy Father. Because God is holy and Jesus has provided for the sins of believers, those who belong to the Lord are holy too.

How wonderful to think that we can eavesdrop on this prayer that Jesus offered to the Father on behalf of himself and those who would follow him. May we be incredibly encouraged as we think about how astonishing our salvation is. Five times, chapter 17 tells us that Jesus referred to his followers as those God "gave" to him. When we ponder the things Jesus revealed in these eleven verses, we must confess that salvation is by grace alone. Jesus went home, and soon we will be there with him. For those who trust in Jesus, the glory and wonder we will experience are unimaginable now. We know with confidence that because the Father has given us to Jesus, we are eternally secure. He is the one who keeps us. Jesus will never let us go. Be assured in Christ today. Just as an earthly father lovingly and protectively carries his child from one place to the next, God will get us to our true home when our time is up.

december
EIGHTEEN

JOHN 17:12-26

Jesus prayed again for his followers, or those the Father had given him. Verse 12 tells us he mentioned Judas, the son of destruction, as the one who was lost. Did Judas "lose his salvation"? No. Judas wasn't called the son of destruction because he was saved and then unsaved himself. Judas never was regenerate. Though he was with Jesus and his disciples, he wasn't there for the right reason. He held the group's purse, and following Jesus had a lot to do with control of the money for Judas. In fact, the Scripture foretold that Judas would betray the Lord. So Jesus excluded Judas from his prayer, because he knew that Judas was not really one of them. Those who are honestly saved will be saved tomorrow, saved in ten years, and saved in one hundred years. Jesus prayed not only for the disciples with him, but for those who would come to him through the gospel. He prayed for all who would believe, including you, if you are a Christian today. He prayed that we would all be one, just as he and the Father are one. When we are unified as one, the world will believe that the Father sent the Son. How can we say we belong to Jesus when we can't get along with one another? It makes no sense.

God told Moses to have Aaron, his brother, bless his people with the beautiful prayer of hope and encouragement found in Numbers 6:24-26. It begins with the phrase "may the Lord bless you and keep you." Thousands of years before Jesus prayed to his Father expressing his ability to keep those the Father gave him, God told Moses to bless the people in the same way. It always has been the Lord who keeps those who are his. And he is able to keep all until the very end. Because of this, we are called to stick together. The genuine followers of Jesus will be together for eternity. It has been rightfully said that you will be closer to your Christian "enemy" in heaven than you were to your dearest friend on earth. If you and your Christian sisters are warring and fighting with each other, stop. See the heart of Jesus in his farewell prayer, and be willing to do whatever it takes to line up underneath his desire for unity among his people.

december
NINETEEN

JOHN 18:1-11

Jesus and his disciples came to the Garden of Gethsemane, where they met often. This was the garden where Judas gave Jesus over to his enemies, and Jesus knew that Judas would be there. He wasn't trying to hide from anyone or escape from the will of God; he was ready to do whatever the Father knew best. Judas arrived with two groups of people: Roman soldiers and Jewish religious leaders. Many Roman soldiers would have been employed in Jerusalem at this time to keep the peace during the crowded Passover festival. John records that Judas came with a "band" of soldiers. The Greek word translated "band" is *speira*, a military unit containing about six hundred men. Can you imagine six hundred men, plus the Jewish leaders, gathered together to arrest Jesus? Probably more than a half a thousand men joined together to get Jesus that night. In addition, they came with lanterns, torches, and weapons. What drama they created to "capture" Jesus. Imagine how Jesus felt as he watched hundreds and hundreds of men pour into the garden to arrest him. Jesus didn't try to get away. Instead, he approached and asked, "Whom are you looking for?" They told him they wanted Jesus of Nazareth. Jesus responded by literally saying, "I am." The "he" in English is implied as the Greek uses only the words *ego eimi*. Remember the seven "I am" statements recorded by John? Jesus used the phrase again here, and when Jesus made this statement, the hundreds of men fell to the ground. What a scene that must have been!

Jesus again asked them whom they were looking for. And again, Jesus said, "I am." Then he told the mob to let his disciples go. Even during his arrest, Jesus was looking out for the safety of his disciples. After Peter tried to fight back by cutting off the ear of Malchus, the high priest's servant, Jesus reminded Peter that he was fully prepared to drink the cup the Father gave him. That cup included the wrath of God, which Jesus voluntarily experienced to atone for those who followed him. Jesus made no attempt to get away. If you are a Christian and you are feeling overlooked, unloved, or even rejected today, remember what Jesus did for you. The cup he drank included the punishment you earned for your sin. Jesus chose to protect you from God's wrath. Respond with an honest prayer of gratitude and appreciation today.

december
TWENTY

JOHN 18:12-18

Jesus was betrayed by Judas and arrested by Roman soldiers in the Garden of Gethsemane. He was then taken to Annas, the father-in-law of the Jewish high priest, Caiaphas. The Jews took Jesus to Annas instead of Caiaphas because, according to Jewish law, the high priest was high priest for life. Annas held the role for about 20 years, then in 15 AD, the Romans took him out of his official office. The Romans feared what might happen if one man had too much authority over the Jewish people. So although his son-in-law, Caiaphas, held the role of high priest at the time of Jesus' execution, the Jews knew that Annas was the true force behind Caiaphas, just as he was with his others sons who served as high priests. After Jesus was betrayed by Judas, Peter and another disciple followed Jesus to the residence of Annas. Again, Judas was never a true follower of Jesus, which is why he betrayed him. But even worse, Peter, his dear friend and a member of his most inner circle, denied him. Jesus loved Peter, and Peter loved Jesus too. But Peter was afraid and went into self-preservation mode. John had just recorded that Peter picked up his sword and cut off the high priest's servant's ear, but now that nothing made sense to Peter, fear overwhelmed him. So during Jesus' darkest and most intense hour, he was truly alone.

Who was the other disciple? Most scholars say it was John, the author himself. The other disciple got Peter into the residence of Annas, because the high priest knew this other disciple. Apparently, John's family, though fishermen, were somewhat wealthy and may have been familiar with the high priest. This unknown disciple entered the courtyard with Jesus, but Peter stood at the door until the other disciple gained admission for him too. And what did Peter do with his access to the unusual night trial of Jesus? Did he support his Lord and friend? No, he denied him. This should remind us that not one human is capable of perfect loyalty. The only exception is Jesus himself. Jesus was flawlessly obedient to the Father and completely committed to us, his followers. If you are a Christian today, extend kindness to those who have failed you, remembering that Jesus is kind to you when you fail him.

december
TWENTY-ONE

JOHN 18:19-27

With an unknown disciple's help, Peter was able to get into the courtyard of the Jewish high priest. A servant girl was stationed at the door, and as Peter walked by, she asked if he was one of Jesus' disciples. Peter said he wasn't. It was cold, so to get warm Peter stood next to a coal fire in the enclosure. Soldiers and servants gathered by the fire too. This so-called trial was technically illegal. According to their own laws, the Jews were not permitted to hold court in the night. In addition, witnesses were necessary for a proper trial. In addition, the accused was not supposed to be interrogated at all, but rather the witnesses. Annas directed questions at Jesus that focused on two issues: his disciples and his teaching. Jesus responded by reminding him that he had taught openly for years. Why did Annas now ask as if something was done in secret? Whatever Jesus taught in private, he also taught openly. Jesus prompted Annas to ask witnesses, as he was supposed to do, and not question Jesus directly. Jesus was smacked in the face for his suggestion. Jesus asked the servant who slapped him the reason for this action. Had Jesus said or done something wrong? If so, what was it? Annas was done. He sent Jesus to his son-in-law, Caiaphas, who had the authority to send Jesus to the Romans.

While Peter was still in the courtyard, warming himself by the fire, those around him asked if he was one of Jesus' disciples. Peter said he wasn't. Then a relative of the man whose ear Peter had just cut off noticed him too. He also asked Peter if he was a disciple of Jesus. And Peter denied it again. As soon as Peter betrayed Jesus the third time, a rooster crowed, just as Jesus said. Peter seriously believed he would stand up for Jesus even to death, but Peter denied his relationship with Jesus in front of a few servants. Jesus knew every single detail of what would happen, yet he still chose Peter, revealed himself to Peter, and remained committed to Peter. Have you let Jesus down recently? If so, be encouraged by the account of Peter's failure. Confess your sins to Jesus again and keep following him. Jesus knew everything you would and will do after surrendering your life to him, and he chose to reveal himself to you anyway. Nothing you have done has caught him by surprise.

december
TWENTY-TWO

JOHN 18:28-38

Jesus was taken from the house of Annas to the house of Caiaphas, the acting high priest, and then to the headquarters of the Roman governor, Pontius Pilate. Because Pilate held the local seat of Roman authority, his verdict was crucial. Historical accounts attest to the hostility between Pilate and the Jewish people. At the time of Jesus' crucifixion, Pilate was worn down by the Jews and tired of reporting back to his leaders about continued local tension. Interestingly, John records that the Jews themselves didn't go into the governor's headquarters. They didn't want to defile themselves by entering a Gentile residence. So, ironically, they turned Jesus over to Pilate and stayed outside to remain pure. They sought to pursue every detail of God's Law, yet they were in direct opposition to the God they claimed to serve. How many out there today try to pay attention to every single detail of what they believe God calls right and wrong, only to miss Jesus? Pilate went out to the Jews and asked what they accused Jesus of and why it involved him. The Jews said they brought Jesus to him because Jesus was evil. Pilate didn't want anything to do with this mess. So they conceded that Pilate alone had the authority to crucify Jesus, and that's why they brought him there.

Pilate asked Jesus, "Are you the king of Jews?" Jesus told Pilate that his kingdom is not of this world, and if it were, his servants would be fighting for it. Jesus' kingdom is completely different from anything Pilate had ever experienced or imagined. Jesus came into this world to bear witness to the truth about God to humanity. The truth is that Jesus is the King of heaven and earth. Pilate thought he had great authority over Jesus, but in fact, Jesus is the King and Pilate would give an account to him. And not only Pilate, but every man and woman will stand before the King. And all that will matter is what we did with Jesus. It won't matter if we were righteous by man's standards, like the Jewish people who wouldn't even defile themselves by entering Pilate's residence. And it won't even matter if we are like Pilate, who agreed to the righteousness of Christ. Have you given your heart to the King of heaven and earth? If not, do it today. If you have, then thank Jesus for allowing you to see and respond to truth.

december
TWENTY-THREE

JOHN 18:39 - 19:16

On the Passover, one criminal was traditionally freed as an act of good will. Pilate presented Jesus for release according to this custom, but shockingly, the crowd demanded the freedom of another prisoner named Barabbas, whose name means "son of the father." According to some scholars, Barabbas' first name may have also been Jesus. So the crowd insisted on the release of Jesus Barabbas, or Jesus "son of the father," a notorious criminal, while they demanded the crucifixion of the real Son of the Father. Pilate took Jesus back and flogged him. This process consisted of viciously whipping a prisoner until even his bones were exposed. The Romans believed that practically beating to death a man sentenced to crucifixion would accelerate the execution process when the prisoner was placed on his cross. After the extreme whipping, a purple robe was placed on Jesus, and a crown with very long and sharp spikes was shoved into his skull. The soldiers began to violently mock and strike Jesus so that he would seem anything but a king. At this point, Pilate brought him out before the crowd again and declared before them, "Behold the man!" Why did Pilate say this? He probably wanted to show the crowd that Jesus was no threat to them. Their hatred should have been satisfied, and they should have let him go. The crowd didn't care. Instead, it continued to repeatedly shout, "Crucify!"

Again, Pilate tried to release Jesus, but the Jews wouldn't have it. Then they revealed why they wanted him dead: he claimed to be the Son of God, making himself equal with God. When Pilate heard this, he was really stressed out and asked Jesus, "Where are you from?" But Jesus said nothing. Pilate told Jesus to talk because he could set Jesus free. Jesus told Pilate he really couldn't release him. God had planned all of this from before the foundation of the world. Pilate had no idea how much power he did not possess. Although Pilate attempted from then on to release Jesus, his fear of what the crowd could do to him was stronger than his fear of putting Jesus to death. What about you? What are you most afraid of? What is most important to you? Our fears often reveal our priorities. Learn from Pilate: make sure your primary concerns are in line with God's priorities for your life today.

december
TWENTY-FOUR

JOHN 19:17-27

Those sentenced to death carried the horizontal bar of their execution rack to the vertical pole planted in the ground at the crucifixion site. Jesus was expected to haul this crossbeam from the governor's house in Jerusalem to Golgotha. When Jesus arrived at the place of execution, his hands were nailed to the crossbeam, and that beam was attached to the pole fixed in the ground. A sign was attached to the top of the vertical pole above each condemned man's head, publishing his crimes. Pilate wrote that Jesus was executed because he was the King of the Jews. The Jewish leaders didn't like that at all. They appealed to Pilate, asking him to change the sign to read Jesus "said" he was the King of the Jews. Pilate rejected their request. The charge against Jesus stood: the King of the Jews. Jesus' clothes were then divided up between the Roman soldiers. Four soldiers each got one item of his clothing. The only garment left over was Jesus' tunic, which was made from one piece of fabric. It was valuable, so rather than rip it apart, the soldiers gambled to see who would get it. Those crucified were stripped totally naked to totally humiliate the criminals and remove all personal dignity as they struggled for their few final breaths of life. None of this was easy for Jesus. And yet, as John mentions, this was all exactly what the Old Testament said would happen concerning the Messiah.

John mentions that Jesus' mother and his aunt stood nearby. Can you imagine Mary's horror? She knew he was innocent. Jesus looked right at his mother, and then he looked at the Gospel's author, John. He addressed his mother as "woman," a term of honor, and committed her to the care of John. Even in his last few moments of life, Jesus thought about others. Mary was a widow at this time, and Jesus didn't want to leave her alone. From that day on, Mary lived in John's house. What a picture of Jesus and his compassion. Jesus realized that his mother and his beloved disciple were broken and hurting too, and he made provision for both. The pain and suffering he experienced were unimaginable, yet he didn't forget the heartache of his followers. Like Jesus, determine to look out for the interests of others today, even if you are in pain yourself.

december
TWENTY-FIVE

JOHN 19:28-37

Jesus naturally grew extremely thirsty as he hung on the cross, bloodied and beaten in the midday sun. His thirst was exactly as foretold by Scripture. The bystanders lifted a sponge with sour wine to his mouth to relieve him, just as David records in Psalm 69:21. The sponge was extended to Jesus on the end of a hyssop branch. Some note that hyssop was used in the Passover ceremony and is another reminder that Jesus was the Lamb of God. The Father was in control of every last detail of his Son's crucifixion. Not one thing happened outside of his perfect plan to redeem all who would trust in him. Jesus took the sour wine and declared, "It is finished." This is a familiar statement, and has great theological significance. One Greek verb, *tetelestai*, is translated "it is finished" in English. The verb tense literally communicates the idea of a completed past action with present implications. Jesus finished his work, and we benefit from it. The root word, *telos*, means "to complete an activity or process, bring to an end, or finish." The mission of Jesus was accomplished. In the local marketplace at this time, when an item was paid for in full, it was stamped *tetelestai*. Jesus fully paid for each and every one of the sins of those who trust in him.

After Jesus made this statement, he died. The Romans were anxious to make sure the crucified bodies were dead and get them off their crosses, as the Sabbath was about to begin. To expedite death, the soldiers broke the legs of those condemned so they could no longer push themselves up to get air. When they got to Jesus, there was no need to break his legs. One soldier pierced Jesus' side with his spear, and both blood and water came out, displaying that he truly was dead. John notes that the Scripture foretells not one of the Messiah's bones would be broken, and yet he would be pierced. Why did God allow such horror to come upon his own Son? Because the only way you or I could be reconciled to God is through Jesus' payment for our sins. There was and is no other way. Take a few minutes to thank Jesus for dealing with every single one of the debts you owed our holy God. All in Christ have been made perfect.

december
TWENTY-SIX

JOHN 19:38-42

Joseph of Arimathea was a member of the Sanhedrin, the highest-ranking Jewish group of religious leaders at the time of Jesus. Although the Sanhedrin sought the death of Jesus, Joseph saw things differently. He was looking for the kingdom of God and was a follower of Jesus, yet because he was afraid of the Jews, he followed in secret. Joseph was not only powerful, but very wealthy. He stepped into the light and courageously asked Pilate for the body of Jesus so that he might give Jesus a proper burial. Normally, the bodies of those who had been crucified were left out for vultures to attack. Relatives of the crucified could bury their corpses, but to keep them from defiling others, executed bodies were not permitted in the Jewish family tombs. Outside the city lay a common gravesite for criminals. Joseph used his influence and riches to provide for Jesus even after his death. God foretold all these events. Isaiah 53:9 states, "And they made his grave with the wicked and with a rich man in his death, although he had done no violence, and there was no deceit in his mouth." Although the Messiah did nothing wrong, he was executed with the wicked, but he was with a rich man in his death. God revealed the details about the life and death of the Messiah to prove he was who he claimed to be. Joseph of Arimathea owned the tomb, located somewhere close to the execution site, into which Jesus was placed. Nicodemus, another Jewish leader (probably of the Sanhedrin too), stepped forward and helped by providing anointing oils for Jesus' body.

So what happened to Jesus between the time of his burial and the time of his resurrection? The physical body of Jesus was clearly dead, but the soul of Jesus was with the Father in Paradise. Two men, Joseph of Arimathea and Nicodemus, risked their reputations, their positions in their community, and sacrificed financially because they recognized Jesus' true identity as the King of Kings. If you are a follower of Jesus today, learn from the example of these two rich and powerful men. Be willing to give to promote Christ, and be willing to risk your personal peace to do what is right. May we continue to trust that not one thing we do for the sake of God and his Son will be wasted.

december
TWENTY-SEVEN

JOHN 20:1-10

John begins by noting that it was the first day of the week. According to the Jewish calendar, the week closed with the Sabbath, which lasted from Friday evening to Saturday evening. So the first day of the week was Sunday. When Mary Magdalene went to the tomb and discovered that Jesus was no longer there, it was Sunday. Because the resurrection took place on Sunday, traditionally Christians have gathered together on the first day of the week to celebrate Jesus by worshipping together as a community of believers, being taught the Scripture, and participating in the ordinances of the church. Although other women went to the tomb of Jesus early that Sunday morning, John mentions only Mary Magdalene. He also notes that it was still dark. Mary came to the tomb very early. When she arrived, she was devastated. Someone had removed the stone that sealed and guarded the body of Jesus. She ran back to Peter and John and let them know that Jesus' corpse had been taken. Peter and John ran to the grave as quickly as they could and saw that what Mary's report was true. Then Peter and John went back home.

The linen cloths Jesus had been wrapped in, along with the cloth that draped Jesus' head, the face cloth, were neatly folded. Why would someone take the body of Jesus, unwrap him, and then neatly fold the burial cloths? John realized this was no robbery. In fact, verse 8 notes that when John went in, he saw or perceived, and he believed. John got it! Jesus rose from the dead and went right through the burial cloths and the stone that sealed his tomb. But if Jesus was able to go right through the stone, why was it rolled away? The stone was rolled away to let his disciples in. If you are a believer, think about what Jesus has done to "let you in," allowing you to perceive truth about who he is and what he accomplished for your soul. He loves you so much that he rolled back the stone or removed the veil from your eyes and allowed you to see the empty tomb. Realize that because Jesus lives, we will live with him. We will have new bodies no longer limited by the consequences of sin and death, but liberated to be all that we desire and long for.

december
TWENTY-EIGHT

JOHN 20:11-23

Mary Magdalene arrived at Jesus' tomb early Sunday morning and found it empty. She ran back to alert Peter and John, who rushed to verify her report. They saw that all was as she said and returned to their homes, but Mary remained and wept outside of the place where Jesus' corpse was placed. This time, she looked into the tomb and found two angels sitting where Jesus had been. They asked her why she was crying and she answered because the body of Jesus was gone and she had no idea where it was. She turned around and saw another man, who asked her again why she was crying. Now the other man who asked Mary why she was crying was actually Jesus, but she thought it was the gardener. Why didn't she recognize him? Maybe she had cried so much that her eyes were puffy and she couldn't see right. Or maybe she had no expectation whatsoever that Jesus would be there, conversing with her. She asked the one she supposed to be the gardener where he put the body of Jesus. Then Jesus said, "Mary." The moment she heard him speak her name, she knew in whose presence she was. She cried, "Rabboni!" and literally clung to Jesus.

As soon as Mary heard Jesus speak her name, she knew who it was. Earlier in John's Gospel, Jesus taught that his sheep knew and would know his voice. Mary knew the voice of her Lord, and she wasn't going to let him go. Then Jesus said, "Don't cling to me, for I have not yet ascended to my Father." Why did he say that? Although scholars have spilled much ink working to understand exactly what Jesus meant, a simple solution may be the best one. At this point, Mary was horrified, thinking she was going to "lose" Jesus again, but he let her know he was staying for a while. In fact, he would stay forty days before he ascended to the Father. He finished his work of redemption, and he would be with her to the end of the age. Jesus asked Mary to tell the others the good news. When was the last time you told someone about Jesus? May the truth of Jesus' resurrection cause others to reconsider their own lives, deaths, and eternities as you graciously testify to humanity's need to repent and believe the gospel.

december
TWENTY-NINE

JOHN 20:19-31

After the disciples learned from Mary Magdalene that Jesus had risen from the dead, the very same night he appeared to them. They hid themselves in the upper room where they had recently celebrated the Passover with Jesus. They were afraid of the Jews, so they made sure the door was locked. Jesus supernaturally went through the locked door and greeted them, "Peace be with you." Interestingly, John quotes Jesus using this phrase again in verses 22 and 26. Two times (14:27 and 16:33) before his crucifixion, Jesus promised his followers peace. They were now recipients of the peace pledged to them by their Messiah. Jesus charged the disciples to finish his work on earth, and then Jesus breathed and said, "Receive the Holy Spirit." The Greek word for "spirit," *pneuma*, is the same Greek word for "breath." In breathing out the words "Receive the Holy Spirit" (the "on them" is not in the original text), Jesus let his followers know he accomplished what he needed to do in order for them to receive the Holy Spirit, who would fully indwell them soon at Pentecost. We just saw that Jesus promised them peace, and he earned it for them through his death and resurrection. Earlier, Jesus washed the disciples' feet and pronounced them all clean, except for Judas (John 13:10). Though Jesus hadn't actually atoned for their sins yet, he declared them clean. Now, in the same way, Jesus promised them the Holy Spirit, whom they would receive shortly.

Thomas wasn't present when Jesus first appeared to the disciples, and he didn't believe their report. Eight days later, Jesus stood in the presence of the disciples again. This time, Thomas was there. Jesus told Thomas to touch his hand and his side to see and to believe that it really was him. Thomas was awestruck and worshipped Jesus, declaring, "my Lord and my God." Did Thomas actually touch Jesus? He didn't need to. He saw the resurrected Lord, and that was enough. Jesus responded by asking Thomas if he believed because he saw. Then Jesus declared, "Blessed are those who have not seen and yet have believed." Jesus alluded to the fact that soon his followers would trust in him based on the testimony of Scripture. Have you believed in Jesus because of what the New Testament records about him? If so, you are blessed. God's favor rests upon those who believe what the Bible teaches.

december
THIRTY

JOHN 21:1-14

Seven of the now eleven disciples got together, and led by Peter, they decided to go back to fishing. Clearly, Peter was still discouraged. The last time we saw him, he adamantly denied being a follower of Jesus three times. Jesus looked at Peter, and then the rooster crowed. Peter had carried the pain of this guilt and shame since that incident. Peter was a fisherman, so he decided to fish. Although the disciples spent the entire night fishing, they caught nothing. Standing on the seashore, Jesus yelled out something like "Hey, guys, did you get anything to eat?" They told him they didn't. So he instructed them to throw their net out again on the right side of the boat. They did as he instructed, and the net filled with fish. The light bulb went on! John said, "It is the Lord!" When Peter heard it was the Lord, he put on his outer garment (possibly tucked in) and jumped into the sea. When Jesus initially called Peter, the incident was similar. Peter caught nothing after fishing through the night. Jesus told him to cast his net in again, and reluctantly, Peter did. When the net was full, Peter knew he was in the presence of someone greater than he, and Peter asked Jesus to depart from him. He was convicted, and he wanted distance between himself and Jesus. But this time, Peter rushed to be near Jesus. He didn't care about the fish. All Peter wanted was Jesus!

The disciples caught nothing after fishing all night. When they listened to the words of Jesus and threw their net to the right of the boat, they had a full load. In a moment, Jesus did for them what they couldn't do on their own after working all night. So who caught the fish? The disciples? Jesus? It seems the answer is Jesus. He told them to throw the net back in, and he clearly directed the fish to their net. But verse 10 tells us Jesus directed, "Bring some of the fish that you have just caught." Jesus said the disciples caught the fish. In the same way, Jesus works through us and rewards us for the work he does. This should cause us to bow before him in humble gratitude, and it should motivate us to work more for the Lord than ever before. Jesus brings the fish, and yet he recognizes our "part" in the process. What a gracious and generous God we serve!

december
THIRTY-ONE

JOHN 21:15-25

Before he was crucified, in his deepest hour of need, Peter denied Jesus three times. Peter and six of the other disciples went fishing all night and caught nothing. Early in the morning, Jesus appeared on the shore and asked them to throw the net in again. When they pulled up a net full of fish, Peter realized who Jesus was and jumped into the water, rushing to be near him. The disciples and Jesus then ate together, and after their breakfast, Jesus spoke specifically to Peter. Jesus asked Peter, "Simon, son of John, do you love me more than these?" When Jesus asked this question, he used the Greek verb *agapao* for "love." This word describes the most committed form of love. What did Jesus mean by "more than these"? More than Peter loved the fishing boats? More than Peter loved the other disciples? Or more than the other disciples loved Jesus? Many say the last is the proper answer, as Peter had failed greatly, and now, totally restored, would love in proportion to the grace he had received. Peter said he did, and then added that Jesus knew this. When Peter answered this way, he used a different Greek verb for love, *phileo*. This word describes brotherly love and isn't as intense as *agapao*. Does this mean Peter didn't love as much as Jesus wanted? Probably not. Different verbs were used for stylistic variety, just as we avoid over-using the same words when we write.

In response to Peter's declaration of love, Jesus told Peter three times to feed or tend his sheep. Throughout the Gospel of John, Jesus called his followers his "sheep." Jesus bought each and every one of his sheep with his blood, and he knows them all by name. Those who love Jesus must invest in his people, and Peter, as a future pastor, was charged to feed the children of God. So why did Jesus ask Peter three times? Peter denied Jesus three times. Jesus knows exactly what his followers need to be reconciled to him after disobedience, and even after great failure, Jesus wants his children restored to him. The dialogue between Jesus and Peter should motivate us. When we fail, let's get up as quickly as possible and get things right with our Lord. And when we have repented and made things right, out of gratitude, let's invest in others who follow Jesus. Love Jesus by serving the people of your church.

a quick note from
THE AUTHOR

Thank you so much for "Following Jesus" along with me this year. If you have any honest feedback, please email me and let me know your thoughts.

I pray that you have seen your need to place your trust in Jesus and turn from living for yourself to living for God. May you go on to be more and more like Christ with each passing day as you faithfully proclaim the good news to any and all who are willing to hear. May the Lord grant you great spiritual success in this life and a rich reward in the life to come.

Stephanie Schwartz
stephanie@compasschurch.org

BIBLIOGRAPHY

Arndt, William et al. *A Greek-English Lexicon of the New Testament and Other Early Christian Literature* 2000: n. pag. Print.

Bock, Darrell L. *Luke: 1:1–9:50*. Vol. 1. Baker Exegetical Commentary on the New Testament. Grand Rapids, MI: Baker Academic, 1994.

Bock, Darrell L. *Luke: 9:51–24:53*. Vol. 2. Baker Exegetical Commentary on the New Testament. Grand Rapids, MI: Baker Academic, 1996.

Carson, D. A. *The Gospel According to John*. The Pillar New Testament Commentary. Leicester, England; Grand Rapids, MI: Inter-Varsity Press; W.B. Eerdmans, 1991.

Edwards, James R. *The Gospel According to Mark*. The Pillar New Testament Commentary. Grand Rapids, MI; Leicester, England: Eerdmans; Apollos, 2002.

Hughes, R. Kent. *Luke: That You May Know the Truth*. Wheaton, IL: Crossway Books, 1998. Preaching the Word.

Morris, Leon. *The Gospel According to Matthew*. The Pillar New Testament Commentary. Grand Rapids, MI; Leicester, England: W.B. Eerdmans; Inter-Varsity Press, 1992.

Sproul, R. C. *John*. Lake Mary, FL: Reformation Trust Publishing, 2009. St. Andrew's Expositional Commentary.

Walvoord, John F., and Roy B. Zuck, Dallas Theological Seminary. *The Bible Knowledge Commentary: An Exposition of the Scriptures*. Wheaton, IL: Victor Books, 1985.